Disciples of All Nations

Oxford Studies in World Christianity

DISCIPLES OF ALL NATIONS
Pillars of World Christianity
Lamin Sanneh

Disciples of All Nations

Pillars of World Christianity

LAMIN SANNEH

OXFORD
UNIVERSITY PRESS

2008

OXFORD
UNIVERSITY PRESS

Oxford University Press, Inc., publishes works that further
Oxford University's objective of excellence
in research, scholarship, and education.

Oxford   New York
Auckland   Cape Town   Dar es Salaam   Hong Kong   Karachi
Kuala Lumpur   Madrid   Melbourne   Mexico City   Nairobi
New Delhi   Shanghai   Taipei   Toronto

With offices in
Argentina   Austria   Brazil   Chile   Czech Republic   France   Greece
Guatemala   Hungary   Italy   Japan   Poland   Portugal   Singapore
South Korea   Switzerland   Thailand   Turkey   Ukraine   Vietnam

Copyright © 2008 by Oxford University Press, Inc.

Published by Oxford University Press, Inc.
198 Madison Avenue, New York, New York 10016

www.oup.com

Oxford is a registered trademark of Oxford University Press

Library of Congress Cataloging-in-Publication Data
Sanneh, Lamin O.
Disciples of all nations : pillars of world Christianity / Lamin Sanneh.
    p. cm. — (Oxford studies in world Christianity)
Includes bibliographical references and index.
ISBN 978-0-19-518960-5; 978-0-19-518961-2 (pbk.)
1. Church history—20th century.   2. Church history—21st century.
3. Christianity—20th century.   4. Christianity—21st century.   I. Title.
BR481.S26 2007
270.8—dc22   2007010411

9 8 7 6 5 4 3

Printed in the United States of America
on acid-free paper

Dedicated to the Memory of

Richard Gray (1929–2005)
Scholar-Statesman, Teacher, Exemplar, Friend

With Devotion and Gratitude

Acknowledgments

The idea for this book and of the series as a whole was several years in gestation, and although the responsibility for both the book and the series falls squarely on my shoulders, the credit should go to many people. When I approached him with an outline sketch, Theo Calderara at Oxford University Press was prompt and encouraging, and moved swiftly and devotedly to guide the proposal through the editorial process for approval and to lend his editorial skills in the writing process. I am very grateful to him personally and to his colleagues at the press for their attention to the book and to the series. I owe an enormous debt of gratitude to the anonymous readers whose encouragement and confidence have been invaluable. I hope this book justifies the faith and trust they placed in me.

Richard Gray was indefatigable and unstinting in his support and guidance right from the conception of the book, and in his role in convening at short notice a group of academics at the School of Oriental and African Studies at the University of London (SOAS) to discuss the project as a whole. He kept in close touch with me as the book developed, and was unfailingly available for help and advice, placing at my complete disposal his deep knowledge and incisive grasp of the field, and always nudging me when needed. With gentle firmness Richard challenged me to make rigorous scholarship an ally of a humane and sensitive understanding of history. It was not just Christian history that concerned Richard but the place of Christian history in the unfolding sequence of the struggles and hopes of the peoples and societies of the world. I appreciated from Richard that scholarship is an apprenticeship to the truth, and to service and solidarity. He impressed on me the fact that commitment of the scholar as scholar cannot be separated from broader commitment to a common humanity. Richard was untiring in challenging me to lift my eyes to see the world in all its complexity and intractability, as well as in its promise and richness. In a more than formal sense, Richard is the inspiration and invisible hand of this book and of the series itself. He died suddenly in August 2005, barely a week after we made arrangements to meet for further discussions, and had earlier left written messages for me when speech failed him. I dedicate this book to his memory in recognition of his role in the book and much more profoundly in my life and work.

I wish to mention also many other people who have encouraged me in all sorts of ways. At Harvard I benefited immeasurably from the work and encouragement of John B. Carman and the late Wilfred Cantwell Smith, whose historical view of the study of religion has influenced my own. The late Tom Beetham, a giant of his day, was an early and much overlooked pioneer of the field, and was a steady influence on me. His deep knowledge, wisdom, and humility were a source of inspiration to students of my generation. Thanks to him, the archives of the Methodist Missionary Society were lodged with the School of Oriental and African Studies at the University of London, there to become a boon to scholarship. I owe Tom more than words can convey.

At Yale I am grateful to George Lindbeck for our lunchtime conversations; to President Richard Levin for his unfailing support and interest in my work; to Dean Harry Attridge for his support; to Adela Collins for her helpful comments and suggestions on the New Testament material in the book; to Serene Jones, Michael Holquist, and Owen Fiss for their collegiality; and to my colleagues at St. Thomas More Catholic chaplaincy for the stimulus of life and companionship there. I owe a word of thanks to Archabbot Douglas Nowicki and to Fr. Tom Hart, both of Saint Vincent Archabbey in Latrobe, Pennsylvania, for their legendary hospitality and encouragement. I am also grateful to Jon Bonk, Judy Stebbins, and to their colleagues at the Overseas Ministries Study Center in New Haven, Connecticut, for their hospitality and friendship and for agreeing to host the series project. I owe a great debt, too, to Ryan Keating and Jane Jeuland, my student assistants at Yale.

I must thank Phil Lundman, friend and philanthropist, for reading through the entire draft manuscript and for his insightful comments, and to the Lundman Family Foundation for its confidence and support of the series as a whole. Phil Lundman's acute observations compelled me to attend to matters of detail and substance, and for that I am grateful. Vinay Samuel has been a friend and colleague over many years, and I have learned a great deal from him about the demands and opportunities presented by currents in World Christianity.

I am grateful for the honor of presenting the Jordan Lectures at SOAS in April/May 2005, and to Paul Gifford and his colleagues for their help in doing so. I am similarly indebted to the officers of the China Graduate School of Theology for the invitation to deliver the 2006 Josiah S Mann Lectures, and to Titus Pressler for the invitation to deliver the Paddock Lectures at General Theological Seminary in New York in 2006. I am grateful to Dean James Hudnut-Beumler of Vanderbilt Divinity School for the honor of delivering the Cole Lectures in 2006, an opportunity that I used to refocus the book. To my students and former students at Yale and Harvard I am indebted for their interest and support. I owe Barbara Alber of the Summer Institute of Linguistics at Dallas a huge debt of gratitude for her expertise and for her much unmerited forbearance with the maps.

I must thank many others for their friendship and companionship over the years. Jack Faal of The Gambia has been a much valued and unfailing friend over many decades. I am thankful, too, for the thoughts and support of Archbishop Obinna and Archbishop Onaiyekan, both of Nigeria. I continue to learn from my conversations with Bill Burrows, Andrew Walls, and other colleagues in the Yale-Edinburgh Group of mission scholars. While on appointment at the John W. Kluge Center at the Library of Congress, I benefited enormously from the friendship of Prosser Gifford, then-director of Scholarly Programs, as I did from the warm welcome of James Billington, the librarian.

Christianity in its current post-Western phase has seen its share of travail and tragedy, but also many heartening examples of indomitable hope and patience. I am grateful for having known some of the people who have stood undaunted at the center of the storm. I trust that this book in a small way is faithful to the spirit that sustains them.

I thank my family to whom more penance is due from me than can be discharged in a lifetime of devotion. In particular, Sia gave me invaluable help from her expert knowledge of ancient Rome, and Sandra read through a draft of the book and gave me many helpful ideas and comments about style, consistency, and clarity. K remains a source of constant inspiration in his lucid and energetic exposition of contemporary American popular culture, including popular religion. I hope they will all see something of their influence in this book.

X ACKNOWLEDGMENTS

The title of the book, *Disciples of All Nations*, represents the idea of Christian variety and diversity united by a common foundation of Jewish monotheist ethics. The human factor in the Christian movement has to do with the experiences of real people embedded in living traditions and cultures. That view represents—and modifies—an aspect of Wilfred Smith's conception of religion as a human phenomenon implicated perhaps in God, but certainly in the historical process. In my view, history bears and marks, but does not replace or account for the religious spirit. Context is a frame rather than the arbiter of religion. Like the sun, Christianity appears in its own light.

The extent to which the current awakening has occurred without the institutions and structures that defined Western Christendom, including the tradition of scholarship, learning, and cosmopolitanism, is an important feature of World Christianity and its largely hinterland following. In the current resurgence monasteries, theological schools, and hierarchical agency, for example, have played comparatively little role, nor is there much evidence of state facility, except as a problem and a burden to overcome.

Indeed, colonialism was often a drain and an impediment. The advantage of the colonial impetus in the missionary expansion was, accordingly, twice offset by the disadvantages of nationalist resistance and the charismatic reaction it elicited, leaving Christianity free to develop its own local appeal. Similarly, foreign missionary agency has been marginal, at least in the surge of conversion. To a surprising extent, the cosmopolitan characteristics of classical Christianity have few parallels in the post-Western developments. There have, for example, been no heresy trials, no bloody battles of theological difference, no spectacles of killing of religious enemies, and no campaigns of state-sponsored military conversion. On the contrary, World Christianity is remarkable for its civil character, its relative peacefulness, and its nonreliance on the state instrument. The intercommunal breakdown in Catholic Rwanda leading to the 1994 genocide was an aberration, and even there was not based on religious division. Also striking is the fusing of old and new in the charismatic dimensions of the resurgence without the disruptions of theological strife that afflicted Christian Europe. The vast majority of new converts belong to mainline historic churches with the difference that theological feuds—as between or among Catholics, Orthodox, and Protestants, for example—have been much less sharp than used to be the case in the West. Charismatic inspiration is a factor in the new openness.

I have tried to keep footnotes to a minimum by staying close to references mentioned in the text, and by supplying relevant details in the bibliography. And finally, it goes without saying that I bear full and final responsibility for the opinions expressed in this book and for any defects, inadequacies, misjudgments, and errors. I offer the book not as an exhaustive statement or even as a complete case study, but as an ecumenical conspectus of the field of World Christianity as I have seen and encountered it in my professional work, especially in its interreligious manifestation. I gladly and respectfully submit it to the reader in the spirit of shared interest.

Contents

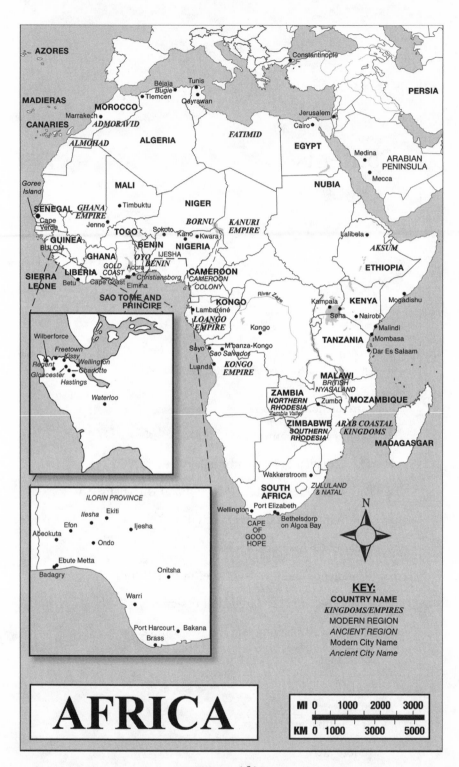

MAP I. Africa

xiv

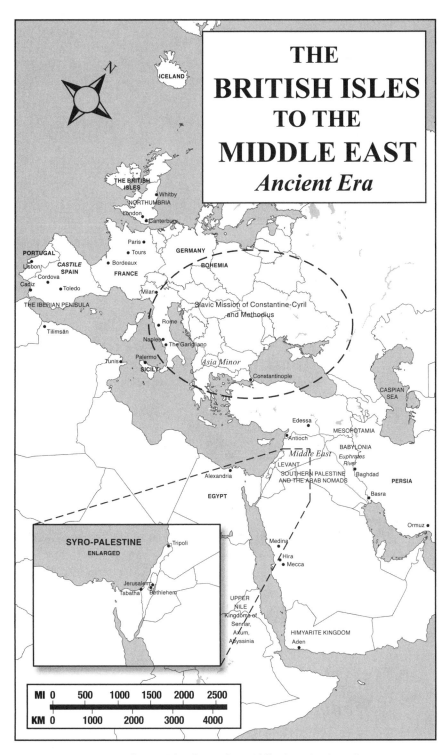

MAP 2. The British Isles to the Middle East (Ancient Era)

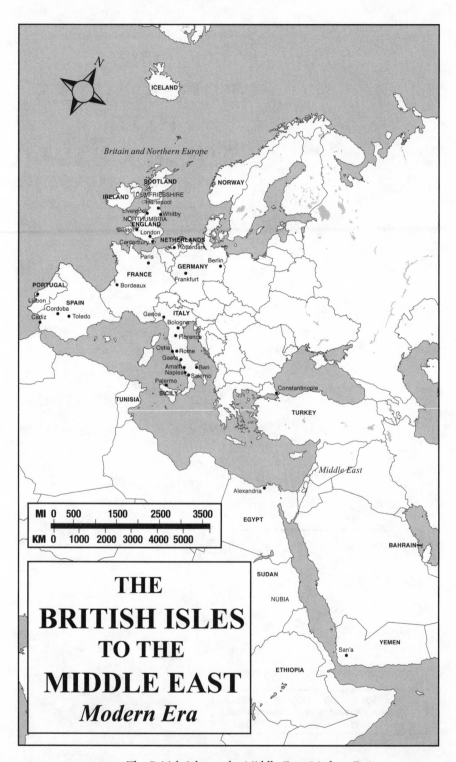

MAP 3. The British Isles to the Middle East (Modern Era)

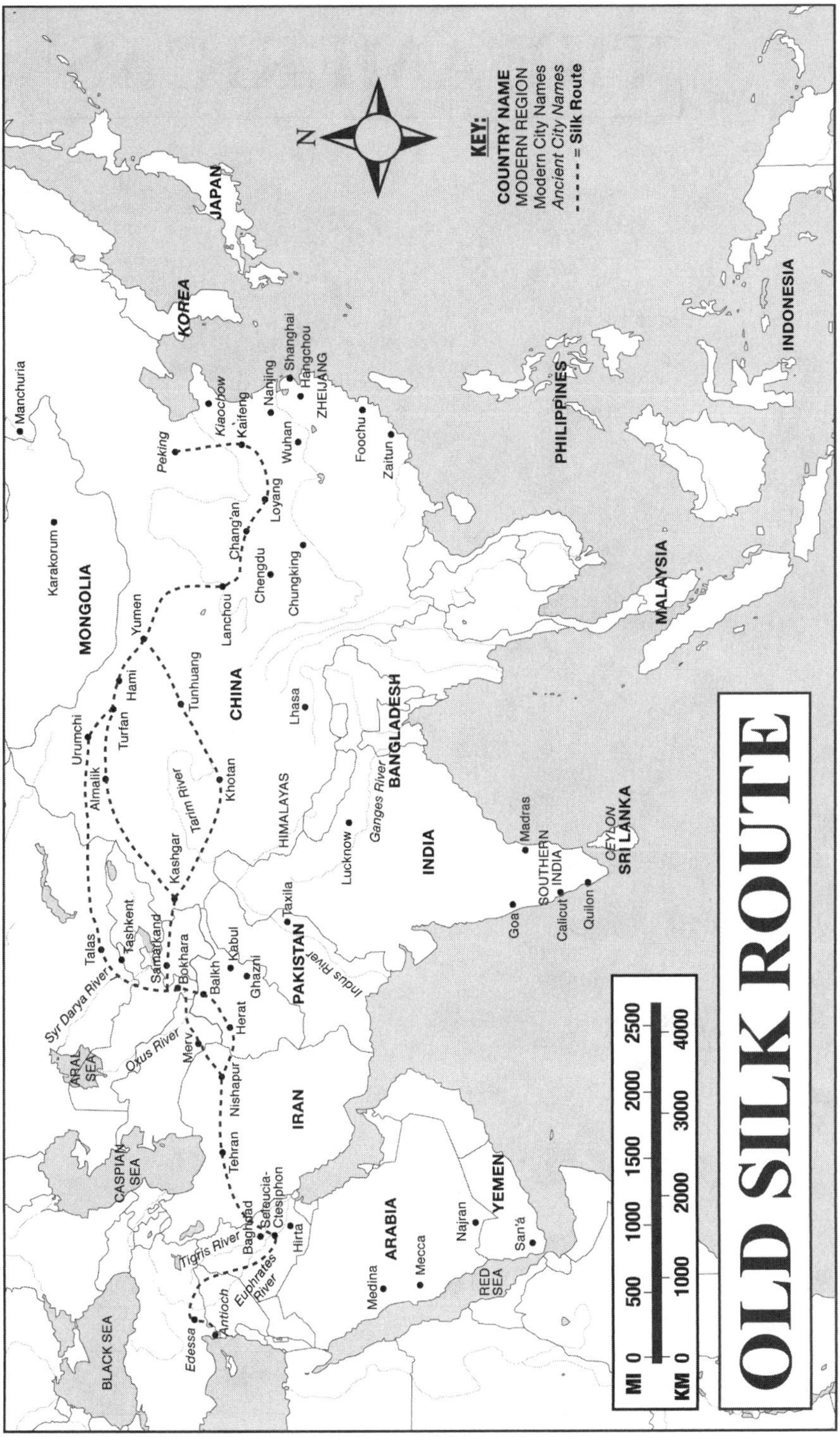

MAP 4. Old Silk Route

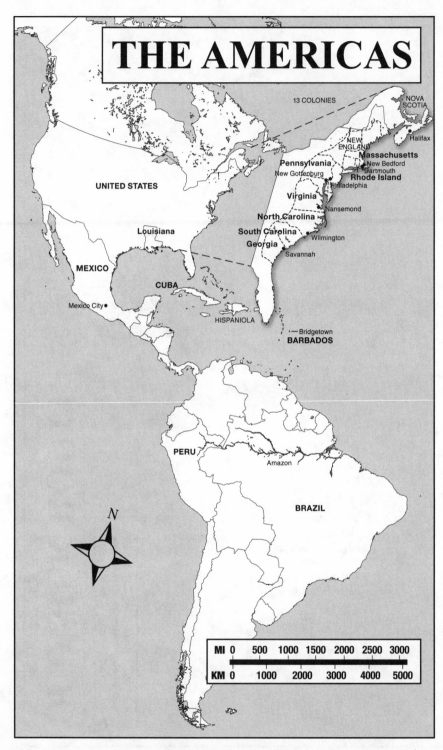

THE AMERICAS

13 COLONIES

NOVA SCOTIA

Halifax

NEW ENGLAND

UNITED STATES

Massachusetts
New Bedford
Dartmouth
Rhode Island

Pennsylvania
New Gottenburg
Philadelphia

Virginia
Nansemond

North Carolina

Louisiana

South Carolina
Wilmington

Georgia
Savannah

MEXICO

CUBA

Mexico City

HISPANIOLA

— Bridgetown
BARBADOS

PERU
Amazon

BRAZIL

N

| MI 0 | 500 | 1000 | 1500 | 2000 | 2500 | 3000 |
| KM 0 | 1000 | 2000 | 3000 | 4000 | 5000 |

MAP 5. The Americas

Introducing the Oxford Series

Among the many breathtaking developments in the post–World War II and the subsequent postcolonial eras, few are more striking than the worldwide Christian resurgence. With unflagging momentum, Christianity has become, or is fast becoming, the principal religion of the peoples of the world. Primal societies that once stood well outside the main orbit of the faith have become major centers of Christian impact, while Europe and North America, once considered the religion's heartlands, are in noticeable recession. We seem to be in the middle of massive cultural shifts and realignments whose implications are only now beginning to become clear. Aware that Europe's energies at the time were absorbed in war, Archbishop William Temple presciently observed in 1944 that this global feature of the religion was "the new fact of our time." An impressive picture now meets our eyes: the growing numbers and the geographical scope of that growth, the cross-cultural patterns of encounter, the variety and diversity of cultures affected, the structural and antistructural nature of the changes involved, the kaleidoscope of cultures often manifested in familiar and unfamiliar variations on the canon, the wide spectrum of theological views and ecclesiastical traditions represented, the ideas of authority and styles of leadership that have been developed, the process of acute indigenization that fosters liturgical renewal, the production of new religious art, music, hymns, songs, and prayers—all these are part of Christianity's stunningly diverse profile.

These unprecedented developments cast a revealing light on the serial nature of Christian origins, expansion, and subsequent attrition. They fit into the cycles of retreat and advance, of contraction and expansion, and of waning and awakening that have characterized the religion since its birth, though they are now revealed to us with particular force. The pattern of contrasting development is occurring simultaneously in various societies across the world. The religion is now in the twilight of its Western phase and at the beginning of its formative non-Western impact. Christianity has not ceased to be a Western religion, but its future as a world religion is now being formed and shaped at the hands and in the minds of its non-Western adherents. Rather than being a cause for unsettling gloom, for Christians this new situation is a reason for guarded hope.

Today students of the subject can stand in the middle of the recession of Christianity in its accustomed heartland while witnessing its resurgence in areas long considered receding missionary lands, but that is the situation today. In 1950 some 80 percent of the world's Christians lived in the northern hemisphere in Europe and North America. By 2005 the vast majority of Christians lived in the southern hemisphere in Asia, Africa, and Latin America. In 1900 at the outset of colonial rule there were just under nine million Christians in Africa, of whom the vast majority were Ethiopian Orthodox or Coptic. In 1960, at the end of the colonial period, the number of Christians had increased to about sixty million, with Catholics and Protestants making up fifty million, and the other ten million divided between the Ethiopian Orthodox and Coptic churches. By 2005, the African Christian population had increased to roughly 393 million, which is just below 50 percent of Africa's population.

It is estimated that there are just over two billion Christians worldwide, making Christianity among the world's fastest growing religions. In terms of the languages and ethnic groups affected, as well as the variety of churches and movements involved, Christianity is also the most diverse and pluralist religion in the world. More people pray and worship in more languages and with more differences in styles of worship in Christianity than in any other religion. Well over three thousand of the world's languages are embraced by Christianity through Bible translation, prayer, liturgy, hymns, and literature. More than 90 percent of these languages have a grammar and a dictionary at all only because the Western missionary movement provided them, thus pioneering arguably the largest, most diverse and most vigorous movement of cultural renewal in history. At the same time, the post-Western Christian resurgence is occurring in societies already set in currents of indigenous religious pluralism. In addition to firsthand familiarity with at least one other religion, most new Christians speak a minimum of two languages. It is not the way a Christian in the West has been used to looking at the religion, but it is now the only way.

Increasingly, and in growing numbers, Third World churches are appearing in the towns and cities of the West, while Third World missionaries are also arriving to serve in churches in Europe and North America. This suggests the commencement of the process of the reevangelization of a secular West by orthodox Christians of former missionized countries. It is sobering to reflect on the implications and political impact of such a sharp cultural encounter. The empty churches of the West are being filled or replaced with mounting numbers of non-Western Christians whose orthodox religious views will pose a radical challenge to the secular liberal status quo, while institutions of liberal theological education are busy redefining themselves to preempt a cultural collision with the post-Western Christian resurgence. Liberal theological institutions as well as departments of religious studies in State colleges and universities have been far slower in appointing Third World scholars of religion than their conservative counterparts. Orthodox Christian groups in the West are, meanwhile, positioning themselves to effect a complex strategic alliance with the new resurgence.

Mainline denominations have already felt the force of this shift. In the Roman Catholic Church the structural adjustment of Vatican II has allowed the new wind of change to sweep through the church (if at times it has been impeded), producing movements in several different directions and across the world. The New Catholic Catechism reflects the change in language, mood, and style, and the rapid creation of bishops and cardinals in the non-Western church, accompanied by a steady stream of papal encyclicals, testifies to the fresh momentum of post-Western Christianity. The papacy has been not only an observer of the change but also an active promoter of it, and, in the particular case of Pius XII, the source of a well-tempered preparation for it. Similarly, churches and denominations comprised in the Protestant ecumenical movement have felt jostled in unexpected, uncomfortable ways by the sudden entrance into their ranks of new Third World churches. The worldwide Anglican Communion has been reeling under pressure from the organized and concerted Third World reaction to the consecration and installation of a practicing gay bishop by the Episcopal Church USA. The other Protestant churches with sizeable Third World memberships have paused to reflect on the implications for them of such a culture clash. Not since the Reformation has there been such a shake-up of authority in the Western church, with unrehearsed implications for the West's cultural preeminence.

In the meantime, the number of mainline Protestant missionaries is decreasing, while evangelical missionary numbers are increasing steadily, complemented by a rising tide of African, Asian, and other Third World missionaries, including more than ten thousand from South Korea alone. In 1950, Christians in South Korea numbered barely half a million; today they number some thirteen million, and are among the most prosperous and mobile of people anywhere. It is likely that churches in South Korea, rather than churches in the West, will play a key role on the new Christian frontier about to open in China, which might well become a dominant axis of the religion, with hard-to-imagine implications for the rest of the world.

These facts and developments afford a unique opportunity and challenge for cross-cultural study of the asymmetry of the turnover and serial impact of Christianity, where a dip here is followed by a bounce there. The intersection of the path of decline in the West with the upward swing of momentum of post-Western Christianity makes the subject a compelling and deeply rewarding one for comparative study and critical reflection.

The new reality brought about by the shift in the center of gravity of Christianity from the northern to the southern hemisphere provides the context for the volumes in this series, which are designed to bring the fruits of new research and reflection to the attention of the educated, nonspecialist reader. The first volume offers a panoramic survey of the field, exploring the sources to uncover the nature and scope of Christianity's worldwide multicultural impact. The agents, methods, and means of expansion will be investigated closely in order to clarify the pattern and forms as well as issues of appropriation and inculturation. The cultural anticipations that allowed the religion to take root in diverse settings, under vastly different historical and political circumstances, will be assessed for how they shaped the reception of Christianity. Similarly, Christianity's intercontinental range, as well as its encounter with other religions, including Islam, elicited challenges for the religion in the course of its worldwide expansion. These challenges will be examined.

The subsequent volumes will be devoted to specific themes and regions within the general subject of Christianity's development as a world religion. While each volume is conceived and written individually, together the volumes are united in their focus on post-Western developments in Christianity and in the elaborations, variations, continuities, and divergences with the originating Western forms of the religion.

Disciples of All Nations

Introduction

*Missionary Pillar: New Testament Bearings
and the Cultural Alignment*

Gentile Frontline

Through the drama and trauma of Roman imperial repression in
Palestine the fledgling Christian religion embarked on its world errand deeply conscious of its claim that it was a religion destined
for all time and for the whole world, and not just for one time, place, or
people. The apostles looked upon the shifting political winds of the
time as a moral lesson about not placing faith in things of the passing day but in God who ruled in all creation and endured forever.
When the faith was taken from Jerusalem to Antioch,[1] Christianity
acquired a worldwide cultural and geographical orientation. These
two external forces of imperial pressure and the Antioch experience
were matched internally by a steadily growing consciousness of
Christianity's world mission.[2]

Peter's historic apostolate began with a watershed that breached
ethnic/national boundaries. He testified how as a devout Jew he
was led to the house of Cornelius, a Gentile, saying he was authorized in a vision to break the cultural taboo of associating with a
Gentile, and declaring: "You yourselves know how unlawful it is for
a Jew to associate with or to visit any one of another nation; but
God has shown me that I should not call any man common or unclean. So when I was sent for, I came without objection."[3] Upon
hearing Cornelius's account of why Peter was sent for, Peter

responded: "Truly I perceive that God shows no partiality, but in every nation any one who fears him and does what is right is acceptable to him."[4]

Peter's contention about every nation being anticipated in the moral teachings of Christianity sets the tone for the full-scale mission to the Gentile world, what J. B. Phillips called "the young church in action," his title of his translation of the book of Acts.[5] When Peter says it is common knowledge that it is unlawful for a Jew to associate with a person of another nation, he is identifying a crucial feature in the history of religion, namely, religion as lawful custom enshrined in binding cultural practices. In that conception of religion, God is a cultural marker bound up with matters of identity and communal pride, with religion set up to require conformity to a set of institutional social norms.[6] Peter's insistence that true religion cannot be restricted to mere institutional adherence signals a radical shift to the idea of God as boundary-free truth, of God as one who is without partiality and who, as such, is open to the genuine moral aspirations of all humanity. The idea is the rock upon which God's free offer of salvation is founded, and it demands ethical change, as the witness of all Israel makes clear.

That view of religion confronts Christianity with a momentous challenge. How can Christianity maintain its commitment to culture, insofar as culture embodies faith in a concrete way, while avoiding the sort of cultural idolatry that fuses truth claims and exclusive national ideals? How is cultural commitment compatible with religious openness? The history of Christianity, it has to be admitted, demonstrates an uneven record in balancing cultural specificity and theological normativeness, and the field is littered with failed attempts at reconciling Christ and culture. Yet, on the basis of his newfound faith, Peter felt it was a challenge he should meet head-on in order to justify and validate his mission to the Gentile Cornelius. Under Christendom, however, this idea of religion as civilized imperial prerogative resurfaced with clamorous force, and non-Christian populations at home and abroad, including Jews, were corralled as subject people, with native lands fair game. The outstanding exceptions to such prerogatives were Muslim lands, but that was by force of circumstance, not from any intrinsic respect.

From the apostolic mandate to practice mission and from the pressure to expand in the Roman Empire, the Christian movement spread beyond Jerusalem and Palestine and penetrated predominantly Greek-speaking areas. Personal conversion to God as redeemer and judge, rather than kinship or cultural qualification, became the new rule for membership in the church. Christianity was an "old" religion insofar as its ethical foundations were grounded in prophetic Judaism—and Jesus was a striking embodiment of the Jewishness of Christianity. But its conception of faith as grounded in the sovereign conscience of the individual was radically new. The faith it preached was derived from moral conviction, not from genealogy or social custom. As R. G. Collingwood pointed out, "The whole of Christianity depends for its value on the assurance that God is revealed in us; and that implies on our part some faculty capable of accepting revelation. That is the primitive Christian conception of faith."[7] Peter's role as architect of the Gentile mission was fundamental to the genesis of Christianity as a world religion, a role that is well summarized by Adolf von Harnack:

> Henceforth Peter, probably with one or two others of the primitive apostles, took part in the Gentile mission. The last barrier had collapsed. If we marvel at the greatness of Paul, we should not marvel less at [that of] the primitive apostles, who for the gospel's sake entered on a career which the Lord and Master, with whom they had eaten and drunk, had never taught them. By adopting an intercourse with Gentile Christians, this Jewish Christianity did away with itself, and in the second period of his labours Peter ceased to be a "Jewish Christian." He became a Greek.[8]

Pauline Watershed

Many writers claim that Paul expanded the subtle yet momentous shift in the understanding of faith that Peter taught. The subject is well trodden, but for our purposes consideration of a few works should suffice. The Oxford theologian C. H. Dodd drew attention to the shattering of Paul's old confidence in the religion he inherited from his ancestors. Whether as Jew or as Christian, Paul believed that the "Law of Moses" was absolute, impeccable law, and within the sphere of law there was nothing higher or more perfect. Paul saw an identical principle at work among the pagans. The pagan sense of right and wrong was God's law written on the heart—the same law as that delivered on Sinai, Paul would have said. Stoic philosophers developed a stream of pagan thought in which we encounter this problem of the search for perfect wisdom by the most relentless and pious of seekers, as shown by Diogenes, so that many Stoic passages come to us tinged with a melancholy evoking the moving transcript from Paul's experience. In the end, for the age-old longing for perfect wisdom Christ became the fulfillment, he being the ageless "wisdom" of God who is now made manifest.[9]

What all this suggests is that concerning divine law and human inadequacy we confront what is at bottom a human problem, and not a specifically

Jewish one. Yet Paul's own bitter experience in Pharisaic Judaism lent a cutting edge to his awakened conscience. His theological studies had told him that God was loving and merciful; but he had thought this love and mercy were expressed once and for all in the arrangements through the law that God made for Israel's blessedness. That was what he and his own people understood as "the plan of salvation." It was a new thing now to be assured by an inward experience admitting of no further question that without qualification God loved him and others, and that the eternal mercy was God's free forgiveness of sinners without regard to their moral record, spotty as that is.[10] Love does not choose the blade of grass on which it falls.

From his encounter with the Jesus of Calvary and Easter Paul arrived at the personal idea that the center of Christianity was in the heart and life of the believer, whoever and wherever the believer is. In Paul's view, one need not conform to one cultural ideal or standard to be saved. He brooded long and hard on how he knew no way of dealing with religion except as a question of inheritance and birthright until he was shown another way. He testified how that change came to him unsolicited with wrenching force, though in retrospect it seemed too obvious to miss. How did he miss it?

Paul was once constrained to defend himself in Jerusalem in the face of a hostile crowd who accused him of defiling religion by bringing Gentiles into the temple. Surprising them with his impeccable "Hebrew," Paul responded by stressing that he was himself of proud Jewish stock, who not so long ago and in the company of many who were present on this occasion tried to beat back the new Christian movement, believing it to be a blasphemy against God. "I am a Jew, born at Tarsus in Cilicia, but brought up in this city at the feet of Gamaliel, educated according to the strict manner of the law of our fathers, being zealous for God as you all are this day. I persecuted this Way to the death, binding and delivering to prison both men and women, as the high priest and the whole council of elders bear me witness. From them I received letters to the brethren, and I journeyed to Damascus to take those also who were there and bring them in bonds to Jerusalem to be punished."[11] Paul was then mysteriously struck blind on the road to Damascus, until one Ananias, a devout Jew living in Damascus, restored his sight and commissioned him as a missionary of the new religion. "The God of our fathers," Ananias assured him, "appointed you to know his will, to see the Just One and to hear a voice from his mouth; for you will be a witness for him to all men of what you have seen and heard. And now why do you wait? Rise and be baptized, and wash away your sins, calling on his name."[12] As a leading persecutor of Christians, Paul's conversion to Christianity was nothing short of a scandal in the eyes of his fellow Jews.[13]

For Paul himself, however, his Jewish ties were indissoluble, and they allowed him to range far and wide across the new Christian terrain. When he offered an account of his new experience of religion he drew on his Jewish background: not simply on the covenant in the light of which "the Way" of the followers of Jesus was, Paul once thought a grave heresy, but particularly on the temple, God's hallowed sanctuary. Paul was now able to extend that idea of sanctuary by affirming that the temple was not an immutable building centered in Jerusalem or anywhere else, but the believers themselves whose redeemed bodies, as such, are God's temple.[14] The idea of faith as something personal made possible a mobile, nonterritorial response. The offer of salvation was premised on the honest and sincere conviction of persons as free agents, not on possessing a promised land. Territoriality ceased to be a requirement of faith.

Several writers have assessed Paul's significance for world Christianity, and it would repay us to consider their work in the broad context of our study. Paul's Epistle to the Galatians shows that Greek believers expected that they would serve a cultural apprenticeship under the Torah and conform to the idea of religion set out therein.[15] Intending it as an inclusive gesture, rabbinic literature compared God-fearing Gentiles to stags whose habitat was in the wild but who were now given provisional leave to graze with sheep of the flock.[16] As Christians under Jewish auspices these Gentiles of Galatia were happy to be considered stags in borrowed fields, not sheep in their own meadow.

As Greek converts, the new Christians acknowledged Jesus to be Israel's Messiah, and would gladly submit to be cut in the flesh to assume an indelible and a venerable mark of the covenant, since that was how they understood participation in the covenanted faith of Israel. Religion for the first Christians was religion as known and lived by committed, observant Jews, and the argument that Jesus was Israel's Messiah who had come to save his people was authoritative and binding for Gentile Christians, too. For those Gentiles who had followed the path of devotion to the synagogue and kept what parts of the Torah they could manage, but who, nevertheless, had stopped short of the final step of circumcision, this might be the time of victory and favor they were waiting for when Jesus appeared as Israel's hope and consolation.[17] In the first decades of its existence the church was the church of zealous Torah-observant Jews who were committed to the age-long project of Israel's messianic restoration and to sharing in Israel's satisfaction when the Torah would flourish in triumph.[18] Pentecost, to them, was all about this ultimate achievement.[19]

Left to themselves, the early Christians would have been thus content to seek shelter under the safe, consecrated shadow of the synagogue and to abide as sincere followers of Christ. But they were not left to themselves, thanks in large part to the intervention of Paul and his company of fellow apostles.[20] Paul's reaction to the appropriateness of the Mosaic code for Gentiles was not just disagreement, it was what Andrew Walls calls "white-hot indignation." Paul's "emotions are so strong as to strain his syntax, and his language becomes so robust that some English versions translate rather coyly."[21] Paul was determined that for those new Christians who were brought up as Hellenistic pagans, even the notion of adopting the lifestyle of very good, devout, observant Jewish believers should be rejected. In that reasoning, the new Christians are not just followers of Jesus; they are a new creation in the sense of their being baptized in him, of their being partakers in the redeeming life of Christ. They are, in fact, converts rather than just proselytes. The gospel was not just about religion as "the Way," or as "ethnic dressing" so that followers and adherents could parade in borrowed garb (though that was how it all appeared to the first Christians),[22] but about religion as a personal, faith-filled fellowship with God.[23] The believer is now Christ-indwelled, not just God-designated.[24] In Harnack's vivid phrase, "Paul wrecked the religion of Israel on the cross of Christ, in the very endeavour to comprehend it with a greater reverence and stricter obedience than his predecessors."[25] Yet "the religion of Israel" was far from wrecked as the church continued to debate the matter even after all the major leaders had adopted the position that Paul had taken at the risk of his life.[26]

In one celebrated case, Paul confronted Peter about precisely that issue. Peter had come to Antioch, a center of Christian Gentiles, and was quite happy socializing with the Gentiles—until, that is, James's party showed up, at which point Peter withdrew from the company of Gentiles so as not to offend pious Jewish sensibilities. Paul was livid. "I opposed him to his face . . . for before certain men came from James, he ate with the Gentiles; but when they came he drew back and separated himself, fearing the circumcision party."[27] Peter was acting insincerely, Paul charged, and leading many young believers astray by his open inconsistency. Although it was understandable against the force of inherited national custom, Peter's prevarication still threatened to undercut the whole basis of Christianity's unique mission. Paul rebuked Peter not because Peter's conception of the gospel conflicted with Paul's, but because Peter's conduct on that occasion seemed to violate the consensus that both of them shared and which the Jerusalem church duly ratified. Salvation was by faith, not by national custom and social affiliation, Paul asserted.[28] Peter could not disagree.

Yet neither would Paul disagree that it was only through the Jewishness of Jesus that the whole world could be incorporated into the people of God. "The very issue of universality," Jaroslav Pelikan contends, "which has been taken to be the distinction between the message of Paul and Jewish particularism, was for Paul what made it necessary that Jesus be a Jew. For only through the Jewishness of Jesus could the covenant of God with Israel, the gracious gifts of God and his irrevocable calling, become available to all people in the world (Rom 11:17)."[29]

That is the sense in which we must take the words of Paul addressed to the church in Macedonia and Achaia concerning their obligation to the church in Jerusalem: Christian Gentiles, Paul admonished, are indebted to the Jewish church by reason of having received the faith from it. The Jewish church has rights against Gentile believers by virtue of spiritual election and also has a moral right of material support from them.[30] Whatever he might advocate for the Gentiles, Paul continued to share with his fellow Jews the national pride and sense of superiority warranted by the Law of Moses.[31] Indeed, the Law of Moses makes explicit the truth of which Gentiles had only fragmentary glimpses, and to accede fully to that truth, the Gentiles urgently needed a parallel moral structure. The name of Israel in translation, as tribe, nation, and vocation, would adorn the lips of Gentile peoples with glad songs of peaceful Zion. "From the outset," Marx observed with real insight, "the Christian was the theorizing Jew. Christianity overcame real Judaism only in appearance. It was too *noble*, too spiritual, to eliminate the crudeness of practical need except by elevating it into the blue. Christianity is the sublime thought of Judaism, and Judaism is the common practical application of Christianity."[32]

Paul envisioned for Hellenistic Christians a continuation of Hellenistic social and personal patterns of life and thought, with Christianity in its Jewish temper challenging and upsetting the pagan premises of those patterns. This would effect a radical change where necessary, but only from within, with Christians engaging the implications of their faith in closest proximity to the ideas and institutions of their society. It was their responsibility to make Christianity feel at home rather than to implant someone else's national custom in their midst.

The early Greek Christians felt empowered to embark on a wholly different way of practicing religion that became the primary intellectual mission of Hellenistic society in the Roman East Mediterranean world. As a consequence, Hellenistic social and family life bore the imprint of the Christian impact. Christian Greeks had now to renegotiate with their own culture, not with someone else's, and what emerged revealed surprising possibilities. New and different social situations arose, and a fresh intellectual environment came into being. Influences from Greek philosophy, Roman law, Eastern mysticism and spirituality, and astral science gave rise to questions that believers had before never encountered. That intellectual setting fostered the development of a distinctly Christian religious thought that culminated in the great theological systems of the church.

All of this must have struck the old-style Jewish believers as dangerous deviation from the established pillars of the received code. What assurance was there that harmful innovation might not follow from the decision to embrace untested, extraneous ideas? In their view, Christians were stepping into uncharted territory and courting grave error thereby. As a religious community the early church was striking out on a radically new path wholly without precedent. As Andrew Walls noted, "Had the Jesus community retained the proselyte model, Christians would almost inevitably have been taken out of the intellectual mainstream and shut up to their own sacred books. But as converts, believers in Jesus were required to turn their processes of thought toward Christ, to think Christ into the intellectual framework of their time and place. The eventual result was Christian theology as we know it."[33]

The distinction between proselyte and convert emerged out of the ferment of Hellenistic transformation, whence Christianity embarked on its consequential world errand. It was an intellectual shift that offered a way forward for other cultures and societies, and a break from the obligation to follow precedent and imitate past examples. As honorary members of the faith community, proselytes were hampered in the religious life because it was not their natural inheritance. As outsiders, proselytes were not held accountable for the tradition; their status was not that of a freehold, and could change with circumstances. Proselytes followed where others led, while converts led and went beyond what proselytes were permitted. Converts were deemed to have permanent tenure. That distinction defined the characteristic missionary task of Christianity: the church was in the world as moral light and leaven, not as a cultural implant trailing short-term establishment ideas. The prevailing cultural practice of regarding religion as a matter of birth and social connection would have been much easier for the church to adopt than the radical choice involved in conversion. "Judaizing" forces for that reason contended seriously with the call for spiritual conversion, and only bold apostolic leadership enabled it to withstand the forces of hallowed custom.

The issue was dear to Paul's heart, as he was at pains to drive home to the Galatians, saying that their instinct to remain tied to the synagogue in the belief that religion was a matter of birthright was fatal to their faith in Christ. In the new faith the idea of a birthright was superseded by the call to a second birth. Consequently, a demanding task of "inculturation" was now required of them because a radically new historical epoch was inaugurated with the coming of Jesus.[34] Before then, Paul noted, Gentiles were placed under guardianship and trusteeship, "until the date set by the father...in the fullness of time," when the Gentiles would be allowed to enter into their inheritance as new heirs: "So that the law was our custodian until Christ came, that we might be justified by faith. But now that faith has come, we are no longer under a custodian; for in Christ you are all sons of God, through faith. For as many of you as were baptized into Christ have put on Christ. There is neither Jew nor Greek, there is neither slave nor free, there is neither male nor female; for you are all one in Christ Jesus. And if you are Christ's, then you are Abraham's offspring, heirs according to promise."[35]

Christianity was unique in its claim to a revelation and in the imperative of the call to repentance, faith, and life in the fellowship. Natural religions that proliferated at the time, by contrast, identified themselves with a cultural system and with the mores of social convention. To these religions the idea of revelation, of a truth and a power outside and above the natural sphere, was anathema, since it implied that the lives of men and women could be regulated by laws and norms that had their source outside society and above human power. In contrast, the mystery cults were counter-currents in which initiates moved away from the social assumptions of natural religion about member-ship as a matter of kin and nature to the idea of transcendent religion as a matter of divine-human relationship. The mystery cults were a real *praeparatio evangelica* for Christianity, and their recognition that the human being was *capax dietatis*, a soul in the making, resonated with the Christian idea of faith as a spiritual journey of understanding and obedience. In its ritual of formation of new members, for example, the church of Antioch confirmed the notion of the Christian fellowship as the community of revealed teaching by describing neophytes as *Christianoi*—not as followers of Christ simply, but as Christ-initiated, in fact, as God-indwelled men and women who were incorporated into him.

J. S. Trimingham expanded on the Christian teaching about the indwell-ing nature of faith by setting it against the natural religions of Syria and Mesopotamia. Those religions represented the idea of divinity within the human spirit, whereas Christianity taught of a transcendent God whose action in history required assimilation and transformation in society. "Consequently, where the Gospel was adopted it had to be assimilated into social life. Such a process of assimilation would inevitably change society, and the process could well be painful. For this reason, society took ways to neutralize the Gospel. The basic Christian Gospel was as exclusive as Judaism. Anyone who sits at the Lord's table, Paul emphasizes, has abjured the table of the gods" (1 Cor 10:21–22).[36]

While Christians were instructed to shun traffic with pagan cults, they adopted many ideas and customs from that source, thus putting them in the novel situation of accepting the new religion with the resonances of the old practices. Total rejection of the old was as unfeasible as complete surrender to the new. Converts were not cultural orphans or undiscriminating neophytes; rather, by virtue of the choice they made, converts were involved in judgment and discernment at the same time that they were involved in appropriation and assimilation.

By a process of fresh combinations and permutations new believers expanded Christianity's multicultural horizon. Materials that so recently defined the world of non-Christians were retrieved to serve a new function. Prayer and sacrifice sanctioned at the old shrines and altars were reconstituted to serve a new purpose rather than abandoned. The old vocabulary was filled with a new theme and burden. The imperial context and cultural demands failed to constrain Christian motives; it's the church's background in a Pharisaic legalism and existence under Roman subjugation, for example, that armed it with a sense of reawakened religious resolve as well as political realism. The Christian movement expanded from intrinsic as well as extrinsic pressure, so that the religion acquired its peculiar temper from both temple and the empire: to serve and witness to the one sovereign God in a world organized, instructed, and administered by others.

I

Whither Christianity?

A Study in Origin, Thought, and Action

Pillar of Empire

In the footloose and protean milieu of the Christian diaspora, it suited
the disciples to recall the assurance of Jesus: "For where two or
three are gathered in my name, there am I in the midst of them."[1]
Christianity was not belief in an axis mundi, and so could flourish
anywhere as experience-based personal faith. The idea of holy place
was not an immutable, timeless place or dwelling; it was wherever
believers found God. Dispensing with maps and pictures, academic
theology gave little credence to the importance of geography; Jerusalem and Bethlehem quickly became abstract timeless symbols. As
such, Bethlehem was emptied of cultural content and elided to a
universal incarnation and Jerusalem to a figurative heavenly city, a
practice at variance with apostolic teaching concerning the kerygmatic
importance of Palestine as the historical home of Jesus. Jerusalem was
a city of unique religious significance, and the disciples felt vindicated when Pentecost occurred there, an event that constituted the
birth of the Christian movement. The idea of a promised land survived
in the church but only in a radically transformed sense, as a concept of open multiple locations rather than of a fixed axis mundi.
Jerusalem was a prototype of a Christian particularity without borders.

Both Peter and Paul saw confirmation in the Scriptures and
compelling meaning in the short lifespan of Jesus between Bethlehem
and Jerusalem. They drew the conclusion that Christianity had no

inalienable birthplace and the church no territorial patrimony to defend. Jesus might have been born in Bethlehem, but he was now bred in the hearts and minds of believers anywhere and everywhere.[2] As the ancient scribe foresaw, in the age of true religion God's name would no longer be confined to one place but would be known and honored everywhere among the Gentiles.[3] The witness of believers that God was their only dwelling place had been validated.[4] Prophecy had been fulfilled, and so a future age of promise could begin. There were as many birthplaces of the religion as there had come to be new communities of faithful people, and as many visitations of Pentecost as there had been hearts and minds set aflame and occasions of bold witness. Christianity was a religion for all seasons, fit for all humanity. Whatever its core was, it was not in any one time, in any one place, or in any one language. The prophets had dreamed and spoken well.

From accounts written by the members themselves we get a sense of how this new conception of religion accounted for the birth of new communities of faith and new forms of social life, independent of official endorsement and without the necessity of a promised land or the advantage of cultural privilege. Lactantius (ca. 240–ca. 320)—a native of North Africa who in his old age became tutor to Crispus, eldest son of Constantine—says that the Christian notion of equality is very different from the Roman and Greek idea of it. Lactantius was determined to defend Christianity against the charge that it was peddling visions and other delusory teachings, claiming there was more to the religion than that. Of particular note, he says, is its concept of equality, which implies not equity, the virtue of giving judgment, but the sense of justice, of treating others as one's equals—what Cicero calls "equability." Yet Plutarch noted how Cicero viewed justice as part of rhetoric. Cicero contended, "how invincible justice is, if it be well spoken."[5]

A revered veteran of the battle of wits, Lactantius was celebrated in the Renaissance as the Christian Cicero on account of his classical erudition. He gave equality a specific religious underpinning, intending to set it above simply a political or legal understanding. Lactantius stressed that the God who gave being and life to all was the same who wished us all to be equal, and to be alike in our status as moral agents. God laid down the same terms of life for us all, giving us the capacity of wisdom and a longing for eternal fellowship. God excluded no one from the benefits of heaven just as in our earthly lives God gave everyone a place in the daylight, nurtured the earth for the benefit of all, and provided nourishment and precious, relaxing sleep. With God there was no slave or master: our freedom derived from our status as freeborn children of God. No one was poor in God's eyes, except where one lacked justice; no one was rich except in moral qualities. All human beings were placed under the same requirement of accomplishing the stages of moral growth in fulfillment of their human potential. And that, explains Lactantius, was why neither the Romans nor the Greeks were able to sustain justice, "since they had so many levels of disparity in their societies, separating poorest from richest, powerless from powerful, the obscure from the most elevated dignities of royal state. Where all are not alike, there is no equality; and inequality is enough to rule out justice, the very point of which is to afford like treatment to those who have entered this life on like terms."[6]

A century earlier, Tertullian (ca. 160–ca. 240) similarly had taken up the argument, saying the Christian view of community life offered a revealing contrast to the existing world. Tertullian was an erudite educated Roman citizen brought up in Carthage, North Africa. He is considered the father of Latin as the language of the church, a claim that would resonate with St. Boniface (675–754), a later fastidious promoter of ecclesiastical Latin.[7] Tertullian's stringent views of religion led him in about 206 to join the Montanists, a fledgling group of disaffected charismatics who had a radical social agenda. Tertullian defines the social characteristics of a faith community, declaring that they entail a new and radical vision of citizenship and civil society.

In their radical obedience to God rather than in their compliance with prevailing mores, Tertullian challenges, Christians became responsible and productive members of society, an argument Augustine of Hippo (d. 430) defended with great eloquence two centuries later. A running theme in Tertullian's discussion, as well as Augustine's, is the idea that Christians are not a secret society, that their beliefs and rituals are open to public scrutiny, that membership and duties in the fellowship are voluntary, that religious office is not for sale, that believers practice mutual aid, and a common fund existed to help the poor and needy. Since the world had not seen anything like that, Tertullian argued, it was imperative—equally for the safety of Christians and for the peace and wellbeing of society—that Christians, like everyone else, be allowed to represent themselves rather than being condemned by slanderous analogy with disreputable cults. "Give the congregation of Christians its due," he pleaded, and judge the church by the same standards by which others judged and were judged.

Tertullian wrote under a sense of siege, yet still went on the offensive to defy the prevailing permissive code of society.[8] Toleration of Christians or of members of other religions was not part of Roman administrative law, for "no Roman propounded the view that Rome should respect the religious liberty of other peoples."[9]

Writing in the third century AD, the historian Cassius Dio justifies the need for a policy of strict religious establishment that outlaws nonsanctioned religions. In an imaginary speech he put into the mouth of Maecenas, Dio has advice for Octavian in 29 BC: not only must Octavian "worship the divine everywhere and in every way according to ancestral custom, and force everyone else to honour it; but you must also reject and punish those who make foreign innovation in its worship, not only for the sake of the gods (since anyone despising them will not honour anyone else), but also because such people who introduce new deities persuade many people to change their ways, leading to conspiracies, revolts and factions, which are most unsuitable for a monarchy. So you must not allow anyone to be godless or [to be] a sorcerer."[10] In that view, religion is a state monopoly; for, without such a monopoly, religion's sectarianism can turn it into a faction. A state monopoly neutralizes religion's potential to be a faction, and thus renders it amenable to control. It is a view claiming that God's injunction will be allowed only by Caesar's edict, not in spite of it.

The career of Herod, son of Antipater and a Nabataean Arab on both sides of his family, demonstrates this. Described by Josephus (AD 37–ca. 100) as being at the time in great favor with Emperor Tiberius, and well known for his reputation as a political survivor and a master at juggling religious and political interests to his advantage, Herod was appointed king of Judea by the Roman Senate at Mark Antony's prompting. He subsequently changed allegiance to Octavian, who defeated Antony in 31 BC. Herod professed Judaism and fostered it with the building of the temple in Jerusalem associated with his name. But, true to his imperial political role, if also to the unmitigated scandal of his fellow Jews, he built temples for the gods to please Augustus, his new master. The year of his death in 4 BC is believed to be contemporaneous with the birth of Jesus, an event that immortalized Herod for history.[11]

Free alike from doubt and subtlety, the Romans considered Christianity to be not so much a religion as a superstition, something akin to a clot in the circulatory system. For the Greeks, by contrast, religion belonged with the experiences of the body. As people of antiquity were urged by Pindar (ca. 518–ca. 447 BC), "become what you are." That view survived, so that when Greeks of a later age encountered Christianity as a religion, they made it necessary to deal with Christianity's truth claims about God. The Romans were different; they saw Christianity as a structural anomaly, and dealt with it as a political problem. In the words of Tacitus (AD 55–ca. 120), Christianity as "the deadly *superstitio* was checked for a time (with the execution of Christ), but broke out again, not only in Judaea, the origin of the evil, but even in the capital, where all hideous and shameful practices collect from every quarter and are extremely popular."[12]

With the stylus and with the sword, and (for dramatic effect) with wild beasts in the stadium, Roman officials waged war against the Christians.

Christianity was placed under penal surveillance as the empire adopted a robust and uncompromising posture toward Christian converts, determined to use the full force of the law and the supporting cultural prejudice to drive Christians into the ground and eradicate the faith. It was an environment rife with charges of treason, imputations of violence, cannibalism, irrational and dissolute conduct, terrorist plots, dishonesty, corruption, and extremism, and it led to horrendous sanctions. Minucius Felix bears witness to such charges, saying Christians were accused of immorality, blasphemy, sedition and general moral turpitude.[13] Yet this was barking up the wrong tree. Even allowing for a convert's pious gloss, Justin Martyr testified about how it was well known that, before they became Christians, people like him took pleasure in debauchery, practiced magic and sorcery, valued above all money and possessions, turned away strangers, and generally were inhospitable.[14]

Persecution stalked the Christians everywhere. In July 180, for example, Carthage was the site of a deadly outbreak of anti-Christian persecution with believers being charged with treason for following an illegal religion. Rejecting the offer of a thirty day grace period to recant, the Christians stood their ground, and invoked in self-defense their moral and ethical way of life: they paid the tax; abhorred murder, theft, and bearing false witness; and although they yielded their hearts only to God, they gave honor to Caesar as Caesar. Responding to their defiance, the proconsul Saturninus read out a sentence of death, and twelve of them, seven men and five women, were immediately beheaded, creating the Scillian martyrs.

Even in their death the "Christians were made an object of mockery: covered with animal skins, they were torn to pieces by dogs; or nailed to crosses, [and,] when daylight failed, they were set alight as torches to lighten the darkness," Tacitus commented wryly. The ominous clouds that hung over the heads of Christians finally burst after 249 in the form of ruthless persecution under the emperor Decius (d. 251) who declared that he would sooner have a rival emperor in Rome than a Christian bishop. In 303 under Diocletian (d. 316) the persecution recurred. Decius adopted a policy of reinstating the state cults with which Christianity was in open contention, while Diocletian adopted a policy of not exempting the provinces from the full force of Roman imperial jurisdiction, a policy that gave him the range he needed to crush Christianity. Dating from the persecution of Decius, the Christian legend of the Seven Sleepers has survived; it describes how after escaping to a cave near Ephesus and sleeping there for 309 years the Sleepers awoke to find that their country had converted to Christianity.[15] In any case, the persecutions called for unflagging, consecrated commitment, and—for the stout of heart—a dash of derring-do.

Endowed naturally with generous gifts in that regard, Tertullian was not shy about responding, and so he grasped the nettle of anti-Christian prejudice. His statement here has all the force of a prosecutor's mind, and belongs appropriately in the context of the evolving values of a new faith community struggling to save itself in the face of a hostile establishment. Borrowing his critics' method of rational discourse, Tertullian offered a model of ironic reasoning in response to critics who might glimpse in his rhetorical tour de force flashes of the brilliance they associated with a fading golden age. We may today take such values for granted, but in Tertullian's day Christians were allowed no such luxury. His statement has an instructive resonance with the straitened circumstances of the Christian movement among threatened marginal and minority populations across the centuries, and for that reason alone it bears citing at some length. I have added paragraphs for ease of reading.

> We are a body knit together as such by a common religious profession, by unity of discipline, and by the bond of a common hope. We meet together as an assembly and congregation, that, offering up prayer to God as with united force, we may wrestle with Him in our supplications. This violence God delights in. We pray, too, for the emperors, for their ministers and for all in authority, for the welfare of the world, for the prevalence of peace, for the delay of the final consummation. We assemble to read our sacred writings, if any peculiarity of the times makes either forewarning or reminiscence needful. However it be in that respect, with the sacred words we nourish our faith, we animate our hope, we make our confidence more stedfast [sic]; and no less by inculcations of God's precepts we confirm good habits. In the same place also exhortations are made, rebukes and sacred censures are administered.
>
> There is no buying and selling of any sort in the things of God. Though we have our treasure-chest, it is not made up of purchase-money, as of a religion that has its price. On the monthly day, if he likes, each puts in a small donation; but only if it be his pleasure, and only if he is able, for there is no compulsion; all is voluntary. These gifts are, as it were, piety's deposit fund. For they are not taken thence and spent on feasts, and drinking-bouts, and eating-houses, but to support and bury poor people, to supply the wants of boys and girls destitute of means and parents, and of old persons confined now to the house; such, too, as have suffered shipwreck; and if there happen to be any in the mines, or banished to the islands, or shut up

in the prisons, for nothing but their fidelity to the cause of God's Church, they become the nurslings of their confession.

For you abuse also our humble feasts, on the ground that they are extravagant as well as infamously wicked. To us, it seems, applies the saying of Diogenes: "The people of Megara feast as though they were going to die on the morrow; they build as though they were never to die!"[16] But one sees more readily the mote in another's eye than the beam in his own.... The Salii cannot have their feast without going into debt; you must get the accountants to tell you what the tenths of Hercules and the sacrificial banquets cost; the choicest cook is appointed for the Apaturia, the Dionysia, the Attic mysteries; the smoke from the banquet of Serapis will call out the firemen. Yet about the modest supper-room of the Christians alone a great ado is made. Our feast explains itself by its name. The Greeks call it *agapè,* i.e., affection. Whatever it costs, our outlay in the name of piety is gain, since with the good things of the feast we benefit the needy.

As the feast commenced with prayer, so with prayer it is closed. We go from it, not like troops of mischief-doers, nor bands of vaga-bonds, nor to break out into licentious acts, but to have as much care of our modesty and chastity as if we had been at a school of virtue rather than [at] a banquet.[17]

Tertullian has set out the social and historical demands of the Christian movement. "We pray, too, for the emperors, for their ministers and for all in authority, for the welfare of the world, for the prevalence of peace," he writes, indicating a necessary relationship of moral responsibility between Chris-tianity and the social order. Christians had a vested interest in the stability of the empire because, affirms Tertullian, "we know that mighty shock impend-ing over the whole earth—in fact, the very end of all things threatening dread-ful woes—is only retarded by the continued existence of the Roman empire. We have no desire, then, to be overtaken by these dire events; and in praying that their coming may be delayed, we are lending our aid to Rome's duration." Solely on the grounds of Christian integrity, believers could claim that "Caesar is more ours than yours, for our God has appointed him.... Never will I call the emperor God, and either because it is not in me to be guilty of falsehood; or that I dare not turn him into ridicule.... To call him God is to rob him of his title. If he is not a man, emperor he cannot be."[18] All this amounts to saying that Rome is not God's kingdom; the empire is not an eternal dispensation; the emperor is not God's messiah; and political obligation is not immutable.

Christianity is at home in the empire, argues Tertullian, for the same reason that it would be at home anywhere else.[19]

From ignorance or fear of the unfamiliar, Tertullian argues, the pagan world moved to place Christianity under penal restrictions, but in that case it is ignorance and fear that are the real enemies of society, not Christianity. It is perhaps quite understandable, Tertullian suggests ironically, for a beleaguered pagan world, in crisis from its betrayal of its own ideals, to pin the blame on Christians, since harm could only come from those already marked for ill-treatment, but that was doubly unfair. The smoke from the banquet of Serapis was so great that it set off fire alarms, and yet, says Tertullian, the modest supper-room of the Christians alone caused a great fuss. By pursuing Christians as enemies, Tertullian charges, the empire had chosen to overlook a much greater menace from its own excesses. As the saying has it, the darkest place is under the candlestick, and a society threatened by the organized call to heed the voice of conscience was likely to trample on those powerless to defend themselves in spite of holding the key to society's tranquility and welfare. It is a harmful and reckless policy, Pius XII would declare from bitter experience, to do battle with Christianity, for the props used to replace the religion "are not strong enough to support the edifice of human worth, freedom, and well-being."[20] An embattled government in dire need of a political vision instead became schizoid and turned for remedy to the petty local cults, caucuses, and coalitions that sapped public morale.

Instead of harassing the Christians, the authorities could have reflected with profit on how Christians prayed and worked for nothing more sinister than the delay of the end time and the elimination of moral apathy. Yet by acting thus, Christians placed themselves in jeopardy from the actions of hostile authorities. With the fraternal bonds forged in the celebration of their feasts, the Christians went out thence to benefit the needy. If there was one principle that marked the basis of belonging to the Christian congregation, insists Tertullian, it was the voluntary principle. There was no compulsion in membership, none in the continuation of it, and none whatsoever in making contributions. Whatever sums were thus collected represented piety's deposit fund that had, as its object, the well-being of those who became beneficiaries of their confession. Pope Nicholas I (858–67) cites a psalm (54:6) to support an identical contention about compulsion being the denial of sound religion. "What someone does not choose he neither desires nor loves; what he does not love he easily despises. There is no good which is not voluntary."[21] The foundations of sound government resided no less in that voluntary principle. In the sphere of personal ethics where the state's role was far from constructive or adequate and where civil society led the way, the tail must wag the dog.

Philanthropy and the New Ethic: An Evaluation

Philanthropy offered one of the clearest examples of state deficiency in foster-ing a climate of social ethical responsibility. Tertullian's reflections on the cause of Christian voluntarism should be set against that fact and in the specific context of contemporary attitudes toward philanthropy and benevolence. Phi-lanthropy occupied a rather minor place in the Greek and Roman world, thanks to the assumption that slaves would do all the hard manual labor and that in an emergency the state, rather than wealthy philanthropists, would step in.

The reforms of Solon, admittedly, were motivated by high social ideals in seeking to improve the lot of poorer citizens, but such reforms were state-directed. In his *Politics* (vi. 5) Aristotle confirms that philanthropy was not a homegrown virtue when he commended benevolence as a foreign practice, thus regretting its conspicuous absence among his fellow-Athenians. A ten-dency toward egoism made the Greeks unwilling to make sacrifices for the common good. John Henry Newman noted that Athenians, "feeble all to-gether," worked best when they did so one by one for their personal advantage. Even the gathering Macedonian threat failed to deter fourth century Athenians from spending lavishly on public games and festivals,[22] such being the spell cast by their carefree *douceur de vivre*.

Among the Romans philanthropy enjoyed no greater prominence than it did among the Greeks, partly because in an age of political mobilization— Roman citizens had the vote—philanthropic ideals were promptly seized as a matter of state policy, and also because the prevailing social unrest fudged the line between altruistic action and political agitation.

Under Stoic influence there appeared around the first century of the Common Era lists of hospitals and private infirmaries. Several of the emperors also established endowments under the control of municipal administrators, called *alimenta*, for the support of selected children of poor parents.

Gibbon observed that the Romans were deficient "in the amiable qualities of benevolence and generosity.... A grateful return is due to the author of a benefit ... In the case of a friendly loan, the merit of generosity is on the side of the lender only; in a deposit, on the side of the receiver; but in a pledge, and the rest of the selfish commerce of ordinary life, the benefit is compensated by an equivalent, and the obligation to restore is variously modified by the nature of the transaction."[23]

The scale of what Christians had to overcome to promote the culture of philanthropy is indicated by a leader in the third century BC who lent three talents to a city in difficult financial straits, on condition that the city mortgage all of its own property as well as the property of citizens and resident aliens. The lender was afraid of a revolution that might prevent the honoring of financial obligations, and an elaborate net of safeguards existed in law to entangle and to deter even the most erudite of scholars who wanted to promote philanthropy. When in the same era Cleomenes III of Sparta intervened with a draconian social program to ameliorate the condition of distressed farmers, including redistribution of land and the abolition of debts owed to landlords, he set in train a social revolution that spread to the rest of Greece and whose motto was division of land and cancellation of debts. One leader of the Cynics, himself an aristocrat, preached philanthropy and urged his fellow aristocrats to heal the sick and to give to the poor before it was too late. In words that read like a prophecy from the book of Amos, he wrote:

> Turn the greedy cormorant to poverty.
> Give to us the riches uselessly wasted.
> Ask God Almighty; when the rich set their hearts
> On nothing but money, God should take away their swinish wealth.
> Give to the frugal, who drink from a common bowl,
> The money he [the cormorant] squanders on extravagances. Is
>   justice blind?
> The sun unseeing? Righteousness bleary-eyed? Vengeance is coming
> And Victory. Storms will overwhelm the rich, the proud.
> Once swallowed, the whirlpool will never vomit them up again.[24]

It is striking that in the authoritative *Oxford Classical Dictionary*, described by its subtitle as "the ultimate reference work on the classical world," there is no entry on philanthropy. Juvenal (ca. 60–ca. 140), a biting satirist who turned his wry wit against the vices of Roman society, may have penned the most fitting epitaph for philanthropy as a lost cause when he observed that the misfortunes of poverty carry with them nothing harder to bear than exposing their victims to public ridicule. The church, in contrast, rallied members to promote social philanthropy and thus lifted the odium of ridicule and callous indifference the classical world attached to poverty.

In the classical understanding, philanthropy lacked the idea that is truly its essential foundation; namely, to give to others what in an absolute sense is your own without hope of reward or gain. Philanthropy implies no obligation of restitution, whereas, as Gibbon noted, making a gift under the rules of justice requires repayment of some kind. Grounded in love for humanity, philanthropy is social in character, and is practiced solely for the good of the other and not for the gratification of the giver or for propitiating God. The ancient world valued other things. In the *Burgundian Code* of 516, Sigismund, king of

Burgundy, softened Roman law in order to improve the plight of foundlings, suggesting that unamended Roman law had little scope in it for philanthropy as a social ethic. The old code behaved as if gifts crippled the law. Rooted in the radical ethic of philanthropy, and in the widow's mite as a collective pledge, Christians used their system of social aid to endure times of state repression and social ostracism. Even dripping water can hollow out a stone.

Diversity and Innovation

Tertullian had much wider vistas in mind than the fate of the empire when he took up the Christian cause against its detractors. He saw the importance of the multiform cultural idioms that continued to shape the Christian movement in the empire and beyond, and he challenged his opponents with that argument, asking:

> On whom else have all the nations of the world believed, but on Christ who has already come? . . . with others as well, as different races of the Gaetuli, many tribes of the Mauri, all the confines of Spain, and various tribes of Gaul, with places in Britain, which, though inaccessible to Rome, have yielded to Christ. Add the Sarmatae, the Daci, the Germans, the Scythians, and many remote peoples, provinces, and islands unknown to us, which we are unable to go over.[25]

Irenaeus (ca. 130–ca. 200), bishop of Lyons, spoke of how the quest and moral insights of antiquity were evocative of Christian teaching, and how Christianity united all the scattered and remote contributions of past ages in the person of Jesus, "who was formed from the contributions of all."[26] Irenaeus referred to the cultural diversity that the Christian movement created, saying apostolic teaching took root whatever the language spoken and wherever the sun shone. Variety was the religion's genius.

> For although the languages of the world are varied, yet the meaning of the Christian tradition is one and the same. There is no whit of difference in what is believed or handed down by the churches planted in Germany or in Iberia or in Gaul or in the East or in Egypt or in Libya or in the central region of the world. Nay, as the sun remains the same all over the world so also the preaching of the church shines everywhere.[27]

Believed now to be a third century document, the *Epistle to Diognetus* preserves a sentiment that belongs with the earliest picture of Christianity as a world religion. It asserts that Christians take their earthly responsibilities seriously while knowing that they have their citizenship in heaven. Understanding loyalty as more than lip service, Christians obey the laws appointed for all while, in their own lives, surpassing the letter of the law. Christianity is a world religion by virtue of its visible diversity and its invisible transformative power.

> The difference between Christians and the rest of mankind is not a matter of nationality, or language, or customs. Christians do not live apart in separate cities of their own, speak any special dialect, nor practice any eccentric way of life.... They pass their lives in whatever township—Greek or foreign—each man's lot has determined; and conform to ordinary local usage in their clothing, diet, and other habits ... they are residents at home in their own countries ... they take their full part as citizens.... For them, any foreign country is a motherland, and any motherland is a foreign country.
>
> To put it briefly, the relation of Christians to the world is that of a soul to the body. As the soul is diffused through every part of the body, so are Christians through all the cities of the world. The soul, too, inhabits the body, while at the same time forming no part of it; and Christians inhabit the world, but they are not part of the world. The soul, invisible herself, is immured within a visible body; so Christians can be recognized in the world, but their Christianity itself remains hidden from the eye.... The soul, shut up inside the body, nevertheless holds the body together; and though they are confined within the world as in a dungeon, it is Christians who hold the world together.[28]

A parallel idea was expressed by Collingwood when he pointed out how Christianity made its home in the Greco-Roman world not by surrendering to it, in which case it would be no different from any of the numerous proliferating cults, but by pioneering a new conception of social life with a theocentric focus.

> For the Christian, all men are equal in the sight of God: there is no chosen people, no privileged class, no one community whose fortunes are more important than those of another. All persons and all people are involved in working out of God's purpose, and therefore the historical process is everywhere and always of the same kind, and every part of it is a part of the same whole. The Christian cannot be content with Roman history or Jewish history or any other partial and

particularistic history: [she] demands a history of the world, a universal history whose theme shall be the general development of God's purpose for human life. The infusion of Christian ideas overcomes not only the characteristic humanism and substantialism of Greco-Roman history, but also its particularism . . . Greco-Roman ecumenical history is not universal history in this sense, because it has a particularistic centre of gravity. Greece or Rome is the centre round which it revolves. Christian universal history has undergone a Copernican revolution, whereby the very idea of such a centre of gravity is destroyed.[29]

Translatability and Openness: Intercultural Turn

The characteristic pattern of Christianity's engagement with the languages and cultures of the world has God at the center of the universe of cultures, implying equality among cultures and the necessarily relative status of cultures vis-à-vis the truth of God. No culture is so advanced and so superior that it can claim exclusive access or advantage to the truth of God, and none so marginal and remote that it can be excluded. All have merit; none is indispensable. The ethical monotheism Christianity inherited from Judaism accords value to culture but rejects cultural idolatry, which makes Bible translation more than a simple exercise in literalism. In any language the Bible is not literal; its message affirms all languages to be worthy, though not exclusive, of divine communication. That implied Biblical view of culture goes beyond culture as a matter of mere mechanical manipulation, including its takeover in religious translation. Accordingly, the vernacular in translation was often invigorated rather than overthrown. The relationship of the Christian movement to culture was shaped by the fact that Christianity is a translated—and a translating—religion, and a translated Christianity is an interpreted Christianity, pure and simple. "Original" Christianity is nothing more than a construction.[30]

The New Testament was not written or dictated by Jesus, and the Greek language in which the Gospels are written is not the language in which Jesus taught or prayed and worshipped. Christianity spread as a religion without the language of its founder—in striking contrast, for example, to Islam. In the ancient tussle between the two religions, Muslim scholars have argued that this language deficit discredits Christianity.[31] As such, the church's recourse to liturgical Latin concedes the Muslims' point that Christians have abandoned Jesus' own language, though it should be stressed that this is in obedience to Him.

Without a revealed language and without even the language of Jesus, Christianity invested in idioms and cultures that existed for purposes other than Christianity. As these idioms and cultures became the carriers of the religion, they anticipated and embodied Christianity. Being a translated religion, Christian teaching was received and framed in the terms of its host culture; by feeding off the diverse cultural streams it encountered, the religion became multicultural. The local idiom became a chosen vessel. As Irenaeus pointed out, the gospel did not strip nations of their distinctions; those distinctions were the rich tapestry adorning the communities of faith. It is a striking feature of Christianity's expansion that it seldom arrived as a surprise. Rather, what people had vaguely divined appeared in the form of Christianity as a confident and reassuring validation. A Palestinian born of settlers in "Flavia Neapolis" (Nablus) and who converted in 133, Justin Martyr testified that the God the Christians worshipped was none other than the One who was from the beginning of creation. Even Jesus was the one "whom the prophets foretold would come as a herald of salvation and a teacher of good disciples." Recognizing the impact of the religion on his fellow Arabs, Justin Martyr celebrated Christianity as a world religion by declaring: "For there is not a single race of human beings, barbarians, Greeks, or whatever name you please to call them, nomads or vagrants or herdsmen living in tents, where prayers through the name of Jesus the Crucified are not offered up to the Father and Maker of the Universe."[32]

Justin Martyr's insistence that Christianity was destined for the whole world is vindicated by the fact that the religion does not only bring what is new; it also adopts what is old and precedes it. With good reason the missionary vocation of Christianity has accorded an esteemed place to the pre-Christian dispensation, creating the irony that preexisting cultures have themselves come to claim a Christian origin, as happened, say, with the Greek of the New Testament, the Latin of Jerome, the Italian of Dante, the German of Luther, the French of Calvin, and the English of the King James Bible. And who knows yet how that logic of serial origin will work itself out in the post-Western Christian awakening? It is because of this that when we try to disentangle Christianity from culture we hit a roadblock, in part because the serial origin means history does not repeat itself, and in part because the language we use is what gave us the subject of our inquiry in the first place. What has occurred in the contemporary Christian resurgence should throw in high relief the many centuries of unjustified wanton attack on ethnic cultures.

By way of contrast, Islam went about its mission in a different way. Its canon of an inalienable sacred Arabic is a dramatic example of the Arabic culture becoming the prescribed, irreplaceable bedrock of religious orthodoxy. In movements of Islamic reform, leaders have sought a reassertion of the Arabic canon of faith practice against the syncretism of local accretions. For its part, Christianity lost any meaningful ties to its founding Aramaic culture, and instead embraced the practice of open-ended naturalization of the message. Thus, in spite of their origin in Jesus' tongue, Aramaic references in the Gospels came to sound foreign and remote to New Testament readers.

Under the banner of Islam, the Arabs gave their fledgling culture the prerogatives of a religious birthright, while a translated Christianity allowed Europeans to interpret it as something they could domesticate by repackaging its truth claims as their own preferred ideas. In time, with currents of irreversible assimilation, Europe transmuted the religion by separating ethics and economics as well as public and private morality. Christianity was thereby disarmed. In their different ways, Machiavelli and Marx exploited the distinction for their purposes. Perhaps the Western impact will force separation on Islam, though the idea seems only credible where a culture lacks the sense of an original religious birthright, as Madison observed with respect to America's adoption of separation. Madison stressed the fact that an unaffiliated Christianity would all at once allay the fear of political theocracy, advance democratic liberalism on the principle of an unfettered conscience, and leave Christianity that much closer to its own origins—and how right he was. Unlike Muhammad, Jesus never founded a state.

Christianity's translated status exempted Christians from binding adherence to a founding culture. There was, however, a positive side. Tertullian hinted at it when he explained that, given Christianity's critical and necessary investment in what preceded it in society, believers could say that Caesar was more the Christians' than he was the Romans'. Tertullian was not just making a rhetorical point, in spite of the considerable advantages he enjoyed in that regard, nor was he being obsequious—"because it is not in me to be guilty of falsehood." He was affirming a basic Christian insight. Affirmation of the empire staked Christian claims on things originally non-Christian, including language. As the religion resounded with the idioms and styles of new converts, it became multilingual and multicultural. Believers responded with the unprecedented facility of the mother tongue, and by that step broke the back of cultural chauvinism as, for example, between Jew and Gentile. Christianity's indigenous potential was activated, and the frontier beckoned.

Christianity's appeal was an appeal to the indigenous milieu. Converts were twice so in the sense that membership in the church was paralleled by membership in one's natural community. The one God was a part of, rather than apart from, one's formation in culture and society. The theme surfaces more than a millennium and a half later in the story of a soldier recently converted to Christianity. The attitude of soldiers like him to authority, he said, was "not with eye-service, but as the servants of Christ, doing the will of God from the heart." Translation on the cross-cultural frontier carried with it the duty of a dual, rather than a divided, loyalty. Christianity aligned itself with earthly affairs so that, as Augustine of Hippo showed, the universal divine purpose could transform the politics of local identity by reclaiming it. Human belonging was given a double heritage, an earthly and a heavenly one.

Accordingly, at Cornelius' beckoning and out of range of the synagogue, Peter as a devout Jew overcame centuries-old obstacles to speak about how honoring God in the Gentile world involved no dishonor to Peter's own sense of God. God's magnanimity overspilled hallowed frontiers to overwhelm cultural strictures. Cornelius' response vindicated Peter and set a new standard and a new direction for the church. From its assimilation in the world's languages and cultures the Christian movement was transformed into a form of deferred homecoming, arriving for the first time where it had always belonged. The movement of Gentile cultures into Christianity and the movement of Christianity in its missionary message were two sides of the same coin. Salvation was not merely an export commodity. Whatever the merit of ascetic renunciation, the early Christians did not shut themselves up in a dialogue of the deaf. On the contrary, they believed that being a Christian in the empire involved reciprocal encounter of give-and-take, not a prickly exceptionalism; for both the church and the empire existed to serve the common good. Trust in the God of all life and goodness was in harmony with the demands and obligations of common citizenship, although divine sovereignty limited the power of the state over its citizens, Christians included. Christian teaching took a commodious view of worldly arrangements for human wellbeing, and was subversive only of the idolatry of power. Rulers were entitled to the prayers of Christians, but that did not give them license from God to do evil.

When he evaluated Christianity's appeal as a world religion, Adolf von Harnack, prominent for his Enlightenment interpretation of religious truth claims, underlined the spirit of local versatility that animated the mission movement. The reasons for the rich and diverse cultural expressions that distinguished Christianity, he wrote, were native to the very essence of the religion (as monotheism and gospel). The versatility of Christianity was reflected in its amazing power of adaptation. From one point of view, it is difficult to determine the relative weight of the different components of Christianity's appeal; to determine, for example, how much of that appeal "was due to its spiritual monotheism, to its preaching of Jesus Christ, to its hope of immortality, to its active charity and system of social aid, to its discipline and organization, to its syncretistic capacity and contour, or to the skill with which it developed in the third century for surpassing the fascinations of any superstition whatsoever."[33] The Gospels testified to Jesus being born of the spirit, not of flesh and blood. In spite of that, his followers soon learnt to be at home in the world. From another point of view, Christianity was a universal religion with the unique advantage that it brought to people what each individual craved spiritually. By that means Christianity became a church for the world.

Harnack's argument that Christianity emerged already equipped with the right spirit for its world errand needs to be elaborated further. Christianity spread through established cultural patterns—sometimes flowing with the tide, and sometimes grinding against the flow—but always making local appropriation of its claims a necessary prerequisite. Christianity's cultural convergence was, in the first instance, an affirmation of what preceded it and, in the second, a critical interface with the cultural materials it encountered. For the apostles, Christianity was culturally adaptable by virtue of its transcendency—it transformed the cultures it encountered. I have employed the language of translatability and its corollary of reciprocity to underscore this complex feature of the religion, a characterization that fits well into Harnack's rationale of Christian expansion.

> From the very outset Christianity came forward with a spirit of *universalism*, by dint of which it laid hold of *the entire life of man* in all its functions, thoughts, and actions. This guaranteed its triumph. In and with its universalism, it also declared that Jesus whom it preached was the Logos ... From the very first it embraced humanity and the world, despite the small number of the elect whom it contemplated. Hence it was that those very powers of attraction, by means of which it was enabled at once to absorb and subordinate the whole of Hellenism, had a new light thrown upon them. They appeared almost in the light of a necessary feature in that age ... [Christianity] was ... something which could blend with coefficients of the most diverse nature, something which, in fact, sought out all such coefficients.[34]

Thematic Shift

The defense of Christianity mounted by Tertullian and others is steeped in urban cosmopolitan assumptions, and that urban milieu has stamped the religion with the highbrow values and ideas of establishment society. Christian

Hellenism was its culmination, and Christian theology its outstanding intellectual legacy. Harnack refers to this urban background, saying that the exceptional facilities, the growth and security of international traffic, the well-constructed roads, the blending of different nationalities, the interchange of wares and ideas, the fluid social relations, the fleet-of-foot merchant, the soldier, and the professional academic to be encountered from Antioch to Cadiz, from Alexandria to Bordeaux—all were part of the world Christians lived in.[35]

According to this cosmopolitan view, the means were available, and the population of the large towns was heterogeneous and devoid of a commanding past, all of which predisposed people toward Christian teaching. Writing in 1882, Ulhorn describes this cosmopolitan process as having reached an advanced stage by the time of Christianity's advent, contending that in "the Roman empire there had already appeared a universalism foreign to the ancient world. Nationalities had been effaced. The idea of universal humanity had disengaged itself from that of nationality."[36] Harnack states that Christianity mocked the barriers of nationality while appealing directly to the conscience. The cosmopolitan character of the religion derived from the blending of states and nations, a combination of forces that produced the idea and the ideal of a universal empire. Cosmopolitanism thereby became a reality. This cosmopolitan development, in turn, produced a culture of individualism that expressed itself in a real demand for purity, consolation, and healing. Looking to the individual conscience, Christianity arrived equipped to meet the demand for personal consolation and spiritual security.[37]

Yet, as Gibbon pointed out, in spite of its undeniable cosmopolitan appeal, Christianity was firmly entrenched off the beaten track in the provinces where imperial authority was weak, or where Christian advances allegedly weakened it.[38] Whatever merit to that conspiracy theory, what rattled the authorities may not have been so much the subversive reputation of the religion for colluding with a renegade Cincinnatus from the provinces as the fear that Christianity might spawn disloyalty within and beyond its cosmopolitan confines.

Pliny the Younger, for example, was puzzled, and told Emperor Trajan that the spread of Christianity appeared to be reviving temple festivals and sacrifices that the authorities thought had long been defunct.[39] It was not the kind of hard evidence Roman jurisprudence required to make criminal charges stick, but it was still circumstantial enough to warrant vigilance. The authorities preferred to have the Christians trounced as scofflaws, but, failing that, they had them tripped under the law for sharing dubious company that was nefarious by its unauthorized ubiquitous appeal. Not only cities and urban centers but also remote villages were affected, as Tacitus was eager to point out.

Christianity had revived the problem of religion for the empire. Rome could not let down its guard for a moment, Pliny advised the emperor, saying that people of every age and rank and both men and women continued to be gravely imperiled. Owning to a sense of urgency, Pliny resorted to panic in describing the Christian movement as the contagion of a superstition that had infected cities and had festered in villages and hamlets. Yet all was not lost, he re-assured the emperor, affirming that it was still possible to check and beat back the new religious movement.

The task was daunting, however, because the Christian movement ap-peared to stimulate and revive temple worship; to suppress it would require widening the target. The religion's urban appeal, combined with its provincial impact, defied a simple solution. Faced with the awakened religious appetite, the authorities tried to strike a balance between isolating Christianity and alienating a far wider circle. Under Christian influence, for example, the de-mand for sacrificial victims, which had been in a slump, had picked up con-siderably, suggesting that Christianity was a moving target.[40] Thanks to Pliny's honest scruples as a tireless enforcer, we have rare glimpses into the popular basis of the spread of Christianity in the empire.

Many scholars, Harnack among them, have pointed out how Christian syncretism made it difficult to pin down the religion sufficiently to make it a steady, consistent target for repression. Christian syncretism was the syncre-tism of a universal religion that had learned and borrowed from all and sundry, to the utter distraction of purists.

Thanks to its roots in Jewish monotheism, Christianity was not originally syncretistic, for neither Jesus nor the apostles belonged to any circle of pagan ideas.[41] However, as the early Christians began to formulate their ideas of God, Jesus, sin, redemption, and life, they drew upon the materials acquired in the general process of religious development that culminated in the imperial *cultus*. In that syncretistic environment, the Christian movement possessed an unacknowledged ally, even though it was one it would cleanse, purify, unite, and (in time) complicate. As a consequence, the religion came to resemble a "patched wineskin filled with mixed wine." There were few religious practices from which Christianity had not drawn something for itself. Indeed, these religions prepared the soil for it, and the new Christian seed planted on that soil sent down its roots and grew into a sturdy tree. Thus could Irenaeus speak with confidence about how with one design and desire all the great spirits of the past pointed unerringly to Jesus Christ. Here was a religion that touched, and was in turn touched, by everything in its path, and yet at its core remained simple and singular: the name of Jesus Christ filled and united it. Integration in the material life was accompanied by reconciliation in the moral life, which made Christian syncretism, in turn, appealing and challenging. It was a case of affirming through discernment.

Confident of the religion's future and secure from any risk of it dissolving into any of the petty local cults, contemporary Christian thinkers dealt generously and leniently with a superstitious world. The revival of the old religions and cults was allowed to proceed, with guardian spirits presiding over the different sectors of provincial life and its agrarian calendar. Assured of the benefits of the spiritual life, the church embraced the material world in all its variegated forms and profuse relationships. Miracles, visions, magic, dreams, and healings accumulated and were plausibly attributed to saints and holy figures, while fables, legends and hagiographies multiplied to cater to the appetite. The reputation of Christianity as a menace and nuisance gave way to that of Christianity as accessible.

Impetus, Setback, and Improvisation

In spite of its cosmopolitan achievement, however, Christianity pursued its mission beyond the empire eastward into Central and East Asia. The epicenter for the Asian mission was Arabia, and in particular Persia. Constantine even wrote to King Sapur commending him for Christian expansion in his kingdom: "I am delighted to learn that the finest districts in Persia also are adorned with the presence of Christians."[42]

By AD 150 Christianity had penetrated regions in Babylonia and lands west and southwest of the Euphrates. When Pantaenus traveled to southern Arabia in about 177 he found Christianity already established there. The entire province of Arabia eventually became studded with church buildings, known as "houses of prayer," the period of the greatest construction projects being between the fifth and sixth centuries. Pantaenus, a convert from Stoic philosophy and a missionary in south Arabia, became head of the Catechetical School of Alexandria where (in about 200) he was succeeded by his pupil, the famous Clement. One Bishop Pamphilos of the nomad Arabs of Mesopotamia was present at Nicaea as an observer.

Rather than blazing its own trail the church adopted a path opened for it. Such was the position of churches particularly in Syria and beyond, leading to the reputation of Arabia as a land fertile in heresies (Arabia haeresium ferax). The deviations and multiple theological interpretations that abounded gave the Syriac and Aramaic-speaking churches a means of self-defense against the meddlesome edicts of official religion.[43] The region of Najrán adopted Christianity around the end of the fifth century and became a satellite of the Axumite kingdom of Ethiopia. A civil war broke out among Najrán's Arab population, with Arab Jews and Arab Christians fighting and tearing down each other's religious buildings. Religious difference trumped ethnic solidarity.

In 523 Ethiopia responded to appeals with a show of force on the side of the beleaguered Christians. That provoked the attack on the Christians and in 525 precipitated a full scale Ethiopian intervention of 70,000 troops, to little avail in the end. A widespread slaughter of Christians followed, with the attackers committing outrages that horrified the Christian world. On the order of the Himyarite king, Dhú Nuwás (522–525), some 427 clerics, monks, and nuns were burned alive; 4,252 Christian adults killed; and nearly 1,300 children and young people enslaved.[44] Ethiopia's Himyarite sway ended in 575. The massacre of the Christians in Najrán and its rallying effect on the whole Christian world show the scope of the religion in Arab ranks.[45]

In Najrán's religious war the involvement of Axumite Ethiopia (its dynastic ally), Byzantium (Byzantium's Justin I was the brother of Ella Asbehá of Axum), Persia, and other regional political interests showed how religion and imperial politics formed a volatile mix. The puppet Himyarite king whom the Ethiopians installed failed to carry the people with him and was deposed by the independent-minded Abraha who established a new capital at San'á. Instead of unifying the area's rival jurisdictions, however, Abraha's action intensified the rivalries at the ultimate expense of the Himyarite kingdom. San'á threatened Mecca's dominance of the pilgrimage trade, with Abraha eventually setting out to sack the Ka'ba, the center of Mecca's annual pilgrimage. The sack of the Ka'ba fanned the flames of hostility with Mecca's Bedouin patrons led by the Quraysh, the tribe of the future prophet of Islam. It was 'Abd al-Muttalib, the prophet's grandfather, who led a counter-attack to repulse Abraha's forces. An oblique reference in súrah 105 to the elephant is taken by commentators to apply to Abraha's elephant-led charge against the Meccans. The attack is claimed by Muslim writers to have occurred in the year of the prophet's birth, though that is unsupported by any contemporary record. Thus saved, the Ka'ba retained its venerable role as the preeminent site of pagan Arab dominance embodied in the privileges enjoyed by the Quraysh. It was in this context that Islam rose to ensure that Christianity would have little future as a force among the Arabs.[46]

Pantaenus makes an intriguing reference to a primitive Christian community existing in India—meaning south Arabia, a gateway to India—a reference that bolsters claims by the St. Thomas ("Mar Thoma") Christians of India that the Apostle Thomas, from whom they took their name, carried the gospel there. Although the claim lacks documentary proof, the contention of an Indian connection with the apostolic mandate is maintained by the extant community of St. Thomas Christians in Kerala.

The church adhered to the Syriac liturgy, claiming the Syriac language was the language of Jesus. Yet, that claim notwithstanding, Syriac had only restricted use as a liturgical language and was never spoken by the people, an indication that the Syriac claim likely evolved rather than being received *ab initio* from the apostles. The churches of apostolic foundation, for example, were predominantly Greek speaking, though apostolic inspiration was claimed for non-Greek-speaking churches founded elsewhere, as seems to be the case with the Syriac churches. The first recorded use of the expression "Christians of St. Thomas" is in a ninth century reference by Patriarch Timothy (779–823) concerning his community in southern Persia, who claimed Thomas as authority for its jurisdiction in order to separate it from the Catholics of Seleucia.[47] It is not improbable, though by no means certain, that the Thomas tradition in India stemmed from that well-established Persian connection.[48] It is a cautionary lesson here that the historian must abandon as futile and distracting all attempts at seeking empirical proof. The mystery of precisely how the gospel reached India in the ancient period is beyond the capacity of historians to solve. What matters is the continuity, not the historical unassailability, of the Thomas tradition in India, and there we are on the kind of firmer ground where once again history can be useful.

References to early Christian pioneers exist in several sources. A late third century source mentioned David, bishop of Basra, who was a missionary in India, thus demonstrating Arab Christian range. John the Persian, who was present at Nicâea, represented what he called the churches of the whole of Persia and of Great India. Another source identified Theophilus the Indian as an advisor of the Emperor Constantius (d. 361). The references continue unabated well into and beyond the sixth century, suggesting a remarkable centuries-long tradition of interest in the ancient world concerning Christianity on the Indian sub-continent.[49] It was a Nestorian monk from Baghdad who arrived in China in the tenth century to report that Christianity had died out in the country.[50]

Traditions carry the Thomas connection farther, saying the Apostle himself took Christianity to China from India. In historical accounts, however, Christianity made its appearance in China only in 635 during the reign of Emperor Taizong (627–49) when the monk Aluoben arrived with books and pictures. Thanks to the Silk Route, a vigorous Sino-Christian interaction ensued, centered on the establishment in 638 of a monastery in the imperial capital. In 642 the first Christian texts were translated into Chinese. Some scrolls discovered in 1907, describing themselves as "Jesus Sutras," indicate how Christian teachings were received and adapted to conform to local Chinese ideas. One of these sutras describes Jesus as a lamb that goes silently to be slaughtered, bearing in his body the punishment of the Law. He suffered out of love to remedy the sin of Adam. Yet he did not die, only his Five Attributes passed away while he himself was released after his death. "Through the holy wonders of the Messiah all can escape becoming ghosts. All of us are saved by his works. You don't need strength to receive him, but he will not leave you weak and vulnerable, without *qi*," the sutra assured.

Successful Christian expansion provoked Buddhist opposition and persecution, but in 745 the emperor Hsuan-tsung lifted the ban (though not for long, as persecution returned under the emperor Wu-tsang). In the era of promise, Christianity's cross-cultural momentum guided it on the Chinese political and spiritual landscape, and left evidence of that in stone on a stele erected in 781. The stele carried an inscription in Chinese and Syriac devoted to the propagation of what the Chinese called Persian Christianity, termed in the inscription the "luminous religion." The existence of such a long-range Sino-Christian connection was maintained only in oral tradition until the stele was discovered in 1623 and the historical trail could be securely established once more. Inscriptions testify to the spread of Christianity on the west coast of Sumatra where churches dedicated to the Virgin Mary were established. Presumably these churches served Persian Christian traders and merchants who traveled there on business. An Italian traveler in the mid-fourteenth century met "Nestorian" Christians in Java. It is known that a Nestorian bishop was consecrated at Palembang in eastern Sumatra in 1502. Thus, long before there was an organized effort in Europe to propagate the religion, Christianity had embarked on its long-range world errand.

Cleaving faithfully to venerable tradition, the St. Thomas Christians of India coalesced around the rite of the apostle and formed a distinct, well-defined community of their own amidst the teeming Hindu population. Arrogating to themselves the rights and privileges proper to an elevated caste but remaining rooted in a recognizably ancient Christian tradition, the St. Thomas Christians rebuffed attempts by outsiders to dissolve and incorporate them. In the early sixteenth century, for example, the Portuguese reported a stern rebuff from the St. Thomas Christians, saying the priests of these Christians closed the door to any traffic with Europeans. Yet this resistance to Europeans must, in mitigation, be set against a remarkable openness to the surrounding Hindu environment. The church of St. Thomas Christians overcame the barrier of an alien faith and pioneered the earliest and most sustained genuine interface between Christianity and the religions of India. It says a great deal about their cultural shortsightedness that in the early modern period European witnesses of this interface denounced it as syncretistic, and yet at the same time tried to put in its place a no less syncretistic substitute in the name of European civilization. The principle of serial origin in Christian history, here today and there tomorrow, seemed difficult to grasp or to concede. That principle represents a crucial thematic shift with unprecedented implications for vernacular conversion movements, as the example of northern England in the West illustrates. To that we must now turn our attention.

Vernacular Pillar: Conversion of England

The Venerable Bede (673–735), the monk of Jarrow, in his classic account of the conversion of the English in Northumbria that early in the seventh century relates that the young prince Edwin of Deira was in exile where he was tormented by inward fires that brought him no light. Suddenly, in the dead of night, he saw in a vision a strange man whose appearance alarmed him considerably. The stranger approached him and greeted him, inquiring as to why Edwin was sitting by himself on a stone, wakeful and alone at an hour when everyone else was asleep. The stranger proceeded to speak directly about what was on Edwin's mind that caused him such lonely distress. He said he knew precisely who Edwin was, what his troubles were, and the impending evils he dreaded, in particular the enmity of Redwald, king of East Anglia. His power on the rise, Redwald hedged his bets with Christianity by keeping a small pagan altar next to the Christian altar. He offered victims to devils on the pagan altar while the Christian altar remained in use.

The stranger offered Edwin a deal that sounded like a godsend: the offer of a person who could deliver him from his troubles, including a promise that Redwald would not harm him or betray him to his enemies. Not only that, but he also promised Edwin that he would attain the throne, vanquish his enemies and become the greatest king the English nation ever had. If Edwin could achieve all this, what reward would he give to the one responsible for such an agreeable turn of events? Edwin answered that he would give ample proofs of his gratitude. The stranger pressed, asking Edwin what further reward he would give to that person who was able not only to foretell such good fortune but also could grant him better and wiser counsel for his life and salvation? Would Edwin promise to follow the advice of such a person? Upon that promise, the stranger placed his hand on Edwin's head, saying, "When you receive this sign, remember this occasion and our conversation, and do not delay the fulfillment of your promise." The stranger then vanished, at which point Edwin came to, realizing that he had seen a spirit in a vision.

Still at the spot and feeling heartened by the message of his mysterious visitor, Edwin was pondering in his heart the identity of his visitor when a loyal friend announced himself with a cheerful greeting to bring the good news that the king who had threatened Edwin had had a change of heart. That king's queen had shamed him into abandoning his evil designs against Edwin. Chastened by the spousal reprimand, the king turned on Ethelfrid, his erstwhile ally, whom he defeated in battle. The victory handed Edwin the throne of England. In spite of the fulfillment of the prophecy made to him, Edwin continued to prevaricate, sitting alone for hours pondering what he should do: whether to remain loyal to his pagan forebears or to fulfill his vows and embrace Christianity. The issue tormented him to distraction, and he was not able to make up his mind which religion he should follow.

Then one day, a man of God came to him and, laying his right hand on his head, asked him whether he remembered that sign. At that the king trembled and would have fallen down had not Paulinus, the emissary of Pope Gregory, come to his aid and raised him with the reassuring words: "God has helped you to escape from the hands of the enemies whom you feared, and it is through His bounty that you have received the kingdom that you desired. Remember the third promise that you made, and hesitate no longer. Accept the Faith and keep the commands of Him who has delivered you from all your earthly troubles and raised you to the glory of an earthly kingdom. If you will henceforth obey His will, which he reveals to you through me, he will save you likewise from the everlasting doom of the wicked and give you a place in His eternal kingdom."[51]

Edwin felt convicted, but asked for more time to consult his principal advisors. Perhaps a push from them would be less hazardous than the jump he was unwilling to take. His strategy would be to obtain a public consensus, so that he and they might all be cleansed together in Christ the Fount of Life. Coifi, the royal chief priest, led the deliberations with an opening remark about how the old religion had lost its potency. Coifi said he had watched with gathering dismay how his prayers and appeals to the gods returned to him unanswered, his devotion and faithfulness to them unrequited, and his zeal in their service unrepaid. This was a premonition of what seemed to lie ahead, and, Coifi argued, if the new teachings could be shown to be better and more efficacious then he and his people, including Edwin, should not hesitate to accept them. Here was a new religion that had the power to peer into the mystery of things and to obtain knowledge that promised uncounted blessings and favors to the people; one, furthermore, that could fortify the people against any contagious fallout from the displeasure of the slighted gods.

It was a weighty decision, and Edwin would not be jostled. He would roll the dice one more time and take counsel. At this point, another senior court officer stepped forward to make a plea, employing for the purpose a figure of speech (such being the occupational hazard of professionals of the art). Addressing the king, the senior official explained that Christianity presented a challenge; under the waning dispensation of the old order, he and the people assembled there were at a great disadvantage when they tried to compare the world from which they took their bearings with the world of the future life about which they knew nothing. Perhaps recalling many a scene he personally witnessed, he said he could only liken it to the swift flight of a single sparrow through the king's banqueting hall on a winter's day when the king's noblemen and counselors were assembled in his presence. In the middle was an open fire, and outside the storms of winter rain or snow raged. The sparrow flew swiftly in through one door of the hall to emerge as swiftly out of another. While the bird was inside it was safe from the harsh winter elements, but after a few fleeting moments of security and comfort it vanished into the world from where it came.

The sum of accumulated knowledge that the old religious craft gave him and the people, he acknowledged, was nothing more reliable than that all too-fleeting episode of the vanished sparrow. Earthly existence, he concluded, straining to make his metaphor work, was like that sparrow's flight. While it was in the hall, the sparrow operated within the scope of human comprehension, and so it was with human beings. With all the accumulated wisdom of their ancestors, the priests of the craft could account for virtually nothing about what preceded this life or what lay after it; therefore, if it could be determined that Christianity brought any more certain knowledge on that front, he would call for adopting the religion. The issue was that clear, and that pivotal. As the herald of an eternal and more auspicious world, the dove of Christian teaching seemed destined to abide.

It was time to hear specifically what the new Christian teaching had to offer, so Coifi asked for the king's permission to have Paulinus summoned to take the stage that had been cleared of his competitors and was now available for his uncontested possession. Paulinus duly appeared and seized control of the occasion. He preached to great effect, it transpired, resulting in a decision to cut loose from the old religious moorings and to embrace Christianity. Coifi asked Edwin to deconsecrate the moribund temples and altars and bring them down, and allow Paulinus to be installed as the new royal chief priest. Coifi was given a warhorse and a spear with which to pull down the shrine. It is significant and appropriate that it was Coifi and his fellow priests, and not Paulinus, who undertook the work of revamping the past by dismantling the pagan temples and altars, and significant, too, that the disavowal occurred only in the light of a plausible substitute. Paulinus stayed for over a month while he baptized converts in the River Glen.

It could not have been lost on all in attendance that it was Coifi who asked the king to elevate Paulinus to the consecrated position that he, Coifi, had until then so eminently occupied. Edwin and his people converted to Christianity not because they had no religion or because their minds were empty, but because the old religions had disposed them to find in Christianity what had failed them in their own. For them, Christianity was a strategic restoration, with power of renewal.

In the compressed narrative of Christian conversion, Bede preserved all the essential elements of the vernacular foundations of religious change. The political and social structure depended for its integrity, stability, and identity on the old rites. It was the much-threatened function of these old rites that Christianity came to fill. The gods appeared to have reneged on the people when the people were in peril and their leaders distracted. In spite of unstinting devotion and public demonstration of zeal, unanswered prayers took their toll. Amidst the ruins of the old assurances and in the wake of the flight of the gods, Christianity arrived equipped in everything in which the old religions were deficient, trailing demonstrable results. With its roots in the soil, Christianity would demarcate spheres of church and state, as well as prescribe for the security and destiny of the soul. It was impossible—and perilous—to ignore it.

It was the right time for all concerned to cut a deal and to make peace with the new order. Edwin and his people would occupy their rightful place in the church with the prospects of a strengthened and revitalized society. Except in historical hindsight, and perhaps in the blinding mirror of pious dogma, it was by no means a foregone conclusion that Christianity would win out; up to the last moment there was always a chance, however diminished by that stage, that the old guard might step in and, appealing to the old die-hards, mount a resistance to hold the religion at bay. People could still be roused on behalf of the halcyon days of yesteryear when the gods reigned and the earth was fruitful and at peace. In any case, Christianity would not be allowed to take root merely by the means of a secret, arcane deal cobbled together in the dead of night, and with someone not fully in possession of his rational powers.

Christianity was, accordingly, put through a stringent round of public scrutiny in which its foremost proponents had been its foremost competitors and those who had the most to lose. Edwin was baptized in 628, and lived for only a few more years. He died in battle in 632 in a war between Celtic Christian kings and a pagan warrior from the Midlands. Christianity collapsed in Northumbria, and Paulinus and his fellow Christians, including Edwin's

Kentish widow, fled by sea to Kent. The cause in Northumbria was taken over and revived from Iona where Edwin's successor and his once exiled enemy, Oswald, had been baptized. Christianity north of the Humber in Northumbria lay within the orbit of Scottish and northern Irish Christianity and had its center in Iona where in 563 the religion was brought by Columba (d. 597). He produced the monks and monasteries that provided the structures of rule and identity uniting the country.

Columba sent missionary monks to the Orkneys and founded houses at Melrose and Dunkeld to maintain the faith. Cuthbert entered the monastery at Melrose to emerge as the center and symbol of the church in all the north. Durham Cathedral remains a living monument to his heritage. A similar drive south from Iona into England resulted in the widespread adoption of Christianity. From that sprang the first bloom of English Christian piety, with the great saints of the north—Aidan, Hilda, and Cuthbert—appearing as national heroes. The "holy living and dying of the northern saints evoked a literature of legend, miracle, and salvation, which stamped Christianity on the soul of the people . . . Heaven and earth seemed very near together in this age of the North."[52] The Christian star that rose in Iona for a while eclipsed religious developments to the south in Saxon Britain.

The real achievement of Bede in laying down the lines of national, vernacular identity was considerable, and its significance for the emergence of a sense of cultural patriotism is noteworthy. Christianity was an indigenous religious movement.

> In Bede's writings we can watch, as seldom elsewhere in Europe, the process by which Christianity came to create notions of "national" unity that would (for good or ill) look straight to the present day. Within one crucial generation, between 700 and 731, two regions of the British Isles received, from the pen of Christian, Latin writers, legends that would prove decisive for their future sense of identity . . . Bede gave the nondescript patchwork of military adventurers who had settled in eastern Britain the common name by which they have come to be known in later ages—the "English." Centuries later, but also under the influence of readers of Bede's *Ecclesiastical History*, they would come to speak of their country as "England."[53]

In the fullness of time the language of the English people, as indeed the other myriad languages of the world, would one day become a common language within the worldwide Christian movement. It took several centuries, but eventually the Christian movement of fifteenth-century England rescued English from its stigma as an unclean and prohibited language and launched it as a language of Scripture, worship, and prayer.[54] Bede was himself reportedly in the course of translating the Gospel of John at the time of his death in 735. The Christian epoch marked a change in Britain from what Lord Macaulay called the age of fable and myth, or of isolation and secret cults, to the age of faith and statesmanship. Lost to view as Britain under the Romans, the country reappeared as England, and few achievements secured England's name as the Bible in English, "a book which, if everything else in our language should perish, would alone suffice to show the whole extent of its beauty and power," Macaulay wrote in 1828. He noted the far-reaching impact of Christianity on the nation, saying it was no longer brute force but intellectual and moral power that shaped the affairs of people as Duncan the priest replaced Penda the warrior. Christianity was "a system which taught the fiercest and mightiest ruler that he was, like his meanest bondman, a responsible being."[55]

The vernacular work of King Alfred of Wessex (r. 871–899), which gave the English literature that was unparalleled by any vernacular literature in Europe, was suppressed by the Norman Conquest. During the many centuries of Latin domination that followed, English was reviled as a harsh tongue, "like the grunting of pigs or the roaring of lions." In this period it would not have occurred to anyone to write in British (that is, Celtic), nor would people have known how to do so, Latin being the only language of writing.[56] Yet, such cultivated prejudice notwithstanding, the forces favoring the mother tongue gathered pace, and as a consequence English was revived in pockets of national cultural awareness. Eventually, the numerous dialects that constituted English yielded to the East Midland stream in which first Tyndale, and then Shakespeare, were steeped and which the printers adopted to great effect. Many were literary precursors. Chaucer (ca. 1340–1400), for example, wrote his treatise on the Astrolabe for "litel Lowis my sone, under ful lighte rewles and naked wordes in English," because "Latin ne canstow yit but small, my lyte sone." Purvey, a disciple of Wycliffe, translated Luke's gospel "for the poor men of his nation which con little Latin or none, and be poor of wit and of worldly chattels and nevertheless rich of good will to please God." The implications for mother tongues of the Gentile revolution in religion affected the whole range of national life and customs as well as moral ideas.

Conversion of Iceland: The Makeover

That there should be any coherence in the message of Christianity or that it should flourish amidst the vicissitudes of the conditions and circumstances of the peoples without the safeguard of central control and direction is testimony to the natural affinity between the religion's message of *one* savior and the *many* tongues of a varied and diverse humanity. Harnack referred to the issue when he spoke of the powers of attraction upon which Christianity cast the affirming light of recognition. The flickering cultural potential was thereby ignited as a necessary and essential feature of the age, showing Christianity retrieving and invigorating the spirit by blending with local influences of the most diverse and unsuspecting nature. That way the religion became the uncapped vein of a strong-flowing vernacular stream. In the quest for truth and salvation, and for a common purpose for organized society, Christianity appeared as the expected promise. Anything less would have betrayed the spirit of the age. The Church Fathers had been pagan for a purpose.

Sometimes the change Christianity engineered occurred amid stress and potential conflict. That was the case in the conversion, for example, of Iceland. Iceland's neighbors had tried in vain both direct and devious means to bring about the conversion of the people. By then in the Christian camp, the king of Norway had despaired of achieving the conversion of Iceland and, old warrior that he was, threatened to kill the people for their recalcitrance.

Hjalti and Gizurr, two Icelandic Christian chieftains, returned after leading a delegation to Norway to offer assurances that Iceland would, in time, embrace the new religion—precisely how or when, they forgot to say. They then embarked on a pivotal mission to bring their compatriots into the Christian fold, but first they had to pick their way delicately through the minefield of pagan sensibilities. They decided to head straight to the center of the national cult located near the great lake—some ninety miles away. The controversial Hjalti, compromised for having on a previous occasion insulted the gods and aroused bitter opposition, decided prudently to drop back and to allow Gizurr to go to the place of assembly alone. Some two miles short of his destination, Gizurr sent a message to the pagan leaders saying he was ready for a meeting. In the meantime (and contrary to arrangements) the outlawed Hjalti, accompanied by others, stormed in, to the consternation of Gizurr. The Christian peace mission now threatened to escalate into a battle against the pagans for whom the sight alone of Hjalti was tantamount to a call to war. Had Gizurr duped them?

Thankfully, cooler heads prevailed on both sides and a public peace meeting wasarranged. The following day, Hjalti and Gizurr reassembled with the followers of the gods. With extraordinary eloquence, reportedly, they made their case for why the people should accept Christianity, which only served to inflame feelings on both sides, with the Christians and pagans hurling mutual recriminations. When the Christians called for their leader to declare a state of unilateral independence from the pagans, he wisely declined. He offered bribes instead and pleaded with the veteran code-bearer of the pagans, Thorgeir, to declare Christianity the new national religion. Yet the code-bearer would not act precipitously either way, and instead retired to the cult booth where he lay down covering himself with a cloak—a well-known divinatory technique for incubating dreams of guidance. Thorgeir remained there all day and all night under ritual silence. The next morning he sat up and, ready to announce the results of his sacred exercise, sent out a message for everyone to gather at the Law Rock.

He addressed the assembled people by warning that great harm would come if the people did not all follow the same law. The whole country would be ruined by the discord and hostility that would follow disagreement. It would then be meaningless for one side or the other to speak of winning or losing—all would share the same fate. Force could not and should not settle the issue, he counseled. People should look for a compromise, with each side giving something. "Let us all have one law and one faith," he urged. "If we tear law asunder, we tear asunder peace."[57]

The assembly agreed to let the code-bearer himself decide the issue. The code-bearer said that, on one side, the people should accept Christianity by having themselves baptized while, on the other, the old code should stand as far as it concerned the exposing of children and the eating of horseflesh. As such, child sacrifice would continue in secret if people still felt a compulsion to do so, though a penalty of banishment for three years would be imposed on those convicted on the testimony of witnesses. The old custom of exposing children in the sacrificial rites was a sticking point for Christians, and so, to resolve the impasse, the compromise pact took due account of that by driving it underground. This event took place around 1000, and the first account of it was written by Ari (ca. 1068–1148) between 1122 and 1133, and preserved in subsequent Icelandic sagas. Iceland's conversion in this account is a story about the unity and preservation of the nation, and echoes many of the themes Bede describes of Northumbria. The king of Norway may have precipitated the crisis, but it was the people of Iceland and their national custom that were decisive in the final outcome. In the end, it was the great monasteries of Iceland that emerged as the engine-room of the country's national heritage by documenting, translating, preserving, and transmitting the sagas, including *Njáls saga*, the thirteenth century literary masterpiece.

Icelandic historical and literary materials noted the change from a Roman Christ to a vernacular Christ for non-Romans. An Icelandic poet, for example, celebrated the passing of the age of Thor—once greeted as sky-king, owner of the strength-belt, the wagon's god, and destroyer of giants and evil beings—and the dawning of the age of Christ who was once Rome's mighty king but who has now "put on new strength in the lands of the powers of the mountain."[58] The following assessment of Iceland's encounter with Christianity seems a judicious historical summary and a fitting tribute to the indigenous basis of religious change. It has echoes for other societies.

> In Iceland Christianity encountered a people of religious mood. They were aware of the numinous and had firm respect for forms, formulas and ceremonies, for commands and prohibitions derived from religious observance as well as from secular law. Already in this may be seen the prerequisites for the adoption of the new order, not least when the Christian dispensation could fulfil three conditions: it could preserve the old legal system and the idea of one nation; it could satisfy the need for religious reverence, now with worship of a novel deity, mightier than the old gods, not subject to Ragnarok but ruling through eternity; and in its early stages it could adapt itself to existing social forms. The place of the *hof* built and kept in repair by the chieftains was taken by churches erected by the leaders on their farms. The local thing-men of the *goði* attended his church, as they had once attended the sacrifices he had organized and the feasting at his *hof*. Contributions that members of a cult-community had previously made to maintain their religious practices must now have come in some form to the church and its owner, and they were finally regularized in tithe-payments. Burial in consecrated ground was an assured benefit in return. *Eyrbyggja saga* [chap. 49] tells of a church built by Snorri goði near the hill of ancient heathen veneration, Helgafell, soon after the Conversion. According to the saga, the chief assured that a man was guaranteed places in heaven for as many of his followers as could stand to hear the service in the church he built. And this, the text says, "much encouraged men to build churches."[59]

The social background to the conversion of Iceland was quite complex. There had been a mass influx into the country of Irish slaves, with a major demographic shift as one of its implications. Women were also coming into their own, as illustrated by the career of Aud the Deep-Minded. She was an influential landowner who brought Christianity with her when she migrated from faraway Dublin Bay and came to settle in Iceland. Her story, representing a different and perhaps even rival tale of the conversion of Iceland, may be as significant as the better known version tied to the séance under the cloak.

Indeed, Christianity opened a range of hitherto unknown opportunities for women, including widows. Eanygh, mother of Heaburg, assumed her leadership position as abbess with an undaunted spirit against prevailing views about the public role of women, apprising Boniface in a letter of the superhuman challenges she still faced, including the king's hostility toward her and her relatives.[60] In the ancient Irish *Annals of the Four Masters* women leaders are mentioned frequently; some were renowned for their hospitality and piety, some for their intellectual achievement. One such was described as "nurse of all the poets and strangers and all the learned." As early as the sixth century, St. Brigid and her successors exercised control over a monastery of men, an example without parallel elsewhere in Europe. A notice in 932 about the death of Ullach, daughter of Muimhnecan, described her as "Chief Poetess of Ireland." In England, convents founded at Hartlepool and Whitby, for example, became renowned as intellectual centers presided over by abbesses, an innovation that followers of the old customs frowned upon.[61]

Christian Roots and Vernacular Bloom

It is important again to stress that the pattern we discern of the parallel movement of local response and Christian adjustment is not just the benefit of historical hindsight but was recognized at the time in the formulation of policy for missionary practice. In a letter to the Abbot Mellitus, Pope Gregory asked for certain instructions to be transmitted to Augustine (d. ca. 604), bishop of Canterbury, relating to the matter of how best to shepherd the new English converts. The letter is dated June 17, 601, and is a classic text on indigenous assimilation. Augustine was instructed that under no circumstances should he allow the old pagan temples to be pulled down. They were, instead, to be consecrated with holy water, altars set up in them and relics deposited there, and the places rededicated to the worship of the one true God. It would steady the religious nerves of the people if they were able to continue to gather at their old places of worship, even with a different God enthroned. The people needed to be discouraged from abandoning the old rites entirely so, on the occasions when they were accustomed to make sacrifice of oxen, a Day of Dedication or Festivals in honor of the martyrs should instead be instituted, shelters of boughs set up as shrines, and the rites celebrated with solemnity and devout feasting, all dedicated to God rather than to the devil. Gregory's reasoning was unimpeachable, for, he determined, "It is impossible to eradicate all errors from obstinate minds at one stroke, and whoever wishes to climb to a mountain top climbs gradually step by step, and not in one leap." That was even more applicable when the mountain in question was not thrust up by a recent volcano, nor followed by the aftershock of alien occupation.

The question of accommodating vernacular practices within Christianity's missionary mandate was a recurrent one. Pope Nicholas I, for example, was asked by the Bulgars whether, having converted to Christianity, they could still wear trousers, perform rituals of rainmaking during a drought, or go to war flying fetish-like horses' tails from their battle standards. In making room for the church, the materials of the old pagan heritage assumed a new, dynamic orientation. King Alfred, accordingly, committed to memory the sagas of the pre-Christian heroes, and his Christian descendants learned them along with the Psalms.

In Northumbria the expanding Christian movement bore strong vernacular strains of its impact there. This achievement was reflected in the poetry of Caedmon, the cowherd of Whitby, the first recorded English Christian poet, who was inspired in a dream to sing of "the Father of Glory" who made for humanity "heaven for their roof and then the earth." In the "Dream of the Rood" a local poet sang of a tree more holy than any in their forests—"the Healer's tree," on which stepped Christ, "the young hero," "the lord of the folk kin," "of the tree's agony, pierced with nails, and the moment when, as darkness covered the earth, soldiers lifted down the King and left the Tree all with blood streaming."[62] "The Dream of the Rood," composed in the rhythms and cadences of Anglo-Saxon religious poetry, was the rallying embodiment of a visionary experience infused with the idea of the Holy Cross, and in about 700 it was carved in runic script on a stone cross in Dunfriesshire, Scotland. It enshrined an example of local response to the universal religious theme of the drama of salvation, a subject of deep devotion across the Christian world. In the "Dream of the Rood" the passion of Christ was fused with the call to personal penance, and a core theme of the gospel assumed authoritative local force.

Whitby was home also to a remarkable monastery where the Abbess Hilda (614–680), baptized in her teens by Paulinus, presided to general approbation over both nuns and monks. Hilda "taught the observance of righteousness, mercy, purity, and other virtues, but especially of peace and charity. After the example of the primitive Church, no one there was rich, no one was needy, for everything was held in common.... So great was her prudence that not only ordinary folk, but kings and princes used to come and ask her advice in their difficulties and take it. Those under her direction were required to make a thorough study of the Scriptures and [to] occupy themselves in good works, to such effect that many were found fitted for Holy Orders and [for] the service of God's altar."[63] Everyone who knew Hilda called her Mother "because of her wonderful devotion and grace," her life the fulfillment of a dream that her mother had when Hilda was an infant. In that dream, the infant Hilda was designated as a brilliant light whose splendor lit all of Britain. Whitby was known as "a house which became a nursery of bishops, a centre of unity, [and] a school of literature."[64] It happened that the first life of Pope Gregory the Great (d. 604) to appear in Europe was written at the Whitby of Hilda's inspiration.[65]

The general Christian movement set up deep patterns of local response and initiative without the burden and handicap of foreign imposition. The papacy was the unbroken apostolic validation for local religious potential. Thus was Augustine of Canterbury, as we saw, instructed to apply this policy of enlightened vernacular adjustment to local need.[66] The policy invested the idea and practice of conversion with a more nuanced and a more resonant meaning. The policy subjected the principle of transmission to the dynamics of reception and adaptation, while the notion of Christianity depending on foreign expertise took a back seat to the primacy of indigenous appropriation. Policy and practice combined to serve, and sometimes yield to, local need. Olympian pronouncements by foreign agents gave way to local priority.

For the ancient church in the West the norms of a literate society set the pattern of Christianization, and that pattern was based on the written culture of Latin. The conversion of the people of northern Europe was modeled on the cultural norms of Western Christendom, though the monastic tradition that first developed in Egypt offered a contrast to the diocesan model of Latin Christianity, as did the vernacular materials that were introduced with the conversion of Arabs, Armenians, Copts, Persians, and Slavs. Hugh Williams noted that the history of Christianity in Britain took a turn in 603 on the occasion of Augustine's meeting with British bishops at "Augustine's Oak" which marked the change between the "old British" and the "new Roman" church.[67]

Latin continued to hold sway in Scripture and liturgy, and that engendered a sense of unity in the church, but at the cost of marginalizing vernacular languages as the home languages of practicing Christians. That vernacular reality, in the end, forced the recognition that Christianity had no revealed language, and those who knew full well that it was not the language of Jesus, or even of the Gospels, imposed Latin on the church. Jerome's Latin Vulgate of the fourth century, based on the Hebrew text rather than the more acceptable Greek Septuagint, was controversial and divisive at the time.[68] Augustine of Hippo warned Jerome against allowing the Vulgate to go forward for fear of splitting the congregations.[69] It is important to remember that it was from the encounter of the Roman legions with the ancient Gauls that a pidgin Latin emerged that would have scandalized Cicero. That pidgin Latin became French, demonstrating creative cultural synthesis from foreign encounter.

Convened in 794, the Synod of Frankfurt had earlier handed down a decision in Canon 52 protesting against the exclusive use of the three ancient languages, Latin included. The bishops declared: "It is not to be believed that

God is only to be worshipped in the three languages. Because God is worshipped in all languages, man is heard if he strives in pursuing the right."[70] That statement echoes Peter's argument about God showing no partiality—that everyone who did right was acceptable to God.

The impetus for the vernacular came from very high quarters indeed, from the Emperor Charlemagne himself, whose preferred model of Christian conversion was the muscular imperial one rather than what he considered the feeble, long-winded style of Roman edicts, or the uncertain give-and-take involved in preaching and dialogue. He opted instead to preach to the Saxons with the inflexible edge of the sword, and gave his empire (*imperium christianum*) the prerogatives of the "City of God," a title Augustine had reserved for the heavenly city in which the faithful had their true and final citizenship.[71] Charlemagne introduced the inquisition, with panels of bishops set up to conduct inquests on delinquent parishioners, who were denounced. Under Pope Innocent III (1198–1216) the inquisition was reintroduced as the third of a three-stage process of accusation and denunciation in a system concerned with clerical discipline.

In that regard, it was Charlemagne—and not Constantine—who was Christendom's iron-willed architect. Yet for all his emulation of Roman imperial grandeur as the "Augustus of the North," as the Christian "caliph" of the Holy Roman Empire, and as God's "shadow on earth,"[72] with no half-measures or second thoughts about imposing his personal will on strong and weak alike, Charlemagne remained at heart a northern European with his roots in the vernacular. The new imperial capital he carved for himself at Aachen in the countryside was abstemious by the standards of other emperors, though opulent by those of the four classical Muslim caliphs, known as "the rightly guided."[73] Charlemagne began a grammar of the vernacular, believed to be of the Rhenish-Franconian that he spoke himself. In the conversion movement initiated by missionary activity, the vernacular question was brought to the fore.

> The impetus to write vernacular still came from the mission-field and to it the emperor had something to say. There can be no doubt that to him, as well as to all his contemporaries, the language of Christianity in the liturgical sense remained Latin, one of the three sacred languages. But the Anglo-Saxons and the Goths had shown that the language of religious exposition could be vernacular; and this was to be encouraged. Most significant . . . are the very large number of vernacular glosses, sermons, hymns and confessions that survive. This wide-ranging reach of the written vernacular for religious and educational purposes throughout the Carolingian world is of first

significance.... That people should understand underlies a large part of all surviving vernacular translation of the period.[74]

Such a confident endorsement of the vernacular was precisely the point made by Constantine-Cyril (d. 869) and Methodius (d. 885) his brother, architects of the Slavic mission. By 879, when Methodius was summoned before Pope John VIII to answer charges of violating sacred teaching by celebrating Mass in Slavonic (considered a "barbaric language"), the issue of the vernacular had acquired unstoppable momentum. Constantine-Cyril was himself challenged on the subject at a meeting in Venice where church officials "gathered against him like ravens against a falcon." Constantine-Cyril responded: "Does not God's rain fall upon all equally? And do we not all breathe air in the same way? Are you not ashamed to mention only three tongues, and to command all other nations and tribes to be blind and deaf?...We know of numerous peoples who possess writing and render glory unto God, each in its own language. Surely these are obvious: Armenians, Persians, Abkhazians, Iberians, Sogdians, Goths, Avars, Turks, Khazars, Arabs, Egyptians, and many others."[75]

The case for Latin as one of three sacred languages authorized for Christianity rested on no more secure a foundation than the instruction of Pilate to place an inscription at the head of the cross in Hebrew, Greek and Latin,[76] and Methodius could point out that Pilate was scarcely a safe authority for church teaching! In support of his own claim, Methodius cited several passages of Scripture.[77] John VIII backed down and approved the vernacular. But the anti-vernacular forces in Rome were awakened, and under the pontificate of Gregory VII (1073–1085) an order was handed down to suppress the Slavic liturgy. The Czech king, Vratislav II (1061–1092), treated the order as mere blustering and ignored it, allowing the vernacular liturgy to stand. In 1096, however, the persecution of Slavic Christians commenced, dealing a mortal blow to Slavic liturgy and letters in Bohemia. Nevertheless, the Old Church Slavonic and the Cyrillic alphabet remained the foundation of religious and cultural life, creating a contrasting Eastern tradition to the church in the West.

Classicism and the Pillar of Historical Intelligibility: Assessment

The emphatic and authoritative hand of the political historian has been in evidence in much of what has come to be accepted about the general course and impact of Christianity in the empire and beyond, with justifiable reason. The empire was the milieu of Christianity's formative self-image, and the religion embarked on its historic mission imbued with the values and ideas of its cosmopolitan imperial beginnings. Thanks to the empire, "the narrow world had become a unity; the barbarian world had become Greek and Roman: one empire, one universal language, one civilization, a common development towards monotheism, and a common yearning for saviours."[78]

Yielding to the cosmopolitan logic, historians felt justified in assuming that a certain level of political centralization—in terms, for instance, of organized societies and markets, consolidated military power, the founding of libraries, and legal institutions—was a necessary accompaniment to the spread of the religion, which launched Christianity as a distinctly urban civilization. Christianization meant the process by which a motley patchwork of tribes and clans banded together to create social institutions, national communities, organized states, regional power blocs, and long-range trading contacts, sweeping triumphant kingdoms and empires.

It was a powerful vision, adopted even by modern Protestant missions who preached the trilateral creed of civilization, commerce, and Christianity—in that order. The great objects of civilization, exulted John Philip, the Protestant Scottish missionary, are to the mind what the sunbeams are to the flowers: they paint the colors and ripen the fruit. As Solomon says of pride, idleness is not made for man, for it shrinks the impulse of civilization. That is why, Philip persisted, religion is necessary to conduct the process of civilization, from planting the germ of civilization on the icy hills of heathen Greenland to sowing the seed of social virtue on the sultry plains of primitive Africa.[79] Accounts portrayed the missionary vocation as pushing the frontiers of civilization among hinterland tribal groups, with sanitation, education, good roads, sobriety, frugality, and a strong work ethic among the fruits of the Spirit. The church was but the machinery for promoting a detribalized progressive social order, and it had no local parallel.

Such an elegant model of religion and civilization as commensurate mutual reinforcement is, however, too sweeping and at the same time too restrictive to account for the influence of local materials in the broad and narrow paths of Christian expansion. A model Christianity based on the Roman idea of political domain remains a religion confined to its originating circumstances without regard to the dynamics of reception and adoption. Roman officials, for example, viewed Christianity as an evil of foreign origin, and thus prone to disloyalty and sedition. Officials were united in the view that provincial manifestations of the religion posed a real threat, and that view was adapted at the hands of Charlemagne to reduce Christianity to a court religion. The provincial non-Western manifestations of the religion were deemed to be heretical and disloyal.

It was from the Romans rather than from the apostles that Charlemagne and his successors inherited the idea of religion as an authorized official edict, a view that is demonstrably inhospitable to Christianity's appeal as a world religion. An official Christianity thus turned the apostle's "letters written in tablets of the heart"[80] into a matter of political edict. Tacitus's idea of religion as political prescription ironically survived in Christianity as "Christendom," as a mandate of political submission. It was, in fact, Christian "islam."

Salvation and History

Yet Christianity's worldwide appeal in the ancient world and in late antiquity points to an implicit Christian philosophy of history, which is that local and personal efforts at truth and the righteous life have significance within the scope of God's intention for general human life. The teaching of Peter, for example, that God is no respecter of persons, proclaims the idea of one human family on the basis that God's covenant is one and the same for all persons. That oneness is not because the state administers one set of laws and rules for its citizens. Classical disdain for provincial culture is echoed in colonial disdain for tribal societies, while Christian teaching in both cases appealed to all and sundry without regard to geography, race, status, or learning. That implies an ethical rather than a cultural interpretation of normative equality under God, and that Christian perspective challenged the assumptions of Greco-Roman historiography, producing a positive advance for the problem of historical intelligibility. A similar advance is possible today provided the flagging fortunes of a post-Christian West are not confounded with the robust potential of a post-Western Christianity. An assessment of classical historiography should elucidate the issue.

When classical writers reflected on their circumstances, they came upon a vexing problem: how you might know much about events without the power to change or influence them, particularly when events seemed locked in a wheel of inexorability. It led to a sense of existential futility, as expressed in the telling words of a classical poet:

> If better life beyond be found,
> The darkness veils, clouds wrap it round;
> Therefore infatuate-fond to this
> We cling—this earth's sunshine-gleam:
> Nought know we of the life to come,
> There speak no voices from the tomb:
> We drift on fable's shadowy stream.[81]

Experience taught that unforeseen events brought unforeseen castigations. Thus did the quest for the principle of historical intelligibility fail from the very attempts to save it. Crusted over with a prickly pessimism, Diogenes' lantern, it turns out, could shed no more light on the purposive impulse in human affairs. And so we are back to the problem that Herodotus began with, and back to the issue of salvation and the theory of history. Justin Martyr's confidence that the pre-Christian and non-Christian world was not excluded from the scope of God's grace had the consequence of giving history a structure of intelligibility. "To the Christians the failure of the classical historiography was the result of its inability to discover the true 'cause' of human being and motivation. Accordingly, it pointed to a substitution of the *logos* of Christ for that of Classicism as a principle of understanding."[82]

The ancient writers had a tantalizing premonition of what would emerge fully as a Christian idea. In his valedictory work, *Oedipus at Colonus*, for instance, Sophocles (ca. 496–406 BC) looks wistfully to Olympus for immutable assurance against the besetting difficulties and uncertainties of fickle nature. He writes that the word that makes all earthly difficulties go away is love, but that this love is sealed in unshakeable, incontestable laws that remain impersonal and remote. To those so minded, Christianity in its turn fulfilled the Sophoclean urge by teaching a "plan of salvation" whose central premise was a loving relationship between the God of forgiveness and redeemed humanity. The resulting moral relationship brought into play a God who was concerned with the lives of human persons; that assurance gave value and purpose to individual experience and to the affairs of organized society.

When he reflected on the defeat and ruin of the empire, Augustine saw a meaningful lesson in terms of history serving God's purpose. The choice that confronted people was between a paralyzing pessimism rooted in the idea that change is a sign of a corrupt, imperfect order on one hand, and, on the other, hope of salvation in the church and of renewal in the world. In attempting a coherent and satisfactory account of the affairs of human society in their fullness—specifically in the experience of defeat in the face of the collapse of the Roman Empire—Christian historiography, in the hands of Augustine, engaged in history's unified significance fact and value, evidence and meaning, as well as actions, intentions, their unforeseeable consequences, and their cumulative import. The historian is not a fortune-teller, at one extreme, or a mechanical recorder of random facts and anecdotes at the other. Historical events, like human language, are not so contingent or so opaque that they cannot bear transcendent meaning, nor so elevated or so unambiguous that they become monolithic and irrevocable. A Christian view of history affirms change as the stuff of reality rather than a changeless universal law in which events and actions are irrelevant. Events would have no significance if they did not happen. Events such as the Crucifixion and the Resurrection, for example, could not have the importance they do unless they happened.

Paul expressed a corresponding sentiment with his reflections on his conversion, saying religious or cultural entitlement is not a substitute for a faith that is the actionable gift of the God of history. The new Christian historiography resonated with that sentiment when it rejected the possession of material or intellectual resources as the exclusive qualification of historical significance and instead expanded the limits of historical significance to include all human existence. Thus, in Augustine's vision it was not the city of Rome—known instructively to its contemporaries as the Eternal City—that was the center stage of history, but the "city" of God in which no age or society had closer or more distant affinity or nearness, or enjoyed greater or lesser advantage, than any other. In both his philosophy of history and in his theology, Augustine remained committed to the view that historical realism was not devoid of the light of truth, that no instance of human existence, however otherwise negligible in material terms, was without value in the overall scheme of humanity's struggle for meaning and dignity. The "manifest destiny" of humanity was equal citizenship in the fair and felicitous city of God. It is within that Augustinian framework and stimulus that we must refocus the historical searchlight to shed light on the Christian movement in its general and specific character. As we shall see, the new Christian frontiers emerging beyond the West show Augustine's insights to be all the more pertinent.

Diversity and Unity of Experience

The work of Peter Brown is extremely helpful, particularly in its detailed exposition of the network of cells, centers, scholars, and specific religious materials that knit Christianity in the ancient Western world. He has advanced our understanding by focusing with lucid learning on hitherto overlooked aspects of the social and intellectual history of the religion. Brown provides a corrective to the political school of historiography by stressing how Christians could be everywhere, not because they converted everyone, but because they were embedded in a highly flexible web of practices that required little by way of a complicated or an expensive infrastructure.

Given all of that, the somewhat old-fashioned title of Brown's book, *The Rise of Western Christendom: Triumph and Diversity*, is surprising, since the book is not about triumphant Christianity as Charlemagne's culminating imperial legacy or about the expansion of papal jurisdiction (though arguably a case may still be made for that).

Brown is eloquent in stating that the conception of faith as dynamic and personal was an advantage in allowing Christianity to dispense with heavy-handed transplanted systems and ponderous safeguards and to foster a sense of coherence in European society when memories of the Roman Empire à la Pirenne were too weak, and loyalty to the papacy à la Dawson too sporadic, to provide a clear center. In this situation, the mere possession of the sacred Scriptures made the Christians

> a potentially worldwide "textual community." The reader should meditate . . . on the implications of those humble fragments which show the same book of the Psalms being copied out, at the same time, as a writing exercise by Christian children, both in Panjikent near Samarkand and in northern Ireland. The basic modules of Christianity, also, were remarkably stable and easy to transfer—a bishop, a clergy, a congregation . . . and a place in which to worship. Such a basic structure could be subjected to many local variations, but, in one form or another, it travelled well. It formed a basic "cell," which could be transferred to any region of the known world. Above all, Christians worshipped a God who, in many of his aspects, was above space and time. God and his saints could always be thought of as fully "present" to the believer, wherever he or she happened to be. In God's high world, there was no distinction between "center" and "periphery." In the words of the modern inhabitants of Joazeira, a cult site perched in a remote corner of northeast Brazil, Christian believers could be sure that, even if they lived at the notional end of the world (which, in western Europe in this period happened, quite correctly, to be the west coast of Ireland) they had "Heaven above their heads and Hell below their feet."[83]

In spite of Christianity's intrinsic character as a worldwide religion subject to many local variations, it was framed, nevertheless, in the uniform terms of Christendom, with imperial Rome or monarchical authority as the model. In consequence, a heavy price was exacted as a result of the transmission and imposition of Christendom in the newly created colonies of the Spanish and Portuguese empires, as we shall see in the next chapter. Such a linear, Euro-centric understanding of Christianity happens to conflict with much of the available evidence, such as Brown has presented, and with the many manifestations of the religion in the twentieth and twenty-first centuries, all of which calls for a fresh orientation of scholarship and perspective.

We need to divest Christianity, if not of the baggage of empire and power entirely and of the accompanying guilt complex, then at least of the presumption of the advantages of civilization. Such a shift will allow scholars to break out of their preoccupation with the European heartland and its structures of power, and look to the frontier, scarce in institutional assets but with a teeming diversity that attests to the religion's genius for fostering a spirit of unity along with a variety of styles and idioms. For instance, Anthony was no less a model Christian for having his roots in the countryside rather than in Alexandria. His disadvantaged background of captivity did not detract from his importance or merit. It is one of the strengths of Brown's book that it presents Christianity precisely in that "antistructural," unofficial fashion.

Whither Christianity? The Gentile Pillar

The question here is not simply whence, but whither Christianity, especially with regard to its living, dynamic character. It is not so much that Christianity has been framed and limited by its natural birthmark, or by the plethora of official birthmarks created for it—whether in terms of its Jewish origins in the one case, or in terms of the proliferation of multiple denominations in the other—as that the religion has grown and multiplied, thanks to the unqualified Gentile benchmark it adopted.

I do not mean here that the historian should embrace the beguiling notion that "truth is the daughter of time," that the past should be jettisoned as erroneous in favor of today's fashions. Rather, I mean that the conventional rules of historical selection, which yoke the historical craft to the high profile appeal of rulers, elites, armies, markets, libraries, cathedrals, harbors, states, kingdoms, and empires, have been singularly deficient in accounting for huge tracts of the immense worldwide Christian movement whose otherwise humble cathedrals of faith have provided still persuasive evidence of the religion's interconnectivity. Structures of faith did not come into being by law and order; they came into being often in spite of deliberate legal obstacles.

The New Testament describes Christian Gentiles and others as bonding with Christianity not by tying themselves to the apron strings of Jesus' Jewish origins but by clothing themselves with the authentic vestments of their own culture. Jewish Christian leaders themselves, chiefly Peter and Paul, were the first and the most adamant in urging upon the Gentile church such a radical move. It is, consequently, not a betrayal of faith for believers elsewhere to embrace Christianity and to fold it into their native traditions rather than to turn against their culture. As Pius XII put it in 1944, "The herald of the Gospel and messenger of Christ is an apostle. His office does not demand that he transplant European civilization and culture, and no other, to foreign soil, there to take root and propagate itself. His task in dealing with these peoples, who sometimes boast of a very old and highly developed culture of their own, is to teach them and form them so that they are ready to accept willingly and in a practical manner the principles of Christian life and morality . . . Catholic inhabitants of missionary countries, although they are first of all citizens of the Kingdom of God and members of His great family, do not for all that cease to be citizens of their earthly fatherland . . . The Church is no obstacle to the native talent of any nation, but rather perfects it in the highest degree."[84] The gospel exists not to alienate but to invigorate and transform. It conflicts only and unavoidably with idolatries of race, nation, and power.

The requisite transformation of culture and society is necessarily tied to aspects and phases of the dynamic reception and inculturation of the gospel, not simply to its mechanical organized transmission. The idea of what Christianity should look like back when it was conceived and launched from its base in metropolitan centers often bore little relationship to realities on the ground once the religion was adopted. On the contrary, those who adopted the faith often expanded and transformed the assumptions of those who transmitted it. Thus, the history of Christianity has become properly the history of the world's peoples and cultures, not simply the history of missionaries and their cultures. It goes without saying that the gospel has necessarily been conveyed in the cultural vessels of missionaries, yet only in the crucible of indigenous appropriation did new faith emerge among the recipients.

2

The Christian Movement in Islamic Perspective

Comparative Pillar

Footloose Beginnings: The Arab Legacy

Christianity owes a great deal of its organized and institutional character to the Roman Empire, in the same way that its theology was shaped by Greek ideas. Christianity's primitive temper was ascetic: to keep oneself blameless and harmless in the midst of a crooked and perverse generation,[1] and yet to shine as a light in the world.[2] In the *Didache*, a document reputedly of the second century, Christians are warned to

> be watchful over your life; never let your lamps go out or your loins be ungirt, but keep yourself always in readiness, for you can never be sure of the hour when our Lord may be coming. . . . all the past years of your faith will be no good to you at the end, unless you have made yourselves perfect.[3]

In due time, however, the early Christians modified the call to ascetic purity by embracing the world and adopting the advantages of social organization provided by Roman imperial life. When kings and rulers converted, they facilitated the process of religious institutionalization, with cultural assimilation reinforcing the process.

A notable exception was Christianity's stalemate with the Muslim world, where Islam presented an insurmountable barrier, and viceversa, as in later centuries the Ottomans discovered to their cost. In spite of Christianity's ancient roots in Palestine and North Africa, there was little by way of mutual attraction between the two religions, and a stalemate ensued, culminating inconclusively in the drama of the Crusades. Meanwhile, in North Africa Christianity remained largely cut off from non-Romanized populations and from the rest of the continental mass south of the Sahara, although Nubia and Ethiopia were early centers of Christian impact. In any case, the impressive flowering of the church in North Africa in the first centuries of the religion offers an instructive example of contrasting patterns of growth and isolation, of promise and failure. The example was repeated elsewhere and at later times, such as when coastal and urban churches developed because of the presence of European traders only to languish subsequently from lack of hinterland response, often reinforced by Muslim opposition.

This feature of early Christianity should offer a valuable insight into the circumstances that are most conducive to long-term resurgence and stability, hence its relevance to our study. We should keep a close eye on matters of reception and adaptation of the message, without overlooking issues of transmission and cultural co-option. Eusebius (ca. 260–ca. 340), the father of ecclesiastical history, records a tradition that John Mark, author of the Gospel of the same name, traveled to Egypt to establish churches there, a tradition kept alive in the Coptic Church of Egypt, which accords a special reverence to Mark as its founder. A parallel tradition claims that in about AD 52 the apostle Thomas came to Egypt and did missionary work there before continuing on to India. An obscure reference also claims an Ethiopian association for Thomas. Whatever their veracity, such claims hint at the worldwide cross-cultural appeal of the fledgling Christian movement.

The new religion received a striking personal response in the conversion of Antony (251–356). Antony sparked a movement that took Christianity outside the study and debating halls of Alexandrine society, and beyond the ambit of imperial urban culture and its philosophical Greek, into the idiom of indigenous Egypt and beyond. His story was written up and publicized in Greek by Athanasius (ca. 296–373), bishop of Alexandria, and an unlikely biographer of a simple Coptic hermit. At any rate, Athanasius's account of Antony, which in its Latin translation had a role in the conversion of Augustine, introduced the West to the institution of monasticism.[4] Antony's model Christian life, based on a radical view of Christian faithfulness marked by sacrificial poverty, constant vigil, and unsparing abstemiousness, cut against the grain of the cultural indulgence of the age, as Augustine noted. Antony's style of holiness was "a flagrant antithesis to the norms of civilized life in the Mediterranean."[5] Freed from the grip of ideas of cosmopolitan advantage, this model Christian life, once institutionalized, became the flywheel of the early missionary movement, doing far more than any other comparable institution to convert and redefine a good deal of Europe. In Islamic Spain, however, monasteries had less of an impact.

Antony's conversion movement stoked the forces of the indigenous discovery of Christianity, and diminished those of the Christian discovery of indigenous societies; it stirred, without inflaming, the Egyptian countryside. Villages were swept in the new fervor. The grassroots basis of the conversions contrasted strikingly with, say, the conversion of the Saxons, over which the emperor presided. Going beyond the boundaries of hegemonic Roman power and appealing to charismatic gifts of the spirit, Antony triggered an anti-status quo, countercultural impulse in the Christian movement. Too preoccupied with keeping watch by night, Antony and his circle of Christian perfectionists, for example, slept too little to have time for dreams and instead looked to angels and visions to vindicate and reward the pure in heart. Antony spoke of wrestling valiantly to overcome the devil, an idea rooted in pagan society. New Christian converts and their pagan peers thus shared a close bond in their desire for the company of angels and for an unsullied apprehension of the divine. That bond helped to legitimize in the new Christian setting the ancient divinatory system, with Antony, for example, requiring only that new Christian joy replace the old pagan fear as the validating principle.[6] Visions became common currency binding the far-flung Christian world, with images and icons as material embodiments of the experience. Visions, dreams, ecstasy, exorcism, and healing featured prominently in the mission of Christianity for many centuries,[7] with charismatic signs an enduring thread across languages and cultures.

Dreams, visions, and prophecy linked Christianity to the old religions, and through them lay and ordained alike had access to the divine. The connection with pre-Christian inspiration was a central element of the genesis of post-Western Christianity.[8] For example, twentieth-century charismatic prophets like William Wadé Harris of the Ivory Coast and Isaiah Shembe of South Africa share kinship with, say, St. Patrick's account in the fifth century of his call to evangelize Ireland, if not with his being taken captive or with his limited education. "I saw in the vision of the night a man coming as if from Ireland.... And I was greatly pricked at the heart and I was not able to read further and so I woke up."[9] When it came to his commissioning, Patrick (d. ca. 460) allowed knowledge from the heart to have primacy over knowledge from reading.

The monastic orders of Antony's inspiration were among the most effective and most fully developed carriers of Christian ideas in a world of uneven social change. As transnational and culturally diverse organizations, the monastic orders represented a stabilizing powerful variation on the diocesan model of Roman Christianity, and became the motor of the Christian movement; they engaged local materials and ideas to produce distinctive patterns of religious life. Monasticism in Eastern Christianity became "endowed with such prestige and standing," declared Symeon of Thessalonica in the fifteenth century, "that practically the entire church seems to be governed by monks."[10] Monasticism was a force for social change. Irish monks and priests from the sixth to the eighth centuries wielded ax and spade to strip manual labor of its demeaning stigma. Learning and industry flourished in the monasteries. According to the accounts, abbots and bishops, some of them related to rulers, could be seen sowing, reaping, planting fruit trees, carrying sacks of corn on their backs to the mill, and working as smiths. By hammering out distinctive styles of religious living, monasteries redefined mainstream culture. The spare habits cultivated in intense devotion, consecrated labor, scholarly pursuit, and spiritual exercises helped define the ethos and character of the wider society.

Unsubstantiated reports speak of an early translation of a part of Scripture into Arabic, but in the eighth century, John, bishop of Seville, produced an Arabic translation from Jerome's Vulgate. Christianity was mediated to the Arabs through the establishment of monasteries that struck root in the pre-Islamic world. A dominating figure of fourth-century Arab Christianity was a holy man of Sinai known simply as Moses, probably the same as the person identified as the Monk of Rhaithou in the oasis of Phárán. His fame spread to the Christian West where he received canonization. Pope Gregory III, for example, invoked him as a saintly missionary model to try to persuade a reluctant St. Willibald to join Willibald's uncle, St. Boniface, in the mission to the Germans. Figures like Moses dominated the Christian landscape of the region, including the Sinai and the Negev.[11]

Ancient Arab Christianity is memorialized in an apocryphal New Testament document called *The Arabic Gospel of the Infancy of the Saviour*, based on an original Syriac source, and compiled from different sources, chiefly from Luke and Matthew, and from the acts of James. The document resounds with the sentiments of its Arabic milieu, with the miracles of Jesus recounted in the rolling, caravanlike steps of the steady, surefooted mastery of an Arab storyteller. The Gospel ends in stylized form with supplication and with celebration of the largesse appropriate for an oriental host whose guests benefit handsomely from their patron's open-handed hospitality and bounty. The open arms of the crucified Jesus are blessed tokens (*tadhákir*) of divine solicitude now configured in the accessible idiom of the open arms of Arab hospitality, with its sense of giving unstintingly for the security and well-being of the client and guest (*dayf*).

The ancient Arabs made protection of the guest a pillar of the honor code (*hilf*). *Shukr*—fulsome gratitude—is the appropriate human response to such unmerited graciousness. In ancient cultures this gratitude took the form of praise-songs offered on the occasions when patron and client became united during social acts of bestowing and receiving gifts. *Shukr* united in trust the destitute sojourner and the host as generous benefactor. Its counterpart in religion was the doxology as thankful praise, in recognition of grace bestowed and acknowledged:

> This is He whom we adore with supplications, who hath given us being and life, and who hath brought us from our mothers' wombs; who for our sakes assumed a human body, and redeemed us, that He might embrace us in eternal compassion, and show to us His mercy according to His liberality, and beneficence, and generosity, and benevolence. To Him is glory, and beneficence, and power, and dominion from this time forth for evermore. Amen.

Hospitality (*diyáfah*) was one of the three pillars of Bedouin pride, along with fortitude (*hamásah*) and manliness (*murú'ah*), and, enshrined in oral tradition, it stamped the coming of Jesus among them with the culturally prescribed ways of acknowledging God's unfathomable hospitality. One can only imagine the Arab cultural possibilities for a Hellenized Christianity, and for the world, had the Scriptures from the start been available to the Arabs in their own tongue, for then, imbibing from the genealogy of the Prince of Peace and inspired by his example, their freewheeling nomadic zeal might have taken a wholly different religious direction.

In the ancient *Odes of Solomon*, believed to be of first-century origin, we have an example of how Christianity evolved in an eastern, Jewish direction, though still significantly short of real Arabic inculturation.[12] The *Odes* were composed in Syriac, and probably emanated outside the Roman Empire in Edessa. We have in the *Odes* the picture of a faith community whose quotidian routine is marked by the rhythm of worship, prayer, and hymns. Giving evidence of contiguity with the early disciples, the *Odes* affirm the Jewish roots of the faith, upholding the Virgin Mother who "laboured and bore a son" without need of a midwife, a detail that places the *Odes* firmly in the frugal, earthy directness of a peasant Jewish society. That Spartan leitmotif gives rise to the ascetic and monastic note of the *Odes*, with the love of God rising like a great river to quench the thirst of devotees and to give new life to all believers.[13] Some scholars try to press from the *Odes* hardboiled doctrine on Christology, say, but are disconcerted by the exuberant and fluid devotional language of the document. Yet such scholars forget that the *Odes* are a performative register of faith practice, not a rulebook of right belief. The turn that Christian theology took in its analytic slant accounts for scholars' prickliness about devotional literature being hard to pin down.

In any case, the conversion of St. Hilarion (ca. 291–371), and Antony's ascetic practice illustrate Christianity's profound impact on the Arabs of the trade routes. Born to pagan parents in the village of Tabatha, some five miles south of Gaza, Hilarion converted to Christianity while attending school in Alexandria. He then sought out Antony after that and served an apprenticeship under him among the anchorites in the Egyptian desert. In 306 he returned to Palestine, and on finding his parents dead, he renounced his worldly belongings and, adopting the life of a solitary monk, retired to a small cell south of the Gaza, "earnest in conduct, grave in discourse, and a good memory and accurate attainment in Sacred Writ."[14] At his solitary retreat his life was often interrupted by the influx of disciples who were drawn to him by stories of his sanctity and of miraculous healings at his hands. These disciples subsequently formed retreat centers of their own in the desert. Hilarion died in Cyprus, but, given the considerable pilgrimage value at stake, a leading disciple stole the body from there and brought it to Palestine to be interred in the disciple's monastery. An annual pilgrimage rite to the monastery commenced, acquiring the status of a national festival. Jerome, Hilarion's biographer, writing in about 391, recounts how Hilarion's influence spread in southern Palestine among the Arab nomads who received regular visitations from him. Jerome's account makes some very pertinent references to the role of monks and monasteries in the conversion process as well as to the deeper cultural changes that were in continuity with older observances. Conversion did not appear to be at the complete expense of the old.

> On one such visitation [Hilarion] arrived at Elusa [south of Beersheba]
> on the very day when the people had assembled on the occasion
> of a festival in the temple of Venus [Athar]. This goddess the Saracens
> worship as the Morning Star, to whose cult all their tribes are dedi-
> cated. The town itself, because of its situation, is semi-barbarian.
> When the news spread that St. Hilarion was passing by, for frequently
> he had healed many Saracens by freeing them from possession by
> evil spirits, the men swarmed out to meet him, along with their wives
> and children, bowing their heads in supplication and crying out in
> Arabic, "Bárikná" [Bless us!]. Receiving them with grace and humil-
> ity, he beseeched them to turn from the worship of idols to the wor-
> ship of God. Weeping and gazing up to the heavens he promised
> them that if they would but believe in Christ he would visit them
> frequently. Wonderful, indeed, is the grace of God! They would not
> allow him to go before he had traced out on the ground the plan of

a church. And the priest of Venus, wreathed as he was, he marked with the sign of Christ.[15]

In the sources on the origins of Islam the scattered references to Christianity create a rather confusing and incomplete picture of knowledge of Christianity among ancient Arabs, quite understandable given disagreements among the Christians. The reference, for example, by Ibn Isháq, the first biographer of the Prophet, to Waraqa ibn Nawfal, a cousin of Muhammad's wife, Khadíja, as a Christian who knew the books, could only mean that Waraqa was acquainted with portions of the Bible in Syriac, for there was then no Arabic translation of the Bible.

In spite of its geographical and historical proximity to Arab society, Christianity remained peripheral. Its Jewish Messianic message had little resonance with the polydaemonism of tribal Arab society, while the Greco-Roman influences of Christianity's Christological idiom estranged it from the realism of the Bedouin code. Instead of the disputations of theologians entangled in the intricacies of philosophical opinions, the Arabs embraced the teachings of Islam because those teachings gave instructions directed to the members of the body rather than to the spin of a cultivated mind. Jesus became a Greek philosopher and promptly left the Arabs to turn to prophets from God. In its Greek temper, Christianity postulated faith as a proposition for rational inquiry; in contrast, Islam established religion as a rule of regular practice. "Perform the religion, and scatter not [into sectarianism] regarding it,"[16] the Qur'an enjoins.[17] In the Arab world, Christianity was a Greek religion, whereas, at its core, Islam was untouched by Greek influence. It set up a polarity.

It puzzled and offended Muhammad, for example, that against one another Christians carved up the God-affirmed reality of Jesus, son of Mary (Îsá ibn Maryam), into splintering disagreements about his nature, with Monophysites, Nestorians, Melkites, and other groups each declaring victory in the sectarian enigma to which they reduced Jesus.[18] The Greek Christ ended up trumping the Jewish Jesus, a civilizational split that had irreversible consequences for all history. The failure of the Jewish Jesus occurred because Christian theology "did not translate into Arab acceptance since it came in partly alien form and was harnessed to external interests which sought to impose themselves politically on a subject, or a hostage, people."[19] Without the gospel in their language, Arab Christians existed as religious clients beholden to Byzantine Constantinople when relations with the Muslim caliphate were fraught. In 668, from about 673 to 680, and again in 716 Byzantine power was faced with complete annihilation by the Umayyads. The Scripture of Arab

Christians was foreign to the Arabs, and that deficit Islam supplied with decisive authority with its exclusive Arabic Qur'an.[20]

In spite of such limitations, Christianity's gains among the Arabs were by no means negligible. The monastic call to penitence and to discipleship reverberated throughout Palestine and beyond.[21] In the late fourth century a monastery was built on the island of Bahrain in the Gulf of Bahrain. Hayyán, a Yemeni merchant, converted to Christianity in the fifth century and took the gospel from his native Hira to adjoining regions. Under the leadership of Queen Máwiyya, the Tanúkh Arabs embraced Christianity and for inspiration looked to monks, the "servants of God," who presided over their religious life.

Arab Christianity Adrift

In reviewing the prospects of Arab Christianity in the first six centuries, Trimingham underlines the surface character of Arab Christian life and thought. A more realistic title of his book would have been "Christianity among the Aramaeans," he said. Christianity failed to awaken the Arab world from its dormant state, and there is not the slightest hint in the records that Arabs felt inspired to witness to their faith through the medium of Arabic. An indigenous Arab church failed to arise. For the most part Arab converts were transient persons, people whose connections brought them into wider contact and who otherwise were on the move as they traversed different worlds, becoming, by that fact, marginal to centers of Arab thought and culture. That was the case with the *Arabic Gospel* referred to earlier, which originated in a Syriac source. "Syriac Christianity touched merely the surface life of Arab Christians," proving incapable of penetrating Arab life and transforming it from within.[22] The exposition of Christianity in a language entirely foreign to Arab ways of thinking ensured its alienation, and in any case official dogma offered little incentive or room for alternative idioms. Theologians became wordsmiths rather than the bearers of real life experience.

The exigencies of nomadic life demanded and fostered a this-worldly code. Nomads did not need religion as a habit of the mind, and so nomad Arabs shunned creedal Christianity. The force and solidity of nomadic life required muscular loyalty and commitment, and the abstract account of Christian faith failed to compete with the Bedouin's elemental solidarity, 'asabiyáh, a concept Ibn Khaldún analyzed with great originality. Religion was a dependent variable in that scheme, and the Arabs changed their gods as often as they changed their social allegiance. Religion was social custom, and since Arab nomads' social custom was effectively cut off from the cultural currents of Christianity, the

Arabs were bypassed by the religion. In contrast, Islam was effective in responding to this social basis of religious allegiance, and in its urban and imperial sequel Islam provided amply for allegiance through power and by rewards, incentives, bonuses, and a status to go with them. Imperial conquest and the sultanate offered the means and opportunity. The Qur'an acknowledges this ancient Arab recalcitrance thus: "The Arabs are more stubborn in unbelief and hypocrisy, and apter not to know the bounds of what God has sent down on His Messenger" (9:98; also 49:13). The Arabs added Islam to their muscular worldview to give Arabness a global religious momentum, so that Islam's Arab center of gravity fixed and projected its worldwide appeal.

The Eastern Church might have afforded a hospitable environment for Arab Christians, but it was too absorbed in bouts of theological hair-splitting to spare a thought for its neighbors. While the church in the West looked to the unity of the community of Christians in spite of the diversity of religious opinion, the Eastern Church pressed for complete agreement in belief as the rule of Christian unity.[23] In a special study of the subject, Richard Bell paints a dispiriting picture of the contemporary state of play. The Eastern Church lost itself in the mazes of intellectual and philosophical problems. The church was rent by strife and schism, its intellectual life more and more restricted by tradition and fanaticism. Dogma was favored over thought.

The problem was not so much intellectual activity and speculation per se as it was the church's impatience with any manifestation of independent thought on religious matters, and the haste with which it rushed to force the issue against hesitating or unwilling fellow Christians. "The persecution of Christian by Christian, if less bloody, was if anything more bitter in spirit than the persecution of Christian by Pagan had formerly been. Thus the speculations of theologians became the watchwords of party strife—the seals of orthodoxy, forcibly stamped upon many who little understood them."[24] In that sense, had "the Meccans become Christians, they would inevitably have become in some respects subject to the Byzantines."[25] The Eastern Church was the barrier preventing Arab Christians from making Christianity their own.

The monastic tradition can claim credit for much of the Christian influence that survived the initial onslaught of Islam. From Scotland to Armenia, that monastic ideal acted to unite and inspire the Christian spiritual community well into the seventh century, and long before there was any comparable imperial structure to do so.[26] A stringent Christianity remained deeply compatible with acute forms of local commitment, and offered a lifestyle choice not dictated or controlled by Roman or any other imperial mandate. Monasteries, as independent communities, often supplied the vocabulary of local response, and acted as a shield against arbitrary imposition. Monasteries became

effective vehicles of cultural transmission, setting the standards by which society determined its ideals. Indeed, overlooking the Egyptian origins of the
practice, Europe in the Middle Ages decided to lay claim to the tradition of
monasticism, arguing that the monastic life originated in the Solomonic por-
tico where the apostles gathered to be of one mind and heart and where they
had all things in common.[27]

This all goes to show the deep appeal of monasticism as a Christian ideal.
Yet power and privilege corrupted that monastic ideal, which provoked a reaction, such as occurred in the Reformation. It is interesting to reflect on the
related idea that the Reformation failed to take root in a once Muslim Spain,
perhaps because of the Qur'anic stricture against the idea of monasteries.[28]
The condemnation is reiterated by Ibn Mubárak (d. 797) to the effect that no
one has corrupted religion save "kings and evil priests and venal monks."[29]

Related social institutions flourished under the Christian impact. In spite
of his declared antipathy, Edward Gibbon (d. 1794) observed that the Christian
societies that were instituted in the cities of the Roman Empire were united
only by the ties of faith and charity rather than by state direction. "Independence and equality formed the basis of their internal constitution. The want of
discipline and human learning was supplied by the occasional assistance of the
prophets, who were called to that function without distinction of age, of sex, or
of natural abilities, and who, as often as they felt the divine impulse, poured
forth the effusions of the Spirit in the assembly of the faithful."[30]

The roots of indigenous Christianity reached back into the style first developed in the early centuries in Egypt and elsewhere, rather than in any current, newfangled theories of liberation and inculturation. In an important
sense, the monastic movement was vernacular in character. Striking root in a
diversity of cultural and historical circumstances, monasticism took common
materials of faith and obedience to expand the church's range and appeal.

Axum, Nubia, and the Axial Shift

In time, Christianity spread to the Upper Nile in the kingdoms of Sennar,
Axum, and beyond to Abyssinia in northern Ethiopia. Based on the Red Sea
trade, the Axumite Empire had a glorious history, being the most important
ivory market in northeast Africa. Its ships plied the Indian Ocean, and its navy
was the largest of its time. Tradition claims that King Ezana converted to
Christianity, though scholars have disputed that on the grounds that Ezana,
like Constantine, remained a devotee of the old gods. In any case the Christian
connection with statecraft recalls a familiar theme. An inscription found at

Meroë around AD 360 describes the political motivation of Ezana's adoption of Christianity. The inscription invokes the power of the Lord of Heaven who is mightier than everything that exists on earth. This Lord of Heaven is perfect creator, reigns through all eternity, and is invincible to the enemy. Ezana claims Him as his personal maker and defender against his enemies. "No enemy shall stand before me, and after me no enemy shall follow. By the might of the Lord of all, I made war upon Nuba."[31] Later interventions in this conversion story had a precocious Ezana professing faith with the Trinitarian formula.[32] It suggests an ongoing contest between the old and new religion.

In pre-Christian times the Axumites were Jews who cherished their Israelite ties through Menelik, the reputed son of King Solomon through the Queen of Sheba. The Axumites maintained a legend claiming that when Moses led the exodus out of Egypt, some of his Hebrew people dispersed to the south and east, settling in Ethiopia. For these Hebrews of the dispersion, Ethiopia was a promised land. The Ethiopian Jews developed a distinctive religious tradition of their own. The Pharisaic Judaism that developed in Palestine and elsewhere bypassed them, and so rabbinic law was absent in Ethiopia, leaving the Torah as the supreme authority. South of Egypt the Axumites were the first African civilization to develop a writing system.

In the adjacent kingdom of Nubia, Christianity made its impact felt starting in the mid sixth century. The Byzantine emperor, Justinian, felt that Nubia would be of strategic advantage to him in his rivalry with Persia. Theodora, Justinian's wife, sought to displace the Orthodox brand of Christianity of her husband's persuasion, and so she secretly dispatched a mission of her own representing the Monophysite school, of which she was a member. Longinus became the first Monophysite bishop of Nubia in the 570s, though Justinian's rival mission also made some headway among the Nubians. The languages of Christianity became Greek and Old Nubian, which was written in Coptic characters. Through smart political maneuvering, Nubia kept close ties to the patriarch of Alexandria, which helped to preserve Nubia's independence. With the coming of Islam, however, Nubia's independence began to crack, and was saved only by submission to a *baqt* treaty of tribute. The new Muslim Arabs took Nubian slaves as *baqt* tribute, and so well established was the practice that traditions, purporting to go back to Muhammad, claimed that he directed Muslims to go to Nubia if they wished to find slave concubines. Relations with Fatimid Egypt were cordial, and Dongola, the capital, played host to the caliph, while the bishop, Georgios I, visited Baghdad in 836 to reaffirm the *baqt* treaty. Thanks to Saladin's forces, the Fatimids were toppled from power in Egypt, and their successors, the Sunni Ayyubid dynasty, looked less favorably on a Christian outpost to the south. Finally, in the early fourteenth century, Dongola was subdued and Christianity waned in the state. After the large-scale conversion of the Funj people to Islam in the sixteenth century, Nubian Christianity became a thing of the past.

Things were different in Ethiopia, where in the late tenth century, Christianity came under attack from forces allegedly led by the Jewish warrior-queen, Judith. Wars engulfed the kingdom and dynastic controversy beset it from within. In its Jewish mold Christianity became intertwined with the interests of the monarchy, leading in due course to the creation of the *Kebra Nagast*, "the Glory of Kings,"[33] a Judaizing document of the sixth century that had gone through several recensions until, in the fourteenth century, it was adopted and translated from the Arabic. Promulgated as the country's inspired national charter, the *Kebra Nagast* is the distillation and defense, at the same time, of its religious custom. The *Kebra Nagast* celebrated Ethiopia's Jewish connections to the Queen of Sheba and to King Solomon, who is presented as being superior to the emperors of Byzantium, and it defended the Monophysite cause against its Byzantine detractors.[34] The *Kebra Nagast* considered Ethiopians to be African Israelites.[35]

The Mediterranean world's realignment with Europe left Christian Ethiopia an island adrift in the surging tide of Islamic power. Accordingly, Ethiopia appealed to the Judaic roots of its new faith to dispel a sense of claustrophobia and to assert its right to international recognition. Such international considerations were part of the calculations, then, and at other times, which often entered into the adoption of Christianity and the establishment of new faith communities. In the Ethiopian case, however, there was the added and urgent sense that paying respect to the ancestors of the Abrahamic covenant would confer legitimacy and blessings on the New Israel of which Ethiopia was becoming a neglected but still necessary part. The instinct of an Ethiopian connection to a primordial Christian faith was several things at once: a rejection of foreign imposition, a charter of orthodox unity and credibility, and a stake in indigenous leadership.

Christianity offered a convincing rationale for established societies—such as Axum, Nubia, and Ethiopia—as well as for those undergoing rapid internal change. The dynamism associated with Christian teachings, and with the church as the possessor of a revitalized moral code of social aid and public practice gave the new religion an appealing and expanded range. People admired the fact that Christianity "made no social distinctions; it accepted the manual worker, the slave, the outcast, the ex-criminal ... above all, it did not, like Neoplatonism, demand education. ... Its members were bound together not only by common rites but by a common way of life and ... by common danger [in the face of official persecution]. The Church provided the essentials of social security: it cared for widows and orphans, the old, the unemployed, and the disabled; it provided a burial fund for the poor and a nursing service in time of plague. . . . Christians were in a more than formal sense 'members one of another.' "[36]

The primitive Christians deemed their relationship to God as one of filiation, and saw in that a transformed kinship to their pre-Christian ancestors.[37] These Christians pioneered a new sense of social solidarity based on baptism and the redeemed life.[38] No comparable system of ideas and institutions existed at the time to compete with the church in that respect, except, that is, the morale-sapping fratricidal divisions and rivalries among Christians themselves. The strong Christian presence in Edessa, the royal capital of Mesopotamia, with some two-hundred-strong clergy, was in the end broken up by the decision to counter regional forces and impose Greek forms of the Antiochene rite upon the Syriac Church. King Abgar of Mesopotamia is reported to have converted to Christianity after a prayer he addressed to Jesus. He was healed following a visit, at the apostle Thomas's instigation, by one of the seventy disciples.[39]

Although Edessa was a city predominantly of Syrian Christians, probably with significant Jewish elements,[40] it belonged, still, in the same spiritual corridor as Antioch, a cosmopolitan center of Greek Christians and the birthplace of St. John Chrysostom (d. 407), patriarch of Constantinople.[41] Rivaling Alexandria, Edessa eventually grew into a strong center of Christian intellectual life.[42] Ephraim the Syrian settled in Edessa. The bishops of Edessa traced their spiritual lineage to Antioch's Bishop Serapion (190–203). Theodore Abú Qurra of the ninth century, who was a leader of the lively intellectual exchange conducted in Arabic with Muslims, was born and reared in Edessa.[43]

When the city came under Roman control after the third century, the attendant political pressure caused the church to retreat into its Syriac milieu, which still thrived in the surrounding countryside.

> The Syriac-speaking communities separated from the Byzantine
> Church through a painful process by which they attached themselves
> to two main lines of interpretation that acquired the designations of
> Monophysite or Jacobite (in Syria) and Dyophysite or Nestorian.
> The first in broad terms was the line that Christians within the Roman
> sphere took, and the second that of those who fell within the Persian sphere.[44]

King Shapur II, who ruled for an astounding seventy years, from 309 to 379, turned on the Christians when he learned that his archenemy, Constantine, had recognized the religion. Thousands of Christians were killed as a consequence. Christian fortunes improved shortly thereafter as relations improved with the Roman Empire. At the great council of Ctesiphon in 410 the breach with Rome was healed.

Muslim scholars were eager to see such splits among Christians as evidence of cultural fragmentation. For those who needed it, it was ample proof that no difference of theological opinion seemed able to alienate Christianity. One contemporary Muslim scholar noted lamentably how religious differences among Christians and Muslims alike had in common only the indomitable dexterity with which the partisans chopped logic. In that regard, Orthodox Byzantium, which enjoyed its golden age in the sixth century under Justinian (527–65), expanded its imperial domain under Heraclius (610–41) to embrace Asia Minor, Syro-Palestine, and Egypt, with a protectorate over Abyssinia. But the debilitating campaigns it conducted in northern Europe and against the Persians in the east combined with long endemic struggles between the iconophiles and the iconoclasts to drain Byzantium's strength from within. Orthodox Byzantium was unable to stem the tide of Islam, and was subsequently overwhelmed in Egypt and the Levant.[45]

The Islamic code on cultural boundaries and on cultural representation had an impact on neighboring societies. Some writers, for example, have suggested that Christian iconoclasm was inspired by Islam's antipathy to images, and have seen Muslim influence in the iconoclastic edict of Emperor Leo the Isaurian in 725. Yet it is likely that Leo only brought to a head the campaign against images that had a much older history. In a letter to Serenus of Marseilles, Gregory I (590–604), for example, issued a condemnation of images, showing that the iconoclastic movement had been underway considerably earlier than the time of Leo. It was John of Damascus (ca. 675–ca. 749), writing, ironically, under the patronage of the Muslim caliph, who offered an argument to reconcile Christianity's divided mind on the matter. He withdrew to a monastery in 716 to write his influential work, *The Fount of Wisdom*, a work that for many centuries had considerable impact on the church in both the East and the West. In some isolated pockets, the Christian movement was not necessarily impeded by Islam.

Islamic Enlightenment and Cultural Momentum

In the end, the defining challenge to the scale and depth of Christianity's social and cultural achievement came not from internal strife and splits, but from the meteoric rise and expansion of Islam in the seventh century—first in the Arabian peninsula, in the Near East with the spectacular fall of Jerusalem, in

Egypt, North Africa, and then beyond to Nubia and the Ethiopian kingdom. The relentless and successful penetration of Islam into areas previously dominated by Christianity precipitated the most serious territorial recession for the church in the Byzantine Near East and in Monophysite Egypt.

Assured of their control of the Mediterranean, Muslim forces turned their attention to southern Italy. In the ninth century, Muslim fleets from Tunisia and Sicily commenced their raids against Italian ports. In 841 they took Bari, the main Byzantine base in southeastern Italy. In 842 the Lombard Duke of Benevento invited the Muslims to help him against Salerno. The Muslims took that opportunity to plunder fields and monasteries that lay in their path. Alarmingly, in 846 a Muslim force of 1,100 men landed at Ostia and marched up to the walls of Rome, plundering the churches of St. Peter and St. Paul.

Without an adequate combined Italian response in the offing anywhere, Pope Leo IV stepped in and organized Amalfi, Naples, Gaeta, and Rome into a temporary alliance, and together they constructed a chain across the Tiber to halt the Muslim advance. When in 849 the expected Muslim attack materialized, the Italian coalition under the pope was able to mount a successful counterattack to hold the invaders at bay, though not for long. In the end the papacy was forced to pay an annual peace ransom equivalent to $25,000 to spare Europe disaster and humiliation at the hands of the Muslims. It was only in 916 that the combined forces of the pope, the Greeks, and the Germans put down the Saracens on the Garigliano.[46] Rome thereby escaped the fate that two centuries earlier had befallen Spain.

There was cause for concern. Where they were successful, the Muslim victors preached conversion, but only *to* Islam, not out of it. The inequality in Qur'anic law between Muslims and non-Muslims accelerated the conversion process. Christian and Jewish subjects, considered *ahl dhimma*, were granted a protected or *dhimmi* status so long as they adhered to the rule of not converting Muslims and in other ways not threatening Muslim authority. And so under the Islamic code, submission and compliance were rewarded; backsliding and defiance punished; dissent and resistance crushed; power sequestered; and activities curtailed. The entire Mediterranean basin began to overheat from the sudden pressure of Muslim forces buoyed by steed and sword as they stormed the strongholds of Byzantine power.

Europe was saved, but not spared, as the Muslim Arabs took Spain in the early eighth century and threatened elsewhere. With the exception of lands to the north, Islam completely encircled the Mediterranean, with Baghdad as the new gravitational center. It was from Baghdad in 907 that a Nestorian monk traveled to China, only to find Christianity had become defunct there. An imperial decree in 845 had effectively rooted out Christianity along with

Zoroastrianism as foreign threats to China's customs. As Ibn Khaldún put it in an arresting phrase, Christians of the Mediterranean world could float not even a plank upon the sea.

Yet Christianity had not been entirely eclipsed. Despite mixed reviews from travelers there, Constantinople, the seat of Byzantine power, for example, continued to enjoy unquestioned respect and admiration even in the Muslim world. In Baghdad, the capital of the Abbasid Islamic Empire, Greek diplomatic missions were welcomed by the caliphs in the name of the superiority of Greek learning. The caliphs of Baghdad had recently embarked on an energetic project of promoting the Greek enlightenment with the collection, preservation, and translation of Greek philosophical and scientific works into Arabic, using Greek-speaking citizens of the caliphate for the purpose.[47] A contemporary poet devoted a panegyric to Baghdad's brilliance, describing the city as the seat of learning and art, its suburbs vying in beauty with the blue vault of the sky, the banks of the Tigris teeming with beautiful damsels, with thousands of gondolas on the water dancing and sparkling like sunbeams in the air.[48] It depicts a city of free and liberal temperament—and few embodied that spirit better than Hasan ibn Hani, known by his sobriquet, Abú Nuwás, who under caliphal patronage wrote poems to wine and sin, to public acclaim.

At several points of their convergence, Christianity and Islam produced mutually beneficial effects. That was how Ibn Rushd, known as Averroës to Europe, emerged as the foremost scholar of Aristotle in his day and well into the nineteenth century.[49] Averroës described a just society as one that allowed every woman, child, and man to develop unhindered the possibilities God gave them. Largely owing to Thomas Aquinas (d. 1274), however, Averroëism in the Middle Ages acquired a heretical reputation as a system of freethinking and infidelity, mainly as a result of the misinterpretation of Averroës by Siger of Brabant, a Latin Averroëist, to the effect that faith and reason are mutually contradictory. More accurately, Averroës himself was interested in harmonizing faith and reason, not in arguing for faith and reason as being separate and mutually exclusive. That harmonizing was the case he tried to make in his *Fasl al-Maqál, On the Agreement Between Philosophy and Revealed Religion*. As such, Averroës was a major influence on Aquinas, especially with reference to Aquinas's claim, first stated by Averroës, that God's knowledge embraces not only universals but also particulars.

With uncanny anticipation of Averroës, al-Kindí (d. 866), an early Arab philosopher, encouraged his fellow Muslims not to retreat before Greek science and not to be ashamed to acknowledge truth from whatever quarter it came—even if it came by means of former generations or from the hands of non-Muslims. Al- Kindí spoke uncompromisingly about how for anyone who

sought truth there was nothing of higher value than truth itself. That sentiment had parallels in Christian thought, and it was not surprising that, to the
shock of fellow Muslims, al-Kindí wrote an *Apology for Christianity*.

Another Islamic enlightenment figure was Abú Bakr al-Rází (d. 925),
better known to the medieval West as the Rhazes. He was the author of a
famous encyclopedia of medicine called *al-Háwí*, translated by Farragut into
Latin as *Continens*, and published five times between 1488 and 1542. He was a
great admirer of Socrates, about whom he wrote, "And if we confess ourselves
his inferior, we do not thereby demean ourselves; for that is the plain truth, and
it is always nobler and more honourable to acknowledge the truth." Rhazes
defended the search for truth, saying knowledge must be allied to justice. "It
is hateful to [God] that we should be unjust and ignorant; He loves us to
have knowledge and to be just."[50] Defending his decision to honor a Muslim
woman saint, Faríd al-Dín Attár (b. 1119), author of the famous *Parliament of
the Birds*, asserts that it is an unimpeachable teaching of Islam that our outward appearance is not decisive for our status before God because attainment
of the divine does not lie in appearance but in sincerity of purpose. For Attar,
the sex line either way is not indicative of our moral worth.

Al-Jáhiz of Basra (d. 869) was similarly respectful of the debt Muslim
scholars owed to the Greeks. "Did we not possess the books of the ancients in
which their wonderful wisdom is immortalized and in which the manifold
lessons of history are so dealt with that the past lives before our eyes, did we not
have access to the riches of their experience which would otherwise have been
barred to us, our share in Wisdom would be immeasurably smaller and our
means of attaining to a true perspective most meager." Al-Jáhiz was a major
intellectual influence in Spain, his adopted country. There are echoes in his
statement of the views of Justin Martyr: both of them gladly acknowledged
their debt to the ancient Greeks on the grounds that there was only one source
of wisdom, who was God.

To prove that the intellectual advantage had shifted to the Muslims,
Baghdad was also the setting for a remarkable encounter between Muslim
ideas of religion and the claims of Christianity, in this case Nestorian Christianity.[51] The caliph al-Mahdí (775–85) summoned the Nestorian patriarch,
Timothy I (779–823), to a public debate. At issue for the caliph was the non-
divine authorship of the Gospels, the allegedly false doctrine of the Trinity that
corrupts belief in one God, and, a defining question, the status of Muhammad
in Christian teaching. The caliph interrogated the patriarch closely and with
dogged persistence, focusing on the Trinity and the nature of God, and in
his answers the patriarch cited the Qur'an where God uses the first-person
plural pronoun with respect to Jesus.[52] That led to an extensive theological

disquisition on the attributes of kingly office and of God's sovereign majesty. On God's nature and attributes, the patriarch cited the Psalms (*zabúr*),[53] as well as several other passages of Scripture.[54] He left no stone unturned.

Aware of the importance of not giving offense and yet not sounding evasive, Timothy's wise and irenic answers left the caliph still wishing that Timothy had accepted the authority of Muhammad, but he appeared content to settle for a stalemate. In this context, it is not irrelevant to note that the caliph instituted an inquisition (*mihna*) against infidels and heretics, and in the ensuing purge the Manichaeans, known as *zindiks*, were driven eastward into Central Asia.

For his turn, the patriarch spoke of the gospel as the precious pearl of faith, a phrase dear to Muslim Súfís, saying this pearl of true faith fell "in the midst of all of us. . . . God has placed the pearl of His faith before all of us like the shining rays of the sun, and everyone who wishes can enjoy the light of the sun."[55] It was the caliph's prerogative to end the two-day meeting, and so he rose duly and went inside his audience chamber. In the atmosphere of intellectual equality and of such refined courtesy, it was possible for the caliph and the patriarch to engage in open theological exchange even if the outcome left the religious status quo unaffected.

Yet the crux of the issue was the caliph's contention that in the final analysis Muhammad rendered Christianity invalid, and so he opened the proceedings on that point. "What do you say about Muhammad?" he asked sharply. Wisely, the patriarch answered deferentially: "Muhammad is worthy of all praise, by all reasonable people, O my sovereign. He walked in the path of the prophets, and trod in the track of the lovers of God. All prophets taught the doctrine of one God and since Muhammad taught the doctrine of the unity of God, he walked, therefore, in the path of the prophets." That deft reply was sufficient to allow the meeting to continue, though it served notice of the power the caliph held in reserve. It put the patriarch on the defensive, all too aware of his subordinate role. He lost no opportunity to sing the caliph's praises, using blandishment to mask the caliph's inquest and shield himself from self-incrimination. In other situations nothing less than the full acknowledgment that Muhammad is the seal of the prophets (*khatam al-nabíyín*) would satisfy Muslim demands, as the patriarch well knew. Mutual affirmation knew its limits.

At once familiar and unsettling for Christians, the rival Muslim claim has dominated and complicated the centuries-long civilizational stalemate between the West and Islam, and to it the contemporary secular West seems not to be particularly attuned or immune. In the present climate of renewed tension between the two civilizations, the claim may be ignored, but it is difficult to see how cultural accommodation can succeed in spite of it.

A word is necessary about a principle of self-preservation in situations of personal risk or danger, a principle that seems to lurk behind much of the patriarch's cautious and circumspect response. This is the doctrine of *taqíyah*, literally guarding one's self, caution, concealment, disguise. It is the technical term in the Muslim lexicon for dispensation from the requirements of truth when one is under compulsion, suspicion, or risk of injury.

The Qur'an permits the denial of faith under duress;[56] the eating of forbidden food under blackmail;[57] and befriending unbelievers.[58] *Taqíyah* is a versatile tool that allows believers to withhold, tweak, conceal, or disguise the truth in order to save themselves and their community from harm. Under *taqíyah*, the duty to witness boldly to one's faith is suspended, and compromise sanctioned, without moral or legal prejudice. It is a form of damage control in which one is granted relief from duty (*rukhsa*) for stinting on the truth where that is a lesser evil than the consequences of open defiance.[59] As one Muslim authority affirmed, "If any one is compelled and professes unbelief with his tongue, while his heart contradicts him, to escape his enemies, no blame falls on him, because God takes his servants as their hearts believe."[60] Accordingly, the caliph would have been all too aware of how, under the rules of *taqíyah*, the patriarch's modulated answers were permissible in the interests of safeguarding conscience.

It is relevant to Baghdad's dominance to point out that when Constantine-Cyril and Methodius set out on their historic mission to the Slavs they reported first to the caliph in Baghdad. At the urging of the Byzantine emperor, Constantine-Cyril was later involved in a major theological debate with Muslim critics (837–43), called in the account "Hagarites," after Hagar, Sarai's Egyptian handmaid.[61] Constantine-Cyril set out immediately to refute Muslim charges of blasphemy with respect to the Trinity by appealing to the Qur'anic verse that appears to lend support to Jesus as the Second Person of the Trinity. He insisted that all the prophets and the fathers of the church support the call "to glorify the Trinity, the Father, the Word and the Spirit, three hypostases in one being. And the Word became flesh in the Virgin and was born for the sake of our salvation, as your prophet Mohammed bore witness when he wrote the following: 'We sent our spirit, to the Virgin, having consented that She gave birth.'[62] From this I apprise you of the Trinity."[63] Even when it was fraught with danger, Christian thinkers welcomed the opportunity for dialogue because dialogue offered the chance to overcome mutual stereotypes and the uncharitable spirit.

In a very tangible way, the European enlightenment owed no small part of its origins to the ninth-century Islamic enlightenment fostered by Caliph al-Ma'mún (d. 833).[64] In that connection the Byzantine link served the Muslims' interests and at the same time extended Christianity's cross-cultural range. Christian ideas were familiar to Muslim leaders and scholars, as the career of Ibn Hazm (d. 1064) of Córdoba illustrates. He wrote a book on comparative religion called, *The Book of Religions and Sects*, where he discussed Judaism, Zoroastrianism, Christianity, and Islam. With rambunctious confidence in Islam's superior intellectual merits, Ibn Hazm said he was unimpressed by the claims of Christianity, which seemed to him contrary to reason. In his *Ring of the Dove*, Ibn Hazm described God's unity as the unity of love, of the lover, and of the beloved, which comes pretty close to a Christian exposition of the Trinity. Still, he said he was surprised that so many nations should fall for a superstition such as the one Christianity teaches.

> Human Superstition need never excite our astonishment. The most numerous and civilized nations are thralls to it. So great is the multitude of Christians that God alone can number them, and they can boast of illustrious philosophers and sagacious princes. Nevertheless, they believe that one is three and three are one; that one of the three is the father, the other the son, and the third a spirit; that the father is the son and is not the son—that a man is God, and that he is not God—that the Messiah is in all respects God, and yet that he is not the same as God—that he has existed from all eternity, and yet was created. A sect of theirs, known as the Jacobites,[65] numbered by hundreds of thousands—even believe that the Creator was scourged, buffeted, crucified and slain, and that for three whole days the Universe was without a ruler![66]

Al-Ghazálí picked up the gauntlet, saying that Christians, "biting with their wisdom teeth," clung tenaciously and on blind authority to the teaching of the divinity of Christ in spite of it running counter to good sense. In a detailed and probing examination of the Gospel of John, al-Ghazálí concluded that the divine sonship of Christ was nothing more than a figurative way of saying that all human persons were God's children by virtue of their being given life by the Creator. The literal sense Christians gave to the title was unwarranted and in flagrant breach of logic and of God's transcendence.[67]

Like Ibn Hazm before him, al-Ghazálí felt, after tussling with Aristole and the Ismáí'lís to his own satisfaction, that it was a relatively easy task next to demolish Christian teaching, and so he dispensed with the customary rigorous methods of philosophical argumentation to employ polemics instead. Al-Ghazálí protested, with a tone one part sarcasm and one part condescension, that Christianity was nothing short of impudence toward God. "There is no disgrace more shocking than that of a people who believe that God the Knower was buried, [and] saying that one should fast on a particular Saturday because 'the Maker of the world was buried on that day.'"[68] For al-Ghazálí as for his religious cohorts, Christianity was not a worthy opponent, though if it became a nuisance measures could be adopted to deal with it. Otherwise the religion would be allowed to wither on the vine.

The Muslim confidence in its superior attainment vis-à-vis the West rested on solid foundations of political and cultural achievement, and that legacy made deep inroads in European life and thought. The Muslim scholar known as Abulcasis to medieval Europe, but otherwise as Abú al-Qásim Khalaf ibn 'Abbás al-Zahráwi (d. ca. 1013), was the author of a major work on surgery. The work was translated into Latin by Gerard of Cremona (d. 1187) and published in various editions at Venice in 1497, at Basel in 1541, and at Oxford in 1778. It was the authoritative manual on surgery in Salerno and Montpellier, among other places.

Another Spanish Muslim medical scientist was Ibn Zuhr (d. 1162), better known by the appellate of Avenzoar. Averroës, who himself wrote a famous treatise on medicine called the *Kullíyát*, hailed Avenzoar as the greatest physician since Galen. An expanding chain of intellectual exchange bound together Spain, Sicily, and North Africa, with a radius connecting areas in Provence and the Alpine passes extending to Germany, Central Europe, and across the English Channel into England. In 953 Otto the Great, king of the Germans, sent a monk as an envoy to Spain, who stayed for three years in Cordoba studying Arabic and collecting scientific manuscripts. Lorraine, Liége, Gorze, and Cologne, for example, became centers of Arab learning and scholarship. The Scotsman Michael Scot (d. ca.1236), a founder of Latin Averroism, studied and worked in Muslim Spain before moving to Sicily as court astronomer to Frederick II. He translated numerous Arabic works into Latin, thus introducing them to the West. Michael Scot subsequently moved to Bologna, and from 1227 served at the imperial court.

By this time Toledo had established itself as a center of Islamic scholarship, a reputation it maintained even under Archbishop Raymond I (1126–51). Scholars, such as Robert of Chester, came to Toledo from Britain, as well as elsewhere. Robert's translation of a treatise on algebra by a Muslim scientist was the first such work in the West. The first Latin translation of the Qur'an in 1143 by Peter the Venerable was done from Toledo. The Dominican, Ricoldo of Montecroce (d. 1320), based in Baghdad, did a translation of the Qur'an, though he said Muslims opposed it. In 1250 the Dominicans established in Toledo the first school of Oriental studies as preparation for mission and engagement with the Muslim world, suggesting how the missionary movement became the catalyst for opening the West to the heritage of the rest of the world. As we shall see presently, a case in point is Voltaire's acknowledgment, centuries later, of the work of Ricci in China, which helped expand Europe's enlightenment horizons. Voltaire dedicated his book, *Mahomet*, to Pope Benedict XIV.

As argued by Miguel Asín Palacios, the Europe in which Dante emerged to create his *Divine Comedy* was steeped in Islamic materials or in materials that came through Islamic or Islamized channels.[69] Dante's eschatology owed its inspiration to Islamic eschatology, and Dante knew many Latin translations of Arabic writings. The whole allegorical structure of the *Divine Comedy*, with its evocative hints of the Súfí idea of *salak al-taríq*, consisting of traversing the path of enlightenment through the threefold stages of *balá* (torment), *faná* (abe-negation), and *baqá* (subsistence), shows unmistakable familiarity with Islamic sources. It has been suggested that the Spanish Muslim Ibn 'Arabí (d. 1240), perhaps the greatest, if also most complex, speculative mind of Islamic *ta-sawwuf*, mysticism, was an influence on Dante as he certainly was on Jung.[70]

For example, Dante's three stages of the soul's journey to Paradise, Purgatory, and Hell occurred in a twelfth-century Islamic source, and such materials circulated widely in southern Europe, including Italy. Ibráhim al-Faquim, a Jewish doctor active in the reign of Alfonso X (1264–77), translated from Arabic into Castilian a work of allegory that contains remarkable resemblances to the structure Dante established for the *Divine Comedy*.[71]

Al-Faquim's translation makes it clear that what gave rise to the Ascension motif in the literature was the Prophet's *mi'ráj* in Jerusalem, and this became very familiar in literary circles in the Middle Ages. A thirteenth-century Codex of Uncastillo mentions it; as does Rodrigo Ximénez, also in the thirteenth century. Ricoldo of Montecroce, who worked in Baghdad in 1291, circulated a popularized and polemical version of the Ascension. Fazio degli Uberti crafted a poetic version of the story in his *Dittamondo*, and it is beyond dispute that Dante was familiar with that work. None of these inquiries, however, is meant to question Dante's literary originality, but only to make the historical point that Islamic materials that suffused so much of the Western Christian world that Dante inhabited made a positive contribution to his original creation. A well-directed Islamic stimulus suffused the Western Christian outlook at its core, and in his great achievement Dante retained evidence of that. Islamic contact thus deepened the West's heritage of variety and diversity.

Affinity and Estrangement

Unlike Islam, Christianity was born with the cultural complex of having lost for good its birthplace in the Holy Land, and the attempt subsequently in the centuries of the Crusades (1096–1271) to lift that weight ended in ignominy, with the shame of it later used as justification for excluding Christian missions in the Muslim world. It left the encircled Christian communities and floating client families with a crippling dilemma: the faith in their hands survived as a private, orphaned religion, subversive if it avowed its Palestinian roots publicly, and belittled if it abjured those roots openly. In deference to Islam, the claim of a Christian promised land was abandoned as ruinous folly, though if Christianity wished to maintain its right to be considered a world religion and the equal of Islam it could not forsake its origins entirely, if only as historical memory. Hellenization foreclosed on Christianity's debt to its Palestinian origins, and exposed it as an upstart faith. The religion was adrift in the tide of cultural assimilation, and Christian writers gave up any credible resistance. Muslims concluded it was because loyalty to culture supplanted loyalty to truth.

Writing in the tenth century, 'Abd al-Jabbár took up this charge of Christianity's cultural slipping, arguing that Greek and Roman influences contrived to stage a wholesale takeover of Christianity and to strip it of any authentic claim to a divine warrant. Al-Jabbár accused Christianity of being a surrogate religion that was indebted to Roman imperial power—it was not Christianity that converted the empire but the empire that converted Christianity. It was only illusion that led people to call this an example of religious change rather than religious co-option, al-Jabbár insisted. Muslims never had to face a moral disqualification of that kind, thanks to Islam's claim to a revealed language and to the unbroken legacy of devotion and veneration of Mecca and Medina, Islam's territorial core.

Al-Jabbár would not relent, saying the absence in Christianity of a revealed language and of any sense of a founding territorial warrant condemned Christians to dealing with religion as social construction rather than as divine command. He implied that without a doctrine of *jáhiliyáh*, of the imperative of a clean break with an unredeemable pagan past, Christians were unable to distinguish between true religion and false religion, and thus powerless to resist corrupting religion.

That sentiment bound the Muslim world as one in its view that Europe could lay claim only in a bogus sense to true religion, which might explain why in trade and industry, traffic with Europe flourished, but why in religion, relations remained fraught, where they existed at all. The inquiry of Harún al-Rashíd (785–809) of the hard-pressed Timothy, the Nestorian patriarch, about which of the two he would consider the true religion of God hints at how the caliph rated Christianity. Timothy answered adroitly, if less conclusively, that it was the religion whose teachings conformed to God's injunctions. Faced with a choice between dishonesty and apostasy, the patriarch slipped the dilemma by choosing discretion as the better part of valor. Dignity aside, Timothy could not for one moment forget who had the upper hand; it justified his grubbing for a margin of safety.

It left a defiant Islam entrenched. No amount of exegesis and hermeneutics, of elaborate and polite phrases of dialogue and interfaith solidarity, no mount of shock and awe, or of contrition and restitution, and none of the devout wish for a secular alternative, or of enlightened calls for a discourse of inclusive diversity could conceal, evade, or budge the one stumbling block in relations with Islam's unshakable conviction that it alone possessed God's truth. Falling short of that truth, the Bible, for example, might be redacted in concession, but not the Qur'an, deemed the purest source of truth. Even with a discounted Bible, or because of it, Christians were considered infidels, and that view created a firewall of estrangement between the two religions, a case of east is east, and west is west, and never would the twain meet.

Christian Europe was cockeyed about Islam. On one hand, European society lived in complacent ignorance of Islam on the principle that what you don't know won't hurt you, and yet, on the other hand, Islam's culture was regarded as alien, and its values threatening. In place of active engagement, Europeans settled for pragmatic coexistence. Many reasoned that a genial agnostic attitude toward things religious would appease Muslims and win their trust; by not parading offensive Christian dogma, appeasement would avert Muslim antagonism.

Internal divisions and debilitating strife may explain why Europe adopted the path of secularization, and, besides, secular traffic with the world of Islam gave Europe crosscultural access without a religious handicap. Yielding to local Muslim sensibilities, European nations sponsored and supported their citizens in Muslim lands only as foreign trading communities, though a showdown seemed inevitable given the accelerating secularization process in Europe where the tide of national self-determination was surging and that of Christianity's public role ebbing. The dissolution of the monasteries commenced that secularizing process, and since Islam had no monasteries, secularization could be promoted without incurring Muslim animosity—or so it was hoped. What the architects of secularization overlooked was that secularism would spark a smoldering centuries-long anti-Western Muslim antagonism not because a puritanical Islam would reject the fruits of the good life, but because the good life demanded as its price repudiation of God. Pride in the normative claims of the secular achievement competed with the requirement in Islam of acknowledgment of indebtedness to God's bounty.

In the aftermath of the 1789 French Revolution, cross and tricolor became warring symbols for Europeans who responded with a radical prescription for church, state, and society. In matters of public interest, organized religion abdicated to the organized sovereign state, while in matters of the truth claims of religion, the institutional church deferred to the individual and society as sovereign arbiters, as the work of Friedrich Schleiermacher and of Émile Durkheim demonstrates. For Schleiermacher, religion was individual experience shorn of objective dogma and organized structure, so that, as Alfred North Whitehead put it, religion was what individuals did with their own solitariness. It gives an insight into the mainstay psychology of liberal Protestantism whose central affirmation, in the words of H. Richard Niebuhr, is that a God without wrath brought men without sin into a kingdom without judgment through the ethical injunctions of a Christ without a cross. In that understanding religion is torn from its roots in the cumulative witness of the prophets to become just a cultural modifier.

In the sociological view, conversion was to be made to society's norms and constraints, not to God as such. For that matter, Durkheim found that religion's origins lay in the collective consciousness and in society's common values implemented in individual conduct and behavior. But Jane Harrison, a contemporary, argued rightly that Durkheim's view creates a tension in that man's body obeys natural law while his spirit is bound by the social imperative. The imperative to seek freedom from necessity conflicts with Durkheim at this point.[72] It was left to Karl Marx to tweak this Durkheimian dualism into the classical dialectic of religion as an opiate or false consciousness of the masses.[73] The civil religion that Niebuhr described was the appropriate liberal concession to Marx.

The brilliant salvage operation of Max Weber, in restoring rationality to religion, or to Puritan forms of religion, saved rationality, but not necessarily religion, except that, tellingly, Islam survived his method. Or did it? According to a recent assessment, "Weber sees Islam as transforming itself more and more into a legalistic religion oriented towards feudal property."[74] Weber claimed that Islam was really never a religion of salvation.[75] Weber exempted Islam because he considered Islam anticapitalist, but he did not discount, thereby, Islam's truth claims. Marx, perhaps, had the last word: class dialectics, if not the imperatives of a well-ordered society, displaced revealed ethics, which ruled out any role for religion.

Some Christian thinkers tried to fill the breach, but without significant success. Because of religious discounting and in light of the failed liberal proposals of someone like Lamennais (d. 1854) for a religious reconciliation, the secular tide continued to surge. Conceding the ground at home, European leaders pursued abroad a defensive policy. France and Italy, for example, covered for their respective Roman Catholic compatriots living in Muslim countries, while Russia intervened on behalf of Orthodox believers living under the Ottomans. For Russia, Turkey was the "sick man of Europe." Operating under the millet system, such foreign enclaves were cordoned off, and as such had only marginal influence on the strengthening of local Christian life that continued to suffer from growing popular disaffection within and steady defections to Islam without. Europe's globalized economic interests eclipsed Christianity's local credibility.

An aching sense of déjà vu pervades the modern scenario of Western defensiveness in the face of reports of repression and discrimination against post-Western Christians. Encircled Christian communities in the early centuries, for example, were steadily depleted by infiltration from a class of opportunity-seeking, mobile Muslim groups. The cities were coming under the control and dominance of imperial officials and of a burgeoning middle class, which left little room for the demobilized elements of the caliphal armies. The Muslim rural expansion that followed initiated a process that remorselessly turned rural Christians into a class of the dispossessed and impoverished. Economic disability combined with a sense of inferiority to deny Arab Christians pride in their religion and to turn them into cultural exiles on home ground. The Islamic version of "orientalism" allowed the Muslims to embark on a relentless cultural campaign of depicting Christians as those who knew only enough Arabic to point to things.[76]

An Arabization assimilation process aimed at establishing the unrivaled preeminence of Islam commenced. It caused Arabization and Christianization, and the accompanying cultural tolerance, to diverge decisively. The strong tradition of toleration of the *dhimmi* was reversed. Jews and Christians would have had intimations of that reversal in the guidance to forego harshness that the caliph 'Umar ibn 'Abd al-'Azíz (717–20) gave to one of his governors, namely, that "the sheep [i.e., the *dhimmi*] should not be dragged to the slaughterer and one must not sharpen the slaughtering knife on the head of the cattle that is being slaughtered."[77]

The heavy hand of taxation (*istikhráj*) and other economic hardships fell on the long-suffering Jews and Christians alike. For many of them, apostasy offered a way out. In Jerusalem the Jews were forced to resort to special collections to avoid being crushed by the tax burden. But even there many Jews were imprisoned because they were unable to pay the heavy debts they incurred in order to pay their taxes. "Many died from the terrible torment of being required to pay the tax and in some cases, of subjection to physical torture."[78] The scandalized author of a Syriac chronicle dealing with the eighth century, the Jacobite patriarch Dionysius I (d. 845) of Tel-Mahré, lamented bitterly the fact that the mass of Christian villages in the Near East was turning to Islam faster than sheep running to water.[79] Only a few villages survived this process of emptying out the Christians.

In other ways, the death penalty was instituted for apostasy from Islam, and such restrictions turned Christians inward for their own safety and survival. In the ensuing centuries the desire to safeguard Christian communal survival took precedence over the promotion of distinctive Christian teachings, and local clergy became minders to their own people who lived in a cultural cul de sac. There were few theological schools to offer education and training, and little by way of viable Christian support to maintain them. A deep sense of inferiority corroded the will and eroded the imagination to challenge the terms of capture and stigma placed on Christians who now lived on sufferance under Muslim rule, alike under the Mongols and the Ottomans.[80]

For a good part of the Aegean and southern and eastern Mediterranean world in the premodern period, Christianity remained an "enclaved" religion of millets, rather than a matter of vital local faith. When it was not about Christians as subdued clients, the religion's history was in large measure the history of Europeans in those societies, and it produced the irony of Europe—those fragmented and isolated in their religious life overseeing those fragmented and isolated Christian communities overseas. Richard Forster, the first English consul at Tripoli in Syria, for example, was instructed in 1583 to proceed warily so as not to run afoul of the other European nations represented there, chiefly the French and the Venetians, and to do whatever was necessary to protect the commercial interests of his country.[81] National differences were a factor in Europe's intellectual fragmentation until the Enlightenment arrived to give Europe the cultural cohesion that Christianity once did, and then some. The Enlightenment created a "narrowcast," slim-fit, "enlightened" Christianity that was held within the bounds of sovereign reason alone. Olympian logic produced the outlook of disembodied detachment: what one knew was torn from the roots of what one experienced. It explains al-Farábí's objection to making Islam's God accountable to reason rather than, as he thought proper, making reason accountable to God. For the philosopher with a lucid pen faith could check the roaring machine of loquacious discourse.

It is instructive to reflect on the position of Prince Otto von Bismarck, the German chancellor, who announced at the Berlin Congress of 1884 that the colonial powers should among themselves preside over the religious affairs of their colonies by favoring and aiding all religions, an enlightened position from which the chancellor beat a quick retreat when Turkey, a Muslim state and a signatory to the convention, demanded the inclusion of all Muslim missionaries in that policy. By "all religions" Bismarck meant, and was understood to mean, all the varieties of Christian denominations in Europe, a fine point Muslim Turkey may be excused for not grasping.

Among themselves, Christians would understand if Muslims looked askance at what the unifying standard was for the scattered pieces of a many-splintered Christianity. Without a formal protocol on the question, however, the European assumption of religions as denominations, and as endorsement for imperial achievement, became the operative policy on the ground. The European practice of trading in Christianity as a national dividend promoted the religion's fragmentation abroad and complicated immensely perceptions of its status as a world religion. On the occasion of the arrival of the coffin carrying the remains of Cardinal Lavigerie—who died on November 26, 1892—in Tunis from Algiers, one observer commented on the huge public demonstration, saying, "Religion triumphs, and France grows in stature in the eyes of the infidel, astonished by so much pomp and splendour."[82] Almost everywhere in the colonial empires Muslim communities, whatever their size, regarded the presence of Christian missions as secular foreign intrusion, to be resisted as such. Like the Romans before them, Muslims felt little inclination to treat Christianity as a true religion, only as provocation in the politics of colonial hegemony. That perception has survived in historical accounts of the Western empire, though, in contrast, Islam is spared in accounts of the Muslim empires.

The Enlightenment spawned a cultural attitude that left little room for large-size religion; that should encourage us to free ourselves sufficiently of the movement's excesses to come to grips with the return of religion worldwide. Patterns on the ground, for example, often show salvation arriving without sanitation or education, which represents a major break with the prerequisite of social progress.

There are signs of such patterns having breached the barriers of Christian Hellenization. New converts have turned with confidence to a naturalized preindustrial Jesus of Palestine rather than to the urbane, cosmopolitan Christ of Greek philosophy and church teaching. For the elites, the human qualities and sufferings of Jesus occupied a very minor place in their thinking because Greek learning saw them as an embarrassment and a stumbling block. Not so for the masses caught up in post-Western Christian resurgence. The Jewish Jesus and his mother, Mary, throb with heartfelt humanity in the new resurgence; encountered in space and time, Jesus and his mother are an assurance of God's solicitude in the face of flesh-and-blood choices and challenges, creating the rationale of divine kinship with the besieged human family.[83] In the process of showing the cross-cultural limits of a Hellenic universal Christ, Keshub Chunder Sen (1838–84), for example, makes the point well enough in a published public lecture, *India asks—who is Christ?* (1879).

New Vision: Global Expansion and the Limits of Cultural Exchange

By the mid fifteenth century, Latin Christendom had lost its cohesion at a time when Ottoman power was on the rise. The Feast of the Pheasant held at Lille in 1454 served as an official statement of Europe's exhausted cultural impulse. The Knights of the Golden Fleece attended a tournament in which a spectacle was enacted to show the plight of Christian Europe before rising Islam. A huge man dressed as a Saracen of Granada led an elephant on whose back was installed a lady in a little, castellated palanquin. The lady represented the church in captivity to the Muslims. She addressed the noble and gallant company, declaiming in verse the plight of the church since the fall of Constantinople, and appealing to knightly honor to defend the faith. After an interval of more elaborate rituals followed by hearty applause, the knights took an oath to undertake a crusade once more against Islam.

The oath was only for theatrical effect, however, and nothing came of it. At the time England was worn down by the Wars of the Roses; Frederick III's grip on the Roman Empire was precarious at best; under Louis XI France was still recovering from its long struggle with England; the kingdoms of the Iberian peninsula had unfinished business to attend to in North Africa; while the Italian powers were preoccupied with the struggle between Venice and Milan. Repeated papal attempts to unite and galvanize Europe in the circumstances failed. The Venetians broke ranks with the Christian West to broker in 1464 an alliance with the Ottoman Empire to preserve their interests as a Levantine power. At the threat of French invasion in 1494, Alexander VI corresponded with Bayazid II (r. 1481–1512) to seek a pact that would protect Naples and, ultimately, Turkey. At various times Hungary, France, Genoa, Naples, and the Roman Empire had negotiated or concluded treaties with the Ottomans. It led Charles VIII to distrust his fellow European leaders and to open direct negotiations with Bayazid II.[84]

A study concluded that in spite numerous discussions, with the papacy keeping before European governments the need for a crusade, the project of a common European stand against the Turks was never a credible option. The powers of Christendom were too rent by conflicting views and interests to agree on a concerted policy toward the Muslim world. Consequently, fear of an alien religion and an alien culture sat awkwardly with "a policy of accommodation and appeasement, which had, ultimately, the effect of admitting the Turkish Empire as one of the components of the European state system."[85]

Few contemporary European leaders understood more deeply and expressed more eloquently the sense of frustration brought about by Islam's suffocating grip on the world's economic lifeline than Portugal's Prince Henry (1394–1460), a younger son of King John, and called "the Navigator" because of his role as the principal architect of early modern maritime expansion. Henry was determined to break the Islamic blockade of Africa, and decided that maritime exploration offered a viable alternative to the seemingly impregnable Muslim land routes. Europe's power and its faith, he felt, were at stake in such a project.

No other contemporary leader had offered such a strategic vision to lead Christian Europe forward into the future, though no one, least of all Henry, could have foreseen the consequences for the peoples and societies of the southern hemisphere of the low-intensity contest with Islam he initiated from Portugal as a crusader state. Europe unbound would be Europe free to tuck Christianity into its expanding material self-interest and into its appetite for national glory. "Europeandom" and "Christendom" were interchangeable and commensurate. As a consequence, with a few exceptions, the participation of the Third World in the Christian movement eventually would yield to the mandate of dividing the world into European spheres of interest and colonies. Fueled by the forces of the Reformation, the rise of new national communities in Europe essentially began the process of the demise and privatization of Christianity as a force in world affairs precisely at the point where Islam in the Ottoman Empire had commenced its vigorous, if also temporary, forward global thrust. The Turks effaced themselves in Islam to confront a rising Europe freeing itself from religion.

The challenge of Islam shows how perspicacious were the views of Prince Henry. His assumptions about the Near East, Egypt, and North Africa as impregnable Muslim lands lying directly in the path of Europe's southward and eastward expansion were proved right. Islam would not suffer any major territorial recession that would cause it to retreat from its central geopolitical position the way Christianity had, and it was sensible, therefore, to concede that world to Islam and to shift to another theater of operation. That was Henry's insight, understandable in light of nascent Ottoman power, but remarkable for its confident, cogent clarity against what R. W. Southern has described as the loosening of the intellectual cohesion of the Western world. Frederick II's cultural ambivalence two centuries earlier—raising a crusader army that included Muslim conscripts, and cultivating relations with Sultan al-

Kamil of Jerusalem while turning his forces against the pope—demonstrated not just an eclectic reputation that was surprisingly free of the stigma of inter-faith bigotry, but a good sense of where the wind was blowing: the West stood little chance against Islamic power. Filling that breach, Henry's rallying vision helped inspire a distracted world.

Henry addressed the fallout of the widespread intellectual loss of morale and deep social anomie by challenging his generation to move forward and beyond the immovable spiritual barrier of Islam's unquenchable defiance, and specifically Islam's unwavering repudiation of the gospel. In his search for a solution, Henry gave the problem a practical orientation. He took the idea of the Crusades in a totally new colonial direction.

Not untouched by the legacy of Europe's frustration with Islam, Gibbon, for his part, indulged the highly speculative thought that had the Christian Ethiopians been successful in maintaining their power in Arabia before the Persians toppled them, they would have been able to crush Islam in its cradle, and thus prevent a religious revolution that changed the world.[86] It is an admission that nothing of the intellectual confidence of Europe in its Christian heritage seemed to make an iota of difference to the Islamic world's discon-certing resistance to the church, and, as we shall see, even Spain's vast empire in the New World was not enough to make people forget the unyielding Moors and Turks. After all, fear of Islam was a major motivation in New World exploration. On his voyage to the New World in 1492, Columbus remembered that his assignment was to keep alive the spirit of the Crusades. He recalled how earlier in that year the Spanish monarchs had achieved the surrender of the Almoravids in Granada, and the triumph of hoisting the royal banners over the towers of the Alhambra palace. He recalled witnessing the subdued sultan come out of his gates and kiss the hands of the king and queen. He continued: "Your Highnesses, as good Christian and Catholic princes, devout and prop-agators of the Christian faith, as well as enemies of the sect of Mahomet . . . conceived the plan of sending me, Christopher Columbus, to this country of the Indies, there to see the princes, the peoples, the territory, their disposition and all things else, and the way in which one might proceed to convert these regions to our holy faith."[87]

According to Bahá al-Dín ibn Shaddád (d. 1234), his able biographer, Saladin in his time had a related maritime ambition, drawing up a will and saying after he finished off the Christian Crusaders in Palestine, he would "set sail on this sea for their far off lands and pursue the Franks there, so as to free the earth of anyone who does not believe in God, or die in the attempt."[88] It strained the credulity of his biographer that Saladin's sincere love of religion, and deep antipathy to the Christians, should be strong enough to overcome the prevailing phobia of the sea among Muslims. As it happened, it was on the sea that Muslims forfeited their power to the Europeans. A casual conversation over coffee in Muscat revealed to Vasco da Gama the idea of sailing to the Indies to share in the lucrative spice trade. It was the Ottomans, not the Crusaders, who introduced coffee to Europe a century or so after it arrived in the empire via Yemen from Ethiopia, where it originated. Even then coffee still had traces enough of its original Sufi religious reputation of spiritual transformation to inspire the setting up in Europe of symbol-crested coffee houses as fraternal inns.

Cultural exchange left Muslims with the upsetting realization that Christian Europe was one civilization they had encountered but had not conquered, and would be forced to acknowledge as their superior. Divesting itself of the debilitating distractions of Christendom in its pursuit of the Crusades, Europe expanded abroad to amass wealth and acquire territory. The contest with Islam took a different turn, and it altered permanently the strategic balance of power with the Ottomans. An astute Ottoman witness in 1625 tried to rally the Muslim world, saying it was still possible to pursue an economically successful but overextended Europe to its commercial strongholds in the east by first regaining control of the Suez and the coasts of Yemen, Europe's economic lifeline. In the era before the rounding of the Cape of Good Hope, "the goods of India, Sind, and China used to come to Suez, and were distributed by Muslims to all the world. But now these goods are carried on Portuguese, Dutch, and English ships to Frangistan, and are spread all over the world from there. What they do not need themselves they bring to Istanbul and [to] other Islamic lands, and sell it for five times the price, thus earning much money."[89]

The lingering nostalgia over a once flourishing Muslim Spain deepened the disappointment. Cultural exchange seemed like cultural betrayal. Ottoman subjection of Europe might be the remedy, and thus the answer to prayer. The Ottoman Empire, however, fell in the attempt.[90] The prospects of intellectual encounter were thereby diminished as the 'ulamá resorted to modes of orthodox defiance, making religious polarization a legacy of intercultural relations. For example, in a future secular Turkey, mosque and parliament would cater to competing assemblies, one under the mantle of clerics and the other under the remit of political representatives. It made little difference to Europe's age-long resistance to Islam.

3

Old World Precedents and New World Directions

Trans-Atlantic Pillar

Old Ferment in the New Christendom

The stalemate with Islam ensconced in its redoubtable Mediterranean strongholds induced Europe to turn its attention from land routes to the sea-lanes that would henceforth bear much of the world's trade. Europe would thus overtake the Muslim world by colonizing distant societies in pursuit of global economic supremacy, and in that pursuit missions would not be allowed to stand in the way. Accordingly, an ebullient Europe declined the opportunity of open cultural exchange and reciprocal relationship. Instead, officials sent down Olympian orders requiring the compliance of subjects and subordinates without regard for local interests, and without the papacy to create moral obstacles.

Accordingly, in a letter to his viceroy in New Spain, Philip II, whose reign from 1556 to 1592 coincided with the era of Spain's greatest power and influence, recalled that by virtue of papal bulls granted to him and to the Catholic sovereigns who were his ancestors, the right of establishing and directing Christianity in the New World belonged to him. He declared:

> We desire and order that no cathedral church, parish church, monastery, hospital, votive church, or any other pious or religious establishment be erected, founded, or constructed, without our express consent for it, or that of the person who

shall exercise our authority; and further, that no archbishopric, dig-
nidad, canonry, racion, media-racion, rectorial or simple benefice, or
any other ecclesiastical or religious benefice or office, be instituted,
or appointment to it be made, without our consent or presentation, or
that of the person who shall exercise our authority, and such presentation or consent shall be in writing, in the ordinary manner

Philip II's interpretation of the papal bulls had the popes implausibly abdi-
cating to him in ecclesiastical affairs, and so he buttressed the power of the
crown over the church with administrative sanctions to secure Christendom
abroad. Yet even so, was Christendom abroad viable or defensible?

It did not take long for cracks to appear in the contrived structure presented as Christendom. In Brazil a system of economic exploitation was created in the form of plantations, called *fazendas*, on which lived some 90 percent of the colonists. The owners of these plantations possessed far more
power and authority than the bishops, a situation rather inauspicious for the
church, not to mention for the Indian laborers. Accordingly, missionary morale took a toll, prompting the archbishop of Mexico to write to Seville in 1556
bemoaning the state of the church. "There is great rivalry among the Orders,"
he noted.

Each defends its territory as if the villages were its own property. There
has been and is great feeling between the Orders, not about which
can best care for the flock, but which can have the greatest number of
places and provinces in its hands; and so they go, occupying the best
centers, building monasteries close together ... not wishing to live
in the difficult and needy places. ... So great is the fear which the Indians have of the friars because of the severe punishment they practice
upon them that they do not dare to complain. And if this is true of
the province of Mexico, what of the mountains? [On account of
this,] very little fruit, it may be suspected, has come of the gospel
among the people. [1]

Gerónimo de Mendieta, a Franciscan missionary living in Mexico, cor-
roborated the archbishop's gloomy view when he wrote in 1562 lamenting
what was happening under Spanish occupation, and describing the situation
as desperate and deplorable. "From what we see and hear in our congregations,
everywhere the superiors are resigning. In visiting the convents one hardly
finds a single monk who is content and happy. Discontent is manifest everywhere; many are seeking leave to return to Spain. It is a miracle to find a friar
who is seriously trying to learn the language, for those who know it use it with

so little satisfaction and profit.... The old fervor and enthusiasm for the salvation of souls seems to have disappeared. The primitive spirit is dead."[2]

With abuse on such a wide scale, it was only a matter of time before local
reaction set in. One reaction took the form of a remarkable eyewitness account
by a leading Indian convert, an account in which he gave a rare, intimate, and
detailed record of the abuses, but also in this case details of Peruvian society
and Spanish colonial life. The writer was Felipe Huamán Poma de Ayala (1532–
1615), a descendant of an Inca chief. His matter-of-fact style takes away nothing
from the scandals he witnessed.

> "The priesthood," he noted caustically, "began with Jesus Christ and
> his Apostles, but their successors in the various religious orders es-
> tablished in Peru do not follow this holy example. On the contrary,
> they show an unholy greed for worldly wealth and the sins of the
> flesh and a good example would be set to everyone if they were pun-
> ished by the Holy Inquisition.
>
> "These priests are irascible and arrogant. They wield considerable
> power and usually act with great severity towards their parishion-
> ers, as if they had forgotten that Our Lord was poor and humble and
> the friend of sinners. Their own intimate circle is restricted to their
> relations and dependants, who are either Spanish or half-caste.
>
> "A favorite source of income for the priesthood consists in orga-
> nizing the porterage of wine, chillies, coca and maize. These wares
> are carried on the backs of Indians and llamas and in some cases
> need to be brought down from high altitudes. The descent often re-
> sults in death for the Indians, who catch a fever when they arrive in a
> warm climate. Any damage to their loads during the journey has to
> be made good at their own expense. The priests make a practice
> of confiscating property which really belongs to a church, a society or a
> hospital and putting it to their own uses. In the same way they
> often overcharge for Masses for the dead.
>
> "When these holy fathers are living as husband and wife with
> Indian girls and begetting children, they always refer to the half-castes
> as their nephews. With the aid of a little hypocrisy they make sin seem
> more attractive, so that it spreads and corrupts one girl after another."

To show that he was even-handed, Poma included in his account
reference by name to some good priests he knew, ones "who treated
people of all sorts with respect."[3]

Described by Eric Williams as "among the greatest gifts of Spanish civilization to the Caribbean and the world,"[4] Bartolomé de las Casas (1474–1566)

took up the cause and mounted a campaign to save the Indians from their colonial tormentors. Arriving first in Hispaniola in 1502, Las Casas served in many parts of the Caribbean. He offered firsthand account of the treatment of Indians, saying, with regard to Spanish atrocities, that he had seen with his own eyes "cruelties more atrocious and unnatural than any recorded of un-tutored and savage barbarians."[5] He reproduced a sermon preached by a Do-minican friar, Montesinos, who denounced the Spaniards for their conduct toward the Indians, determined, as the poet put it, "to frighten into hooded shame a money-mong'ring, pitiable brood." Montesinos further demanded:

> Tell me by what right or justice do you hold these Indians in such cruel and horrible slavery? By what right do you wage such detestable wars on these people who lived mildly and peacefully in their own lands, where you have consumed infinite numbers of them with un-heard of murders and desolations? Why do you so greatly oppress and fatigue them, not giving them enough to eat or caring for them when they fall ill from excessive labors, so that they die or rather are slain by you, so that you may extract and acquire gold every day? And what care do you take that they receive religious instruction and come to know their God and creator, or that they be baptized, hear mass, or observe holidays and Sundays?
>
>   Are they not men? Do they not have rational souls? Are you not bound to love them as you love yourselves? How can you lie in such profound and lethargic slumber? Be sure that in your present state you can no more be saved than the Moors or Turks who do not have and do not want the faith of Jesus Christ.[6]

The reference to Moors and Turks shows that fear of Islam survived the jour-ney to the New World, as we saw also with Columbus.

Indigenous reaction to the bruising encounter with Spanish colonization took many forms. One form we just saw with the caustic observations of Felipe Huamán Poma de Ayala. Another was resistance at any price. The context here was the catastrophic decimation of the population of Hispaniola. When Co-lumbus first set foot on the island in 1492, it had a population estimated at some three hundred thousand. By 1508 it had fallen by tragic proportions to 60,000; in 1510 the figure was 46,000; in 1512 it was 20,000; and in 1514, 14,000.[7] When the Indian chief of Hispaniola, Hatuey, was captured in Cuba—where he fled before the invaders—and compelled to embrace Chris-tianity or else be burned alive at the stake, he asked the Franciscan friar in attendance, who urged him to relent and save his soul from eternal damna-tion, whether any Spaniards were in paradise. When told that only the good

Spaniards were, Hatuey is reported to have replied: "The best are good for nothing, and I will not go where there is a chance of meeting one of them."[8] He went down in flames, his defiant words a stinging indictment of his Christian tormentors. As Adam Smith noted, "The pious purpose of converting [the Indians] to Christianity sanctified the injustice of the project."[9]

Local reaction took a different and surprising form in the guise of a poor Mexican Indian peasant, Juan Diego, who testified in 1531 to seeing an apparition of the Blessed Virgin, Our Lady of Guadalupe. Yet this vision, while in conformity with the common experience of Christians elsewhere, was striking in its identification of the Virgin as an Indian peasant woman whose "beautiful countenance is grave and noble, and rather dark." It was a momentous claim that changed (and charged) the face of Mexican religious and national life, and altered for good Mexico's place in the Catholic world. Given the experience of a suffering people and their systematic alienation from their land, the vision was proof of a special protection for native populations. The shrine of Our Lady of Guadalupe became a national symbol, Mexico's Runnymede, where the magna carta of its spiritual freedom was proclaimed. As a result, the merchants of misery and the agents of absolute power, together with the defenders of the religious status quo, were understandably wary.

Luis Lasso de la Vega, who first published the story in 1649, reported the words addressed to Juan Diego that became the charter of Our Lady of Guadalupe: "Know the Mother of the True God in whom we live. . . . I greatly desire that a temple be built me here, that in it I may manifest and give to all my love, pity, help, and defense, for I am your mother, yours and all the dwellers in this land and the others who love me and call upon me and trust in me. . . . Go to the palace of the bishop of Mexico and tell him that I have sent you."[10] Incredulous at the report, the bishop, reputedly Fray Juan de Zumárraga (d. 1548), demanded a sign to prove the veracity of this vision. He duly received this sign in the form of Castilian roses that the Blessed Virgin sent Juan Diego to gather from a hillside in the freezing December weather, though the bishop might have saved himself the trouble and applied, just as plausibly and decisively, Antony's test of joy as final proof that it was the true God who inspired the vision rather than the devil. When Juan Diego brought the bishop the roses wrapped in his blanket, the image of the Blessed Virgin appeared on the blanket, to the consternation of bishop and audience alike, because on the threadbare blanket of a poor, country peasant was etched a particularly poignant vindication of native populations against their new overlords. A shrine to the Blessed Virgin built at Tepeyac has existed from as early as 1555.

Juan Diego's vision showed how a tribesman, or, as described himself, "one of those campesinos, a piece of rope . . . a leaf [blown around at the whim of others],"[11] with little cosmopolitan advantage, could be a persuasive symbol of the faith to the honor of church and nation. Whatever the critical verdict on its historical veracity,[12] Juan Diego's reported experience wrests Christianity from its metropolitan frame of the bishop's palace and puts it firmly in the hands and hearts of the people. In the final analysis, the people's faith breached official Christianity's walls of authorized access to fix the religion in the soul of a nation. It may explain the vibrant resilience of popular Catholicism in Mexico in spite of anticlerical measures later adopted by the state.[13]

That civil pattern of New World religious naturalization was repeated in many places across the world, and its cumulative effect drew Europe out of its intellectual isolation. When it succeeded in breaking free of crown control, the Western missionary movement in both its Catholic and Protestant forms carried the intellectual seeds that transformed Christianity into a world religion, though the mental habits of Christianity as Christendom, of Christianity as political kingdom or as cultural domain, concealed from people the force of that fact. The changes following Columbus's New World explorations were soon reflected in new geographical maps of the world, but the mental maps remained unaltered for many centuries afterward. Globalization meant then, as it has tended to mean now, the corralling of the world's resources by dominant powers, and traversing the globe for that purpose. Intercultural dialogue was out of the question.

Colonial Ascendancy and Missionary Engagement

The rise in modern Europe of missionary associations represented a significant turning point, for Christianity entered its epochal crossover into non-Western cultures. The missionary associations developed the principle of free association outside state sponsorship to carry Christianity abroad into the non-Western world, though this principle was at odds with the calculated strategy of colonial hegemony, and, at first, missions worked within the framework allowed them by colonial governments. It proved an irksome arrangement, however, and as a result Roman Catholic missions slipped from under the terms of the 1514 Padroado dispensation in which Pope Leo X granted the Portuguese crown control of its "conquests" in Africa, Asia, and Brazil.

It was that colonial impediment that drove St. Francis Xavier (1506–52) to cut his ties with Portuguese-controlled Goa—and eventually contributed to the papcy itself denouncing outright the Padroado.[14] Goa was a neglected island within the domains of the Mogul Muslim Empire. Its Hindu inhabitants were smarting from the exactions of the Bijapurese Muslim overlords, eager just as soon to cast off the Muslim yoke. It placed Goa's ultimate loyalty in serious doubt. That gave Afonso de Albuquerque, the Portuguese agent, the pretext he needed to launch an attack in 1510, and after initial serious setbacks from stiff resistance mounted by combined local Muslim and Turkish forces, Albuquerque withdrew, only to return unexpectedly with heavy reinforcements. Goa was taken triumphantly on St. Catherine's Day, November 25, 1510. Positioned midway up the Indian peninsula, with its strategic deepwater harbor safely insulated at the confluence of the Mandovi and Rachol rivers, and boasting a flourishing international trade, the capture of Goa transformed Portugal into a commanding Asian imperial power. As Albuquerque crowed to Portugal's King Manuel, "The capture of Goa alone worked more to the credit of your Majesty than fifteen years worth of armadas that were sent out to India."[15]

Goa gave Portugal overseas a blanket political and moral immunity to colonize in Asia without being accountable to anyone in the field. Culturally cut off from the Indian mainland, with scarce any need to acknowledge or defer to local needs and rights, Goa saw itself tied directly to the court in Lisbon. Missionaries and their converts were accordingly conceived as clients of Portuguese power. Xavier found that colonial environment intolerable, saying he would "flee" to Japan because he could not stand the corruption of the Portuguese officials. He said he felt distressed beyond endurance that it was for him like personal "martyrdom" to see the good work of missionaries being destroyed by official greed and immorality. "Everywhere and at all times," he lamented, "it is rapine, hoarding and robbery. . . . I never cease wondering at the number of new inflections which, in addition to all the usual forms, have been added in this language to the avarice of conjugation of that ill-omened verb 'to rob'."[16] More than a century later, the situation in Goa had not much improved, for we find the Jesuit chronicler, Padre Francisco de Sousa, reporting in 1698 that the Portuguese were at serious risk of losing the respect of the people on account of their failure to administer justice properly. "The Portuguese may well despair of securing the favourable opinion of Oriental natives, in so far as our administration of justice is concerned, until we decide cases in the law-courts with greater brevity and dispatch, like the nations of the North do, who accordingly get on much better with the rural folk."[17] Portuguese power would remain insecure without justice, de Sousa warned, while, as Xavier had contended, mercantile greed made justice all but an unknown commodity.

Prodded by appeals from the field, including the Kongo, the papacy in the 1620s broke with the tradition of imperial sponsorship and created the Propaganda Fide to assume responsibility for missions, though as late as the 1680s Portugal was still resisting any papal interference in its overseas empire. It did not help that the papacy did not recognize the Portuguese Crown, after its separation from Spain, until 1668. Combined with distress calls from the field, such realities disposed the church in mission to commit to shedding its imperial baggage. Eventually, field experience of both local rulers and serving missionaries in South America, Asia, and Africa vindicated the papacy's decision to cut ties with sponsoring maritime European powers, as illustrated by the protests and decisions of figures like Las Casas, appointed "Protector of the Indians"; Xavier, known as the "Apostle of the Indies and of Japan"; and, later, Cardinal Charles Lavigerie (1825–92) of Algeria. Historians, however, refused to bury the hatchet.

Righteous Indignation and the Anachronism of Christendom

The Christian message sowed seeds of critical social consciousness in the minds of new converts and missionaries alike, enough to challenge the idea of uncontested foreign imperialism. The thought is warranted in the light of South America's complex history, and justifies examining whether the claim of total and comprehensive victimization of native populations can be upheld, and whether there were exceptions with examples of resistance and renewal.[18] Such examples might indicate the limits non-Western cultures set for the cosmopolitan assumptions of Western Christendom.

The case today for an alteration in our mental maps, and in our corresponding cultural sensibilities, has never been more urgent and necessary. The Willkien one-world implications of New World colonization required an all-embracing global moral language that Las Casas, for example, attempted valiantly to put in place. "No nation exists today," Las Casas affirmed, "nor could exist, no matter how barbarous, fierce, or depraved its customs may be, which may not be attracted and converted to all political virtues and to all the humanity of domestic, political, and rational men."[19] Las Casas returned to the subject on another occasion when he observed that the Christian religion is destined for all the nations of the world, being open as it is to all in the same fashion. Christianity, he declared, took from none its freedom nor does its truth depend on its promoting a specious distinction between the free and servile status. The entire world, and not just Europe, should, therefore, have a share in adjudicating the religion's standing.[20]

Jesuit chronicler Francisco de Sousa's remarks about the imperative of the common people's right to justice appealed to the same issue of cultural sensibility. A geographically united world should oblige people to accept the solidarity of a common human inheritance, and the mutual ethical responsibility that went with it.[21]

As was clear in the mercantile system, economic processes can repress talent and freedom.[22] It led Adam Smith to propound his famous thesis of the "invisible hand" as a thoroughly domesticated mechanism rather than as one of deliberate global design. He argued that persons acting in a free economic system generally intend neither to promote the public interest, nor know how much they are promoting it. In fact, such persons prefer the support of domestic industry to that of foreign industry; they intend only their own security and their own gain by directing that industry in such a manner as its produce may be of the greatest value. Smith concludes that people as such are led by an invisible hand to promote an end that was no part of their intention. Nor is it always the worse for the society that the end was no part of their intention. By pursuing their own interest, people frequently promote the interest of the society more effectively than when they really *intend* to promote it.[23] The good of the market system lies in its side effects.

The question, as I misleadingly put it earlier, is not whether Christendom was viable or defensible, but that given the fact of global awakening and increased intercultural contact, how soon Christendom's civilizational mandate should be abandoned as outdated. In spite of Columbus, the failure to shift Eurocentric perspectives continued to wreak havoc on non-Western cultures and societies. Globalization was about competitive advantage; the weak, the nonwhite, and the poor became fair game. Theophilus Conneau, a New England slave trader, noted that the cause and course of the slave trade were many and various, but that none was more complicit than the avarice of civilized nations whose commodities caused the wars and injustices that fed the slave trade. The world was no less effectively globalized for paying scant attention to moral or human values. As a driving force, competitive advantage was need blind and culture proof. Apart from speed and spread, it is hard to know what makes it different now. It brings to mind the words of John Maynard Keynes (d. 1946). "The modern capitalist," he wrote, "is a fair-weather sailor. As soon as a storm rises, he abandons the duties of navigation and even sinks the boats which might carry him to safety by his haste to push his neighbor off and himself in."[24]

Catholic Potential in Premodern Africa

Aware of the impetus Iberian maritime explorations had given to the expanding frontiers of Christianity beyond Europe, the papacy became active in pursuing the missionary path in Africa. Yet there would be obstacles to overcome, chiefly the reality of the rising mercantile power of Portugal. In earlier eras Ethiopia sent embassies to Rome to appeal for contact with the Holy See, but these embassies returned empty-handed. Even the offer of expensive and rare gifts failed to move the papacy to establish contact with Ethiopia. One such embassy to the Holy See in 1402 brought four leopards for effect. The Ethiopians persisted with their appeals, and attended the Council of Constance, which recognized Martin V. Still, Ethiopian representatives carried their appeal to the Council of Florence in 1443, a significant event that led to the Portuguese interest in Africa. Finally relenting, Pope Nicholas V in 1451 authorized sending a representative to Ethiopia.

From those early contacts developed real historical knowledge about Ethiopia, knowledge that replaced earlier fanciful concoctions about distant and exotic cultures. Ethiopia attracted the personal interest of Ignatius Loyola himself, who asked to be sent there. The ensuing short-lived Jesuit embassy to Ethiopia in 1554 contained the largest group of Jesuits until then to sail for the mission field anywhere. The popes responded to Ethiopia's entreaties by establishing a hospice for Ethiopian visitors to Rome, which was attached to the church of S. Stefano Maggiore, close to St. Peter's. "By seizing on the imagination of papal strategists, Ethiopia was the first African kingdom to summon Christian Europe to a joint endeavour."[25]

The situation changed with the establishment of Portugal's overseas trading factories. Portugal became the first European sea-based power to colonize extensively in Africa. Portugal was a small monarchy that had arisen during the twelfth-century Christian crusade against the Moors in the Iberian Peninsula. Fortified by Crusader indulgences granted by the pope, and seeking gold and slaves—and perhaps the fabled Christian kingdom of Prester John—fifteenth-century Portuguese kings sent many expeditions to sail ever farther southward along the western African coast and beyond. Although mercantile interests eventually swamped the stirrings of missionary awakening, the Portuguese maritime expeditions brought with them priests, many of whom viewed the explorations as a continuation of the Christian Crusades.

In the early fifteenth century, Portuguese expeditions reached the Canary Islands, which were placed under Spanish jurisdiction; Madeira and the Azores; and, in 1460, the Cape Verde Islands, where a bishop was based from 1532. These islands provided a beachhead for Portuguese expansion into the African mainland, the real focus of commercial interest. In 1482 Ghana was explored by a party landing at Elmina, a promising outpost of the gold trail, which was given the name of São Jorge da Mina. However, it was only in 1572 that four Augustinian priests arrived in Elmina to cultivate a "fortress Christianity" that, in being restricted to castle life, was a stony meadow for missionary prospects. Thus the trading castles provided missionary range, but they also made it possible to afford putting off evangelizing local populations. It is a recurrent theme in the history of the missionary movement that facility of travel brought with it accessibility but also the ability to choose when, where, and how to go. Cultural curiosity ceased to be a motivation, and unfamiliarity a deterrent.

In the scheme of colonial strategizing, with the discovery of São Tomé in 1470, which became an important base of the trans-Atlantic slave trade, the Portuguese secured a platform for penetrating the African mainland. São Tomé was the missionary base for the whole of the Guinea coastline along which the Portuguese were active. It was from São Tomé that Portuguese reached the kingdom of the Kongo, a sophisticated African state along the river Zaire, roughly in the area of present-day Angola. Missionaries arrived there in 1491, and received a warm welcome that culminated with the baptism of Afonso, a powerful leader of the Kongo; the ruler of the nearby Soyo kingdom; and hundreds of their subjects. Called the "apostle of the Kongo" and a "new Constantine," Afonso gained the Kongolese throne as a Christian convert in 1506, and reigned until 1543, one of the longest reigns in the continent's recorded history.

By establishing a Christian monarchy, creating a new Christian capital— called São Salvador—learning Portuguese, building churches, promoting missions, and indeed sending his son, Henry, to Portugal to be educated and commissioned for missionary service in the Kongo, the indomitable King Afonso inaugurated a particularly brilliant epoch of Christianity in Africa. His interest in the religion appeared deep and sincere, as he states in his letters. He did battle with the old pre-Christian cults, and, in an ironic twist, with the corrupt emissaries of Christianity; he accepted the conversion of an old enemy who led an army against him rather than executing him, and, as Dom Pedro, appointed the man guardian of the baptismal waters in the church; and three times he sent the man as ambassador to Lisbon. In a symbolic move, he built a church dedicated to "Our Savior" on the site of the old shrines, and preached after mass. He was tireless in calling for priests to come and serve his people. These priests became the fabled King Stork that Afonso conjured up.

When they arrived, the priests led anything but exemplary lives. Abandoning their vows, they broke away from their religious communities and lived in separate houses that they filled with slave girls as pleasure objects, to the scandal of new believers and to the disdain of local skeptics. The people mocked the king, saying the priests showed Christianity to be a lie. Stung by the remarks, the king pleaded with Portugal: "In this kingdom the faith is still as fragile as glass on account of the bad examples of those who came to teach it. Today our Lord is crucified anew by the very ministers of his body and blood.

We would have preferred not to be born than to see how our innocent children run into perdition on account of these bad examples."[26]

Some semblance of order was restored in later centuries. The Jesuits arrived in the mid sixteenth century and formed Christian villages. In 1596, the Papacy established the diocese of São Salvador for the Kongolese kingdom and for the neighboring territory of Angola. The Jesuits established a college at São Salvador in 1624; the first rector, Fr Cardosa, translated the standard Portuguese catechism into the kiKongo language, and distributed hundreds of copies. These kiKongo catechisms were used by lay catechists, the *maestri*, who, across the generations, handed on the teachings in the villages, much of the time without any clerical presence.

In 1645 the Capuchins, including Italian and Spanish friars, began a mission in the Kongolese kingdom as part of a larger initiative of Propaganda Fide to promote mission activity in West Africa directed from Rome. In what marked the beginning of nearly two centuries of Capuchin involvement in the Kongo, the Capuchins established schools in São Salvador and Soyo, learned kiKongo, and began systematic evangelization in the rural districts. They established confraternities among the Africans, among them the Confraternity of Our Lady of the Rosary, which was formed in Luanda in 1658 and which became a forum for promoting African rights. Between 1672 and 1700, thirty-seven Capuchin fathers recorded a total of 341,000 baptisms. Other Capuchin missions were established on the Guinea Coast and in Sierra Leone in 1644, in Benin in 1647, and in the small state of Warri in the 1650s. Queen Nzinga of Matamba, in eastern Angola, embraced Christianity through the influence of a captured Capuchin priest. She had received baptism in 1622, and then succeeded her brother as ruler in 1627. Thereafter, she promptly lapsed from the faith.

After years of bruising conflict with the Portuguese, however, Queen Nzinga received a message from an oracle that if she accepted to return to the faith the Portuguese would stop making war with her and peace and prosperity would return to her kingdom. In 1656 she relented and she and a great number of her troops were received into the faith by the aforementioned captured Capuchin priest. She sought to create a Christian state, personally carrying stones for the building of the church of Our Lady of Matamba, which was completed in 1665, the year of her death. She was a distinguished example of women pioneers of Christianity in the ancient church, as the following account of her role makes clear.

> In all public places, over the houses and in every corner the sign of our
> Redemption was erected; it preceded them into battle, every neck

bowed to venerate the cross; every breast protected itself with it in any danger. War prisoners ready to be baptised were freed and enrolled to help in the construction of churches. When a missionary appeared from afar, the people knelt down on the way as they waited for his blessing; they walked miles and miles to have their children baptized. No other pious soul could surpass the Queen. When she had received holy communion she distributed goods lavishly and fed the poor. She saw to it that several times during the day the rosary was said, sermons given and processions held, while in the evenings the spiritual joy burst out in a final display of fireworks, music and songs.[27]

After the Portuguese rounded the Cape, they set up colonies in East Africa, including fortified trading cities along the coast. The island-city of Mozambique became the main administrative center of Portuguese East Africa, and the city had an estimated 2,000 Christians by 1586. The Mutapa Empire in Zimbabwe came under Dominican influence in the seventeenth century, and its kings accepted baptism. In the Zambezi Valley, the Portuguese crown made large grants of land (*prazos*) to settlers. Jesuits and Dominicans from Portugal accompanied the colonists, and in some cases the fathers owned *prazos*. According to a Portuguese Jesuit in 1667, there were sixteen places of worship pursuing missionary work in the lower Zambezi Valley—six conducted by the Jesuits, nine by the Dominicans and one by a secular priest. The Jesuits in 1697 established a college at Sena for the children of both the Portuguese and African elite.

For a time in the early to mid seventeenth century, there was a real prospect of the large-scale spread of the Catholic faith in Africa, maintained by a network of African kings and the other members of the ruling elite, and pushed forward by a number of remarkable priests and friars. Christianity's close ties with Portugal's imperial ambition, however, impeded the mission.[28] Still, while many Africans embraced Christianity to please their Portuguese overlords, many others did so out of genuine faith and commitment.

A graphic example bears this out. In 1631 the city of Mombassa was retaken by the Muslims led by Sultán Yúsúf ibn Hasan. Earlier, Yúsúf ibn Hasan had been adopted by the Portuguese as a protégé after his father was treacherously murdered by a renegade Portuguese captain. He was baptized as Jeronimo Chingulia and educated in Goa where he was made a knight of the Crusader Order of Christ. On his return to Mombasa Yúsúf ibn Hasan suffered ill treatment at the hands of the captain of the fort, and that experience gnawed at his resolve as a convert. In an act of vengeance, Yúsúf ibn Hasan had the captain and his guards murdered, and followed it with a full-scale attack on several Christians, who were offered a choice of accepting Islam or death. That seventy-two African men and women, known as the "Martyrs of Mombassa," should have willingly accepted death along with their fellow Christian Portuguese rather than renounce their faith and embrace Islam testifies to their genuine faith and commitment. Another 400 defiant Africans were taken as slaves to Arabia in exchange for ammunition. Carrying the cross knew few bounds.

By the early eighteenth century, however, the prospects for Christianity in Africa had dimmed markedly. Civil war shattered what was once the distinguished Christian Kongolese kingdom, and the power and authority of the king were irreparably damaged. The capital of São Salvador was sacked by a warring faction in 1678 and then was deserted for a quarter century. Reoccupied in the early eighteenth century, its twelve churches were in ruins, and only a single priest, Estavo Botelho, remained in the capital, by which time he had become a slave trader who lived openly with concubines. Of the several provinces of the kingdom, only the coastal province of Soyo retained a significant Christian population. The forlorn Capuchin mission in the Kongo survived with only two or three friars.

By 1750, the continued survival fell to one Capuchin missionary, the remarkable Fr Cherubina da Savona, who bravely carried on traversing the country from 1758 to 1774, baptizing some 700,000 during his lonely mission of twenty-seven years. Although later Capuchins attempted to carry on the mission, the last regular Capuchin priest withdrew in 1795. In some rural villages, the *maestri* continued to convey Christian teachings, and the people observed Christian rituals and chanted canticles. French missionaries discovered one such village north of the river Zaire in 1773, its identity proclaimed by a great cross. Without a regular priesthood empowered to baptize, however, such communities in time lapsed from their Christian faith. Despite periodic but short-lived bursts of mission in Warri and other kingdoms in West Africa, Christianity struggled under severe strains. In East Africa, the religious orders and secular priests increasingly restricted their ministry to the Portuguese ruling class, and by 1712, missions to Africans continued only in Zambesia. Soon these also died out. In subsequent eras, with the onset of colonial suzerainty, Christianity became a mere appendage of the imperial system, and the clergy chaplains to the colonizers and to their apprentices.

Setback

There were a number of reasons for this decline of the Catholic missions. After his conversion to Christianity in 1506, Nzinga Mbemba, who came to be known as King Afonso I, gradually but inescapably came to the realization that while the slave trade enabled him to hold power and to enlarge and strengthen his kingdom, it also made him dependent on the Portuguese slave traders for arms, supplies, and diplomatic recognition that he needed to avert enslavement, in turn, for his subjects—such being the cruel logic of the slave trade and of dynastic survival. Afonso I called on the help of Portugal and Rome to save his people and his kingdom. He pleaded with the Portuguese Crown, saying so great was the calamity caused by Portuguese trading factors that order was threatened, and with it the cause of the gospel. "And we cannot reckon how great the damage is, since the mentioned merchants are taking every day our natives, sons of the land and the sons of our noblemen and vassals and our relatives . . . so great is the corruption and licentiousness that our country is being completely depopulated."[29]

The tripartite alliance of commerce, civilization, and Christianity in premodern Africa was turning out to be a deadly combination, as Afonso I was discovering, and the European connection was a mixed blessing at best. Infiltrated by agents from Lisbon, the Kongo kingdom found all alternative channels of contact with Rome virtually blocked or compromised, and so the kingdom languished in a noose of isolation. The interest the kingdom aroused in Rome led to the decision by the papal Curia to shift control of Catholic missions from Portugal and to create an indigenous priesthood. The Propaganda Fide was set up in 1622 to return control of missions to the Curia. But it was only under the pontificate of Gregory XVI, who as Cardinal Capellari ran Propaganda Fide, that the papacy succeeded in regaining such control.

The waning power of Portugal undermined its ability to recruit and maintain missionaries, while at the same time increased its suspicion of missionaries of other nationalities. Moreover, Rome experienced a declining interest in world mission during the eighteenth century, and, accordingly, the supply of missionaries gradually fell. There were never enough priests for the African mission field, and while many of the missionary priests were exemplary in their piety and commitment, others were appreciably less so. Often isolated and lacking regular episcopal supervision or encouragement, many grew discouraged, took concubines, or became slavers, bringing scandal and disrepute to their church and to their calling.

Missionaries succumbed to the African climate and fever. Of 438 known Capuchin fathers active in the mission to the Kongo between 1645 and 1835, 229 died after a few years in the mission field—a 52 percent mortality rate—while others hobbled home in poor health. Portugal's decision in 1759 to expel the Jesuits from its colonial territories further reduced the number of missionaries, especially in Zambesia. Efforts to recruit and to educate an African priesthood produced meager results, and with the paucity of African priests went a decline in Catholic faith. To compound the problem, Capuchin priests, moreover, were suspicious of the lay *maestri* and often failed to give them the necessary support. These problems and a failure of vision created a setback for the Christian cause.

In spite of early promise, the Catholic involvement in the Ethiopian church hit a stumbling block. When in 1622 the Jesuit Pedro Paëz succeeded in persuading the emperor Susenyos (1607–32) to join the Roman Catholic Church, everyone concerned believed that a new era had arrived for Abyssinian Christianity. But it was not long before those hopes were dashed by the willful and divisive policies of Paëz's successor, Alphonso Mendez, who arrived in 1626. He moved promptly to pursue the logic of the counterreformation by trying to make Roman Catholicism the national faith of Ethiopia, but the implications of foreign domination in such a move antagonized Abyssinian Christians. Mendez adopted a collision course when he rammed through a thoroughgoing purge of the church by suppressing local customs, rebaptizing believers as if they were pagans, having their priests reordained and their churches reconsecrated, and introducing graven images and the Latin rite and calendar. Deeply rooted Jewish customs like circumcision, Sabbath observance, and lunar rites—long revered marks of identity—were proscribed. Ethiopian Christianity's Jewish roots had no analogues in Western Christianity, which viewed them as an offense.

The reforms, accordingly, met with popular insurrection, and a fierce conflict erupted against the Catholic latinization "jihad" against Abyssinian Christianity. The bitter memories of foreign imposition left a century earlier by the jihad of Ahmad ibn Ibráhím al-Ghází (1506–43), nicknamed Gráñ, "the left-handed," were revived by the antagonism sparked by the Catholic attacks on the Abyssinian church. Many Christian chiefs declared that they would prefer a Muslim ruler rather than submit to Portuguese domination. The Muslim comparison must be appreciated for its rhetorical posture rather than taken literally. It was an attack on the Catholic purge of local customs by way of the Islamic analogy. It is doubtful that Ahmad's jihad, which called on the intervention of Turkey to counterbalance the rising power of Portugal, would in reality have been considered preferable even to a meddlesome Catholicism.[30] In any case, Susenyos had no choice but to back down, and so he issued a proclamation reinstating the old faith. "We restore to you the faith of your forefathers. Let the former clergy return to the churches, let them put in their tabots, let them say their own liturgy; and do you rejoice."[31]

Fasilidas (r. 1632–67), Susenyos's successor, declared that the concessions to make peace with Roman Catholicism were, however, too little too late, "for which reason all further colloquies and disputes will be in vain."[32] The Jesuits were expeled, with Mendez transferring to India after sending a petition to the king of Spain calling for the conversion of Ethiopia and saying the only means for achieving that was military occupation of the country. Such ideas about the forcible conversion of Christian Ethiopia, it turns out, occurred also to Muslims nearer home, and in their case regional jealousies among Christians suggested that Christians, too, had an unsettling premonition of such future Christian defections to Islam. The period of rival regional sovereigns, called the *zamana masáfent*, lasted from 1769 to 1855, and was profoundly shaped by the haunting specter of a surging Islam. One witness expressed in 1840 a sentiment that preserves much older attitudes: a widespread feeling prevailed that the nominally Christian Wallo passed their time in the repetition of prayers, while in the meantime a proverb and general belief circulated among them that their country could never be conquered by those who were not followers of the prophet Muhammad.

It impressed Edward Gibbon that for many centuries Ethiopia was shrouded in a haze of obscurity. Gibbon wrote that having slept for nearly a thousand years, Ethiopia became forgetful of the world by which it was in turn forgotten.[33] Yet under the shroud of mystery and far from the prying eyes of hostile neighbors, Ethiopia created from the second half of the twelfth century enduring monuments to its Christian heritage, such as the thirteen rock-hewn churches at the monastic settlement of Lalibela, set at an altitude of some 2,700 meters. Still a place of pilgrimage, Lalibela's architectural achievement is celebrated in legend as the place that angels built. The deep subterranean trenches, the open quarried caves, and the complex labyrinth of tunnels—narrow passageways with interconnecting grottoes, crypts, and galleries—all shrouded in a soft and solicitous holy silence that is filtered with the faint echoes of monks and priests at prayer, justifies Lalibela's steadfast reputation as a historical wonder.

Catholic missions in other parts of the world confronted similar difficulties, however, without the collapse that they experienced in sub-Saharan Africa. What was distinctive about Africa was the social devastation the slave trade caused. While slavery and the slave trade had coexisted with Christianity in the past, in Africa the sheer scale of the trade was unprecedented. From the mid seventeenth century, tens of thousands of Africans were shipped off each year to plantations in the Americas. Portugal's African empire became, above all, a slave quarry. In order to feed the growing demand for human labor, the slavers began seizing whole villages and devastating and depopulating whole districts, which in turn contributed to civil war and social breakdown. It is estimated that 40 percent of the total number of slaves that crossed the Atlantic came from the Kongo–Angola area, a figure out of all proportion to the population of the region, and one of the main reasons for the disintegration of the Kongolese kingdom.[34]

It is a bitter irony, too, that some of the clergy in Africa owned slaves and engaged in the slave trade. For example, Fr Pedro de S. S. Trinidade, who lived at Zumbo on the Zambezi between 1710 and 1754, owned 1,600 slaves and worked a gold mine. He was a larger-than-life figure, and his memory, appropriately, survived in local folklore as a rainmaking divinity to whom people offered sacrifices in times of drought. Nearly all the clergy benefited financially from the slave trade. Yet, the prevailing climate of opinion notwithstanding, many members of the clergy launched a vigorous attack on slavery and the slave trade. Given its vast scale and momentum, however, the slave trade continued unabated in spite of that, with ruinous consequences for African societies and for missions until well into the early nineteenth century.

When the famed Scottish missionary David Livingstone reached Angola in 1854 on his trek across the continent, the only evidence of Jesuit and Capuchin churches he found was in ruins, and Christianity among the Africans was reduced to a folk memory. In 1750 the Jesuits and the Dominicans had decided to baptize converts no more because, acknowledging defeat, they said that Christianity would only bring the people condemnation, not salvation, on account of the ignorant lifestyle of the people. The last Dominican priest there died in 1837. Mission drowned in the surging mercantile tide, raising a disquietening question about the viability of Christianity as a link with commerce and civilization. The recovery of the Catholic missions would come, but from a different equation.

Civilization and the Imperative of Justice

As it developed, the European impulse of colonization was driven as much by the strategic need to circumvent Islam as it was by economic interests, and any considerations of faithfulness to the church's teachings were secondary to calculations of political advantage and monopoly rights. The explosion of maritime exploration, which Catholic Spain and Portugal led, to be joined later by Protestant England and the Netherlands, created the shift from land-based power to sea-based power. Whereas in 1415, before the era of Vasco da Gama (ca. 1469–1524), the dominant world powers were those that controlled the land routes, from the Tell Atlas on the Atlantic Rim to the silk depots of Samarkand. Now the dominant powers were those with unchallenged suzerainty over the sea-lanes, from Lisbon and Genoa, or Plymouth and Rotterdam, to Benin, Goa, and Shanghai.

The social revolution attendant on such a major shift of power arrange-ments brought into play a new mercantile class whose entrepreneurial spirit sent them looking for wealth and profit in hitherto unknown or unexplored lands. As one such adventurer expressed it, they crossed the seas "to serve God and His majesty, to give light to those who were in darkness," but most em-phatically "to grow rich, as all men desire to do."[35] Or, as Columbus expressed it, "Gold, what an excellent product! It is from gold that riches come. He who has gold can do whatever he pleases in this world. With gold one can even bring souls into Paradise."[36] For these entrepreneurs, mission was not just neces-sary; it was profitable.

It is instructive in that light to reflect on how the later Catholic missionary orders that headed for Africa and beyond conceded the economic argument by scrupulously avoiding having their headquarters in Rome for fear of being obstructed. Even when authorized from Rome, Catholic missionaries still had to report to Lisbon for royal approval and conveyance.

In the meantime, Rome's attention was drawn to another crisis, this one of Christian making. The warning note was sounded as early as 1610 when the American Jesuit, Alonso de Sandoval, attacked the slave trade as being steeped in fraud and injustice, publishing accounts by the slave traders themselves to show how uneasy were their consciences. He persisted, "Among human possessions, none is more valuable and beautiful than liberty. All the gold in the world and all the goods of the earth are not a sufficient price for human liberty. God created man free. Slavery is not only exile, but [is] also subjection, hunger, sorrow, nakedness, insult, prison, perpetual persecution, and, in short, is a Pandora's box of all the evils."[37] It is pertinent to Sandoval's argument that gold was the link in the economic chain that sustained slavery.

Slaves or former slaves would themselves seize the initiative to call for an end to the slave trade and slavery. One such person who appealed to papal support was Lourenço da Silva de Mendouça, of Afro-Brazilian origin and an early antislavery activist. He made personal representation in Rome, asking for a papal condemnation of the abuses of slavery and the slave trade. His forceful petition was remitted to Propaganda Fide where it made a profound impact on the Curia, which responded, saying Mendouça's appeals "have caused no little bitterness to his holiness and their eminences."[38] The practices reported by Mendouça were a disgraceful offense against Catholic liberty and an impedi-ment to the mission of the church, Propaganda concluded.

As Francesco Ingoli, the first secretary of Propaganda Fide, much earlier discovered to his chagrin, the Eternal City had a reputation for procrastination, and, accordingly, Mendouça organized to have a petition presented directly to Propaganda Fide at its meeting in January 1686, on behalf of "the Blacks and

Mulattos born of Christian parents both in Brazil and in the city of Lisbon."[39] It resulted in a remarkable series of vigorous, detailed discussions about the evils and injustices of slavery and the imperative of Christian solidarity with the oppressed. The Capuchins seized the opportunity the discussions afforded of seeking reforms in mission, including the need to wrest control of Propaganda from royal patronage. But the issues went beyond that to touch on doctrine. It was on that ground that the Holy Office took up the propositions drafted by the Capuchins condemning the slave trade and its accumulated abuses, and approved them.[40] The highest tribunal of the church thus promulgated a set of formidable and rigorous condemnations of the abuses of enslavement and sequestration of rights.

Stirred to life by the exertions of Mendouça, Propaganda Fide was given new heart and fresh impetus, to result in the uncoupling of the church's missionary endeavor from the control and patronage of Spain and Portugal. It fell eventually to Capellari, appointed Cardinal Prefect of Propaganda in 1826, and subsequently as Pope Gregory XVI (d. 1846), to harness the new forces spawned by the church's missionary expansion and to redirect them to the reinvigoration of the papacy. In his *Supremo Apostolatus* of 1839, Gregory XVI condemned the slave trade and reiterated official teaching repudiating the inferiority of Africans. That was how Propaganda made the strategic alliance with Francis Libermann (d. 1852) whom Pope Gregory invited to Rome in 1840 and who became a champion of the antislavery cause in Africa.[41] Propaganda teamed with Libermann to initiate a movement that began for the first time to rely on a network of local associations for logistic support of Catholic missions. It represented a crucial shift from dependence on the *ancièn régimes* for government support.[42]

Awakening and Recovery

In time, the antislavery note that Mendouça sounded to such effect in Rome became a dominant theme in the renewal of the worldwide missionary movement in Protestant Christianity that had for the most part rejected mission as a Roman Catholic preserve. As the first such Protestant organization, the Society for the Propagation of Christian Knowledge (SPCK), which was founded in London in 1698, had as its stated purpose "to promote religion and learning in the Plantations abroad and to propagate Christian knowledge at home." It decided, however, to allow as a spin off activity the formation of a missionary arm called the Society for the Propagation of the Gospel in Foreign Parts (SPG) with the goal of sending out missionaries and maintaining them. A royal charter in 1701 established the SPG on that basis.

Many SPG agents, in their capacity as Associates of Dr. Thomas Bray (1658–1730), were commissioned for missionary service in the American colonies. Bray himself went up to Oxford in 1674 where he was a student at All Soul's, graduating in 1678. As a philanthropist he was an ardent promoter of missions. Bray was the founding spirit of the SPCK and the SPG. He wrote what he called his "General Plan" "for the Propagation of the true Religion in the Plantations."

Although appointed in 1695 as a commissary in Maryland by Henry Compton, bishop of London, Bray did not leave immediately but rather went on to make wide-ranging contacts in the Netherlands among the Huguenot refugees there, spreading his ideas of doing missionary work among New World Africans, slave and free. He then set sail for North America, arriving in Maryland in March 1700. He returned to England in May but remained active in directing the work in North America from afar. Eventually Bray's missionary plan was separated from the SPCK and the SPG and reconstituted as the Associates of Bray in 1723. Its goal was to do missionary work among Indians and Africans in North America.[43]

Significantly, these missionary initiatives were a response in large part to the presence of Africans in the New World, however much the missions were tied to colonial and New World interests. African Americans loosened missions from their colonial hinge. Among other Protestants, the work remained largely ad hoc and contingent, and often derivative from the work of others. The SPCK's educational and publishing work, however, had an impact at home and on work others were doing in the mission field. In particular, by 1720 there was an extensive program of Bible translation. The SPCK produced 10,000 Arabic New Testaments, 6,000 Psalters, and 5,000 Catechetical Instructions. The targets were communities in the Ottoman dominions, and in Russia, Persia, and India. The SPCK began a mission to the Scilly Isles in 1765 that lasted until 1841.

Direct involvement in Africa was prompted by the needs of trading concerns rather than by any strategic plan to promote Christianity as a world religion. In 1751 a naval chaplain arrived at Cape Coast Castle in Ghana to minister to the expatriate community there only to discover that the neighboring Africans needed shepherding. He made a brief and furtive attempt to commence a mission, but ill health cut short his plan. Four others followed in quick succession, three of whom died, and the fourth was struck down by illness, and was, accordingly, invalided and sent home.

The first pioneers had opened a school within the castle and introduced Bible reading there. The pupils subsequently formed a Bible Study Circle, which met once a week. They drew up rules of daily conduct, and at the weekly meeting studied and prayed together, and in other ways encouraged one another to grow in the Christian faith. Before long, however, the group came under pressure from the local people, while the Europeans at the castle objected to the idea of Africans becoming Christians without missionary supervision. Rumors began to circulate that the group was a subversive political organization, and steps were promptly taken to suppress it. The members were arrested and imprisoned. However, upon learning the true facts of the case, the governor of the castle intervened and had the members released and authorized their meetings.

The society continued to flourish but was impeded by the lack of Bibles and other literature. One of the members had a business contact with the captain of a Bristol trading ship, whom he asked for copies of Scripture. It turned out that the captain was a member of the Bristol Wesleyan Society. The captain joined the Study Circle and became the group's personal representative with the Bristol Methodists, with the governor approving the contact. That contact produced a tangible result with the arrival of Reverend Joseph Rhodes Dunwell at Cape Coast on New Year's Day 1835. The indomitable steadfastness of the members of the Study Circle led to the opening of a new, if uneven, chapter in the religious history of Ghana. The first batch of missionaries died of malaria soon after they arrived.

In the meantime, another front was being opened by organized mission. Between 1752 and 1824 the SPG sent out at the request of the Royal African Company (RAC) English clergymen who were commissioned as chaplains at Cape Coast in the then Gold Coast. One of these clergymen, Thomas Thompson, served for five years and recorded his impressions in a journal entitled, *An Account of Two Missionary Voyages*, published in 1758. Reflecting the prevailing opinions of the RAC, Thompson persisted with the view that slavery was not an evil and he wrote approvingly of the slave trade. But in the attention he paid to the value of African languages in the work of missions, Thompson unwittingly signaled a crucial shift to African cultural materials as the appropriate framework for the transmission of Christianity. He stressed the importance of developing Fanti language and education, and, appropriately, arranged for three Fanti boys to accompany him to England for education. Two of them died, but the third, Philip Quaque, was ordained in the Anglican Church and in 1765 returned to Cape Coast where he served as schoolmaster, catechist, and missionary. He died in 1816 in those positions.

The Danes, too, had been involved at the fort of Christiansborg, Accra, a garrison fortress held by Denmark from which they regulated trade in the adjacent area. The chaplains who arrived in the Gold Coast were not, strictly speaking, missionaries, but, significantly enough, some took a close interest in

African life and religion. For example, Wilhelm Johann Mueller, a chaplain from 1662 to 1670 at Fort Frederiksborg near Cape Coast, argued for missionary effort among the local population and asked for the Bible to be translated into the local languages. He followed his own advice when he collected some 800 practical words and phrases. He also demonstrated knowledge of local religious practices, the first such attempt by an outsider.

Two other chaplains based at Christiansborg found the restricted boundaries of fortress life too confining, and ventured farther afield. One was Johann Rask who served between 1709 and 1712, and the other was H. S. Monrad, serving between 1805 and 1809. Both condemned slavery and the trade that fostered it, and both expressed the classic doubt about the viability of establishing the church in Africa under the compromising shadow of European commercial enclaves. Without a missionary organization behind them, they did the next best thing and encouraged African pupils to enroll in the school at the castle.

Among the bright talents drawn to the school were William Amo of Axim, who obtained a doctoral degree at Wittenberg University; Jacob Capitein, who graduated from the University of Leiden in the Netherlands, producing for his dissertation an ironic defense of the slave trade as not being inconsistent with Christian teaching; Frederick Svane, who graduated from the University of Copenhagen, Denmark; and Jacob Protten. Such early missionary work was the first bloom of the evangelical awakening that eventually spread to Africa. Svane belonged to the Ga people and returned with a Danish wife to serve briefly at Christiansborg as a catechist and teacher before he returned to Denmark in 1746.

Jacob Protten also returned to the Gold Coast but disappeared into neighboring Togoland to emerge for a brief spell in faraway Germany. He was then at Christiansborg between 1756 and 1761, and again from 1765 until his death in 1769.

The haphazard nature of these missionaries' careers was a fitting testament to the centuries of dogged but futile effort to usher Christianity into *Bilád al-Súdán*, "land of the blacks," the designation of Arab geographers for sub-Saharan Africa. In 1776, the year of the American Revolution, and as cruel fate would have it, the year also of the Dutch construction of a slave house on Gorée Island in Senegal, there were in Africa only a few isolated priests overseeing a dwindling missionary flock. The fact that centuries of missionary enterprise showed no more progress than this indicates the degree to which the global strain of the slave trade caused the missionary enterprise to collapse abruptly. Saving souls was less appealing and less convenient politically than selling or using them.

The domesticated and co-opted version of Christianity that accompanied Europe overseas unsurprisingly had little export appeal, unlike Europe's manufactured commodities. The isolation of Christian Europe marched in tandem with the global expansion of secular Europe, which suggested that secular Europe would have to be bypassed if Christianity were to develop its worldwide potential. Europe and Christianity together need not be inevitable or inseparable, and Africans were eager to make that distinction. For instance, the officials' opposition to the long-suppressed demand of New World Africans for unhindered access to Scripture contradicted the gospel officials wished to proclaim. To remedy that situation New World Africans were left with having to assume responsibility for their kinsfolk in the continent of their origin.

Change of that order was afoot, thanks in large part to the unforeseen and far-reaching consequences of the 1776 American Revolution. It is relevant to the larger story of world Christianity as well as to its future potential in modern Africa to point out that what became constituted as the United States contained the largest population of Africans anywhere outside Africa. The vast majority of these Africans were slaves—some 700,000 by 1790—with an additional 59,000 free Africans. Antislavery sentiments acquired a new urgency in the context of the anticolonial politics of the thirteen colonies on the Atlantic seaboard. Many of the leading voices for independence from Britain expressed similar objections to continued slavery on American soil. The first antislavery society was founded in 1775 in Philadelphia, and in 1785 Benjamin Franklin (d. 1790) became its president. Franklin joined emancipation to the national cause of political independence, vowing, for example, to boycott sugar because it was dyed with the blood of slave labor. A related motive in such ideas of boycott was undoubtedly the attack on the economic interests of the plantation system on which Britain's colonial power was based.

The political and economic basis of antislavery agitation connected with the movement of evangelical awakening that was at the time sweeping the American colonies and drawing in throngs of African converts. It was an eventful connection with long-range ramifications for the course of the history of Christianity in Africa. The evangelical awakening brought about an African mass movement in Christianity that was the first of any such movement among non-European populations, and in scale and effectiveness it went beyond anything else that impacted Africa before or since. It dramatized, for instance, the theme of the African discovery of Christianity in its New World adverse circumstances, and its inescapable long-range extension to Africa itself.

As we have seen, individuals such as Mendouça, the Afro-Brazilian, and others in the Gold Coast had embraced Christianity and had striven to expand its benefits to their compatriots at home and abroad, but they were not, as such, a part of a mass movement. Some, like Frederick Svane, Jacob Capitein, and Jacob Protten, were wandering souls after a lost cause. Others were ephemeral, such as Mendouça, who achieved temporary fame and then slipped into obscurity, largely unknown among his own people or beyond his own lifetime, or Abram Petrovich Gannibal, an African slave who was adopted by Peter the Great (r. 1682–1725). Gannibal, the great-grandfather of Alexander Pushkin, lived all his life in Russia, except for a brief spell in Paris where he was a spy for the czar.[44]

Some assimilated and turned their talents to self-advancement. That was the case with Pedro Juan Garrido, an enterprising African who joined the conquistadors in their takeover of Mexico. Writing to Charles V, Garrido explained how he became a Christian in Lisbon "of my own will," and spent seven years in Castile before coming to Santo Domingo. Buoyed by the currents of Spanish colonization, he arrived eventually in New Spain. He was part of Hernan Cortés's *entrada* that embarked on the conquest of Mexico in 1519. He wrote: "I was present at the taking of Mexico City . . . I was the first to plant and harvest wheat in this land . . . and brought to New Spain many vegetable seeds. I am married with three children." Garrido sought to establish himself as part of the Spanish ruling elite by becoming a property owner, including ownership of a gang of slaves who panned for gold in the alluvial plains of northwest Mexico. In the 1530s he reunited with Cortés in the expedition into Baja California, only to return unfulfilled. His personal fate of hope, isolation, desolation, and penury was poignantly emblematic of the Africans of the slave era. He ended his letter to Charles V by declaring that he was "very poor and have nothing with which to sustain myself."[45] His was the voice of Africa's lost children.

By contrast, the Christian surge among Africans in eighteenth-century America was of an entirely different order. In their hands the religion achieved global range and became a multiplying factor by reason of social scale, with long-range trans-Atlantic repercussions for Africa. An oracle might have said of these New World Africans:

> And other spirits there are standing apart
> Upon the forehead of the age to come;
>
> These, these will give the world another heart,
> And other pulses. Hear ye not the hum
> Of mighty workings?—
> Listen awhile, ye nations, and be dumb.
>
> (John Keats [1795–1821],
> poem addressed to Haydon, 1817)

Long before the American Revolution there was a movement, for example, among New England Puritans to suppress the slave trade. Thus in 1640 in the Puritan colony of Massachusetts a slave captain was arrested and his slave cargo confiscated and ordered to be returned to Africa at the colony's expense. When later the slave trade gained in popularity enough to defy Puritan strictures, it was justified on grounds of economic expedience, not on those of religion.[46] In 1773, Samuel Hopkins of Rhode Island, a disciple of the leader of the Great Awakening, Jonathan Edwards (d. 1758), approached a fellow clergyman and a future president of Yale University, Ezra Stiles, about organizing a batch of black converts for repatriation to Africa as the bridgehead of a Christianization errand into the continent. Hopkins in 1775 appealed to John Adams (d. 1826), the future president of the United States, for a contribution to the cause of Christian colonization. At the outbreak of the war in 1776 over $500 was raised from private donations, but the war interrupted the plans. Hopkins returned to the idea even before the war was formally concluded in 1783, and later in 1794, under the aegis of the African Society of Providence, James McKenzie was sent to the West African coast to prospect for a colony.

In remarks from June 1776, timed to coincide with the American colonies' declaration of the war against Britain, Samuel Hopkins challenged his fellow Americans to the effect that a slave-holding America waging war for political freedom was implicated in a profound and untenable moral contradiction. Hopkins insisted that "the occasion of the present war is such, as in the most clear and striking manner to point out the sin of holding our blacks in slavery, and admonish us to reform, and render us shockingly inconsistent with ourselves, and amazingly guilty if we refuse. God has raised up men to attempt to deprive us of liberty; and the evil we are threatened with is slavery. This, with our vigorous attempts to avoid it, is the ground of all our distresses. . . . The very inconsistent part you act, while you are thus enslaving your fellow men and yet condemning and strenuously opposing those who are attempting to bring you and your children into a state of bondage, much lighter than that in which you keep your slaves."[47] As supreme arbiter of the American cause, Washington's complaint about how Britain chose to "make us as tame, and abject slaves, as the blacks we rule over with such arbitrary sway," shows him to have been all too aware of the contradiction of fighting for political liberty while upholding New World slavery. Morality and politics make fickle allies.

The surge of conversion spurred by the Great Awakening affected large numbers of African Americans involved in the American Revolution, and they afterward crossed the ocean back to Africa as new emissaries of the gospel, formed in evangelical piety and tempered by experience. At the conclusion of the war black loyalist troops were demobilized under British command and transported to Canada in 1783. Finally, in January 1792, the freedom armada of about 1,200 of these blacks, disillusioned with life in Canada, set sail from Nova Scotia and arrived in Freetown, Sierra Leone, in March of the same year, to commence a new phase in Africa's experiment with Christianity and with freedom from slavery. The original colony of free London blacks that settled in 1787 at the Province of Freedom in Sierra Leone had from numerous causes disintegrated beyond salvage, and the cause of the new Christian experiment in Africa appeared to all intents and purposes to have foundered. At that point providence intervened in the form of an impetus from the New World, with a gallant British Parliament backing the enterprise by paying the full cost of re-patriation to the tune of £9,600. Perhaps it was Britain's ironic way of repaying the Americans for their disloyalty, as George Washington had reason to suspect.

At any rate, here they were, these New World African descendants of those originally uprooted from their homes, bound in chains, crammed in slave ships, and hauled across the ocean, returning from the horrors of enslavement and racial castigation to better than the source of their misfortune. They came with a new and different message: liberation for captives, release for prisoners, time of favor for outcasts, and good news for the poor. It helped, too, that the new emissaries could grow rich from legitimate trade while preaching the good news.

Old World missions had targeted kings, chiefs, princes, and the other eminences of the land as the principal candidates for conversion, but the kings and chiefs and their circle of officials sooner or later repudiated Christianity if they adopted it at all, reverting instead to the exploitative ways of the old politics that sanctioned slavery and the slave trade. Even as late as 1878 when he sent out specific instructions to Catholic missionaries, Cardinal Lavigerie empha-sized the importance of converting chiefs in order to produce an "African Constantine" as the basis of creating a Christian society. He said that would do far more for the advancement of the mission than the conversion of hundreds of isolated individuals.[48] When eventually a Catholic political sphere was carved out in Uganda, it was "a paternalistic politico-religious system designed to guarantee the Christian moral order."[49] It did not work. Under the rule of *cuius regio eius religio* (the religion of the ruler is the country's religion) chiefs flip-flopped between being Catholic and being Protestant, or being neither, de-pending on the political winds of change. Between 1480 and 1790, missions adhered doggedly to that top-down approach of political adoption, and for as long Africans en masse declined the boon thus extended to them and continued to do the bidding of their rulers.

The spell was broken when, finally, New World ideas of freedom com-bined with the revival message of redemption and personal promise to declare reprieve for outcasts, the downtrodden, and the bound and gagged. Former slaves, ex-captives, victim populations, and marginal social groups stood in the first line of appeal, a situation that represented a stunning public repudiation of the old venerable principle of political pedigree, social privilege, and public custom as immutable law. This message ignited the dormant forces of indig-enous discontent and disaffection, indicating that there was nothing blithely "contextual" about this social revolution, at least not in the sense of accom-modating to prevailing custom. Contextualization was simply victimization.

Thrust up by the events of the American Revolution, New World Africans mobilized a global human rights movement to transform the continent. As the leaders of the Underground Railroad, an antislavery organization, asserted, human rights are the limits of both divine and all human law, and the practices and enactments such as slavery that go beyond those limits are void.[50] Yet, even if these New World Africans failed in their attempt to eradicate the slave trade in Africa, there was no question now of turning their backs on it.

Logs to the Gypsy Fire

Many contemporary blacks felt called to be the emissaries of the gospel to their own people and to the African continent. One such example is Olaudah Equi-ano, an indefatigable antislavery campaigner who worked on both sides of the Atlantic to mobilize progressive opinion to abolish the slave trade and to advance Africa's economic development. There is also the career of another ex-slave, the Fanti Ottobah Cugoano, with whom Equiano joined forces, and who in 1787 wrote the book *Thoughts and Sentiments on the Evils of the Slavery*, possibly with the collaboration of Equiano. Cugoano's work was a scathing indictment of the slave trade and of the Europeans who promoted it in the name of Christianity.

The story of David George is a fitting testament to the unsuspecting be-ginnings of the new Christian movement, particularly the freewheeling char-ismatic style and the circumstances of adversity that would distinguish the religion in the twentieth century. Born in slavery in Virginia in about 1742, George was later converted in the evangelical movement that swept through the ranks of New World blacks. He undertook missionary drives in the South where he succeeded in setting up Baptist churches in Georgia. At the time of the outbreak of the Revolution, George was already an accomplished religious pioneer, as became evident when he was evacuated to Nova Scotia where he arrived in 1782. There he resumed his preaching activity, putting up what he called "a meeting house" and holding revival sessions there. John Clarkson, brother of Thomas Clarkson, who arrived in Nova Scotia after Thomas Peters's

intervention in London, went to one of George's revival meetings and testified about George's talent for the vocation. "I never remember," said Clarkson,
"to have heard the Psalms sung so charmingly in my life before," and that
no business, obstacle, or thought of favor was capable of deterring George
"from offering up his praises to his Creator."[51] When, in 1792, Clarkson, an
"unlikely Pied Piper," led the Nova Scotian blacks "across the sea to the coasts
of Africa,"[52] George, not surprisingly, was among their number. New World
antislavery sentiments crossed the Atlantic to the African continent to decisive
effect, for good and ill.

In Freetown George expanded the scope of his work. He continued with
his preaching duties, naturally, but he assumed an increasing role as community leader and unpaid ombudsman for the settlers. He defended what he
called "the religious rights" of the Nova Scotians against attempts by the authorities to impose an official Christianity as safeguard against seditiously
inclined black preachers. Britain was a recovering protagonist of the American
Revolution, still hostile to republican ideas of religion and the public order, and
still wary of the contagion of open-house religion in the colony. Officials operated in religious matters on "the Christian discovery" principle of central
control rather than on that of the indigenous discovery of Christianity based on
local direction, and were adamant that they should lead and that Africans
should follow, or be made to follow. Yet the settlers would not budge, with
George making the argument on their behalf that the status of blacks before
God as carrying no stigma or prejudice should be reflected in their freedom
and equality in state and society, regardless of how that claim might reek of
republican sedition. The redemptive work of God in personal recovery, George
pleaded, belonged with the cause of religious liberty, a sentiment shared in the
broad stream of evangelical religion.

Officials decried such views as antinomian by instituting the Colony
Chaplaincy as a deterrent, forgetting, or perhaps fearing, that the settlers were
not preaching anarchy or subjective retreat, but a social activism of change and
reconstruction. The antinomian charge was based on a theological misunderstanding, namely, that the settlers were appealing to the doctrine that says that
"to the pure all things are pure," so that those who are saved consider themselves impeccable, and thus above legal, moral, and political ordinances. That
understanding, however, was far from the case with the settlers, for they did
not come to Africa to engage in utopian escape from their problems. For one
thing, the climate encouraged no such complacency, and, for another, missionary labor was not for the impractical.

On a visit to London in 1793, for example, George urged commitment to
the cause of abolition and mission in Africa, pleading with his English friends

to bestir themselves to a similar end in England. On that visit George met John Newton (d. 1807), author of the popular hymn "Amazing Grace" and one time a slave trader on Africa's west coast, who had since converted to evangelical religion.[53] In 1793, we may recall, the idea of overseas missionary service was far from the minds of British churches, though the Wesleyan revival had awakened society to a larger responsibility at home,[54] with William Carey taking such homebred impulses abroad when he set out for India in 1792. George's appeal was, under the circumstances, a significant gesture that placed Africa right at the center of the antislavery movement and of the accompanying missionary awakening. It was a matter of time before the growing sentiment for abolition would prevail in Parliament where William Wilberforce (d. 1833) led the drive to abolish the slave trade in 1807.

The charge of antinomian heresy met with a convincing refutation in the person of Paul Cuffee, an African American from New England, and one of the wealthiest and most influential blacks of the eighteenth and nineteenth centuries. Cuffee's career demonstrates the inevitability as well as long-range trans-Atlantic hazards of the new Christian movement. Born in 1759 in Dartmouth, Massachusetts, Cuffee grew up in the slave household of the Quaker Slocum family, later converting to that religion. The name Cuffee or Cuffe ("Kofi") was adopted in 1778, hinting at his paternal Ghanaian Ashanti origins. He was freed by his conscience-stricken Quaker owner, and at the age of sixteen Cuffee entered the whaling trade in which he rose eventually to great wealth. By 1800 he had achieved the unusual distinction of being a black shipowner when he commissioned the 162-ton vessel *Hero*, a ship that on one of its voyages rounded the Cape of Good Hope. In 1806 he fitted out two more and larger ships, one a 268-ton vessel, the *Alpha*, which traveled from Wilmington and Savannah to Gottenburg, Sweden, eventually returning to Philadelphia.

In the other ship, the *Traveller*, in which he owned three-fourths' interest, Cuffee made the fateful voyage to West Africa. He left Philadelphia in December 1810, traveling via England where early in 1811 he arrived at Liverpool, then a significant slave port. There he obtained the release of a slave named Aaron Richards, having sent a petition on the matter to the Board of Admiralty set up under the terms of the 1807 act abolishing the slave trade. Cuffee consulted widely with leading figures of the antislavery and evangelical movements, including William Wilberforce, born, coincidentally, the same year as Cuffee, and Zachary Macaulay, since retired as governor of Sierra Leone, and the father of the celebrated historian Lord Macaulay. Cuffee also met the Duke of Gloucester, president of the African Institution, an influential and active antislavery and humanitarian organization whose directors included Wilberforce and William Allen, the prominent Quaker leader with known sympathies for the Mennonite cause in southern Russia. Cuffee then resumed his journey to West Africa in September 1811, arriving in Freetown in November of that year. He gave free passage to a British Methodist missionary and three schoolteachers, proof here, too, that the missionary impetus even in Europe was enabled by black initiative. That was even more so in field practice abroad, though missiologists have often ignored that fact.

The immediate impetus for Cuffee's West African odyssey was the act of 1807 that was inspired in large measure by the successful establishment in Freetown of the American blacks from Nova Scotia. His purpose was to establish a center for legitimate trade at the source of the slave trade in an attempt to discredit the human traffic there. He also wished to create a different triangular trade connecting Africa, the New World, and Europe, a trading cycle in which African Americans should form an indispensable link. The goal of this triangular trade was to grow tropical produce by means of scientific agriculture that would be carried to America in ships owned by blacks, the profits from which would then be used to purchase machinery and goods, thus laying the foundations for settling more free and productive American blacks in West Africa. Their example should prove contagious, Cuffee argued. Legitimate trade and profit, as William Thornton, the Quaker philanthropist, also argued in 1785, would thus forge a moral chain to strangle the vicious slave trade to the direct benefit of the long-suffering Africans themselves.

Yet formidable obstacles stood in the way, not least of which was the grip exercised by European traders who reduced their African partners to crippling indebtedness. It was difficult, Cuffee calculated, to raise an African entrepreneurial class against such odds. He confessed that it appeared to him very clearly that a new economic foundation had to be laid with the Africans in the colony. "I had to encourage them to exert themselves on their own behalf and become their own shippers and importers that they may be able to employ their own citizens[,] for at present their colony is stript of their young men[,] for as soon as they are discharged from school they have no business to go into and they enter on board foreigners[.] So the Colony is Continually stript of her [population]."[55]

As Cuffee determined, chiefs also stood in the path of commercial progress, for, whatever their promises of cooperation, their heart was not in abolition, or in legitimate trade, for that matter, with its free enterprise culture. Cuffee asserted, "I May also add further that in conversing with the African chiefs that it was with great reluctance [that] they gave up the slave trade saying that it made them poor and they Could not git things as they used to git when they traded in slaves."[56] In the old order of the slave trade, local rulers and princes shared an identity of interest with the captains of slave ships, and slave profits helped to strengthen indigenous political institutions. Yet, in enslaving their neighbors chiefs risked a similar fate for themselves. Preemptive raids as a strategy and a deterrent increased the certainty of retaliation. Slave raids benefited no one in the long run, though in the short run no one could afford to do without them. It was that short-run imperative that stumped the ameliorative plans of Cuffee and others, and particularly those of the British Parliament.

To push forward his economic ideas, Cuffee founded the Quaker-inspired Friendly Society of Sierra Leone (Quakers call themselves the Society of Friends), and later wrote to its secretary, the African American James Wise, "I instruct thee to endeavor that she, the Friendly Society, may not give up her commercial pursuits, for that is the greatest outlet to her national advancement.—I foresee this to be the means of improving both your country and nation."[57] Cuffee returned to the United States, departing Freetown on April 4, 1813, and arriving after a fifty-four-day voyage.

Thomas Clarkson (d. 1846), the Cambridge antislavery campaigner, in a notice of January 24, 1814, drew the public's attention to Cuffee's Friendly Society, saying it existed "to devise means of disposing of [the settlers'] produce on the most advantageous terms, and of promoting habits of industry among each other. This association continues but," he cautioned, "it cannot carry its useful plans into execution, without assistance from England."[58] Clarkson's apprehensions about the Friendly Society were echoed by William Allen, who rallied to Cuffee's cause, then under attack from white trading interests in the colony.

In spite of his troubles with officials in Sierra Leone, Cuffee's was a much-respected name with the American establishment. He corresponded regularly with members of the U.S. Congress and was in personal contact with the president. From that advantageous position he made a public appeal to the U.S. president and Congress in June 1813, with proposals for shipping materials and supplies to Sierra Leone to assist in its economic development. What the people there needed, he emphasized, was a sawmill, a millwright, a plow, and a wagon with which to haul loads so that people would not have to carry loads on their heads, as was the custom. He pledged his own resources as proof of his commitment, if that was needed. He said in the memorial that he would lay before the American public a specific challenge "in the expectation that persons of reputation would feel sufficiently interested to visit Africa, and endeavor to promote habits of industry, sobriety, and frugality among the natives of the country."[59]

The following year in 1814 a petition was presented to Congress on Cuffee's behalf. The Speaker of the House remitted it to the Committee on Commerce and Manufacture. The Senate then tabled a resolution authorizing the president of the United States to allow Cuffee to leave for West Africa with a cargo of goods, but the measure was defeated on the grounds that it would let British goods elude the blockade imposed by Congress. A similar request to the British Parliament on Cuffee's behalf was turned down as too risky given the current state of navigation laws still dealing with the effects of the Anglo-American War of 1812 as well as the Napoleonic Wars.

Far from being discouraged by such setbacks, Cuffee, undaunted, persisted with his efforts. With the help of fellow Quakers in Westport, he fitted out the *Traveller* again and set sail in November 1815. The *Traveller* was laden with a cargo of tobacco, soap, candles, naval stores, flour, iron to build a sawmill, a wagon, grindstones, nails, glass, and a plow. There were thirty-eight passengers, eighteen heads of family and twenty children, and common laborers who tilled the soil.

On board the *Traveller* was a Perry Locke, a licensed Methodist preacher, "with a hard voice for a preacher," Cuffee commented delicately.[60] Another passenger, Anthony Survance, was a native of Senegal. He had been sold to the French in Santo Domingo and escaped to Philadelphia during the Revolution. He learned to read and write and studied navigation, though, in spite of professional interest, life at sea ill suited him because of his susceptibility to seasickness; Cuffee himself mused privately that Survance would not make a good mariner. Survance joined the voyage at his own expense, intending eventually to make it to his home in Senegal.

The party dropped anchor in Freetown on February 3, 1816. Unbeknownst to Cuffee, the attitude of the Freetown establishment toward him had hardened to the point of active opposition, and so he was beset with landing difficulties. He was subjected to heavy customs duties for his goods, diminishing any hope he entertained of making a profitable going of his venture. It was little consolation that the governor and chief justice granted Cuffee an audience. The Freetown traders and commercial interests who conspired to shut out Cuffee were determined to prevent any American penetration of the West African market. Thwarted, Cuffee returned to America to continue his antislavery and missionary campaign. He died there in July 1817.

Cuffee's conflict with European mercantile interests in Sierra Leone introduces a theme of long-term significance for the assumed natural connection between Christianity and commerce, on the one hand, and the antislavery campaign on the other. The canon of eighteenth-century philanthropy made wealth and profit the natural companions of right and virtue, and saw wealth creation as the remedy for injustice, inequality, and inhumanity, in fact, as the source of all desirable virtues. Yet Cuffee's experience showed how in the hardnosed world of money such sentiments, when crossed with race, took a back seat, and, accordingly, it would require, for example, an influential antislavery force like Thomas Fowell Buxton, Wilberforce's successor in Parliament, to put morality back into the call for a market economy in Africa. Mary Kingsley makes a biting comment that "conscience, when conditioned by Christianity, is an exceedingly difficult thing for a trader to manage satisfactorily to himself."[61] Some three centuries earlier, the Jesuit Alonso de Sandoval made the same point about the uneasy conscience of slave traders. A leading voice of the French Enlightenment, Chevalier de Jaucourt, wrote in 1765 about how avarice and greed, which ruled the earth, never allowed the cry of humanity on behalf of slaves to be heard. However awkward the conscience of a trader might be, religion, or what remained of it, could easily be enticed by profits and worldly gain to bend conscience into compliance.

In that mercantile world, slavery flourished from the successful coupling of self-interest and material reward. Buxton, and Cuffee before him, introduced moral arguments as a halter to hobble that easygoing formula. Understandably, as Cuffee pointed out, the chiefs regarded moral advocates as threats. Thus, it is worth raising a pertinent question as to whether the moral ideas that challenged and ultimately overwhelmed the global, economic system of the slave trade came from the trade itself. Did material incentives have a hidden and an inexorable moral and humanizing effect on the slave trade? Or did such moral ideas originate in sentiments above and beyond the mercantile slavery system, ideas that proceeded from a premise of their own, however radical and controversial that premise? The sunny Enlightenment view that human beings have an inborn will to freedom conflicts with an equally powerful inborn desire for domination, a contradiction that acted to undercut any overweening confidence in natural law remedies. The existence of slavery refutes the notion of freedom as an innate virtue. In its ensconced racial form, slavery was the fatal obstacle that the doctrine of natural perfection could not surmount. In any case, the evidence suggests African chiefs, and their trans-Atlantic partners, the slave captains, regarded slave profits as necessary and beneficial to the status quo that favored them, and so they perceived the moral campaign to overhaul slavery and the slave trade as a direct attack on them. Top dogs might have to change places with underdogs, for example, and, understandably, that prospect disconcerted both chiefs and slave captains. In their own time, the new nationalist leaders would in turn claim economic necessity and moral autonomy to justify similar human rights violations. Samuel Ajayi Crowther (d. 1891) was constrained to observe, somewhat ruefully, that former victims, including the colonized, make bad taskmasters.

As a "Christian Experiment," Sierra Leone was substantially changed for good by the introduction of African "recaptives" following British abolition in

1807. The British Naval Squadron patrolled the extended West African coast-line, impounding slaves bound for the New World and landing them in Free-town. They were resettled into parish communities organized around church, school, and farm. These recaptives hailed from all parts of the African conti-nent and in time formed the backbone of the settlement. They swamped the original Nova Scotian settlers, and took over much of the work of education, community government, and evangelization. From their ranks emerged a new mobile middle class with an effect far beyond its size. That middle class be-came the ironic nemesis of colonialism, and, with tragic consequences, of the successive messianic nationalism of the second half of the twentieth century.

Paul Cuffee's legacy in America was an enduring one, and it led directly to the establishment of Liberia as a settlement for freed slaves from the southern United States. Robert S. Finley, a Presbyterian minister from New Jersey and later president of the University of Georgia, had been campaigning for the creation of a settlement in Africa for freed slaves. He made contact with Cuffee and wrote to him saying, "The great desire of those whose minds are im-pressed with the subject is to give opportunity to the free people of color to rise to their proper level and at the same to provide a powerful means of putting an end to the slave trade, and sending civilization and Christianity to Africa."[62] Finley eventually became an architect of the Liberian colonization venture.

When eventually the American Colonization Society (ACS) was formed in December 1816 in a hall in the U.S. House of Representatives, Cuffee's pro-posals and example were the inspiration, and Sierra Leone the model people had in mind. Consequently, the board of managers of the ACS paid fulsome tribute to Cuffee in a memorial note, praising him for his clear and unwavering judgment, his informed opinion, his unyielding commitment and unstinting devotion, and, above all, for his hands-on experience of life in West Africa, experience that counteracted the effects of unfounded prejudice. The tribute to him ended with the point that any future engagement with Africa would have to be based on partnership of an uncommon order, one in which fact and knowledge would replace prejudice and aspersion, an order that must be eval-uated in terms of its "usefulness to the native Africans and their descendants in this country."[63] With the antislavery cause in West Africa, the African theme in New World Christianity acquired a trans-Atlantic range.

Unfinished Agenda: The Slave Trade as Nemesis

The Christian experiment in Sierra Leone was the brainchild of the evangeli-cal movement and of the revival of missionary interest in general. Thus was founded in 1795 the London Missionary Society (LMS), and other related bodies such as the Netherlands Missionary Society of Rotterdam (1797), the mission school in Berlin (1800) founded by Pastor Johann Jänicke of the Brethren Church, and the Basel school (1815) that supplied recruits for British missions. The Netherlands Missionary Society picked up the African connection established by the Moravians in the 1740s when John Theodore Vanderkemp went out as a missionary to South Africa.[64]

Vanderkemp arrived at the Cape in 1799, establishing a mission to the hard-pressed Hottentots at Bethelsdorp on Algoa Bay, 400 miles east of Cape Town. He made a dramatic entrance into the politics of the slave trade when he purchased from slavery a girl of seventeen whom he then married. The young girl's African mother was from Madagascar. Vanderkemp's personal example of a radical and politically uncompromising evangelical faith that openly endorsed the principle of racial and political equality influenced many who followed him in missionary service. Yet the rigors of frontier life among Africans on the fringes of a colonial white society and on the path of unrelenting land sequestration took a terrible toll on him, and he died relatively young in 1811. The leading agent of the LMS and chief architect of its work in South Africa was John Philip of Aberdeen, Scotland, who was appointed to the position of leading agent in 1820. He was an eloquent and passionate defender of the rights of Africans against whites in South Africa, carrying the antislavery banner into opposition strongholds. His book, *Researches in South Africa* (1828), contains a robust defense of his evangelical and humanitarian views and of the rights of native populations. We shall return to his work in due course.

In time, Catholic missions, too, came to an identical view about the role of a productive African middle class in the advancement of Christianity. Writing from East Africa in 1906, one Catholic missionary noted how the men lay idle while the women did all the work, and said that must be changed if Christianity had any hope of succeeding. The African, he insisted, must not become merely the employee of the irreligious colonialist or the agent of an Indian merchant. Rather, the African must be independent of both and become "owner of his own land and later on the owner of an enterprise, workshop and house. We want to form a Christian society, but one that is African, one which finds all its constitutive elements among Africans.... The foundation of any well-regulated society is private property, [such as] the ownership of a parcel of land, loved, maintained, [and] improved. The foundation of property understood in this sense is work—work on one's own behalf."[65]

In West Africa, the evangelical cause was represented by the Church Missionary Society (CMS) of the Church of England, founded in 1799, although, instructively, the first CMS recruits were German evangelicals, Melchior Renner and Peter Hartwig, who arrived in Sierra Leone in 1804.[66] Evangelical religion was suspect among Anglicans, and churchmen found the idea of missionary service unfamiliar and unacceptable. The idea of missionaries setting out for foreign parts was ridiculed in an article in 1808 in the *Edinburgh Review*. "The wise and rational part of the Christian ministry find they have enough to do at home. But if a tinker is a devout man, he infallibly sets off for the East," William Carey being the intended reference in that rebuke. Such eastbound missionaries were considered "little detachments of maniacs, benefiting us much more by their absence, than the Hindus by their beliefs."[67]

As a consequence, the CMS became by force of circumstance an ecumenical and transnational missionary organization. It was a rocky beginning for the CMS even then. Hartwig abandoned the missionary life, disappeared promptly into Susu country, not to convert Africans but to become a slave trader. Undaunted, the CMS dispatched a second batch of missionaries, all Germans, who arrived in 1806: Leopold Butscher, Johann Prasse, and Gustavus Nÿlander. Nÿlander was to become the pioneer agent of the CMS in Sierra Leone, and he stayed in Freetown as agent of the Sierra Leone Company.[68] He was a man who wore many hats: as chaplain he ministered to a flock of European churchgoers; in the village he taught school and supervised subordinate officials; at home he was husband to a Nova Scotian. The tropics stripped whatever surviving religious habits his European parishioners retained, and they deserted the chapel, leaving Nÿlander with no flock to tend. The chapel fell into disrepair and was abandoned, its functions absorbed into Nÿlander's other household responsibilities.

Nÿlander began to make headway with the mission only when he directed his attention to the country beyond the Freetown peninsula. On the Bulom Shore he commenced in 1818 the language work that was to distinguish missions and Christianity's encounter with modern Africa. He compiled a Bulom grammar and vocabulary, and translated St. Matthew's Gospel into Bulom. It was the first Bible translation in Sierra Leone, although in 1801 Henry Brunton, back in Scotland from the African mission field, published a Susu grammar and some catechisms. Brunton's translations were the first to be published in a West African language.

With respect to Nÿlander's two other missionary companions, a similar pattern can be discerned in their work. Johann Prasse went with Butscher and Melchior Renner to the Rio Pongas for work among the Susu in pursuit of the new CMS doctrine stating that metropolitan Freetown was an inauspicious environment for mission, and accordingly shifting the focus to indigenous hinterland populations. It was a policy change representing a quiet but momentous repudiation of Christianity and civilization as natural bedfellows, and it ran counter to prevailing settler opinion about the irredeemability of so-called uncivilized "tribes." In the spirit of malice that marred relations with indigenous Africans, the colonists lifted a line from the *Te Deum* and fixed it on the tribes whom God proceeded to address as those "unto whom I swear in my wrath that they should never enter into My rest."[69] Butscher eventually returned in 1814 to Freetown to head a settlement of new recaptives in Leicester.

Butscher's experiences from living among the Susus led him to formulate some sharp ideas about the deep impact of the slave trade on societies beyond the coast, and noted the facilitating but limited role of colonial guardianship alone in addressing the problem. What he said on the subject has echoes, for example, in a Roman North Africa that was blissfully oblivious to hinterland realities, and was in a significant measure far in advance of his time. It was not till 1837, when Thomas Fowell Buxton (1786–1845) published his much acclaimed *The Slave Trade and Its Remedy*, that belated attention was drawn to what Butscher had described as far back as 1812. From his experience, Butscher said the slave trade was the most important source of income for inland societies and that the recent abolition had threatened the very foundation of their economic survival. Seizing slaves on the high seas, as was the policy of the British government, did not strike at the root cause of enslavement; what was needed, Butscher said, was an export commodity that could profitably and effectively replace slaves as precious cargo. It should therefore be the single most urgent objective alike of missions and governments to develop an alternative source of wealth for African societies. Accordingly, Butscher set about seeking to secure the support and cooperation of government authorities, thus suggesting a strong partnership between mission and government, with the flag following the Bible rather than the Bible following the flag, as happened elsewhere.

It was under Butscher's plan that Sierra Leone's Governor Charles W. Maxwell (1811–15) organized an administrative scheme for the resettling of recaptives who were arriving in the colony in increasing numbers. In 1807 Freetown's population was 1,871, including 95 military personnel. In the census of April 1811, it had increased to around 3,500, because of an influx of recaptives. In July 1814, there was a big jump again to 5,520 recaptives. In a report drawn on December 31, 1818, the number of recaptives was put at 6,406. The total population, including settlers, was about 17,300 in 1816. By December 1840 some 67,000 recaptives had been resettled in Freetown.

The rapid rise in these figures is not due exclusively, if at all, to the British Naval Squadron commanding improved techniques of seizure, but, more ominously, to the uncomfortable fact that the pace of the slave trade had quickened, both because of and in spite of, abolition. It is, for example, estimated that during 1810 alone some 80,000 slaves were being illegally shipped across the Atlantic, mostly to markets in Brazil, Cuba, and the southern United States. It was this demographic pressure on the Freetown peninsula that Governor Maxwell was asked to address, though the task fell to his successor, Sir Charles MacCarthy, who for that purpose devised an effective network of supervised village settlements, called the Parish Scheme, if such a lofty rubric was tenable or appropriate for the seaborne indigenous influx it sought to channel.

A Roman Catholic by background, MacCarthy took up the task that fell to him with energy and imagination, responding to Butscher's call for a genuine partnership between mission and government in the cause of African reha-bilitation. We shall return to MacCarthy in subsequent chapters. The recapti-ves were farmed out to newly created villages on the peninsula, each village directed by a clergyman. There was a chapel, with required attendance, which during the week would also serve as a school. Before 1815 there were three such villages: Leicester, founded in 1809; Wilberforce (formerly Cabenda), estab-lished in 1810; and Regent (formerly Hogbrook), founded in 1812. Between 1815, the year of Waterloo, and 1820, ten more villages were created to absorb the newcomers, among them Kissy and Gloucester in 1816; Charlotte and Leopold (the latter renamed Bathurst) in 1817; and Wellington, Hastings, and Waterloo in 1819. After the disbanding of the Royal African Corps in 1819, the demobilized troops were resettled appropriately in Gibraltar Town, named in recognition of the servicemen who served in Gibraltar.

These parish-style villages transformed Freetown into a black diaspora, a bustling entrepôt of refugees at large, with Freetown becoming a creolized, Caribbean-style cultural experience on African soil, a teeming crossroad of Af-rican and Western ideas stirred with an admixture of religious elements, Mus-lim, Christian, and indigenous. African recaptives who originated from many different parts of the continent, some from as far away as the Congo and Mo-zambique, intermingled with those from Nigeria and elsewhere. They had in common only the experience of being uprooted and banished from village, hearth, and shrine, and of the bewildering effects of a life of forcible migration in slave ships and slave camps.

Assessment

For these brittle victims of the global Atlantic slave trade, the availability of faith-based Christian communities offering security and the promise of new life proved to be a compelling incentive. They may be forgiven for putting on airs, so stupendous were the odds against their survival. The shrines and altars of indigenous communities arrived in the settlement with the recaptives and coexisted quite amicably with Christian rituals. Recaptive Yoruba diviners, for example, thoroughly at home in the world of divination, visions, and the crowded company of unseen spirits, welcomed the challenge of missionaries, saying they were happy to add the Christian divinity to the Yoruba pantheon because a place already existed for that. It showed how, in the conditions of dislocation, mobility, resettlement, and reassurance precipitated by the slave trade and its consequences, Christianity was welcomed as African restoration. The transmission of Christianity engaged the terms of indigenous discovery to commence a long-term intercultural process of conversion and readjustment in Sierra Leone and beyond.

In due course the social kaleidoscope of tongues and tribes was expanded with recently arrived West Indian and American blacks. When eventually the CMS German missionary linguist Sigismund Kölle compiled his *Polyglotta Africana* in 1847, he was able to document some 120 different languages spoken in the colony. Such pioneer language documentation laid the groundwork for many disciplines, among them comparative African linguistics and cultural anthropology. The achievements for academic study in that regard were long lasting.

I shall return to the black settlers in a later chapter where I shall examine their religious contribution. Here it is only necessary to say that our story, sad to say, had an anticlimactic ending, for when almost 200 years after its founding Sierra Leone disintegrated into political anarchy amid a bitter civil war, much of what remained of the original Christian experiment was trampled into the ground. The sudden transfer of power at independence in 1961 opened a tragic gap between metropolitan Freetown and the new centers of political power in the vote-rich, much maligned, and ethnic-sensitive hinterland. The new politics of comprehensive national power and total commitment to the state's command dogma combined with ethnic politics to stage a frontal assault on the idea of a Christian-inspired civil society, as well as of government as limited partnership and trust with the people. Colonial rule ended, it turned out, only in the sense of the foreign adjective being ditched for getting in the way. With few qualms, the homebred variety of nationalist overlordship was less scrupulous.

As we have seen, chieftaincy authority was a machinery of the slave trade, and for that reason became the target of the international antislavery campaign. In its place came nationalist dictators who took cover behind the lethal doctrine that indigenous authenticity conferred on them moral immunity and placed them out of range of any international human rights movement able or willing to challenge their excesses. The mantle of nationalist innocence foiled the international community in any attempt to become a real force against the postcolonial debacle. Acts of ethnic cleansing, often rising to genocidal frenzies, gripped the land as they swept off whole populations, to the numbing silence of the rest of the world. Armed with voter registration cards commandeered from village headmen, a predatory state thumbed its nose at the moral case for civil society such as that which Cuffee and Buxton advocated, while churches as civil structures became emergency processing centers for refugees and an ark of hope for the much maligned and much abused. Neighboring Liberia suffered a fate no less enviable than Sierra Leone when war and pillage reduced the country to ruins. The collapse of religion, except as political cannon fodder, suppressed the will to choose and thus removed a safety barrier between the free heritage of the children of Africa and an age of barbarism. Meanwhile, just to show that Africa had crossed an intellectual Rubicon, the epicenter of the Christian impact, with undimmed prospects before it, shifted south and east to Ghana, Nigeria, and beyond.

4

The Yogi and the Commissar

Missions and the Colonial Pillar

Theme

In its vernacular mode, the Christian movement wrought changes in Scripture and church life, lighting a fuse that transformed missionary practice. The vernacular Scripture impacted local ideas and customs, and changed their relationship with missions. Yet this fact has all but slipped from scholarly consciousness, in large part because attention was directed to the priority of foreign transmission rather than local reception; since that transmission focused on organizing the missionary effort in Europe and North America, attention shifted there rather than to the local setting and agents. Missions led to Europe's overseas ascendancy. By accepting this interpretation, historians endorsed the colonial view of events and left standing the connection between missions and colonialism. The conventional wisdom that Christianity provided backing for foreign rule was reinforced, and missionaries became the earnest journeymen of imperialism. In reality, however, the vernacular issue complicated the mission mandate immensely.

In spite of that, the study of missions became little more than Western mischief and its numerous insidious effects on the subject races. That mischief survives, for instance, in the Wolof word for a Roman Catholic, *gourmette*, from the Portuguese for houseboy. Missions were organized, funded, and directed from the West, a fact that made it easy to construe them as colonialism at prayer, and to see colonialism as the West's moral mandate. Suitably chastened, missionary organizations have since beat a retreat by speaking modestly of "missioner," "fraternal worker," "cross-cultural consultant," "ecumenical partner," and anything else so long as it was not the offending word "missionary." On the ground, however, it is hard entirely to defend the claim that missionary activity ignored local realities. Still, as long as missions were regarded as part of the colonial project, it was difficult to escape the colonialist stigma completely, or to defend field gains against the charge of cultural subversion, and of conversions as betrayals.

I am urging a revisionist history without claiming that missions and colonialism were not in cahoots. In many places there was, without question, cooperation between them, with missionaries supporting military force where necessary to establish and to defend their work. The story of Catholicism in the New World and elsewhere makes that clear. But Catholicism is not the sole culprit. When Hope Waddell of the United Presbyterian Mission was about to set out for Old Calabar in Nigeria in 1845, he insisted that he and his party should receive a guarantee of protection from the British Royal Navy, which was given. Almost immediately, and with good reason, the missionaries became locked in a bitter controversy with King Eyo Honesty II, the ruler of Creek Town in Old Calabar. In the end, the missionaries prevailed, reducing King Eyo to a puppet role. They went further by seizing the king's court and converting it into an open-air space for Sunday services. When provocative missionary highhandedness inflamed local feelings by the desecration of local shrines and other acts of wanton recklessness, the missionaries appealed to the British consul to take military action against the Efik population for their recalcitrance.

The Admiralty arrived in the HMS *Antelope*, whose naval gunners razed the town. When a similar punitive action was taken against the city of Lagos, the missionary in charge, Rev. C. A. Gollmer, applauded the action, declaring triumphantly, "I look upon it as God's interposition for the good of Africa[,] and may we not hope that now the word of God will gain free course among the Ijebus, too?"[1] In other words, a similar fate was in store for other recalcitrant Africans.

Assured of Britain's military might, the missionaries in Old Calabar resolved to press their advantage. In the face of a local decision to withhold the people's co-operation, the missionaries sent an appeal for a show of force to teach the people a lesson in submission.

Before long HMS *Scourge* steamed up the coast and put a landing party ashore, which summoned the local chiefs to a conference on board. There they were told that by inviting the missionaries to their country they had entered into a perpetual obligation to help them, that they must never again take any measures against the missionaries, that if they molested the missionaries and the Africans who were being educated by the missionaries, they would incur the extreme displeasure of the Queen of England.[2]

In a relatively short space of time, missionaries completely subdued Creek Town and the adjoining country. Missionary ladies took the local girls and fitted them out in Victorian clothes, thus imposing through its women the constraints and conceits their Western culture deemed appropriate to the gospel. Africans well understood the momentous changes afoot. One old man made bitter lament in his Krio tongue: "Fine ting dis be, white woman come and make law for we."[3]

The complaint acknowledges the truth of hammer blows of an alien civilization on local values, but the evidence is still far short of a logical demonstration of a cultural makeover. Evidence that an alien wind bent the cane is no reason for the sugar to be crooked.[4] In fact the emergence of Christianity in Old Calabar and beyond occurred largely from the effects and consequences of the African-led Niger Mission of 1841 when African agents under Ajayi Crowther (ca. 1806–91) mobilized a powerful vernacular movement to overwhelm the missionaries' imperial presumptions and Victorian scruples. The ready-made missions program did not survive the movement for indigenization.

It all came to a head in 1905 with the creation of the Union Igbo Bible. After initial hesitations and criticisms, Archdeacon Dennis' translation of the Scriptures into Union Igbo was eventually applauded and celebrated as a work of genius. "The beautiful and liquid phrasing of the Archdeacon's Bible, as majestic and chaste in its euphony and its haunting sweetness as our own English Authorized Bible, spoke the grand truths of God and Christ to countless waiting hearts."[5] Union Igbo became a living speech, and pupils used it to express their hopes and dreams, taking it home with them from school. People coming from distant parts found that they could understand each other through this new tongue—new, yet somehow their very own. It was not unlike what Dante had achieved with the unification of the various Italian dialects.

A shift of perspective is needed to see that, in practice, things were more complex than the simple view of Christianity (or even of missions) and colonialism as a united conspiracy. As we saw with the moribund missions in Sierra Leone, the Kongo, and elsewhere, although missions fell from their high moral calling by engaging in slavery and the slave trade, they also transcended them by creating communities of faithful converts. With renewed commitment, many returned to resume, or began afresh to salvage what was left of their work and reputation, whenever and wherever possible.

Ground Rules

The evidence paints a complicated picture of the diverse and unpredictable indigenous responses to Christianity because the premise of missionary hegemony is faulty. There were equally as many examples of Christianity coalescing with anti-colonial activities and movements as there were of imperial collusion and acquiescence. A chain is only as good as its weakest link, and the weakest link in the argument of hegemony is evidence of Christian-inspired protest and resistance, both in the church and in politics. Colonized societies produced a class of national champions as well as imperial supporters, those whom the language of dialectics castigates as collaborators. We may decry such collaborators, but that does little to disguise the point that collaboration was a two-way street, for it suggests that colonial administrators saw advantage, too, in rewarding local talent. To the extent that they shared power with the collaborators, administrators were being manipulated, thus falling well short of the triumphalist dogma with which they set out on their foreign venture. The swaggering rhetoric of enlightened power bolstered by a sense of metropolitan entitlement did little to mince the ambiguities of alien rule. The descent was necessary in order to achieve even the limited objective of conquest, let alone the long-range goal of indefinite rule. Merely to have achieved the establishment of colonial rule carried no assurance that all local obstacles, including religious ones, had been overcome. Sometimes the obstacles only got bigger.

The appointment in 1891 of George (later Lord) Curzon to be Undersecretary of State for India, for example, is reckoned by many historians to have been the catalyst for modern Indian nationalism.[6] As Viceroy—or, unflatteringly, as the Great Ornamental of India—Curzon earned bitter nationalist opposition on account of his partitioning of Bengal in 1905. The order was subsequently rescinded, but the nationalist feelings it inflamed never subsided entirely.[7] Moderate opinion began to shift as a consequence, and was eventually and effectively overtaken by nationalism. Gopal Krishna Gokhale (d. 1915) fired a warning shot when he devoted a seminal address to the Curzon issue in a speech in London at the New Reform Club in 1905. The address was entitled "The Governing Caste," and it challenged Curzon's basic assumption that Indians were entitled to little beyond the restrictions and other disadvantages of colonial tutelage. Indians lamented the fact that the Viceroy of India was screened from all knowledge of India.

Being practical, the British recognized the facts, and, where necessary, they devolved authority to Indian leaders. That was how they adopted the "doctrine of the lapse" which allowed them to assume control of a princely state following the death of a sitting prince. It removed the need for costly military action. Elsewhere, the principle of Indirect Rule was put in place, enabling the colonial administration to rule through established local institutions, called Native Authorities. Where none existed, such Authorities were created. Indirect Rule allowed the British to be an imperial power at long range without the provocation or the burdens involved in direct rule at close proximity. As one eyewitness account put it, Indirect Rule saw Native Administrations as a bulwark of indigenous systems.[8] It used to be said of the empire that the British stumbled on it in a fit of absentmindedness, and Indirect Rule was no less an accident of history. The facts on the ground taught officials that adaptability was less costly and more effective than military force, thus requiring adjustment of the dogma of colonial superiority to reflect local reality. Indirect Rule became shared rule.

Missions faced a similar challenge, and the course they employed muddied the water considerably by adopting local idioms in Bible translation in place of Western forms and ideas. Bible translation acknowledged the priority of local usage over Western usage, thereby causing the colonial system and its missionary allies to become schizoid about Christianity. The religion represented the West's moral superiority over local superstition, a reassuring fact that allowed a certain moral authority to accrue to the colonial project. Yet missions confused the issue unnecessarily by allowing locals to mobilize a naturalized Christianity with all its subversive and so-called heathen implications. Fearing sentiments of liberation, administrators promptly clamped down on the new Christian movements, threatening their followers and sympathizers with reprisals and rounding up and incarcerating their unamenable leaders. Just as the Great Awakening provoked a social crisis in New World slavery, the missionary movement was at risk of fomenting a political crisis in the colonial empire. It was proof that missions were colonialism's Achilles' heel, not its shield.

As nursery beds of conversion, the schools shared in the same complex web of relationships missions initiated. Challenged about why schools failed to live up to their reputation as effective instruments of evangelism, a schoolteacher responded to the suggestion to try other forms of indoctrination by declaring:

We teach [the gospel] all day long. We teach it in arithmetic, by accuracy. We teach it in language, by learning to say what we mean— "Yea, yea, and nay, nay." We teach it in history, by humanity. We teach it in geography, by breadth of mind. We teach it in handicraft, by thoroughness. We teach it in astronomy, by reverence. We teach it in the playground, by fair play. We teach it by kindness to animals, by courtesy to servants, by good manners to one another, and by truthfulness in all things. We teach it by showing children that we, their elders, are their friends and not their enemies.[9]

Missions cultivated local sensibility, and that greatly complicated the language of colonial control. Instead of welcoming this complexity as a boon for scholarship, scholars of mission demurred, reluctant to abandon the claim of foreign mischief and eager to retain their reputation as progressive champions of victims and oppressed groups. But it does not seem convincing to press the hegemonic argument only because it allows you to safeguard your progressive reputation, when doing so conflicts with the local empowerment Christianity fostered. Those who made policy to convert and to civilize subject races had to contend with the historical facts they confronted; the more awkward those facts were, the less possible and the less prudent it was to ignore them. Historians could do worse than follow their example.

Overlordship

Old habits die hard, especially habits of the mind. Scholars insisted that mission "hinged upon the effort of a few men, with loosely shared social origins, to impose an entire worldview upon their would-be subjects, to contrive reality for them as a coherent and closed, uniform and universalistic order." The missionaries, in the words of Jean Comaroff and John Comaroff:

set out to save Africa: to make her peoples the subjects of a world-wide Christian commonwealth. In so doing they were self-consciously acting out of a new vision of global history, setting up new frontiers of European consciousness, and naming new forms of humanity to be entered onto its map of civilized mankind. [They] were not just the bearers of a vocal Protestant ideology, nor merely the media of modernity. They were also the human vehicles of a hegemonic worldview, [purveying] its axioms in everything they said and did. Their assault [was] driven by a universalizing ethos whose prime object was to engage the Africans in a web of symbolic and material transactions that would bind them ever more securely to the colonizing culture. Only that way would the savage finally be drawn into the purview of a global, rationalized civilization.[10]

This argument assumed a life of its own, begetting the view that the intellectual and material artifacts of a global, rationalized Christian civilization had foreign fingerprints all over them. Western hegemony was all the more malevolent for being external and forceful as well as hidden and seductive. Missionaries, for example, punctured the mystique of rainmaking, until then a sacred art to Africans, by staging verifiable experiments to prove condensation. In the material sphere, European tools and techniques mesmerized the natives with dazzling images of a looking-glass world and compelled them to deal with the reality below the surface; to show the tribes, for example, how to dig wells and cause water to appear where none had been before. Missionaries introduced the post-Enlightenment idea of separation of church and state and shattered traditional notions of the seamless unity of life and consciousness (except that, if the Comaroffs are to be taken at their word, Africans had no consciousness to begin with).

In respect specifically to African languages, the intellectual ideas and material culture of the West had a dominant and decisive influence, with orthography, text, and literacy reducing the vernacular to an instrument of the humdrum empirical and mundane world. The Comaroffs claim that in Scripture translation, where local idioms prevailed, language was only a technology of mind manipulation. According to them, missionary linguists were cultural imperialists, though the truth is quite otherwise.[11] For example, in a study of the life of Robert Moffat, an outstanding missionary linguist in southern Africa, the observation was made that the vernacular Bible bridged the old and new. It was a living book in the double sense of being a truthful record as well as a living oracle. Lifting a vernacular New Testament in his hand, an African Christian testified that he and his people once imagined the Bible to be a charm of the white people to keep off sickness, and a trap to catch the people. He knew differently now. "We have never heard of such a thing . . . but now we not only hear with our ears, we see with our eyes, we read it, our children read it. . . . We thought it was a thing to be spoken to, but now we know it has a tongue. It speaks and will speak to the whole world."[12] We find echoes in such testimony of an idea enunciated by C. S. Lewis that if the translated Bible is to return as a book, it must do so as a sacred book.[13] In other words, a convincing translation is better than a correct translation. That observation validates the testimony of converts and proves that Christianity has been a religion of dynamic responsiveness and not a device simply of mind manipulation.

In any case, the Comaroffs press the argument that the Africans' spatial and imaginative worlds were beleaguered, and eventually conquered and subdued by the forces of an alien, rationalized, Christian civilization. Like a teeming river, choices began flooding the Africans' world and forcing a silent but pervasive movement in homesteads and across the tribal landscape. Even resistance and protest did not escape the overrun from the missionary surge. Because of its superior technology and culture, and because of its ability to impose its power, the colonial empire became "the African bleaching ground," as has been said about New World slavery. Native culture was uprooted and "bleached" of its natural elements. "That is why new hegemonies may silently take root amidst the most acrimonious and agnostic of ideological battles," the Comaroffs conclude.[14] Conversion was cultural subversion.

By distilling universal theory from missionary motives rather than looking to missionary actions, this procedure ignores historical contingency. It assumes those motives to be identical with the suspicions of the anthropologist. It is the view that Christianity is not a religion as such and can be explained by nonreligious arguments, as if the sun can be seen without its own light. The only possible outcome is a foregone conclusion that the West dispossessed and dominated the cultures it encountered. Context, variety, and difference served the same hegemonic purpose as surrender, collaboration, and conformity. In the end, that left Africans on the downside of the dialectics of power, and would perhaps be the only example in history where whole populations survived as a delinquent race. What missionaries once did, academic curators must now do, which is to drag "the savage into the purview of a global, rationalized 'explanation'." Conquered in the field by missionaries and in scholarship by theorists, Africans were double victims, without history and without a voice.

Yet all that is to assume that the message of Christianity, launched like a missionary arrow, glided across vast watery wastes, dust trails, and beaten paths, and landed among bemused, hapless Africans. In fact, long before the missionaries dug wells, Africans taught their children that one did not spit into the well from which one drank, especially when the well in question was the well of Samaria. The relevant moral was that missionaries could not denigrate the people who as converts justified the practice of mission. Yet the caricatures persisted. The movie, *The Gods Must Be Crazy* (1980), presented this hackneyed stereotype of Africans, and a fantasy-savvy media world, catering to the appetite, produced several sequels. Yet scholars have less excuse persisting against the evidence and presenting Africans as feckless specimens of nature trapped in a state of suspended bewilderment.

In one respect, the Comaroffs are right to call attention to how, in spite of their close physical and social proximity to Africans, Europeans remained remote and isolated. Admittedly, technology and power narrowed the distance between the two continents, but did not achieve genuine rapprochement in cultural attitudes. In the trenchant words of R. Delavignette, with respect to the French African empire, the European "must put the world in order. This determination has the compelling power of a religion, and the European is its prophet."[15] By performing his own errand, the prophet as colonizer saves the native messenger's hire. Europeans could be in Africa, but, thanks to their technology and messianic ideology, they could afford not to be of it. Familiarity here was the opiate of empathy. Geographical range affected little of the imaginative capacity for intercultural exchange or the willingness for equality. As Basil Davidson observed, the extent of this multicultural intransigence spanned the entire period of Europe's maritime dominance, and, as Anthony Benezet protested, was scarcely improved in the era of the slave trade.[16] "Until the seventeenth century—though rarely even then—[European's] writings are seldom more than laconic tales of adventure or bare recitals of trading profit, laced now and then with more or less fantastic speculations on the nature of African humanity."[17] The limitation of cultural insensitivity was not a credit to the European, or an inadequacy in the African.

Writing in 1776 in his *Wealth of Nations*, Adam Smith (d. 1790) offered some pertinent reflections on the consequences of the global expansion of Europe for indigenous populations. He said the discovery of America, and that of a passage to the East Indies via the Cape of Good Hope,

> are the two greatest and most important events in the history of mankind. Their consequences have already been very great; but in the short period of between two and three centuries which has elapsed since those discoveries were made, it is impossible that the whole extent of their consequences can have been seen. By uniting, in some measure, the most distant parts of the world, by enabling them to relieve one another's wants, to increase one another's enjoyments, and to encourage one another's industry, their general tendency would seem to be beneficial. To the natives however, both of the East and West Indies, all the commercial benefits which can have resulted from those events have been sunk and lost in the dreadful misfortunes which they have occasioned.[18]

Lesslie Newbigin, himself something of a lost child of the Enlightenment, testified to the same effect, saying: "The discovery of the New World was flooding Europe with silver and gold and producing a huge inflation of prices, destroying the ancient balance in society, and making possible a vast extension of trade to the far corners of the earth. Old rules governing wages, prices, interest, and land tenure became impossible to maintain. Capital was no longer primarily the adjunct of the labor of the small craftsman; it became more and more the master that controlled economic organization."[19] Alongside their ir-reversible global structural effects, the forces of advanced economic change created social fractures and personal estrangement rather than securing a world of equality and justice. Global range was different from intercultural equity.

The courageous if forlorn career of Dr. Albert Schweitzer (1875–1965) of Franco-German Alsace, later a missionary in Lambaréné, Gabon, is testimony to the reach as well as the gulf of advanced technology and cultural sophisti-cation. The author of the highly influential study, *Quest of the Historical Jesus,* and the recipient in 1952 of the Nobel Peace Prize, Schweitzer propounded a New Age philosophy of "reverence for life" that took little account of African ideas of God or of the Africans themselves, whom he kept at arm's length though he lived among them.[20]

Schweitzer became an icon of the West, a post-Enlightenment wonder who, in 1913, forsook a lucrative, preeminent career in Europe for a life of danger and deprivation in the jungles of Africa. Yet the Western adulation of Schweitzer for his humility contrasted sharply with African objections to him for his towering aloofness.

The strange controversy that Schweitzer represented happened to be per-fectly consistent with the European idea of religion as reason unimpeded by intercultural understanding. Schweitzer did not believe in evangelizing Afri-cans, only in doing good for them and being somewhat indifferent to their homage and gratitude. For him, Africans lacked the capacity for abstraction, including the refined cultural habits presupposed in a high Christology, and it was the duty and mission of Europeans to remedy that cultural inadequacy without requiring Christianity. It was a strange idea for him that Africans could become Christian without being European, or without possessing the European capacity for universal rationalization, and that circumstance was a double jeopardy. Christianity's universal intellectual legacy in Europe twice precluded access to it by non-Europeans. As a one-man goodwill brigade, Schweitzer built a hospital to treat Africans while admitting, in his own words, to suffering from a Western cultural "hereditary disease" that was incapable of cure. In effect, Europe's high intellectual tradition was not transferable even by proximity, and so the very idea of Christian mission was an oxymoron. On the other hand, colonialism might bestow upon the tribes the benefits of modern science and technology without superstitious religious distractions.

Schweitzer's lean prescription of religion as reverence for life—free of creed and sacrament—appealed to the modern mind because of its elegance, its clinical brevity, its inclusive simplicity, and its self-direction, but it left him with no obligation to learn from Africans. It is little surprise that Africans could not otherwise claim him, though they respected him and protected him as a stranger among them.

As far as one can see, all these considerations are incidental—though arguably not irrelevant—to the argument of the Comaroffs. The hegemony of science and technology that Schweitzer embodied opened a gulf with Africans. But the Comaroffs make little distinction between Europe's mercantile and technological expansion, on the one hand, and, on the other, the missionary movement and the frontier experience that ultimately transformed missions' agenda and modus operandi. Without the distinction, it would be difficult to conceive of Christianity as being involved in a reciprocal relationship, with intercultural exchange and mutual criticism appropriate to it. Hegemony defies sharing and demands conformity.

In the field, the distinction was made repeatedly. An early example of it was the Africans' demand for cultural reciprocity as described by Andrew Ross in his study of David Livingstone (1813–73). The example concerns a Xhosa chief, Sandile, who in an eloquent speech defended the chieftaincy office against attack by white authorities. The speech made an impact on Livingstone who circulated it and cited it often. Sandile challenged the colonial authorities, stating:

> No white man is without a book [the Bible]. Is it God who gave this book bids them think of blood? Some white men come and say the Caffres steal. God made a boundary by the sea and you white men cross it to rob us of our country. When the Son of God came into the world, you white men killed him. It was not black men who did that, and you white men are now killing me. Send this over the sea that they might know my mind. I was not made a chief by Englishmen, your Queen makes men chiefs. She made Smith a chief, God made me a chief. How is it that you are breaking the law of God? I do not know who will make peace in this country. I have given up my life and God may preserve it. I will never give up fighting. If you are able you may take me. If you drive me over the Bashee I will fight there also. If you kill me my bones will fight and my bones' bones will fight . . . I am angry with the English, I am tired of the English on account of their bad conduct.[21]

In his turn, Livingstone adopted the cause of the Xhosa as his own. He said that, while England sympathized with the struggles for freedom that she herself so well enjoyed, she had inconsistently been trying to crush the Xhosa whose struggle for freedom was every bit as important as that of the Magyars of

Hungary. He continued: "We are no advocates for war but we would prefer perpetual war to perpetual slavery. No nation ever secured its freedom without fighting for it."[22] He concluded that, in siding with the Africans, he was siding with the weak against the strong.

A second, much later example was Charles Domingo, a Christian African who embraced the missionary vocation for himself and made the religious-political distinction, saying it was a crucial basis for understanding contradictions in official policy. Apparently from a Roman Catholic background, Domingo was born in Mozambique but found himself adrift before arriving in British Nyasaland, now Malawi. There he took up domestic employment at the Scottish Livingstonia Mission where he eventually became a mission worker. The Scottish Mission placed much hope in Domingo's ability to carry the gospel deep into hinterland Africa. But Domingo was developing his own ideas and style.

At a conference in 1901 at the Blantyre Mission, Domingo specifically defended dancing against missionary condemnation of it as the devil's work. Domingo said dancing played a valuable role in the life of the people. Shortly after that, between 1907 and 1910 to be precise, the independent-minded Domingo became associated with the Seventh Day Baptist Mission in Malawi, and assumed the role of a pioneer agent of the expansion of the mission among Africans. Between 1910 and 1912 several African congregations were founded as a consequence. Seventh Day Baptist teaching adopted the sabbatarian rule that had an appeal for the new converts. Reading materials, including Scripture, were translated and distributed, and received with much appreciation by the Africans for whom literature and education were in short supply. Accordingly, however small its size, each native church tried to establish a school for its members. The schools taught not only religion and literacy, but also ideas that challenged white control. In the hands of the new African leaders "the Bible became, as it has so often become in moments of social tension, a great source-book for the criticism of established institutions, and a mine of authoritative texts which soon acquired the character of political slogans."[23] More than political slogans, however, Scriptural texts provided a narrative structure for community building, for a new Zion of peace and justice. In 1911 Domingo became the Nyasaland editor of the denominational publication, the *African Sabbath Recorder.*

The spectacle of native churches rapidly rising to prominence outside the mainline mission churches produced a predictable reaction from the hegemonic-minded Livingstonia Scottish missionaries, who claimed that "not much more maturity" could be expected of half-educated, self-concerned natives who were impatient of foreign control (as if foreign control deserved any better). Still, the Africans had never claimed that education was a prerequisite of faith or that colonial control was a requirement of membership in the church. Conse-quently, the anticolonial reputation of the new African churches was not in-trinsic to their motivation, but was foisted on them by the provocative social circumstances of missionary life and practice. The inconsistencies Africans observed among the white people—who, as their neighbors and friends, had brought them the gospel—caused deep disappointment, and sharpened the contrasting case Africans wished to make for Christianity. Domingo articulated this sense of disappointment, saying it was hard to find anything distinctively Christian about the Resident's attitude toward Africans. Domingo wrote that he was reluctant to accept the evidence of his experience that, for Europeans, cul-tural primacy had displaced Christianity as an ethical way of life; but he won-dered why the word *Christian*, particularly as an adjective, persisted at all. It is important to notice how early in the history of colonial rule these views were expressed.[24]

Domingo's strictures against "Europeandom" masquerading as Chris-tendom recall similar strictures by Mark Twain: "I bring you the stately matron called CHRISTENDOM—returning bedraggled, besmirched and dishonored from pirate raids in Kiaochow, Manchuria, South Africa and the Philippines; with her soul full of meanness, her pocket full of boodle and her mouth full of pious hypocrisies. Give her soap and a towel, but hide the looking-glass."[25] Equally critically, Mojola Agbebi of Nigeria declared in 1902 that "European Christianity is a dangerous thing."[26]

In the storm of the coming awakening, Agbebi and Domingo were light-ning rods. Eventually a solid throng of spirit-filled witnesses took center stage and filled the African firmament. Furnished with the Scriptures in the ver-nacular, Christianity assumed a frontier imperative and commenced its inex-orable march across the continent, intersecting the path of colonial advance with a magnetic appeal to African empowerment. The hidden appeal of Chris-tianity exerted a powerful impact on the implementation and outcome of the colonial mandate as well as on missions. By giving religion short shrift in their analysis, the Comaroffs (among others) miss this possibility in the sources and, therefore, give no credit to Africans either as agents of history or as possessing "consciousness," to use their language. Yet, enthroned in the conscience, re-ligion as such is weighted with consciousness as well as conscientiousness, as Marx acknowledged in his account of the religious sensibility of Jews.[27]

As archetypes, David Livingstone and Cecil Rhodes (d. 1902) dramatized the contrast between mission and colonialism. Rhodes was the empire builder par excellence, the great entrepreneur whose guiding rule was "philanthropy plus five per cent," while Livingstone was the anti-yogi and defender of Afri-can interests, which earned him the bitter enmity of white settlers. Both dominated Central Africa: Rhodes left a legacy of black subjugation under white domination; Livingstone of irrepressible African aspirations. The contradiction came to a head in the abortive Central African Federation of the 1950s, a federation aimed at uniting—under white minority rule—the territories of Southern Rhodesia, Northern Rhodesia, and Nyasaland, and in its violent sequel of the Rhodesian civil war. These developments showed the clash between "the Exploiter tradition of Rhodes, with [white] settler politicians as its guardians, and the Tutor tradition of Livingstone" whose guardians were the Kenneth Kaundas, the Joshua Nkomos, the Kamuzu Bandas, and the missionaries of the St. Faith's Mission in Southern Rhodesia and the Church of Scotland Mission in Nyasaland.[28]

The contrasting popular depiction of Livingstone and Rhodes is a lesson in classic role reversal and the discounting of historical reality. Rhodes was embraced as the great philanthropist who left a generous academic endowment to immortalize his name, while Livingstone became a favorite target for debunkers of mission. For example, Patrick Keatley, a Canadian writer, was worried that such a caricature had been allowed to overshadow the reality on the ground. After journeying through territories that Livingstone traversed in his own time, Keatley testified: "The best way to make contact today with David Livingstone is simply to talk to Africans. You could do this anywhere, but perhaps best in Nyasaland (Malawi), his beloved land by the lake, where his influence remains most profound. . . . He gave himself no airs, was never pompous, and never underrated the ability of his African students to make excellent missionaries themselves. 'I have no hesitation in saying one or two pious native agents are equal if not superior to Europeans.' "[29]

In summing up the contrasting legacy of Livingstone and Rhodes, Keatley observed that the forces menacing Rhodes' political dream of a permanent white establishment in Central and Southern Africa were the Africans who "were the spiritual heirs of the other empire-builder, David Livingstone. . . . And it is not particularly difficult to predict which of the two empires will last the longer, for Livingstone chose much the sounder foundation."[30] The extreme nationalist ideology that soon entrenched itself in a post-independent Zimbabwe, the former Southern Rhodesia, may be overcompensation for the race politics of Rhodes, but that nationalist ideology in its moderate version was the weathercock's reward for missionary good faith.

That outcome bore out Livingstone's prediction. He explained how it is normal to judge missions by the amount of conversions they made, but how, in his view, that was secondary to what he called the wide diffusion of better principles. He said he did not wish to diminish the importance of personal conversion, especially with regard to the Africans' own sense of its value, "but viewing our work of wide sowing of the good seed relatively to the harvest which will be reaped when all our heads are low, there can, I think, be no comparison.... Time is more important than concentration."[31] In due season, the founding president of Zambia, Kenneth Kaunda, led the singing and dancing at a dedication ceremony in Livingstone's memory, calling Livingstone "the first freedom fighter."[32]

The argument of Western hegemony, with the notion of an accompanying missionary caliphate—what the Comaroffs call a worldwide Christian commonwealth—cannot be separated from white settler politics in Africa, as Rhodesia illustrated. The generalizations in Rhodesia about African inferiority and innate subservience clashed with the teachings of Christianity. African Christian voices like Frank Ziqubu, Bernard Mizeki, and Nancy Jones, an African American, stood out in this respect. But so did the voices of many white missionaries who thereby earned the bitter opposition of white settlers. John White, a Methodist missionary who arrived in Rhodesia in 1894, was denounced by a white settler, who railed at him thus: "These damned parsons ought to be kicked out of the country. Here is one of them, and I have a damned good mind to take it out of him."[33]

The offense of the missionaries was to question the supposedly immutable, divinely ordained order of white settler superiority and the denial to blacks of the normal considerations of justice. The *Rhodesia Herald* newspaper laid the blame for black uppitiness at the door of "Exeter Hall," a reference to the Anglican evangelical wing in London that a century earlier was a force behind the founding of the CMS. The paper faulted Exeter Hall for its pernicious teaching that instilled into Africans "false notions of equality" with whites. The paper said the moral, social, and mental inferiority of Africans was innate and could not be changed even by evidence of bravery among some, such as the Matabele people. It was dangerous folly to try to civilize the African, the paper contended. Africans "are nothing but a horde of cunning, treacherous, cowardly, idle thieves."[34] A settler politician, Hans Sauer, invoked the medical and scientific works of Darwin and Huxley to back his claim of the natural inferiority of the black who, he said, should be governed by white benevolent despotism with a rod of iron.

Before long, such attitudes spread even among missionaries. The Rev. Isaac Shimmin, the head of the Wesleyan Missions, denounced African workers as mischievous and undisciplined. The Jesuit, Farther A. M. Daignault, concurred, saying Africans were grown up children and yet did not possess the virtues of children. White authority was necessary to hold them in check. As the

Rhodesia Herald put it, compulsion was imperative to get Africans to be productive (i.e., to work for whites).

Empire Strikes Back

Arabic chronicles written by Africans engage in considerable discussion about the purposive impulse in decision making, and about choice and consequence in the human endeavor. The accounts focus, for example, on order and justice as building blocks of civilization, and in scholarship on the relationship of events, their reconstruction in facts and sources, and the judgments they allow. Muslim Africans shared that tradition with the wider Islamic world, such as the works of al-Kindí, al-Farábí, and al-Jáhiz.

In his assessment of the impact of Napoleon's expedition on society, for example, the Egyptian historian 'Abd al-Rahmán al-Jabartí (1754–1825/6) refused to be bamboozled by the display of French science and technology mounted at an exhibition in Cairo and instead examined closely French ideas of justice, their interest in learning and the sciences, their discipline and devotion to their country, their effectiveness in getting things done, and—above all—their sensitivity, or, in this case, insensitivity to religion. It was the French who, in investing so much in the dazzling spectacle of an exhibition, showed they were living in a looking-glass world. Toynbee was blunt in saying that al-Jabartí thought "the French mistook the Muslims for children who could be impressed by monkey-tricks, and that this was really rather childish of the French themselves."[35]

Belonging to a family of Abyssinian Gallas long resident in Cairo, al-Jabartí's significance lies in his sensitive depiction of the bruising encounter with the French. Al-Jabartí never lost his touch for the human side of history, so that even when he wrote about conduct among the French that offended him deeply, he did not abandon the rules of factual description. His enemies never lost their humanity, and his outrage fed off that fact. They ought to know better than their deeds suggested. With al-Jabartí we never lose the "feeling that he has his finger on the pulse of life and of sharing in the true atmosphere of the country and of the period."[36]

The Senegalese writer, Cheikh Hamidou Kane pursued the theme of one humanity through a character in his novel *Ambiguous Adventure*. He created a scenario in which the West encounters unsuspected limitations of its power on the colonial frontier. Paul Lacroix, the local French administrator, had arrived to impose a secular French school on a religious community not yet fully recovered from the throes of its holy resistance. Lacroix defended his mission in the name of the superiority of Western science. His African interlocutor, called the knight, objected that science established an allegedly perfect world that merely echoed itself in its own evidence, and was thus bereft of any abiding moral resonance. That left the West with a clamorous despair that stifled the spirit, he concluded. When Lacroix bristled at this and asked impishly to what he might be born, the knight rose to the challenge: "To a more profound truth. Evidence is a quality of the surface. Your science is the triumph of evidence, a proliferation of the surface. It makes you masters of the external, but at the same time it exiles you there, more and more."

On the West's global expansion, the knight pointed out that mainland Europe would itself be changed by the unforeseen consequences of frontier responses. He declared: "Every hour that passes brings a supplement of ignition to the crucible in which the world is being fused. We have not had the same past, you and ourselves, but we shall have, strictly, the same future. The era of separate destinies has run its course. In that sense, the end of the world has indeed come for every one of us, because no one can any longer live by the simple carrying out of what he himself is."

Oral traditions of premodern Africa as well as much creative writing similarly dwell at length on themes of power and responsibility, wisdom and folly, bravery and cowardice, honor and wretchedness, loyalty and guile, restraint and ruthlessness, and so on.[37] All this is evidence that the frontier was not simply a flat placid corridor that was waiting to be annexed without recourse by the forces of metropolitan hegemony, but a theater of ferment where Europe could not dictate the outcome of events. History is not just mortgaged to outsiders or to the future, and the only thing inevitable about history is that it is not inevitable. Choice is at the heart of it.

Cheikh Kane was cognizant of the fact that even in the most unpromising of circumstances, choice may favor underdogs. That was the view he forcefully expressed in a searching critique of Europe's colonial project. A leading character in his novel, the Most Royal Lady of the Diallobé, summons an apprehensive community and directs it to surrender and send its children to the French school. But such surrender, she cautions, is like sowing seeds in roughed up soil and waiting for the results to complicate what otherwise looked like an act of abject surrender. In other words, giving in can be a form of disguised resistance. She continued:

> But people of Diallobé, remember our fields when the rainy season is approaching. We love our fields very much, but what do we do to them? We plough them up and burn them: we kill them. In the same

way, recall this: what do we do with our reserves of seed when the rain has fallen? We would like to eat them, but we bury them in the earth. Folk of the Diallobé, with the arrival of the foreigners has come the tornado which announces the great hibernation of our people. My opinion—I, the Most Royal Lady—is that our best seeds and our dearest fields—those are our children.[38]

We do not normally or credibly think of the class of colonizers or the colonized as in any way being culturally challenged, much less being culturally "nativized," and perhaps that is because we lack appreciation for historical irony. There is, however, no shortage of evidence for such irony. A report in the *New York Times* pointed out that "in many parts of Africa, the church seems embroiled in a phenomenon common to those who conquer, only to find themselves being assimilated into the manners of the conquered. Thus in Zaire [Democratic Republic of Congo] for instance, a churchgoer can see a Belgian clergyman, clad in a cap of monkey skins, leading acolytes who carry spears along with the cross and who equate the Christian saints with the ancestral spirits of animism."[39]

The point is well illustrated in the personal story of Charles de Foucauld (d. 1916), who embarked on the course of imperial hegemony when his path took an unexpected, dramatic turn and he became a hermit apostle to the desert Tuaregs. He had been a lapsed Catholic and was a young officer in the French colonial army fighting in Algeria when he witnessed scenes of Muslim religious devotion that led him to question his carefree dolce vita lifestyle. His biographer gave an account of his experience thus:

> The skirmish continued for a good half hour, with Foucauld calling at last for fresh ammunition supplies. There was no response from his own Arabs who had taken cover with the pack animals. Furious, Foucauld galloped back to read the riot act to his men—only to find them prostrating themselves in prayer . . . On the opposite hillside, too, the firing had stopped. At the risk of being shot like sitting ducks, the Uled Sidi Sheikh (snipers) had emerged from cover, turned their backs to the sunset and bowed down to the east . . . *Allahu akbar*. A strange silence filled the little wadi, a stillness that reminded Foucauld of the awesome quiet of Nancy Cathedral in his boyhood days when he still believed in God. That silence, in fact, had meant to the boy that he was indeed in the presence of God. He had laughed at himself since for such mawkish credulity, but he did not laugh now. These Arabs took God seriously. They had stopped fighting be-

cause it was time to pray. . . . They had exposed themselves to possible massacre to prostrate themselves before their god, refused to neglect prayer even in the face of the enemy.[40]

There are also mundane examples of the genre, such as European commercial adventurers prospecting for trading advantage and finding themselves outflanked by a local agent armed with better intelligence and contacts. The strangers from Europe gratefully accepted a deal for a share, and only a share, in the business. Entire coastlines of the colonial world are dotted with structural relics of such compromises. At the sublime end of the genre, however, Foucauld's experience finds an echo in that of many others, including Louis Massignon (1883–1962), the author of the magisterial four volume study of the Persian pantheist Súfí, Mansúr al-Halláj (d. 922). In a fit of ecstatic frenzy, al-Halláj threw caution to the winds and declared, *ana al-haqq*—"I am the truth," or, "I am God," truth being God's exclusive attribute. To the ears of the pious the statement was deemed blasphemous and deserving of death. Al-Halláj paid with his life. He was seized as a heretic in 922 in the 'Abbásid inquisition and exposed on a gibbet before being decapitated and burned.

Nevertheless, a vogue developed around al-Halláj's name as spiritual aspirants and sympathizers formed cells of devotion in his memory. Al-Halláj's tomb in west Baghdad went on to acquire the sanctity proper to that of a saint. Massignon returned to his Catholic faith after having experienced, while living in the Middle East, the faith-inspired graciousness and warm hospitality of his Muslim hosts who tended him with care and devotion in a time of illness. By way of pious restitution, Massignon set out to rehabilitate al-Halláj's stained reputation for posterity by adding luster to it, a task in which he succeeded brilliantly. With all of al-Halláj's intractable complexity and legendary elusiveness, and in spite of the heavy pall of heresy that fell on him, Massignon repossessed al-Halláj and restored him once and for all to the general stream of Muslim religious thought.

Such examples of intercultural breakthrough are proof that the West's cultural citadel was far from invincible. The missionary movement turned colonial empires into cathedrals of variety, difference, and irony, making religion in the empire a Trojan horse. The idea that Europe could take other lands and impose its own ideas and standards on the people was abandoned in deference to local realities for long-term security and stability. Defending his controversial novel, *Satanic Verses*, Salman Rushdie said that this pluralist view of life was the distinguishing mark of the modern world,[41] though its roots are arguably much older. In its local and localized form, religion demonstrated the limitations of power to trample on the subject races. Europe's own sense of identity and purpose were of necessity implicated in its overseas enterprise. As Kane rightly noted, the era of separate identities had, indeed, run its course.

Uprising

These examples of intercultural exchange and criticism suggest that the boundaries of culture contact were seldom neat and fixed, or the results predictable. Insofar as persuasion and choice were involved, Christianity prospered in that unstable, complex milieu. The public career of Jomo Kenyatta, Kenya's founding president, dramatizes the truth of this view. In his book, *Facing Mount Kenya* (which was published in 1938, two years after he returned to Kenya from London), Kenyatta launched an impassioned nationalist defense of African culture. A student of anthropology under Malinowski, Kenyatta set out the case for African agency under conditions of missionary and white settler politics in colonial Kenya.

On the face of it, Kenyatta supported the charge of wholesale destruction of African religion and culture at the hands of missionaries. He spoke about how missionaries regarded the African "as a clean slate on which anything could be written. [The African] was supposed to take wholeheartedly all the religious dogmas of the white man and keep them sacred and unchallenged, no matter how alien to the African mode of life. The Europeans based their assumption on the conviction that everything the African did or thought was evil."[42] Kenyatta charged that missionaries thought of Africans as depraved souls to be rescued from "eternal fire," and consequently "they set out to uproot the African, body and soul, from his old customs and beliefs, and put him in a class by himself, with all his tribal customs shattered and his institutions trampled upon. The African, having been detached from his family and tribe, was expected to follow the white man's religion without questioning whether it was suited for his condition of life or not."[43]

Among the targets of cultural violation, Kenyatta argued, were the Africans' sense of community and the place that political and moral authority occupied in that scheme. Kenyatta said the missionaries imposed their culture of individualism on the African and, by that process, wrought havoc on all African society. The missionaries compounded the deeply oppressive character of colonial rule in Africa by paving the way for swift and decisive access to the hearts and minds of Africans who, ingesting the bitter pill of political defeat, yielded their *amour propre* and became brainwashed subjects of a white supremacist order. The gospel entered African culture like a tranquilizing needle and came out like the sword of domination. The school represented missionary bad faith, and was more insidious than the peremptory colonial system. The school simultaneously had the qualities of cannon and of magnet. With the cannon, it shared the attribute of the compulsion of armed combat. In fact, the school made conquest permanent and assimilation secure. With the magnet, the school shared the quality of invisible influence, of the power of hidden irresistible force acting on young, impressionable minds. Still, like the magnet and the cannon, or the needle and the sword, the school aspired to fill only a mundane, mechanistic role. There was no question of teaching moral values that transcended the demands of colonial expedience.

Writing always involves a certain recomposition of the facts of experience, the nationalist variety no less so. Yet there is no gainsaying Kenyatta's deep sense of cultural betrayal by missionaries. In his lively, if prickly, account of the extent of colonial and missionary complicity in the assault on Africa, Kenyatta and Africans of his ilk provoked a question that echoes one of our own: namely, how could a system of complete and comprehensive control by mission and colonialism leave any room for objection and resistance? In the event, by taking such objection and resistance seriously, Kenyatta signaled a critical modification of the idea of absolute colonial supremacy that allowed him to sketch out in precise ways the urgent choice he and his fellow political agitators felt it was their paramount responsibility to make. Nationalist protest proved that Africans had not lost all the initiative and that colonial mastery was not irreversible.

The intellectual response Africans mounted showed the crucial role religion played in that nationalist campaign. Accordingly, in 1929 a new religious movement came into being called *Watu wa Mungu*[44] ("People of God"), or sometimes also *Arathi* ("prophets" or "seers"). Partly in response to the Church of Scotland Mission Gikuyu's prohibition of clitoridectomy, the movement soon embraced a wide range of internal cultural and political issues.[45]

Under the *Watu wa Mungu* Africans took the offensive against white domination and missionary interference. The most potent weapon in the struggle turned out ironically to be the very Gikuyu Bible that was the product of missionary translation. That an oracle of the highest and most universal authority was available in the Gikuyu language broke the spell of local stigma and tapped a rich vein in the cultural resolve. The fact that the Gikuyu Bible contained stories of slavery and freedom, captivity and liberation, exile and homecoming, death and resurrection, made it a primer for the decolonization campaign and a godsend for nationalist aspirations. The distinction between a civilized colonial order and an uncivilized primitive Africa could now be superseded by the more authoritative distinction in Scripture between Pharaoh and Moses, between Babylon and Ethiopia, between masters and subjects, and between Caesar and God. Kenyatta declared: "The African, faced with these problems and seeing how his institutions have been shattered, looked again in the Book of Books," called in Gikuyu *Ibuka ria Ngai*, "the Book of God." The God of this book, called by the people Mwene Nyaga, was the God of their history and would deliver them from the hands of their enemies as He did the Israel of old.

In preparation for that time of vindication, members of the *Watu wa Mungu* movement adopted a radical program of commitment to communal life, giving up private ownership of property, including their homes, banding together and adopting an itinerant lifestyle. They composed prayers that blended Gikuyu and biblical materials, and performed their rituals "standing in a picturesque manner. In their prayer to Mwene-Nyaga they hold up their arms to the sky facing Mount Kenya; and in this position they recite their prayers, and in doing so they imitate the cries of wild beasts of prey, such as lion and leopard, and at the same time they tremble violently. Their trembling, they say, is the sign of the Holy Ghost, Roho Motheru, entering in them. While thus possessed with the spirit, they are transformed from ordinary beings and are in communion with Mwene-Nyaga."[46]

In one prayer circulated among members of the *Watu wa Mungu* community, the sentiment of Africans unjustly bearing the yoke of foreign domination—but, on account of it, assured vindication with courage, power, and the gift of prophecy, in fulfillment of ancient promise—acts like a lightning rod to galvanize the hosts, seen and unseen.

> O Lord, your power is greater than all powers.
> Under your leadership we cannot fear anything.
> It is you who has given us prophetical power and has
>   enabled us to foresee and interpret everything.
> We know no other leader but you alone.
> We beseech you to protect us in all trials and torments.
> We know you are with us, just as you were with our
>   ancient ancestors.
> Under your protection there is nothing we cannot overcome.
> Peace, praise ye Ngai, peace, peace, peace be with us.[47]

Recognizing immediately the danger posed to authority by such indigenous mobilization, officials decided to meet the *Watu wa Mungu* head-on. In 1934 bloody clashes with the police took place, with the government claiming that the *Watu wa Mungu* was committed to fomenting a general insurrection aimed at the foundations of the colonial order. Whether that was a self-fulfilling prophecy or whether it showed real insight into the delayed effects of vernacular empowerment, in the end the colonial system did not survive the forces that the *Watu wa Mungu* activated, forces that included the violent Mau Mau rebellion. Kenya was subjected to oppressive rule under a state of emergency declared in October 1952, which remained in effect until 1959. Kenyatta was detained in 1952 under the emergency, and released in 1961. He became prime minister when the country gained its independence in December 1963, and president in 1964 when Kenya became a republic within the Commonwealth. It became immediately apparent that Kenyatta was not the demon colonial propaganda made him out to be and that he embodied the attribute of a genuine patriot who knew what was in the best interests of his people, not to say those who stamped on them. It transformed the relationship between masters and subjects into that of good neighbors and happy citizens, and both as a free and proud people.

Perhaps inevitably, and perhaps also avoidably, under Kenyatta's successors that thrilling possibility of mutual acceptance took a heavy toll, to the disappointment of many on both sides of the race line. Yet that setback fell considerably short of the deluge everyone predicted, thanks in large part to the choice made by Kenyatta and his colleagues in Kenya and elsewhere in East, Central, and Southern Africa at a pivotal stage of the nationalist uprising. It is a remarkable fact that, in spite of overwhelming grounds for class action retaliation by the much-maligned tribes, sub-Saharan Africa was spared the race war that would have been a sanguinary and logical outcome of centuries of abuse and insult. Edward Blyden, the nineteenth-century prophet of black nationalism, once noted that the Africans' relation to the rest of the world had always been strange and peculiar: Africans had not mingled with other races except to serve them.[48]

The politics of decolonization, however, changed that axiom of inevitable disadvantage. Under their own leaders the subject races could embrace reconciliation with their old masters. At the banquet celebrating the country's independence and in the presence of Queen Elizabeth II, Kenyatta expressed sentiments of that order to a surprised and appreciative audience. He intended his hearers to understand that, whatever the odds, the West should not underestimate the capacity of people to shape their own destiny and to participate in what touched their interests and gave meaning to their lives. In that sense, *Facing Mount Kenya* was an impressive achievement for the national cause, its anti-Western strictures appropriate to the milieu of a prime time political audience.

The vernacular Bible supplied the vocabulary for the politics of decolonization even though missionary claims for historical chronology justified the continuation of the colonial system. For a time, the missionary role in the creation of the vernacular Bible was construed as another attempt at regulating African culture, so that rules of grammar and orthography could be fixed with a supremacist goal in mind. Vernacular linguistic ideas were thus confirmed by a successful translation, say, of the Nicene Creed. If African languages coped well enough with the orthodox subtleties of phrases like "true God from God . . . begotten not made . . . one in being with the Father," they were accorded qualified approval.

Yet such foreign assumptions conflicted with the decision to adopt the vernacular names for God as the God of the Christian Scriptures and worship. It made no difference how missionaries arrived at the vernacular names for God; it was enough that they arrived there and nowhere else. As a consequence, Christianity's transplant theological infrastructure underwent radical vernacular reconstruction. In the African idiom God kept crowded company, mixing with superior and minor deities, high and low spirits, lineage, clan, and ancestor spirits, and thus scrambling convergent lines of social status and religious hierarchy. Kenyatta added a political twist to that paradox. His mighty fortress was Mwene-Nyaga.

Ironically, colonial governments, too, felt indebted to the vernacular success of missionary linguists. In North Africa nearly fifty dictionaries and grammars of mother tongues were printed between 1892 and 1914 on the basis of work carried out by the White Fathers. In 1906, Bishop Bazin's dictionary of the Bambara ("Bamana") language was published in Paris by the French government. In Uganda, the Runyoro prayer book was printed in 1907 at the printing press set up by Julien Gorju (d. 1942), the "Vicar Apostolic of Urundi." It was impossible to control the plain import of such vernacular linguistic activity and to restrict it to the confines of the mission station. The effects were irrepressible. As William Sharp (under the pseudonym of Fiona Macleod) noted with respect to the old Gaelic race, the last tragedy for broken nations was not the loss of power and distinction, or even of country. "The last tragedy, and the saddest, is when the treasured language dies slowly out, when winter falls upon the legendary remembrance of a people."[49] Bible translation helped preserve the people's language, and thus averted "the last and saddest tragedy" of defeat and loss.[50]

In consequence, in both the colonial and missionary rhetoric the line separating foreign overrule and local autonomy was often smudged. In theory the colonial and missionary thrust stemmed from a unified impulse, which was the assumption that good government meant rule by whites in the same way that sound religion meant the values of Western civilization. From the point of view of the missionary, the gospel was but a conduit for the material benefits and ideas of Western civilization, and these views were inhospitable to the historical fact of Christianity's vernacular multicultural profile.

Reciprocity

Yet, as F. B. Welbourn argued in his acute study of religion and politics in the decolonization process in East Africa, the symmetry of Christianity and Western culture was mirrored by the symmetry of Christianity and African culture.[51] In the eyes of missionaries, the shift of location to Africa provided the mandate for exchanging Paganism for Christianity, since a Western blueprint was now available to check and correct local ideas and practices. For both sides the frontier was paramount, but for contrasting reasons. With their Enlightenment assumptions, missionaries committed themselves to instituting on the frontier a secular dispensation as a demonstration of the most enlightened and most appropriate form of the gospel. English Protestant missionaries in Uganda promoted the establishment of a British protectorate over Buganda as remedy for the widespread Arab slave trade. For the missionaries who hammered out the Uganda Agreement of 1900, which consolidated British control, the instrument of a secular state was an ally and a fruit of the gospel. Bishops and other members of the clergy filled a dual role as religious officials and cultural agents. The missionary, the explorer, the settler, and the government administrator all shared—and were seen by Africans as sharing—identical interests and objectives. These Western agents also shared a common mind about Africans, who, whether as converts or as colonial subjects, they felt must be changed from what they were before the white man arrived. In its original conception as well as in its effect, conversion required secular vetting to render it desirable.

This brings us to the contrasting African symmetry. Unlike the Comaroffs, Welbourn insists that Western hegemony was not the whole story, for there was an equally powerful African side to the correspondence of Christianity and Western culture. In 1953, when the English bishop of Uganda was consulted about the deportation of the Kabaka, the reigning king, the Kabaka's African supporters struck back by refusing to attend church services. They moved their opposition to the religious terrain by contending that only the old gods could restore the Kabaka. While missionaries took their place in the Executive

Council as representatives of African interests in colonial Kenya, seeing nothing amiss with the church's endorsement of the Western secular order, in Uganda and elsewhere African politicians, including those who were Christian, backed Christian candidates for chieftaincy office whose claim to the title was rooted in dynastic legitimacy. Just as in the West where Christianity endorsed the "traditional" status quo of the secular order, so in Africa Christianity endorsed the norms of lineage politics.[52]

English Precedent

Africans demanded that Christianity be responsive to their situation, implying that a compelling parallel existed in the West with the blessing of all concerned, missionary, explorer, settler, and government administrator alike. The Western church installed many a generous benefactor of good causes as bishops without the slightest twinge of conscience about their religious views or moral character. It was enough that such recognition reinforced the secular establishment. Sir Ernest Woodward gives the example of a bishop whose consecration was allowed to go forward even though he did not believe in the resurrection. The man's many other "excellences" were considered sufficient qualification in the meantime, with the onus for remedying his other deficiencies remitted to the sphere of the work of God's spirit. There was still time, it was said, because divine grace was never content to leave its work unfinished.[53] Officials placed all their confidence in the proposition that, once it was established, the secular sphere would render religion superfluous, and that the secular order would become a substitute religion in terms of giving meaning to human life. Secularization as reverse conversion would wean people from religion. If the religion survived, it would be as a secular foster child, with the church becoming a national trim.

All this implies that godliness was not a prerequisite for national citizenship any more than loyalty was the monopoly of organized religion. Establishmentarianism thus restricted Parliament's role in religion, with the law creating a religious sphere under the Crown. That had an inhibiting effect on sectarian splits which were so widespread in seventeenth-century England and which became endemic in the Free Churches.[54] In theory, under the Act of Supremacy, the monarch was vested with authority to "extirp all error, heresies, and other enormities and abuses." In practice, however, Parliament and the monarch had no role in making doctrine. Thus, even as late as 1646, Thomas Edwards had occasion to list sixteen groups and over two hundred "errors, heresies, [and] blasphemies."[55] The endemic battles of church-state relations and natural selection and creationism that have, for example, recently rocked political life in the United States were largely absent in Britain and elsewhere. Those battles would be what Powell partly had in mind when he spoke of sectarianism.

African Precedent

Yet, in Africa there was a sudden and inexplicable retreat from trust in Africa's venerable customs or in divine grace to look favorably on those customs and make them an acceptable frame for Christian adoption, and an increase in the suspicion of a double standard. Accordingly, Western strictures against African culture elicited African strictures against Western culture, with the African frontier turning that scrutiny into an exercise in local self-defense.

The Africans' disillusionment was delayed. The people had enthusiastically embraced Christianity because they thought that missionaries were their friends and their partners against the slave trade and other injustices that afflicted African societies. But after the 1885 Berlin Congress, which partitioned the continent into spheres of colonial control, a decisive change was seen in missionary attitudes. When African culture came under systematic assault from the new colonial masters, the missionaries connived, leaving Africans feeling betrayed. The hopes of the early days of Christian conversion were dashed, and instead of African society being protected it was being pulled down. In the ensuing widespread disarray and confusion Africans returned to the first assurance they received about the gospel and concluded that the change in missions was not their fault but that of the missionaries. They began looking to themselves for a solution.

As tends to happen with transplant systems, Christianity under African conditions revealed its indigenous potential, but also its objectionable Western presumptions. Africans came to feel that the West had, perhaps, paid too high a price to post-Enlightenment demands for a downsized religion, with the deep discount leaving Christianity too affordable to be worth promoting in its own right, and too domesticated to entrust into the hands of others. It was easier to sell schools, clean water, carbolic soap, good roads, and good manners than to face the awkward claims of Jesus of Nazareth since that might compromise Western paternalism. A polarized value system promoted the quality of life over the quality of faith; the West presided over the quality of life with the authority that it could not exercise over the quality of faith, at least not faith as trust in God directly. In that sense, Christianity itself was interpreted to mean the West's civilizational advantage. The material benefits of the West now being extended to Africa carried the seal of God.

That claim lost its bite in the transplant environment of colonial subjugation. Christianity came into the world already culturally attached, as the apostles made clear. In the African phase, that cultural attachment required an affirmation of local tradition, and a corresponding diminished role for missionary supervision. Missionaries came upon African anticipations of the gospel message with something of a mild shock, not knowing whether they should be pleased or suspicious. As one missionary testified, "It seems as if one were telling them an old story, with which they had been quite familiar but had now half forgotten."[56] Such anticipations were many and commonplace, but missionary ambivalence blunted their impact.

Missionaries were unprepared for the unforeseen consequences of their own work. In a note in 1922, one writer expressed his forebodings, saying the rapid development of Africans in Kenya in a year and a half of missionary education was unsettling. Africans were now in a position to defend themselves against oppression and exploitation. But, he added with disquiet, "What is much more to be feared is native risings led by young educated Christians." Students in mission schools were carriers of ideas that threatened the colonial order. The new generation of young Christians, he warned, posed a challenge that could not be ignored or postponed. Yet all the weapons of war cannot arm fear. From the African side, mission-educated young were preferable to missionaries in representing African interests.[57] The gospel was destined for all people and nations, and would be vindicated by the role of local people, not foster care by expatriates.

With foresight, missionary statesmen of the nineteenth century, such as Henry Venn (d. 1872) of England, Rufus Anderson (d. 1880) of the United States, and Gustaf Warneck (d. 1910) of Germany, were much in tune with the sentiment of "a self-supporting, self-governing, and self-propagating church," which would be reared on local cultural roots and establish itself in former missionary territories. Having tasted power at a safe distance from the home board, however, many serving missionaries flinched. When the conference of Foreign Mission Boards of the United States sent a notice in 1895 to the missionaries working among the Zulu with the request to encourage the idea of a self-supporting church there, the notice was disregarded. But when the circular was translated into Zulu, the words for self-support (*ukuzondla*) and self-government (*ukuziphatha*) completely changed the dynamics on the ground. Reading the Zulu circular, the African leaders promptly concluded "that the missionaries were withholding from them the rights of Congregational

Churches," that is the right to form independent, self-propagating congregations.[58] Such was the potency of translation that the Zulu Congregationalist Church was formed in 1896 as a result.

Missionaries had cause to wonder whether they had created a monster with their vernacular translation projects. For their turn, Africans wondered whether the West had rendered Christianity so nearly unrecognizable from what it was in the hands of the apostles that the religion was unfit for the African hands for which it was primarily intended. A new breed of charismatic prophets stepped forward to contend that God, whom the West claimed as their own, had in fulfillment of the Scriptures spoken in sundry and diverse ways to the tribes of Africa and confirmed it with signs and wonders and with diverse miracles. Christianity's ascetic and monastic ideal of renunciation, for example, had helped to covert Europeans, but for the Africans facing the threat of political subjugation and exile in their countries, the challenge was to resist foreign invaders and to reclaim their culture. After all, Protestant missionaries who considered hygiene and tidiness fruits of the spirit did not come donning the habits of monks.

The religion in African hands became a different custom. The claim of the early apostles, that Christianity was destined for the world in spite of every attempt by the Roman empire to stamp out the religion, made it reasonable for Africans to insist that they should not be made an exception by imperial sponsorship being required of them. Christianity was born in exile, and in Africa it found a homecoming compatible with its exile origins.[58] Exodus was for the intruders.

The reservations Africans expressed about the Archbishop of Canterbury's visit to Uganda in the 1950s were the same as those they expressed about the Queen's visit, for in both cases the issue was about the European ideas of preeminence without regard to local custom. To have ordained priests in Europe making daily supplications in their prayers to God for Queen and country was little different from having priests in Africa making daily supplications to God for office-holders and for the people. The criticism was reserved for fellow Africans who sided with the missionaries. Such Africans had little excuse for abandoning the indigenous cause while wrongheadedly embracing the missionary cause; by making that choice, the Africans placed themselves in the same incongruous position as the missionaries who, at least, had the excuse of a fall back at hand. They could always return home, and nearly all did, fulfilling an African proverb that says "even though he has a bed, a stranger will return home."

Confronted with the missionary provocation that depicted Africa as a subjugated foreign field, Africans appealed to home advantage. Confident of their birthright, Africans regarded their dispossession as a breach of their God-given rights, and demanded the end of colonial rule. As Africans saw it, religion was their ally in the cause of justice and freedom. For the colonial authorities, religion was a matter of establishment entitlement, which did not include Roman Catholicism,[59] Islam, or African primal religions. Africans noticed the discrepancy.

That missionary exclusion was extended to the field of Christian worship, too. The organ, for instance, was a standard fixture in Christian worship in the West, despite a lack of evidence of its requirement in the Gospels, yet the use of the more ancient drum in African was attacked as unbiblical and heathen. The contradiction aroused local resentment.

The drum enjoyed a high status in Ugandan life. On the ceremonial occasion of installing a chief in office, the Kabaka presented him with a drum as an insignia of office. John Roscoe describes the high place the drum occupied in Ugandan national life. When Christianity came, it was met with drums and drumming. Taken around 1900, an old photograph of Namirembe Cathedral in Kampala shows a youth in flowing white robe standing on two layers of bricks to strike a large kettledrum with two wooden rollers. Behind the youth stands an older man also striking a smaller drum slung from his neck. To the left of him is a third drum that appears at the time unattended. In the photograph, the church seems to be a cathedral of drums, allowing a youth to occupy center stage in the act of performing on one. It did not take long, however, for missionary reaction to set in and the drum was toppled from its place in Christian worship. "Allan J. Lush, writing in 1935, reports that although drums were still used, the majority of young Baganda were ignorant about their names and history. He attributes this to the end of despotic rule [sic] and the adoption of Western ideas."[60] Housed in the belfry, the church bell replaced the drum, at least in the colonial rhetoric.[61]

The boisterous nature of African worship that missionaries took delight in attributing to the untamed, unredeemed state of the African soul was, in fact, much closer to the world of David and Isaiah than Western modes of worship, and, like so much else, could be vindicated with explicit scriptural warrant. The psalmist calls on the people to clap their hands and shout to God without restriction as to what instrumental accompaniment is allowed: not only organs, but also high sounding cymbals, timbrel, and dance, including singing aloud even in bed![62] Scripture testified that David, almost naked, danced before the Lord with all his might, paying little heed to those whose cultural sensibilities he offended.[63] Even when it is deemed culturally undignified, uninhibited enthusiasm may not be devoid of spiritual merit entirely, as David showed.[64] The West's Teutonic inhibitions about worship as an expressionless formal activity in which the body is propped up in a state just shy of rigor mortis contradicted every instinct and reflex in African life. It stood little chance of success. A wet blanket cannot muffle a drum. In this matter, the witness of Scripture backed African sentiments against the West's highbrow cultural tastes.

Religion in the African schema included more than denominations; it included Islam and primal religions in their total environment, particularly in the political thrust of their teachings. Confident of the invincibility of a unified secular order, colonial and missionary officials modified their stance and included primal religions under the Pax Britannica. Religious pluralism did not involve plural state jurisdictions: persons might be Anglican, Presbyterian, Methodist, Catholic, Muslim, or pagan and still live in one or more states. In spite of the limitation that primal religions were ethnic based and, in theory, an obstacle to nation building, colonial administrators gave them protection and sometimes even sponsored them as a foil against a competing Pan Islam.[65]

Religious dissent and splintering no longer connoted political sedition and, thanks to the safeguards of secular control, religious differences ceased to carry any structural threat. The modern nation state thrived from the multiplicity of religious allegiance, and became the exclusive embodiment of the transcendent national will in relation to which religion ceded absolute authority. Delavignette was correct that Europe's mission was concerned with its mastery in the world, and that only the European was qualified to undertake it. By extension, only the particular form of Christianity that represented Europe's mastery was accorded a place in that scheme.[66]

Politics as the art of the possible inclined too readily to expedience, and, as Africans were disposed to see it, expedience was too easily co-opted by supervening powers. It was debatable in these circumstances whether the West's cultural takeover could allow Christianity to rise to its potential as a world religion. In hindsight, it is remarkable the extent to which colonial co-option weakened Christianity by presenting it as a freshly minted European creed. Africans rejected that view by circulating the religion as local currency. We might recall that it was in similar circumstances of attempts at colonial suppression that Pan-Islamic anticolonial sentiments brought a renewed Islam to power. In the end, the irony was that, instead of shrinking as a mere colonial instrument, Christianity survived to achieve global range in its post-Western awakening, an outcome that completely befuddled the post-Christian West. It would be helpful in the next chapters to explore further the roots and nature of the new Christian awakening.

5

Pillar of Charismatic Renewal

Obstacles and Horizons

Independency

The eighteenth-century Pietist movement in Europe took a confessional stance against worldliness in the church, demanding repossession of the religion's moral autonomy against the compromisers. Because of the corrupt nature of the world Pietist leaders considered the general diffusion of Christianity in the structures of state and society as tantamount to blasphemy. It was an iconoclastic theology that demanded a Manichaean "discontinuity" between faith and worldly institutions, between the cultivation of piety and the affairs of the workaday world.[1] Pre-dating the formal colonial empires of the nineteenth century, the Pietist movement inspired the founding of the Protestant missionary movement, which spread abroad the idea of keeping well clear of political entanglements, a position adopted, for example, by William Carey and Joshua Marshman in India, Johann Vanderkemp in South Africa, Franz Michael Zahn and Johannes Zimmermann in Ghana and Togo, and J. Lewis Krapf in East Africa. Both Vanderkemp and Zimmerman, for example, married former slaves to defy prevailing racial strictures.

Among subject people this Pietist legacy spawned anticolonial ferment. Here was a Christian group from the West saying government was the enemy of the gospel. It was not difficult for Africans to identify with such a group, and the government in question with colonial rule, so that even the subsequent entanglement of missionaries with the colonial regime did little to shake that faith. In fact, it reinforced it. In 1847, disease and famine ravaged the island of New Caledonia, sparking an antimissionary uprising in which a lay brother, Blaise Marmoiton, was killed. The people attributed their troubles to the landing on the island in 1843 of William Douarre, the first Vicar Apostolic of New Caledonia, who came in a French corvette. A French ship landed after the troubles and rescued the surviving missionaries, transferring them to safety on another island.[2] It was not just sympathetic magic that led people to make the incriminating colonial connection; it was the law of cultural preservation spiked with Pietist scruples.

For the colonial powers the message of Christianity was less important than the medium. Their interest in mission was, therefore, tactical. Under the Third Republic, for example, France set aside its aggressive anticlericalism to sponsor Catholic missions abroad because it saw missions as advantageous to the colonial strategy. Missionaries obliged by acquiescing in the sequestration of native lands, the suppression of local languages in favor of French in order to facilitate assimilation, and the granting of privileges to white settler communities. In the colonial scheme, Christianity was politically useful, and could be utilized to bolster colonial rule. It was resisted as such.

The collaboration of missions contributed to the goal of promoting secular civilization, and that complicated the response to religion. For the people the gospel meant freedom from domination; for Europeans it meant freedom to dominate. The vernacular projects of mission, however, scrambled the lines of authority used to rule the natives. Accordingly, the creation of the vernacular Bible, whose power was fortuitously bolstered by the collapse of the nationalist dream in the post-independence era, upset this complacent attitude about Christianity as a colonial strategy. Religion provided ironic illumination of the circumstances of colonialism, affording Africans a sense of identity more potent than the abstract and contested idea of citizenship. In many places, for example, anniversaries of political independence were far less popular than religious feasts, including those celebrating the birthdays of charismatic leaders, both living and dead.

Concerning loyalty to one's culture, few Africans were revolutionaries in the sense of wielding Ockham's razor against hallowed tradition, intending to replace it with new principles of innovation. Many became rebels in order better to resist the attack on their primal heritage, which they regarded as their birthright. Their revolt was motivated by a conservative outlook, understood as preserving inherited tribal institutions such as veneration of the ancestors, deference to the elders, and respect for tradition.

Instead of permanent alienation or mistrust, a reasonable resolution of the cultural conflict lay in the glad acceptance that Western culture, which once was seeded with Christian values, offered an example for Africa. A direct comparison may be made with respect to loyalty to church and country contained in the Parliamentary act establishing the Church of England. That was the subject of a British House of Commons debate in 1984 calling for the disestablishment of the Church of England. At that debate Enoch Powell, a former senior Conservative MP, but on this occasion speaking as an Official Unionist MP of Northern Ireland, denounced the measure as an attack on the English church and nation and a contravention of the 1534 Act of Supremacy.[3] This cultural establishment that Powell describes echoes African views that the church should assume the forms of their own national cultures free of foreign vetting. The European precedent made African demands historically reasonable and necessary.

Nationalist objection to Christianity being imposed on Africa in its Western garb was not an objection to the West imparting Christianity, but rather to the West's attempt to impose colonial rule as a Christian mandate. In the nationalist rhetoric that sentiment was to the fore, and it led Africans to believe that the West's successful Christianization held a similar possibility for their own societies without the onus of foreign rule.

Mojola Agbebi (1860–1917) of Nigeria, a prominent figure of the movement leading to Christian independency and an avowed admirer of Henry Venn (d. 1872), argued in a sermon in 1902 that the implicit challenge of the success of the English Book of Common Prayer (BCP) for Christian Africans was that they should produce its counterpart in an African Book of Common Prayer. He cited the BCP's preface to the effect that the authors condemn no other nations, nor prescribe anything but to their own people. They would urge every country to use their own ceremonies to set forth God's honor and glory.

Agbebi pleaded for a positive acceptance of Christianity's capacity for cultural adaptability. He pointed out that even the BCP had a diverse history, as per the Salisbury Prayer Book, the Bangor Prayer Book, the York Prayer Book, and the Lincoln Prayer Book. Tastes differ. English tunes and meters, English songs and hymns, many so unsuited to the African reality, had been effective only in sapping the talent for hymnology among Christian Africans. Agbebi continued: the joys of the Christian life are one; redemption is one; Christ is one; God is one; but our tongues are various and our styles innumerable.[4]

For Agbebi, the Muslim contrast, or what he freely construed as the Muslim contrast, backed his plea for a distinctive African Christianity. He wrote:

The African Moslem, our co-religionist [sic], though he reads the
Koran in Arabic and counts his beads as our Christian brother
the Roman Catholic does, and though he repeats the same formula of
prayer in an unknown tongue from mosques and minarets five
times a day throughout Africa, yet he spreads no common prayer
before him in his devotions and carries no hymn-book in his worship of the Almighty. His dress is after the manner of the Apostles and
the Prophets, and his name, though indicating his faith, was never
put on in a way to denationalize or [to] degrade him. Islam is the religion of Africa. [By contrast,] Christianity lives here by sufferance. . . .
European Christianity is a dangerous thing.[5]

Missionary interference with the prospects of Christian awakening taking
root in Africa contradicted the gospel by which missionaries justified their
actions, and that provoked the backlash that Agbebi described. The accepted
general rule that Christian faith is embodied faith was violated with respect to
Africans who were now accused of using Christianity to bolster their political
campaign on behalf of their threatened societies. Europeans professed Christianity with an ample mouth while they continued to observe Western customs, and yet denied that freedom to Africans. Agbebi suggested that a different standard was being applied, whereas the gospel afforded the same latitude
to all.

Africans adopted the Christian path because they were led to believe that
they would gain all that belonged with their welfare and future prospects.[6]
Surrounded by powers seen and unseen, and all too aware of the forces of the
spirit world, Africans were predisposed to believe that the material world was
connected to their spiritual interests, and their spiritual interests to the material world. Missionaries' selective use of Christianity to avoid addressing the
crisis occurring in society as having spiritual significance looked like a deliberate obstruction of God's work for human flourishing.

It was not that Africans were incapable of receiving the gospel; rather, it
was that they would not receive it wholeheartedly in the partial, halfhearted
way it was given to them. The Africans' demand for customizing the West's
preshrunk Christianity opened them to the charge of religious laundering for
political ends, though Africans were only appealing for the recognition that
the gospel preached equality and justice. Shaped by centuries of exposure
to material and spiritual trials, and more recently by colonial subjugation,
Africans believed that Christianity's message belonged with their hopes and
dreams. The gospel proclaimed salvation as good news for a people historically
marginalized, and now ethically empowered, and in that milieu Africans

felt connected and reassured, something very different from the snares of race relations that dominated the colonial era and its surviving academic representation.

Although missionaries stressed the importance of adhering to sound doctrine as a prerequisite of membership in the fellowship, Africans learned from experience that missionaries often failed to undertake a just and loving treatment of others. The failure in personal relationship encouraged Africans to look elsewhere for more authentic marks of Christian community. Africans treated human relationships with far greater seriousness than the missionaries they knew, and often admired. Puzzled by the scant attention missionaries paid to experience and social relationships, and frustrated by the missionaries' paternal attitude toward them, Africans embarked on an independent course to take the drama of salvation into the areas of life and experience where it was eagerly welcomed. Faced with a historic challenge, African leaders made the choice on behalf of their people to reengage the gospel afresh.

It was a bold, courageous move to cut all ties with the mission churches, which was done partly in order to escape their control, but partly also in order to face the claims of the gospel unfinanced, unvetted, and unfettered by outsiders. Support for such a course of action would have to come from Africans themselves, with church workers for the most part giving of their services without charge. The new faith community was structured with a view to sustained engagement with the needs of real people in real time and in real-life situations.

Beginning in 1929, the East African revival got underway. It was an attempt at applied Christianity in the setting of the total cultural environment. The revival made European leadership in the church dispensable. On a more positive note, the revolt against white paternalism was guided by "the spirit of love and loyalty with which it was permeated and the fact that the issue on which the movement has taken a confessional stand, even to the point of martyrdom, has been the refusal to break fellowship with white brethren."[7] For all that, the revival came under heavy pressure from Mau Mau because of the revival's Christian claims,[8] and from the administrators because of the refusal by the revival members to embrace an armed confrontation with Mau Mau. In the end splits occurred within the revival movement, leading in one case to separation from the Anglican Church and the establishment of the Church of Christ in Africa in 1957. Evidence of such splintering led W. M. Eiselen, an anthropologist writing in the 1930s, to bemoan the fate of Christianity in African hands. Calling the splintering a malady, Eiselen warned of "the most injurious effects on the development of a Christian way of living within the well-established old mission churches."[9]

That heavy-weather view of African failure was not shared by the Africans themselves. In rituals around the Faith Healing Fountains that predominated in Soweto, for example, those who congregated there at night were assured: "Nobody is asked whether he or she is Anglican, Catholic, Lutheran, 'A.M.E.' or Zionist. At the Fountain, [at] 'The Lake of Peace,' all are alike: the same anxiety about health and wholeness; the same trust in the blessed water which they are given to take home."[10] Welbourn also took an upbeat view of the challenge of separation and Christian independency in Africa.[11] An African proverb says that the elephant is not thwarted by its tusks, that is to say, a wholesome Christianity destined for the whole human race should not be judged by secessionist outbreaks that appear to impede its progress, and if independency appears as a setback for the unity of the church, it might also be a rallying point for confronting long-standing division and failure in reconciliation among Christians. Christians allowed cultural priorities to weigh heavily on the claims of the gospel, and that stiffened the separatist resolve. Changing that order and making the gospel the discriminating arbiter of culture might place Christians in a stronger position to tackle the politics of exclusion and cultural stigmatization. It was not only Africans who were responsible for that shortcoming.

It is worth reflecting on the effects of multiple political boundaries on the idea of the unity of Christianity. Christianity has been subject to the autonomous jurisdiction of nation states, and the boundaries of these states preclude the idea of faith-based identity beyond national borders. That has made it difficult for Christians to be attuned to the religion's transnational themes. The national state as the basis of identity has overshadowed religion as a source of identity, with Christian experience schematized as national identity. As bearers of religious experience, persons are worth more than their national identity. Perhaps what appears as religious splintering is only symptomatic of a deeper political issue, with religion a silhouette of multiple and separate political spheres.

In the early phase of local resurgence the idea of unity turned on the sheer variety of Christianity and the proliferation of diversity in terms of national idioms, ethnic variety, worship styles, and aesthetic choices. In one example from a different part of the world, we hear echoes of this strain in a plea about our not being misled by the appearance of disunity, which was often the result of newness following the first planting of Christianity. The disconcerting appearance of disunity should not blind people to the fact that the promise of fullness and abundance lay just under the surface, stirred by hidden currents of faith. In the pithy language of peasant society, the hope for Christian unity is likened to the organic life of germinating grain, with the sense of it all brilliantly captured in the prayer of a Filipino as follows: "Lord, make us realize that our Christianity is like a rice field, that when it is newly planted, the paddies are prominent; but as the plants take root and grow taller, these dividing paddies gradually vanish, and soon there appears only one vast continuous field. So give us roots of love and make us grow in Christian fellowship and service, so that Thy will be done in our lives."[12]

Abroad, the seed of the gospel assumed new forms of faith strong enough to overcome the barriers of suspicion, unwillingness, and distrust. As E. Jacottet of the Protestant Paris Mission put it, a little less Europeanism and a little more Africanism would do a great deal of good for the cause of the gospel and for race relations on the frontier in Africa. "Christianity," he challenged, "must lose its European form and colour [i.e., race consciousness], it must become as African a religion to Africans as it is today a European religion to the Europeans."[13] In the words of a nineteenth-century black pastor, the breath of Pentecost had not turned the earth into the polar seas and frozen the waves in eternal fetters, but rather had freed tongues to become like the ocean's unfettered flow where the waves could roll with power, distinct as the billows, but still one as the sea.[14]

The momentum of independency provided movement in an otherwise sluggish, jaded world church, in part because indigenous resurgence bolstered the flagging fortunes of many mainline denominations, and in part because the spirit of independency persisted into the mainline churches without fracturing them. Charismatic elements of independency helped to renew the spirit of worship in these churches.

The bewildering variety and pluralism that seem to engulf the Christian movement today are nothing new. The ancient church had its share of similar diversity, not to mention of challenge and strife. In Carthage, for example, Augustine joined the Manichaean sect as a member for nine years during which time he converted many to that group. Considered as the most authoritative spokesman on the subject in the early church, Tertullian devoted eight chapters to sleep and dreams in his treatise, *On the Soul*. Tertullian joined the charismatic Montanists, who pursued a radical social agenda. Gnostics, who regarded visions and prophecies as authoritative, offered stiff competition. Commenting on the *Shepherd of Hermas*, a second-century devotional work, Clement of Alexandria (d. ca. AD 215), glimpsed something yet of God beyond the restrictions of dogma and boldly acknowledged the necessity of charismatic gifts. Irenaeus (d. ca. AD 200) defended the gift of prophecy against official opponents. Basilides of Alexandria embraced Christianity because it offered him a handy alibi for his abiding interest in Gnosticism. Prophecy, dreams, and visions occupied a place of dominance in the life of the third-century North

African Church.[15] Perpetua, the martyr, as well as Cyprian, were famous for their reputation as charismatic proponents. Martyred in 203 at age twenty-two, Perpetua kept a diary of her experiences in prison where visions became her aid and succor. As for Cyprian, he wrote profusely and gladly about his many mind-bending experiences. In his treatise, *On the Making of Man*, Gregory of Nyssa (d. 394) spoke of sleep as the state in which reason is not extinguished but, heaped with chaff, smolders like a fire and breaks forth in insights in dreams.

Numerous other groups were spreading at the time, with many Christians moving in and out of them. The outlook of these diverse little groups entered the general Christian stream to great effect. In this field, little chips did kindle the fire that the big logs sustained. In any case, says F. B. Welbourn, Europeans are not themselves entirely innocent when it comes to separation and splintering in the church,[16] and so, perhaps, partnership with Africans, he urged, might be the push needed to advance the prospects of Christian reconciliation generally. A seasoned missionary acknowledged that churches in the Third World "co-operate to a far greater extent than they do in Europe," especially in the production and distribution of literature.

United in everything to do with legitimizing colonial rule but divided about the interests of Africans, the church's inconsistent witness was addressed as a matter of urgency. Welbourn's argument, illuminated by his extensive African experience, seems sound, that a fragmented church is not a negation of Christianity but a demand to take it even more seriously. That was certainly the case, for example, at Vatican II.

Africans understood the teachings of Christianity sufficiently to demand an honest reckoning with the need for national leadership. Missionaries, for example, preached at length about Christian love but without a visible change in their attitudes toward the Africans they were in contact with, even though missionaries criticized traditional religions for failing to make a difference to the character of Africans. A step was here missing in the logic of cause and effect. Accordingly, African Christian Independency, also called the African Initiated Church movement, stepped into the breach to close the gap. Specifically, the leaders of independency turned to the concept of *philadelphia*, brotherly love, and infused it with palpable life and purpose. In the eyes of Africans, when they thought of *philadelphia* as love as listening, sharing, sympathizing, and sensitive understanding in depth between equals, they felt that missions had failed disastrously. "Instead of biblical love, there was paternalism; instead of *philadelphia* there was competitiveness [among] a multiplicity of missionary agencies."[17]

In contrast, for the Africans *philadelphia* acted as a Christian validation of the values of corporate life, of the community as the site of interpersonal relationships, hospitality, and a philanthropic ethic. Numerous groups within the broad stream of African Christian Independency consciously adopted names that noted their commitment to "brotherly love," to community, and to serving others. Many such groups in West Africa stressed the Christian virtue of loving one another. In the Congo the Kimbanguists established fellowship cells that allowed them to describe themselves as *Kintwadi*, "the Brotherly Community." David Barrett lists several such groups, including those that adopted the name *"philadelphia"* in their title, such as Filadelfia Church of Africa, the African Sixth Church of God of Philadelphia, the Divine Love of Christ Church, the Luo People of Love, the African Brotherhood Church, and the Christian Brotherhood Church.

Barrett emphasizes the point that even more important than mere titles was the fact that, on a large scale, independent churches established a reputation for undertaking philanthropic work in society. In one case an organization was established called Conseil Supérieur des Sacrificateurs pour les Églises-Unies de Jésus—Christ en Afrique, known by its acronym as COSSEUJCA. It set up an agency for the purpose, Caisse Philanthropique Chrétienne des Sacrifices, which looked after the needy, the sick, and travelers without regard to creed. In Zimbabwe the Reformed Seventh-day Adventist Church, among the Ndebele, looked after neglected orphans and widows. In Madagascar the followers of a female charismatic leader, Prophetess Nenilava, obtained government license in 1963 to establish themselves as a philanthropic body known as Manolotsoa, "Doers of Good," "Philanthropists." In its day the Martha Davies Confidential [Private] Benevolent Association of Sierra Leone supported a wide variety of social programs to alleviate hardship.

The new religious movements practiced philanthropic ministry across a range of social and personal needs, their work distinguished by the fact that it was entirely dependent on money raised by Africans in Africa. No foreign aid or government subsidy was involved; every cent that was expended was given, collected, and distributed by church members themselves. "In short, the movement as a whole has introduced onto the African scene and forcibly drawn attention to a new quality of corporate Christian life and responsibility, a new *koinonia* (sharing) of warmth, emotion and mutual caring in the Christian community, together with a new philanthropy towards all."[18]

Trail

A vital historical clue has all too easily eluded students of world Christianity, who too readily present the case for the African appropriation of the gospel as something that began with African Christian Independency, which was a recent reaction to colonial and missionary assault, or else was evidence of the influence of the contemporary prosperity gospel movement in the United States.[19] Yet the historical trail is much older, stemming in one direction from the eighteenth-century Great Awakening, and in another from the African American missionary impulse.

The two streams merged in the poignant story of Moses Wilkinson, a slave from Nansemond, Virginia, from where, in spite of his being blind and lame, he escaped during the American Revolution. He arrived in Freetown in 1792 with the original Nova Scotian settlers and established a preaching ministry in the community. Like the other preachers, Wilkinson objected to the official Christianity that the authorities tried to impose on the colony. For the officials, religion was "the king's book and the king's proceedings," and thus required a license to be legitimate. Consequently, the authorities insisted that religion should not be allowed to degenerate among the Africans into what an English divine once termed "a shooting-horn to their vanity and gain." In the hands of unlicensed preachers, the pulpit could not uphold sound doctrine and good order nor guard against charlatanry.[20] The sentiment was "If the beard were all, the goat might preach."

In spite of official prejudice, the pulpit as symbol of the unfettered word of God had a formidable status in black Christian culture, described in this vivid account of Austa Malinda French with respect to blacks in wartime South Carolina:

> The real spiritual benefit of these people, instrumentally, seems
> to have been mostly derived from a sort of local preachers, Co-
> lored, and mostly slaves, but of deep spiritual experience, sound sense,
> and capacity to state Scripture facts, narratives, and doctrines, far
> better than most, who feed upon commentaries. True, the most
> of them could not read, still, some of them line hymns from
> memory with great accuracy, and fervor, and repeat Scripture
> most appropriately, and correctly. Their teaching shows clearly
> that it is God in the soul, that makes the religious teacher. One
> is amazed at their correctness and power. They say: "God tell me
> 'you go teach de people what I tell you; I shall prosper you; I teach
> you in de hart.'" They open their mouth in simple faith that
> God will fill it, and are not disappointed. How dear to God, must
> be their perfect humility, perfect trust, perfect love. "Riches by
> far is the heart's adoration, / Dearest to God are the prayers of the
> poor."[21]

The style that distinguished the Freetown ministry of Moses Wilkinson is aptly reminiscent of Mrs. French's account. A colonial official who turned up to mock Wilkinson's effort in the pulpit remained to praise him. Here is his eyewitness testimony:

Moses Wilkinson preached this evening from Isaiah iii: 11 and 12. He gave out his hymns and texts from memory. His manner was warm and animating.... While hearing him I was led to admire the good-ness and wisdom of God in the instruments which he frequently sees fit to use, to advance the interests of his kingdom. Many of the wise and learned in this world, if they were to see and hear such a man as our brother, professedly engaging in endeavouring to lead their fellow creatures from sin to holiness, would at once conclude it to be impossible for them to effect the object which they have in view. Experience, however, flatly contradicts such a conclusion. Numbers have been led by their means to change their lives, and are in-duced from day to day to pursue their conduct which conduces to their own happiness and to the welfare of those around them.[22]

Blacks flocked to revival religion because, knowing suffering of body and spirit, they desired to be led from sin to holiness, and their talents and re-sources, such as they were, they devoted to that high endeavor. Where the officials suspected political conspiracy they found instead a committed seeking after communion with God. The officials were surprised, and although they went on record as to the veracity of what they witnessed, they refused to abandon their political suspicion. As the blacks saw it, going to church was not the same as coming to God, for, after all, all is not fish that comes to net. For the officials, however, the world made sense only in a political frame. The following report of an encounter between Sir Charles MacCarthy, the governor, and a revival preacher sums up the issue:

His Excellency the Governor came here today. He had led the con-versation while we were in the garden to baptism. He wished I would baptize more people. I told him that I could not, unless God first baptized their hearts. He said the reason so many were baptized on the Day of Pentecost was that the Apostles despised none. I replied that they were pricked in the heart. He thought baptism an act of civilization, and that it was our duty to make them all Christians. He spoke in great warmth about these things, and I endeavoured to show him through Scripture passages the contrary. He gave up at last; calling me and the society a set of fanatics.[23]

Not surprisingly, the political frame easily skewed not only African motives but also religion as a distinctive, unique phenomenon. The answer lay in accepting the distinction religious people drew between religious autonomy and political acts. In religion, the seeker pleaded before his or her Creator and Judge; in political acts the citizen wagered with those who possessed power, usually by privilege and for the privileged. Religion, by contrast, was for the soul in need; everyone was equal there.

With a whiff of Pietist distrust of the world, Africans insisted that officials should not conflate or confuse the spheres of religion and politics, and they led a movement for that reason. When a governor of Freetown colony made the charge that a settler preacher was using the Holy Spirit as an excuse to cloak political effrontery, the affected preacher defended God's sovereign prerogative to deal generously and graciously with the seeker without regard to race, office, or social status. The witness of God's spirit in the heart of the seeker was not by written warrant, for the seeker need not be anything else to receive God's favor. Suffering united blacks, but so did religion. Two in distress (or in religion) made trouble less. Such company was not the insubordination or sedition officials alleged it to be, since it merely stated a universal principle of the religious life. As John Blassingame put it, in reflecting on the place of religion among slaves and other oppressed groups, God was not an abstract deity, or even a cultural arbiter, "but a Being who took an interest in the lowly slave and interceded in his behalf. He was the God of freedom to whom slaves prayed for deliverance from bondage. They poured out their troubles to Him and saw visions of Him."[24]

Sermons and testimonies reveal an awareness of the onerous restrictions and reservations placed on religion and on black preachers, but the blacks accepted the preachers' power not because it had the approval of white or other earthly authorities, but because it had the hand of God on it. It was power of the moral not the political kind. Blacks, therefore, rejected the contention of officials that the object of preaching was reverence for magistrates and their office, not the cure of souls. For them, the preacher was a laborer in the cause of the gospel, and the power of his or her word was God's gift, not something for which she could claim credit or reward. In prayer and testimony, the unsealed lip had authority over the magistrate's muzzle.

A contemporary observer, Anna Maria Falconbridge, confirmed the preeminent role of the preacher in the new colony, saying the preachers held forth all night long. "I never met with, or heard, or read of any set of people observing the same appearance of godliness; for I do not remember, since they first landed here, my ever waking (and I have awoke at every hour of the night), without hearing preachings from some quarter or another."[25] Amending the words of W. E. B. DuBois, the preacher became the unique and authoritative figure developed by blacks in America first, and on the African continent subsequently.

Religion was transcendent in the sense that it was not a projection of acquired status, acquired skill, or historical circumstances. In fact, for those who had them, status and skill, as well as trials and tribulations, were at the behest of religion, not religion at the behest of this world. As one much-afflicted settler testified to an official who went to commiserate with him, without tasting of the bread of adversity and wading through bitter waters, there could be no experience of divine grace. Unbeaten clay does not make good bricks, or, to change the figure, one who gets blisters from the hoe handle will not die of hunger. A much-afflicted former slave quoted the lines of a hymn:

> When my faith is sharply tried,
> I find myself a learner yet.[26]

When it crossed the path of politics, religion appealed to standards of scrutiny and judgment, such as freedom, forgiveness, justice, equality, and reconciliation, rather than to norms of political expedience. As Paul Cuffee pleaded, let those whose human rights have been infringed upon step forward and claim the due that belonged to everyone created in the image of God, so that they "may enjoy liberty that God has granted unto all his faithful Saints."[27] In his remarks on the inalienability of freedom cited against the confederalists in the Civil War, John Greenleaf Whittier (d. 1892) affirmed this as the bitterest of all ills:

> Whose load man totters down to death,
> Is that which plucks the regal crown
> Of freedom from his forehead down,
> And snatches from his powerless hand
> The sceptred sign of self-command.

Religion might challenge politics to take an advocacy role in society in matters of justice and fairness, education, the rule of law, common defense, common morality, and individual responsibility, but not to become the means of grace in matters of salvation, Scripture, the church, worship, and the soul's destiny.

Ordinarily, it would have been merely incidental had such views carried political meaning. In conditions of colonial and missionary control, however, the words were fraught with political charge, thus forcing a choice. When in 1796 the governor of Freetown, Zachary Macaulay, father of the famous historian, promulgated an order to regulate marriage among the settlers, the settlers responded with a petition drive to rescind the order and for the first time invoked the sentiment of Christian Independency. The petition was delivered to the governor in the name of "The Independent Methodist Church of Freetown." It declared:

> We consider this new law as an encroachment on our religious rights. . . . We are Dissenters, and as such consider ourselves a perfect Church, having no need of the assistance of any worldly power to appoint or perform religious ceremonies for us. If persons in holy orders are allowed to marry, we see no reason why our Ministers should not do it. Our meeting-house we count as fit for any religious purpose as the house you call the church. We cannot persuade ourselves that politics and religion have any connection, and therefore think it not right for a Governor of the one to be meddling with the other.[28]

The roots of Christian Independency in the Great Awakening and in the first attempt to establish a foothold for the cause in Africa suggest that independency is a threshold phenomenon with a long history, and that, if conditions are right, it will thrive at the boundary between establishment values and the ideals of a people in transition. In that sense Christianity, as a world religion, was not just the extension of mainland Western norms to societies on the outer rim of its global scope, but a religion with pre-thematic local resonance. Whether in the drama of the disruption, dislocation, resettlement, and restoration characteristic of slavery and antislavery, or in the highly compressed conditions of colonial and missionary domination and nationalist agitation, Christian ideas of judgment and redemption assumed a potent, frontier meaning.

In that milieu, the vernacular Bible became a primer of frontier imperatives: Exodus was a moral imperative that repudiated colonial rule; Joseph the outcast was anointed so that he could dream dreams of liberation and healing; Moses was the great restorer of the dignity of the tribes against Pharaoh's exactions; the long-suffering David was vindicated when he prevailed over Goliath; Samuel was a parable of God's reward for Mother Africa, rendered barren by slavery's dispossession; Mary was one whose tears of sorrow flowed like buoys of hope for a continent whose sons and daughters were tossed by alien forces; and victim Jesus was the Africans' Friend and Redeemer whose God-empowered resurrection confounded the enemy and began God's reign. History was full of meaning, particularly for people with a cause and with a homeland motivation.

In the people's idiom Christian Scripture supplied the requisite text for liberty. As a result, Africans rushed to the Bible not only to seek answers to their pressing problems but also because the Bible offered them written assurance of God's unimpeachable solidarity amid the restrictions and other disadvantages of colonial domination.[29] When a local Christian held a translated Gospel in his hands for the first time, he declared: "Here is a document which proves that we also are human beings—the first and only book in our language."[30] Equally exultantly, a Christian in Angola celebrated holding the Gospels in his hands for the first time, affirming, "Now we see that our friends in the foreign country regard us as people worth while."[31] At an assembly of local Christians when a Wesleyan missionary produced the complete Bible, an elder declared, "I know that in my body I am a very little man, but to-day as I see the whole Bible in my language I feel as big as a mountain." Another echoed him: "I wish that I were as big as an ox, or had the voice of an ox, so that I might shout the great joy which I feel."[32] These examples had in common the fact that vernacular translation amounted to a historic event for indigenous populations, and that the mother tongue was fertile soil for the new religion. It had the effect of presenting Christianity as arriving where it belonged, at home in the language of the people. The excitement was understandable.

An important point often overlooked in accounts of the subject is the decisive impact New World Africans had on the missionary impulse in modern Protestantism. As we saw in a previous chapter, Freetown was the center of that New World African impulse, and from there the recaptives took the flame to Nigeria where Martin Delany (d. 1888) broke upon it. Active in New World black consciousness movements in Canada and the United States, Delany had been a vocal critic of the whole idea of black repatriation and mission even though it was the missionary exploits of David Livingstone that inspired him in 1858 to organize the Niger Valley Exploring Party. His goal was to use that as a secular vehicle for black advancement, specifically for the purposes of establishing a cotton industry in Nigeria. Still, E. W. Blyden could extol Delany only in religious terms as the "Moses [who is] to lead the exodus of his people from the house of bondage to land flowing with milk and honey."[33]

Delany saw in other parts of West Africa the achievement of the Sierra Leone recaptives, and that made a convert out of him with respect to the possibilities of the religion in Africa. While still critical of Christianity, Delany spoke admiringly of African agency in the dissemination of Christian values, and concluded that on the African frontier expatriate missionaries had no future role. The missionary imperative had become an African imperative, and nothing clinched that fact better than the multicultural flair of Christian Africans. The Christian awakening converged with an African awakening.

I have not as yet visited a missionary station in any part of Africa, where there were not some, and frequently many natives, both adult and children, who could speak, read, and write English, as well as read their own language; as all of them, whether Episcopalian, Wesleyan, Baptist, or Presbyterian, in the Yoruba country, have Crowther's editions of religious and secular books in the schools and churches, and all have native agents, interpreters, teachers (assistants) and catechists or readers in the mission. These facts prove great progress.... Both male and female missionaries, all seemed much devoted to their work, and anxiously desirous of doing more. Indeed, the very fact of there being as many native missionaries as there are now to be found holding responsible positions, as elders, deacons, preachers, and princes, among whom are many finely educated, and several authors of works, not only in their own but [in] the English language, as Revs. [Samuel Ajayi] Crowther, [Theophilus] King, [John Christopher] Taylor, and Samuel Crowther [junior], Esq., surgeon, all show that there is an advancement for these people beyond the point to which [expatriate] missionary duty can take them.[34]

Foresight

The historical trail is not easy to miss once attention is drawn to the subject. The trail exists in the comments and observations of writers who had their fingers on the pulse of mission as it translated the message into the mother tongue. Much of what came to transpire in Africa with the post-Western Christian resurgence was predicted by writers who made the shift of perspective. Even though he was dogged by much foot-dragging and official obstruction, Diedrich Westermann, for example, contended that Bible translation would contribute to African advancement in education and sow the seeds of cultural renewal as the assured basis for an acculturated Christianity, with an effect on the rest of society far greater than anything secular education alone could achieve. Writing in 1925 from his academic chair at the University of Berlin, Westermann advanced reasons why vernacular translation was essential to the whole psychology of recasting Christianity in the idiom and psyche of an indigenous culture. Translation was empowerment.

In this sense we speak of the soul of a people, and the most immediate, the most adequate exponent of the soul of a people is its language. By taking away a people's language, we cripple or destroy its

soul and kill its mental individuality. . . . We do not want Christianity
to appear in the eyes of the Natives as a religion of the white man,
and the opinion to prevail that the African must become a pseudo-
European in order to become a Christian, but we want to implant
the Gospel deep into the soil of the African mind, so that it may
grow there in its own African form, not as a gift of the white man but
as the gift of God. . . . If this is to be effected, the Gospel and whole
Christian education must take root in the mother soil of the vernacular. Only in this way will it enter into the African mind and become
the medium of the new life—not of new forms of life—and of a
regeneration of the people's soul. . . . If the Christian Church in Africa
is to be really African and really Christian, it must be built upon
the basis of the indigenous peculiarities and gifts of the people, it must
become part of the African genius, and these will for ever be embedded in the mother language.[35]

In views identical to Westermann's, Edwin Smith observed that the mother tongue was the music of the heart and home. Persons might learn many
languages, but they prayed in their own, as they made love in their own. The
speech that comes to people in their mother's milk is the most precious thing
they have. "Every language is a temple in which the soul of the people who
speak it is enshrined. If it is sinful to exterminate them bodily, it is no less
sinful to destroy their individuality."[36] Smith opposed foisting a ready-made
Christianity on Africans, saying the African "cannot be treated as if he were a
European who happened to be born black. He ought not to be regarded as if
were a building so badly constructed that it must be torn down, its foundations
torn up and a new structure erected on its site, on a totally new plan and with
entirely new materials," because "to insist upon an African abandoning his
own language and to speak and think in a language so different as English, is
like demanding that the various Italian peoples should learn Chinese in order
to overcome their linguistic problem."[37]

These statements called for a fundamental change in colonial policy in spite
of the disadvantages involved in promoting African languages without much of
a written literature suitable for use in schools. In 1923 the Education Committee
of the Conference of Missionary Societies in Great Britain and Ireland submitted
a memorandum to the Secretary of State for the Colonies on the subject of
education in the colonies in Africa, calling for greater resources to be devoted
to the issue than the missions commanded. In the memorandum, the mission
societies stressed the importance of religion, broadly understood, and moral
instruction as a safeguard against cultural alienation and disenchantment.[38]

In colonial North Nigeria the administration introduced an education code in 1926 called the Education (Colony and Southern Provinces) Ordinance. It prescribed vernacular languages in primary and secondary education. The preamble stated: "Among infants and younger children all instruction should as far as possible be given in that vernacular or language [sic] by means of which the new ideas presented to their minds are most readily explained.... The free development of their minds must not be hampered by making the assimilation of new ideas unnecessarily difficult by presenting them in a language not readily understood."[39]

The future first prime minister of an independent Nigeria, Abubakar Tafawa-Balewa, became a teacher at Bauchi Middle School under the terms of the education code. Intending to hold the attention of his pupils, Tafawa-Balewa devised an ingenious pneumonic piece on pedagogy called, "The City of Language," in which he compared the grammatical parts of speech to the parts of a hierarchical Hausa city.[40]

Tafawa-Balewa appreciated what the vernacular channel offered by way of a creative outlet for young minds—and for gifted teachers. Without the development of the vernacular in Bible translation, for example, there would have been such a dearth of materials as to make the task an almost impossible one to conceive and to undertake. A teacher in Benin province pointed out that problem, lamenting the fact that no textbooks existed in the language in question, and no standard orthography, either, all of which meant confronting teachers and students with daunting challenges. The one ray of hope came from missionary efforts. The Benin teacher wrote, "As for text-books the rudimentary but laudable efforts of Rev. J. Corbeau may be regarded as pioneer work."[41]

The writer made no claims about Europeans having the power to name new forms of humanity in order to promote their agenda of colonial hegemony, as Jean Comaroff and John Comaroff argue. Instead, the writer turned his attention to the imperative of developing an African consciousness radically different from the Western tradition. "We English-speaking Africans very often forget that the atmosphere, both physical and moral, which shaped the European mind is quite altogether different from ours; and that European literature is the written expression of [the] European mind and the atmosphere which shaped it. If an Englishman wants to study Latin or French he will not be required to make very strenuous mental efforts to enable him to 'think' a Latin or French sentence. The atmosphere is all European, it is there already. But with African languages the position is different; the gulf between the two intellectual developments is wide."[42]

It was that gulf that Tafawa-Balewa was able to bridge with his sensitive, imaginative approach. The challenge of bringing the benefits of modern education to children reared in traditional society led Tafawa-Balewa to expound linguistic principles by analogy with established Hausa political institutions and ideas, thus achieving the double goal of respect for the old amid the new. It might be a new form of consciousness, but if so it was one of the Africans' devising. Because of its vernacular inspiration, such creativity exceeded by far the superficial import variety of imitation and repetition, and encouraged all concerned to look again with fresh, discerning eyes at the world of everyday life. The *malam* (derived from the Arabic *mu'allim*), as the teacher is called in Hausa, was quintessentially an agent with a dual role: he brought frontier ideas to bear on heartland values without undue strain or distortion. The *malam* as transmitter of new ideas was the community's contact point with historical developments and its shield against cultural dispossession, as Malam Tafawa-Balewa so well demonstrated. Westermann's contention that an education that uprooted the child from the soil of its nurture could not achieve much of lasting value seems valid. The vernacular allayed that fear by connecting the child to things of mother tongue originality and assurance.

Assessment

We have seen not only the complex role of missions toward the West's colonial hegemony on the one hand, and, on the other hand, the role of missions toward Christianity's heartland position in Europe but also how an ambivalent religion became unavoidably entangled with the frontier agenda. In several noteworthy cases, such entanglement was inscribed into the very idea of missionary practice. Many missionaries felt there simply was no other way to do business except to uphold the native cause, however begrudgingly, to the alarm of colonial officials but to the critical welcome of Africans. That was the case in South Africa where, as we saw earlier, John Philip took up the cause of the Hottentots; in the case of the Xhosa, where Livingstone stepped into the breach by defending them; and in North Nigeria where Walter Miller, the pioneer CMS missionary, sided with the Africans in denouncing colonial exploitation. They all issued a clarion call to Europeans not to allow colonial shortsightedness to blunt their conscience to the glaring case for legal and social justice, for open equality, and for mutual trust on behalf of the subject people. Philip invoked the system of justice and the rule of law of the Roman Empire to criticize the failure of the British to safeguard the interests and welfare of Africans.[43]

For his part, Miller lodged a protest: "We cannot be content," he insisted, "while men in masses are suffering, are hungry, living stunted, aimless lives.

It cannot be right that great fortunes have been made, and are being made, in the Colonies, and dividends paid to shareholders in Britain, while men, from whose lands this wealth comes, sweat and live like beasts, and even fight to obtain less than a living wage in the plantations, docks, factories, mines, and even fields of their own land."[44] In the view of all concerned, Miller's words carried tremendous weight along with those of the colonial administration and within Hausa society.

Miller's provocative book, *Have We Failed in Nigeria?* (1947), was a rousing manual of decolonization, and was instrumental in transforming hinterland priorities into an agenda of the national cause. It led to the creation of the first organized political party in North Nigeria that laid the groundwork for political independence, thus carrying to a maturing point the incipient divergence between mission and colonialism. In a different direction, the realignment of local forces removed obstacles, including the Western baggage, which had stood in the path of Christianity being able to accede to its role as a world religion. The postcolonial Christian resurgence in Nigeria is proof of that role.

The Anglican Church that Enoch Powell passionately defended has, in its transplant version, succeeded beyond bounds in Nigeria. With the resurgence came unexpected challenges, with the church caught in a culture clash between the resolute objections of Anglican Nigerians and the 2004 historic enthronement of a gay bishop by the Episcopal Church USA. The conflict showed the unforeseen developments that have taken place in Christianity's worldwide expansion. It showed the Third World rejecting the West as the church's final arbiter. Difference and variety have projected a multifaceted Christianity steeped in a pluralist discourse. Pastoral authority was no longer aligned with financial power, so that taking the king's shilling did not concede the king's bidding in matters of doctrine. Still, not to lose sight of an important comparative lesson, the unilateral action by the Americans casts a revealing light on the demand by the Church of England at the first Lambeth Conference in 1868 to ban polygamy in the African church. Although they had colonial subjugation to contend with, African pastors chose to submit to the ban by upholding it as public teaching. Even widespread breach of the rule failed to galvanize a politically correct case for annulling the ban or for drawing up blacklists.

African church leaders reacted cautiously to provocative advice by European mentors to reject too close an association with the European church. Launching an incendiary device into the volatile circumstances of the controversy surrounding the public humiliation and dismissal of Bishop Ajayi Crowther, one Mr. Cust, formerly of the Indian Civil Service,[45] called on the African Anglicans to follow the example of the Americans and break ties with

Canterbury. "You must take care," Cust told Archdeacon Dandeson Crowther, the bishop's youngest son, "to keep your Church principles: *you are members of the Episcopal Church: keep to it*: but you are not bound to remain in the National English Church, any more than the American colonists were bound."[46]

The first African bishop and the most distinguished churchman of his native continent, Crowther was an unrivaled early pioneer of Christianity's post-Western development. His personal circumstances were compelling in the extreme: captured and sold into slavery in his native Nigeria, he was rescued in 1822 from a Portuguese slave ship bound for the New World and released in Freetown where he embarked on his remarkable public career. He was ordained priest and subsequently consecrated bishop in Canterbury before returning to West Africa to lead the missionary drive in Nigeria. His conflict with commercial slaving interests in Nigeria, both local and European, was exacerbated by attacks on him in missionary circles for turning a blind eye to moral lapses among his African clergy. An ecclesiastical trial was mounted in Nigeria in which Crowther was censured and dismissed even though his own conduct was never in question.

It was against that provocative background that Cust challenged local Anglicans to cut ties with the Church of England.[47] His words have an eerie, prophetic ring to them more than a century later in light of the unilateral action taken by the Episcopal Church USA, action that the Americans said at the time only the Second Coming could prevent from going into effect. Still preoccupied in his day with things of the First Coming, however, Dandeson adhered to church teaching.

Disabused of the notion that colonial hegemony was an ally of Christianity, Africans seemed better placed than Westerners to appreciate the obligations of common fellowship in a world church, perhaps because kinship structures instilled values of community deep enough to promote the idea of the church as one family. It is instructive that even the challenge of foreign domination failed to displace the sense of common religious identity nourished by the sacraments. Post-Western Christian hatchlings, so to speak, may be able to offer a lesson for the West about the spirit of mutual bonding as part of Christianity's contribution to the worldwide human family. The missionary frontier once rose above its historical circumstances to engage post-Western ideas and values, trailing a Pietist-inspired legacy concerning the distinction between universal norms of revelation and European instruments of control. The current awakening sprang from the indigenous encounter with the legacy of Europe's complex overseas outreach, and seems firmly set on its post-Western primal course.

6

Resurgence and the New Order in West Africa

Primal Pillar

Seeking a Better World

When we bear in mind that a long shadow of warfare and upheaval fell over much of West Africa in the nineteenth century, while disorder and a sense of alarm spread like wildfire among the people, we are struck by the fact that the region emerged so soon as an important stronghold of the Christian movement. Yet change was in the air, with indications that a strategic turn of direction was imperative for survival. The tide bearing Europeans into the continent had to be reversed, and its consequences faced squarely. The old chieftain structures were too involved in slavery and the slave trade to be able to ward off calamity and offer security to their people. In fact, slavery and the slave trade allowed Europeans to establish themselves in African societies, so it was reasonable to conclude that the encounter with Europeans brought harm because Africans were partners, willing or not. Intending to strike out on a new path, the new African leaders believed that victims condemned themselves the more if all they did was blame others. "Whither Africa?" became a revolving question.

Though painful and demanding, the choice was clear: abandon the centuries-old dealings in human traffic, repudiate injustice, renounce blood-feuds, and place society on a new foundation altogether, one that would uphold a view of the world that was more all-embracing and was radically just. People did not have to sacrifice their roots to bend with the wind of change. With sanguinary sanctions a staple part of their method, the old religions were on the defensive. Up to their last agonies, the old gods made self-imprecation and potent curses the price for seeking their company, with retribution the stipulated prescription. In a clinch, the old religions delivered millennial commands that fed and, in turn, were fed by insecurity and vengeance. Beset by recurrent threats and crises, the African people felt abandoned by the guardian spirits. Christianity arrived as a second wind amid the flight of the gods; instead of people feeling jinxed in a haunted world, they had the incentive to revamp the old code and its residual tribal animus. Even with a whiff of colonial odium, Christianity still felt credible because it was able to fill the gap caused by the collapse of the old structures and ideas.

One example dramatizes what was afoot. One of the new Christian charismatic prophets staked his movement's claim on a spot of ground that evil spirits had placed a curse, which could not be cultivated or otherwise reclaimed. The new Christian leader commanded people to bring all their idols, carvings, charms, and other sacred objects and to heap them in a pile; among the sacred objects was a juju with nails driven through it, called an *aiyara*, which was used to kill one's enemies. The leader doused the pile with kerosene and palm oil before setting it alight; from the ashes, the prophet claimed a trophy convert when the chief of the town was baptized as Solomon.[1]

Africans scrutinized omens with familiar tools of cultural exegesis, such as dreams, dream incubation, dream interpretation, divination, spirit possession, and clairvoyance. Africans concluded that, because of the evils and disruption caused by the slave trade, the old cults were dying and the white man's way of worshiping God was spreading and would one day prevail. In 1863, Samuel Pearse, a local clergyman, reported a conversation with an elderly woman of Badagry, Nigeria, who mused ruefully on the strange times people were passing through, times "when the worship of idols being transmitted from one generation to another was in crisis. The horrors of the wars that ensued doomed many [people] to an untimely dissolution and sold them into slavery. In the state of slavery how is it possible they could do such justice to worship as did their forefathers, and yet the evils came that were never seen nor heard of were the orisas [deities] alive?"[2]

Instead of pitting the older and younger generations against each other in a sudden access of interethnic viciousness—as happened with the elderly Sutu and her son, Sandilli—the new ideas of millennialism joined both young and old in the task of renewal, and of salvaging what was worthy in the old ways. The plea of the old Yoruba woman on behalf of the embattled *orisas* reached the ears of the younger Samuel Pearse and inspired him to embark on a salvage operation with the new orientation Christianity represented.

Throughout the continent it was this hopeful reconciliation of old and new that the work of the new Christian charismatic prophets stood to promote. They took African millenarianism in a new direction by rejecting the status quo and by teaching reassurance, trust, spiritual efficacy, and a sense of community. Provoked by the way Europeans bulldozed their way into much of the continent the old vigilance persisted, but it was vigilance freed of the menace of the avenger and inspired by a vision for the poor, the weak, the dishonored, and the underdog. Armed with such values, the new elites of Africa (including the so-called Creoles) performed an important task by providing a bridge between an exploitative colonial system and an oppressive chieftaincy system. The catastrophic failure that followed their decline is a measure of their importance.[3]

The circumstances behind the emergence of the new modernizing Christian Africans were full of drama and pathos. The tribal ways were being trampled upon by incoming whites, the Africans reasoned, while the guardians of tradition looked on bemused or (which amounted to the same thing) colluded with their exploiters. An old woman diviner made a bitter complaint that the road being built by the colonial administration went through her town and broke her sacred pot. She left the town in protest.[4] The young African who heard her complaint had manned the steamroller used in the road construction, and he later became a charismatic leader prophesying a new millennium. Charismatic power bestowed on the weak and rejected was one way, then, to answer the challenge of tribal disarray and the pain of white domination. Christianity met a real need.

Delta Ferment

In this connection, one charismatic movement with overt political overtones was that led by Garrick Sokari Braide. He was born in about 1882 in the village of Obonoma in Kalabar, east of the Niger Delta. Obonoma—the birthplace, too, of his mother, Abarigania—was a stronghold of traditional religious worship, being a center of pilgrimage to the titular deity, *Ogu*. Garrick Braide, however, grew up in Bakana where his father, Daketima Braide, had settled. Some accounts speak of the young Braide being initiated into the *Ogu* cult at Obonoma by his mother.

Braide's parents were too poor to send him to school, so he grew up somewhat on the margins of the Christianity that was penetrating the area. Braide became acquainted with Christianity from the open-air meetings in Bakana, which began around 1886. The meetings appeared to have had a defining effect on him, for he was an inquirer and participant at the St. Andrew's

Sunday School in Bakana in the 1890s. While there, he came under the instruction of Rev. Moses Kemmer of Brass. The instruction was in the Igbo language, which Braide had to learn. It was a long apprenticeship. He completed his catechetical course and was baptized on January 23, 1910, aged twenty-eight. In 1912, he was confirmed by the eminent Yoruba clergyman Bishop James Johnson.

Braide's mature years increased his sense of personal urgency about the role he would play in his newly adopted religion. Reports mention his regime of withdrawal for private meditation and religious exercises. He went to St. Andrew's Church on weekdays for quiet personal devotions, including prayers of forgiveness for sin and for the personal intervention of Jesus. He carried a Bible and a prayer book.

Braide became a prominent figure in the Niger Delta Pastorate Church, noted for his charismatic gifts of prayer, prophecy, and healing, the gold standard of charismatic religion. People responded enthusiastically to Braide, attracted by public display of his charismatic gifts. He is reputed to have once caused a heavy storm as punishment for those who defied his orders to observe Sunday as a day of rest and prayer. On another occasion, he performed a prayer ritual for rain in order to spoil plans for a local dance that he deemed offensive to religion. His reputation as a rainmaker spread widely, making it difficult to say whether the standard format of the Christian catechism or the divinatory method of *Ogu* was the more powerful motivator.

As if to clear up that ambiguity, Braide launched a campaign against the symbols of African religion, demanding devotees to abandon their charms, confess their sins, and make trust in God their supreme rule in life. Braide seemed to have been driven by a need to deal with the reality of the old spirits; he would not rest until he felt that he had subdued them. Yet his method deepened the paradox of the role that Christianity—or his version of it—played in providing answers to questions that the old spirits once dominated but had long since met with silence. Braide brought his knowledge of traditional religion to bear on his role in Christianity. Like the old village religions, Christianity had power, but it had a greater power and a clearer monotheist message. Christianity was bound to prevail in the contest with the agents of Baal of Africa, just as Elijah did against the prophets of Baal.[5]

While Braide might have succeeded in harnessing *Ogu*'s power to the new Christian teaching, it would be a different matter with the colonial administration. By Braide's time, drunkenness and alcoholism had wreaked havoc on the populations of the Delta towns and villages. Some three million gallons of gin and rum were consumed there every year, a level of consumption that ensured steady income from the excise tax to fill the colonial coffers, while taking a heavy toll on the social fabric. Braide was extremely effective in preaching against alcohol consumption; as a consequence, a temperance drive was launched which brought him to the hostile attention of the authorities. Braide's effectiveness threatened the excise revenue, which turned him into more than a religious nuisance. By 1916, at the height of Braide's movement, the government was showing a massive loss of revenue to the tune of £576,000 in excise taxes.[6]

Meanwhile, at about the same time, the French in the Ivory Coast were closely watching the conduct of another charismatic figure, Prophet William Wadé Harris. Harris was also turning himself into more than a religious nuisance, and the British decided that they should mount a similar surveillance of Braide's activities. As a self-declared prophet, Braide became a lightning rod for local discontent and, the British felt, he could not be ignored. Besides, the events of the First World War had produced deep nervousness in official circles by then: Germany, the common enemy of the French and the British, was entrenched in the nearby Cameroon colony. The British struck. Braide was arrested in March 1916 and tried for economic sabotage and false teaching. He was found guilty and sent to prison. He died in November 1918, a few months after his release.

Braide's preaching boosted the membership rolls of the Protestant, Catholic and Independent churches in the Niger Delta. In 1909 when Braide began preaching, there were only 900 baptized Christians on the membership rolls of all the churches. By 1918, that number had increased to some 11,700. The increase for the Catholic Church in the period between 1912 and 1917 was 500 percent, largely to Braide's work.

The conversions were so great that the new believers could not be contained within the historic mission churches, so a large number reconstituted themselves as a separate body in 1916, taking the name Christ Army Church. This church became, in effect, a rival to the Niger Delta Pastorate Church presided over by Bishop James Johnson. The Christ Army Church applied for affiliation to the World Evangelical Alliance in London in 1917, a necessary insurance policy for an indigenous movement without much educated leadership and caught in the web of global forces. Outside sponsorship would garner local prestige and protection.

Another general consequence of Braide's activity was his adoption by nationalist opinion as an agent and symbol of political freedom. The *Lagos Weekly Standard* espoused his cause in op-ed pieces and in other articles. The *Standard* claimed that Braide was anointed by "the God of the Negro" as an instrument to achieve the liberation of Africa. Braide was defended against the attacks of Bishop James Johnson and of other leaders of the Niger Delta Pastorate

Church. The *Standard* applauded Braide's career as demonstrating that colonial and episcopal structures and hierarchies were out of step with Africa's true needs, saying that Braide should be embraced as a hero by all genuine patriots. In their view, Braide offered an African cultural alternative to Western forms of Christianity and looked to people at the grass roots to lead in the mission effort. His accomplishment was instructive about Africa's desire to be freed from foreign domination.

The period of Braide's activities was a generally auspicious one for revival fervor. Not all winds will steer a boat, but in this case several forces conspired to propel the charismatic and Pentecostal movements forward. One was the worldwide influenza epidemic of 1918, known as the Great Pandemic, during which a series of revival meetings was held across Yoruba country and beyond. The series was partly a response to the urgent need for healing, for the epidemic reached its height in the area in October 1918. Many of the central figures of this revival were disaffected members of missionary-led churches and resolved to break out on their own. Then, the global economic slump of the 1920s—culminating in the Wall Street crash and the Depression that followed—caused great hardship among the people, leading the government to adopt highly unpopular measures. The city of Lagos was ravaged by bubonic plague between 1924 and 1926, increasing the appeal of applied religion and setting the stage for the new religious leaders to offer charismatic solutions: prophecy, prayer, dreams, visions, healing, and a sense of community. To even further increase the sense of depression, there was severe famine in 1932.

The revival meetings were carefully coordinated, with individuals traveling between meeting points and maintaining a resource network of personal contacts and intercessory mediation. The formative period was from 1918 to 1930, when "many implicit views of Christianity by leading Christians turned into something explicit."[7] At the center was a millennial-type figure, Joseph Ayo Babalola (d. 1959). In July 1930, at a vast public meeting at the Yoruba town of Ilesha, Babalola,

> clad in white shorts and shirt, with Bible and handbell, preached to the people to renounce evil practices and witchcraft, and to bring out for burning all their idols and juju, for God was powerful enough to answer all their needs, and to cure them. Furthermore, what became a standard practice, he sanctified the near-by stream by prayer, as *omi iye*, the water of life, as had been revealed to him. A District Officer who attended a meeting noted its purely religious and inoffensive character; it was not dramatic or exciting, and was most impressive when people raised the water-vessels on their heads for Babalola

to bless them. He took no money and the crowds were orderly; the worst confusion was on the roads leading to Ilesha from Ife and Ijebu.[8]

Babalola was born in 1904 in Ilorin Province, now Kwara State, Nigeria. He had a few years of primary school education, quitting at a mature age in 1928. He was subsequently employed as a steamroller driver with the colonial Public Works Department. While engaged in this work, he claimed to have heard a voice calling him to devote himself to preaching the gospel. Like his counterparts in Scripture, such as Amos and Isaiah, Babalola was given a parable of his mission. In that parable, he saw three palm leaves attached to his steamroller: one was dead and dry, the other was wilting, and the third was fresh and green, which represented those who responded favorably to his message. He was commanded to take a bell as the symbol of his commissioning and was given the promise that prayer and the *omi iye* would cure all manner of illness.

When Babalola burst upon the unsuspecting townspeople they were startled by his wild, dramatic appearance: he was naked and covered in ashes, carried a bell, and, in the manner of John the Baptist, called upon the people to repent. Finally, after predictable opposition in several places, Babalola arrived at the town of Ebute Metta near Lagos where, in December 1929, a fellow charismatic preacher baptized him.

Babalola acquired a reputation as a master of powerful prayers. When he was at Ilesha, he prayed in the name of *Oluwa Olorun Alayé*, "Lord God of Life." When news of this reached the town of Efon, it is reported to have impressed the chief, the Alayé of Efon, because of the apparent pun on his own title. When Babalola subsequently arrived at Efon, a rousing hero's welcome awaited him.

The Ilesha revival that inaugurated Babalola's millennial career was soon followed by an outpouring of the spirit in Ibadan from a man who had attended the Ilesha meeting and was now on his way back to Lagos. The cascade swept over a string of other places, including Abeokuta; Ijesha; Ekiti; Ondo; and, most impressive of all, Efon, where Babalola, the prince of prayer, strategically established a center. With some half a million followers, his movement became known as the *Aladura*, a Yoruba word for "prayer." (It is derived from the Arabic, *al-du'a*, supplicatory prayer, to be distinguished from *salát*, canonical prayer.) Before long, charismatic envoys, prophets, and prophetesses were touring the country, preaching, prophesying, organizing, healing, and confirming, reaching places as far apart as Onitsha and Port Harcourt in the Delta region, and Kano and Sokoto in the Muslim north, over a thousand miles apart. Adhering loosely to denominational boundaries, the revival leaders actually helped the mission-led churches increase their membership and experience a quickening of religious interest.

The Roman Catholic Church, in particular, was swept up in the fervor as African Catholics moved to the forefront of the movement. It turned out that the charismatic renewal had gained greater acceptance and support in the Catholic Church than in other mainline denominations. Most Protestant churches had a decidedly negative attitude toward the phenomenon because of the splits the movement caused in Kansas since 1901. Foisted on the charismatics, the term "holy rollers" reflected the hostility with which mainline Protestant leaders regarded charismatic devotees.[9] By contrast, the Catholic environment was less hostile.

Although it would be natural to assume that the charismatic link in African Catholicism was introduced at the hands of local people, in fact it came by way of an expatriate American and Dominican priest named Richard Farmer. He founded a group in Ibadan, Nigeria, in March 1973, and enrolled the members in what he called the *Life in the Spirit Seminar*. Similar groups were started in the metropolitan Lagos area, along with Bible studies, weekly meetings devoted to learning new songs, and a monthly paper, *Living Waters*. The Catholic newspaper, the *Independent*, began carrying articles on charismatic experience written by Fr. Farmer.

By March 1975, some thirty-five articles were published. A year later, some 45 groups in eleven states were active. In the midst of this ferment, a visiting team from the United States arrived led by Fr. Francis MacNutt, a Harvard educated charismatic pioneer. The team held meetings in various towns and cities across Nigeria, praying for "baptism in the spirit." In one public meeting, a crowd of about 1,500 attended; at another, the number was estimated at 1,700. A prominent feature of the meetings was prayer for healing, a subject of study by Fr. MacNutt. A point he made is worth recapitulating here. Mainline Western Christianity asserted that, although healing was unquestionably a central theme of the teaching and ministry of Jesus, there were no grounds for assuming that it was a valid vocation for the church in the modern world. That position, Fr. MacNutt contended, was unsupported by Scripture and by experience.[10]

According to him, Christ intended his healing ministry to continue not only in apostolic times, as the church teaches, but also in our own. MacNutt stressed the fact that the charismatic gift of healing was not intended to dispense or conflict with modern medicine, or even with the mystery of suffering and death. On the contrary, the gift of healing only called upon powers and forces that were beyond human control, thus helping to anchor faith in a God who cared for our wellbeing. God was the source of life, and was within the range of human need and misfortune rather than being impotent in the face of suffering and death.

Armed now with sufficient theological ammunition, MacNutt declared a ringing endorsement of charismatic Christianity as fundamentally consonant with the spiritual quality of African life. He called for the adaptation of Christianity to the African realities of the spirit world, noting that the phenomenon of the *Aladura* revival and its popularity were evidence of a charismatic void in the lives of ordinary Christians who received little help from the mainline churches. MacNutt's observations indicate his awareness that a post-Western reality in Africa and elsewhere had overtaken the churches of the post-Christian West as they scrambled to salvage what they could from their costly truce with secularism.

MacNutt's message had deep resonance with Africans. In a testimony published in the monthly, *Living Waters*, a Catholic charismatic devotee described how he experienced healing and about how he now understood the deeper meaning of healing. He said before he received the baptism of the spirit he was not able to relate to people in a loving way. He easily took offense and was always on guard. He found it hard to forgive, he confessed, and that left him with no peace of mind. Realizing that he was hampered in his relationships, he prayed for the gift of forgiveness, which he said he received and was confirmed reputedly by general approbation. For him, healing was of the body as well as of restoration of relationship.

In the turn it took in its post-Western phase, charismatic religion was more than a spacey rhapsodic binge, just as its effects went far beyond wild spectacles and heady excitement. The West insisted that worship must be of a God who was intellectualizable, because intellectual veracity was the safeguard against mystification and superstition. Yet for Africans, the call for explanation was not equal in its drawing power to the appeal of the living God before whose eternal mystery explanation must exhaust itself in worship. Only the reality of a transformed spiritual life could commune with God, which, in part, was the need that the African charismatic movement existed to meet. The religious experience is about intimacy, connection, trust, discovery, and an ethical life in community and solidarity. As the Wolof expression has it, *njebbel jotewul jaxas*: "the pledge is not with guile." It is true that God welcomes the erudite, but He especially invites the pure in heart to worship Him.

Coastal Surge

Meanwhile, a new tide of charismatic renewal was surging elsewhere on the West African coast. It crested in the religious career of Prophet William Wadé

Harris of the Ivory Coast, whose call to conversion represents one of the most spectacular examples of resurgence in the history of the Christian movement. Harris was born in 1860 in Liberia, and died in April 1929. In 1892, he was employed by the American Episcopal Mission in Liberia as a schoolteacher and catechist. He was involved in several political incidents, including an anti-Republican uprising in 1909 in which the British Union Jack was raised over the Liberian flag. For his part in the uprising, Harris was arrested, tried, sentenced to imprisonment, and fined $500. He was subsequently placed on parole.

Harris took part in the Glebo War of 1910, when he was again arrested and imprisoned. While in jail, he reported a spiritual experience in which the angel Gabriel appeared to him and commissioned him to be a prophet, commanding him to preach repentance, to abolish fetish worship, and to baptize converts. Released later in 1910, Harris began a preaching tour in Liberia. He set out in 1913, striking eastward along the coastal belt of the Ivory Coast and further on to Axim in western Ghana. In December 1914, his meteoric preaching career was abruptly ended when the French arrested him. In January 1915, the French banished him from the Ivory Coast.

In eighteen months of public preaching Harris converted some 200,000 people, who at first opportunity embraced his lean iconoclastic message and went on to suffer a decade of harsh colonial suppression and persecution before European missionary societies responded. Between 1910 and 1913, under the lieutenant governor Gabriel Angoulvant, the back of Ivory Coast's anti-colonial insurgency was broken through a program that military officers euphemistically called "pacification." Angoulvant had the local rulers disarmed and interned, villages destroyed, and people regrouped into newly constructed settlements. He also imposed a poll tax and, to help pay for the tax, instituted the *corvée*, or forced labor. Harris swept into this vortex to add a further twist to colonial efforts at obtaining the prompt and orderly submission of Africans. In effect, Harris opened a new front in the colonial war to take the country. The French realized that they needed to expropriate Harris' moral capital lest Africans be emboldened by it to question colonial legitimacy. Christianity as an uncontrolled moral capital was a flammable ideology in the hands of Africans. Harris was rounded up and expelled, with an armed embargo clamped upon his followers.

The intimate details we know of the Harris movement come from eyewitness accounts and contemporary reports, some of them a bit incredulous—how could an unauthorized native presume to Christianize his heathen brethren?—yet much of it also careful and faithful. Acting under official instructions, Fr. J. Hartz, the Superior of *Missions Africaines* in the Ivory Coast, took notes at a meeting with Harris. Fr. Hartz described Harris as a man in his forties, with a long graying beard, a flowing white robe with broad sleeves, sandals, and a white turban. He carried a wooden cross and a small calabash containing seeds slung in a net decorated with cowrie shells, and carried a Bible which he obtained from the Wesleyans. He claimed to be the envoy of Christ, a new John the Baptist, who came to convert fetish worshippers. His followers included several women, clothed in white like him. Under orders from the colonial administration, Fr. Hartz interviewed Harris who "expounded the purpose of his visit to me in that pure and correct English which does such credit to Great Britain." Here is part of Harris' testimony to Fr. Hatz:

> I am a prophet. Above all religions and beyond the control of men, I draw my authority from God alone, through the mediation of the angel Gabriel. Four years ago I was suddenly wakened in the night. I saw the guardian Angel in visible form above my bed. Three times he struck the crown of my head and said to me: "I demand from you the sacrifice of your wife. She will die, but I will give you others who will help you in the work which you must undertake. Before she dies your wife will give you six shillings; this will be your fortune; you will never need any more. With these six shillings, you will go everywhere. They will never fail you. I will go with you everywhere and reveal to you the mission for which you are destined by God, Master of the Universe, whom men no longer respect." After this revelation the Angel appeared on other occasions, and is gradually initiating me into my mission as the prophet of modern times, of the Age of Peace of which Saint John speaks in the twentieth chapter of the Book of Revelation: the Peace of a thousand years, whose coming is nigh. In fact my wife died soon afterwards, she too having learned of my Mission from the Angel. Before leaving me she foretold the difficulties of succeeding in my Mission. I was a Wesleyan teacher, and preacher, in the minister's absence. I now prepared for my prophetic ministry by prayer, and by reading and studying the Bible. The Angel taught me of things to come: the actions of Gog and Magog, the wiles of the great dragon . . . which is to be found for a thousand years. . . . I am sent by Christ, and nothing shall prevent me from accomplishing the deeds to which he calls me. I am going through this country, driven by inspiration from On High. I must bring back the lost nations to Christ, and to do so must threaten them with worse punishments, so that they may allow themselves to be baptized and instructed by Men of God, both Catholic and Protestant. I must bring men to honour the Natural Law and the divine precepts, and especially the observance of

Sunday, which is so much neglected. I am coming to speak for all the people of this country, White or Black. No abuse of alcohol. Respect for Authority. I tolerate polygamy, but I forbid adultery. Thunder will speak, and the Angels will punish the World if it does not hear my words, which interpret the Word of God.[11]

Jubilant with the results of his preaching, Harris continued to expound his mission to Fr. Hartz, "now with the fire of passionate conviction, now with the smile of a calm and tranquil man who sees that one shares his views and sympathies." When asked for a sign, Harris responded that he could make rain but that the true sign was the presence of masses of people who had understood and turned to him. People were changing their lives and pressing toward him from all directions. Harris sang and danced and played what he called his "celestial harp," the women striking their calabashes, while baptismal ceremonies were being conducted in the foreground. It was an inspired and inspiring spectacle. When Fr. Hartz asked Harris not to baptize, Harris replied that Christ bade him to do it. Fr. Hartz interceded with him again not to baptize. "He thereupon brought hundreds of people to me to baptize myself. When I asked him to wait until Instruction should have made of these people souls capable of understanding the blessing of Baptism, he replied, 'God will do that.' "[12]

In his assessment of the impact of Prophet Harris, Fr. Hartz noted that Harris was venerated as a saint wherever he went. He had a considerable effect on the Catholic Church, causing an irresistible surge of people into the church. In Bassam, for example, the Catholic Church was too small to hold the number of people converted at the hands of Harris. In 1917, there were about eight thousand members on the Catholic rolls; by 1922, there were more than twenty thousand. A Catholic missionary priest, Fr. Gorju, could not resist insulting Harris while also paying him grudging tribute, admitting that "What he did none of us would have been able to do, indeed, because the methods were forbidden to us. That hallucinating man, who was also a charlatan, did, in barely three months, what we, ministers of Our Lord Jesus Christ, were not even able to begin doing in twenty years."[13]

Protestants and Catholics began to compete for Harris' converts, each side claiming Harris for itself. The Catholic Mission that had kept its distance from Harris sought openly to profit from his influence. Father Hartz paid tribute to Harris for creating popular sympathy among Africans for the Catholic Church. According to a report in 1918 by Fr. O'Herlihy of the Catholic Mission at Betu in Kroo country, Harris had assured him that "his mission is not to found any special church but to draw all black men to Christianity, [to] baptize them, and

[to] share them out among the different churches." Father O'Herlihy continued, somewhat tongue in cheek: "last week he had a special revelation—he is a grand pal of Gabriel's—that Mary, Mother of God, was in counsel with the angels to ask God to stop the war."[14]

William Platt described a heady occasion when he first arrived in the Ivory Coast, near midnight, to establish the Methodist Mission there. Expecting a sleeping town he found instead "a town *en fête* with a procession, songs, [and] lanterns awaiting our arrival." Although a large throng of Harris' converts had already signed a deed placing themselves under Methodist supervision, many others made up their minds to join the Catholic Church during the Holy Week vigil, thanks to a Catholic catechist who was stationed in the town.[15] The Catholic appeal appeared to strengthen with the revival fervor that Harris stirred.

However, in his message—or what was purported to be his message—to the churches in the Ivory Coast dictated to a Protestant missionary, Harris advised his converts not to join the Roman Catholic Church if they wished to remain faithful to him. The message is dated September 25, 1926, and seems suspiciously inconsistent with the broad theme of his preaching. Catholic reports about Harris' broad-spectrum ecumenical approach are supported by similar reports in other Protestant accounts, as we shall see presently. At any rate, we may note that as late as 1961, at a conference in Louvain, Fr. Hartz's story of William Wadé Harris appeared in the proceedings under the rubric of non-Christian religions. Europe was obviously slow to recognize Africa as a new and valid Christian frontier.[16]

Father Hartz's contemporary positive assessment of Harris, however, is echoed on the Protestant side, with witnesses reporting on the extraordinary effect Harris wrought on the littoral populations of the Ivory Coast and western Ghana. One of these Protestant witnesses was Pastor Pierre Benoît, a Wesleyan missionary who met Harris in September 1926, by which time Harris had suffered a stroke that left him partially paralyzed, seriously hampering his preaching. Benoît conducted extensive interviews with Harris who was much reduced in vigor but not morale, and the record of those interviews represents the most extensive, detailed portrait of Harris available.

Harris emerges from the interviews as a full-blown charismatic prophetic figure who used his reputation for miracles, signs, and wonders to stir to life a largely peasant backwoods society scattered among an uncoordinated string of village shrines and homesteads. Facing the accelerating machinery of colonial takeover, Harris set Christianity on a collision course with imperial hegemony and thereby gave the African response a popular religious outlet, to the utter befuddlement of officials. The Catholic ambivalence toward Harris, and toward the ensuing Protestant missions—which French administrative officials regarded with equal suspicion—showed a two-faced Christianity occupying the field. It compromised not only establishment Christianity, but also the European claim to being the religion's indispensable agents, in both cases to the begrudged benefit of Africans.

Pierre Benoît painted a detailed portrait of Harris, especially of his physical stature. He said Harris talked very quickly, with vehemence, his chin pointing forward with a gleam in his big eyes as they rolled in their sockets. He had a strong, well-preserved body, his broad shoulders carrying a proud and expressive head. His muscular arms and strong legs were those of an athlete. He weighed about 85 kg. Harris found it difficult to sit still, changing his seat several times and nervously pacing up and down the room. He seemed always agitated, a sign, perhaps, of suppressed spiritual energy.[17] A note of abiding urgency rose in his words as he warned repeatedly of the approaching denouement. He cut a striking apocalyptic figure, mitigated somewhat by his advice to build and organize churches for his converts.

Prophet in Profile

Harris was a subject ready-made for legend and more: invention, exaggeration, and denominational axe-grinding. Harris' own remarkably conciliatory tone was soon diverted by over-eager prospectors, who felt the need to collar his movement for the benefit of home audiences and metropolitan heartland advantage. Even Benoît's otherwise admirably scrupulous reporting did not entirely avoid this partisanship, for one suspects that he leaned on Harris to specify the "Wesleyans" as inheritors of his work. There is much to regret in that outcome, because Harris provided convincing evidence and powerful enough incentive by his own example for others to repair the harm caused by religious divisions and theological differences. Meanwhile, colonialism offered a convenient alibi for ecclesiastical authorities to raise the partisan stakes.

Some of the reports of the Harrist phenomenon provided useful information on the fortunes of Christianity in Africa, as well as on the mixed prospects of missions generally. Missionary observers expressed a sense of incredulous delight at the news that Harris was converting people in droves, and their reports led to a stampede in the field. The trail was blazed by William J. Platt, the senior Methodist missionary based in Dahomey, now the Republic of Benin, since 1916. He wrote an invaluable contemporary study of Harris, *An African Prophet*, and used that information to produce a typology of Prophet Movements in Africa in his book, *From Fetish to Faith: The Growth of the Church in West Africa* (1935). Platt, who assumed personal responsibility for the Harrist converts, was instrumental in getting the younger Benoîts to enter the field. At long range, Platt was overseeing 32,000 of these converts who were maintained in 160 congregations. Platt's understanding of Harris' message noted the prophet's strong monotheist emphasis and his demand for people to abandon their idols, to turn in faith to the one true God of Scripture, and to observe the Sabbath, a remarkable example that of how the Jewish monotheist tradition survived intact in the Harrist movement. That Jewish thread has remained strong in the centuries-long Christian movement, and is a unifying theme in the general post-Western Christian resurgence.

Platt observed that, as far as his preaching work was concerned, Harris was connected to no religious denomination or organization.

> He wanted no money, only the repentance of the people. . . . He preached by interpretation to ten different tribes. He, too, demanded the destruction of the lower religious symbols of magic and witchcraft in the search for God. His movement achieved astounding success, until in 1915 it was calculated by the French Government officials that one hundred thousand people had accepted allegiance to Harris. These folk burned their superstitious symbols, built small churches, said prayers, and paid nearby African clerks from other colonies to teach them hymns. But they had no teachers, no translated Bible, little or no knowledge. Then, again, unworthy "minor prophets" arose to make money out of the credulity and earnestness of these simple pagans, and, fearing disturbance in war-time, the government asked Harris to leave the Ivory Coast. "Wait and pray," he told his people. "Build churches, and one day missionaries will come to teach you the Way." In this remarkable movement we see African prophetism at its best, for its leader brought the people to the very door of the Christian Church.[18]

When Methodist missionaries turned up a decade later, Harris' star had risen to the meridian point, and they hauled some fifty thousand converts into the Methodist church.

> I arrived in one of these villages at midnight. There were hundreds of people in the streets awaiting me, for I happened to be the first missionary. I was taken into a long, low building and found six hundred people seated on the floor. On one wall was a picture of Elijah on Mount Carmel, praying fire from Heaven on his sacrifice while the prophets of Baal looked on. On another wall, John Baptist was seen baptizing in Jordan. These pictures are symbolic of the religion of

those people: standing for repentance and righteousness, but not yet fully Christian. "Harris baptized me ten years ago," the leader of the meeting announced to the crowd. "He told me to preach to the people, and so I have done. Now, Sir," he went on, turning to me, "tonight we hand over ourselves to your Church—two thousand of us in all—if you will only send us a teacher."[19]

The request was for a teacher, we should note, not for an overlord.

Another contemporary report sketched out a roughly identical image of the great work Harris wrought, which is all the more confounding because Harris appeared to bypass the cultural attainment that missionaries regarded as the prerequisite of Christianity. The gospel Harris preached

was elementary: idol worship was wrong and charms unavailing; there is only one God, the Father of all men, and one Saviour, Jesus Christ. In this Name he appealed to his hearers to abandon the fetich and accept the Faith. He had no idea of forming a new sect, but commanded the converts to join themselves to the nearest Church for fuller guidance. He said: "I am not a minister; I am only a voice crying in the wilderness. Repent, for the Kingdom of Heaven is at hand." This man journeyed from village to village, and huge crows followed him. His power was astonishing, and his appeal irresistible. People gathered together in hundreds to burn their idols and charms; fetich priests publicly renounced their works of darkness, and, what was more remarkable still, the majority declared themselves willing to renounce polygamy, the greatest stumbling block to the progress of Christianity in Africa. The wandering preacher disappeared as suddenly as he came. His ministry covered only a period of three months, and then he passed into French territory, when, in the midst of similar scenes, he was arrested by the authorities and imprisoned, and finally expatriated as a disturber of the peace.[20]

Cultural Matrix

There is an unmistakable Muslim flavor in Harris' public persona. His flowing white gown and white beard surmounted by a white turban, the suspended gourd decorated with cowrie shells, a bowl mounted on a Bible in his left hand: all of that was in the style of the ambulatory mendicant Muslim cleric festooned with turban, robe, sacred book, staff, and vials of ink so familiar on the bush tracks and wattle-fenced hamlets of Africa. Harris was not weighed down by the past, but instead proclaimed the gospel in the present tense. Harris' disciples carried his message in the tradition of traveling Muslim novices disseminating the word and *barakah*, grace, of their *muqaddam*, master. Harris embodied, in his own person, the charismatic message he broadcast. He was a living, walking specimen, an oracle of wisdom and deliverance, a vivid manifestation of prophet, preacher, and healer combined. The unadorned bamboo cross in his right hand and the Bible in his left hand were symbols of hope and renewal, and his white turban the seal of his high calling. His open face showed that he had unmasked the spirits and looked into the face of angels. Everything about Harris suggested urgency, movement, mobility, economy, brevity, lightness, poise, and alertness. The common thoroughfare, not the walled manse and its guarded doors, seemed eminently suitable as his stage. He made Christianity a religion of the open road, a religion without borders, and left introspective Catholic and Protestant missions equally in his debt.

Harris established Christianity on the central primal pillar of its post-Western dispensation, and thereby set it against the terms of metropolitan entitlement. Indeed, he wrested Christianity from colonial control and compelled missionaries to face a totally different direction if they wished to see the work of God. The thousands who were converted at his hands, and who stood firm in defiance of the armed containment of colonial sequestration, vindicated his surefooted grasp of their yearning for salvation. Between the French in the Ivory Coast and the British in the Gold Coast, Harris promoted frontier Christianity as a reality transcending the cultural and political boundaries designed for a vanquished people. Salvation-without-strings was the antidote to conversion by civilization. When Harris taught his followers that God was their friend, and that this mattered more than the view that Europeans might be their enemies, he became the epitome of the age. He was the people's prophet, and they embraced him with uncommon devotion and honor.

Reflecting on why the church was making painfully slow progress in his time, one missionary issued a parting plea in 1910 to his colleagues in the field to adopt a more relevant and effective lifestyle, and the model he held up for emulation was the itinerant Muslim teacher, the proverbial footloose Bookman of preliterate societies. The attributes he lists might have come from an advance preview of the style Harris adopted. Writing rather too faintheartedly, the missionary issued a valedictory challenge:

> When we have a policy . . . it will take time and money to work it
> out. . . . Force and cruelty are no longer being used to spread Islam . . .
> the Mohammedan teacher is everywhere. He needs no society

behind him, no funds to sustain him. He goes forth as the first Christians went with his staff and his wallet, and wherever he goes he is at home! He is everywhere welcomed- though perhaps no more freely than the Christian teacher would be. Both have the prestige of being Bookmen and God men. The Christian teacher goes as a stranger among foreigners and must be supported from without. The Mohammedan teacher gets paid in kind for blessing crops, sells charms etc. and he doesn't do anything for nothing. The Christian teacher is debarred from these methods of livelihood, and consequently must be kept or starve. . . . The wonder to my mind is, not that Mohammedanism has spread among the pagan tribes, but that it does not spread more rapidly, and that it should make no impression on the multitudes of professed Christians whose Christianity is so immature and all whose instincts and tradition are in this direction. . . . Even the native ministers and European missionaries show not only lack of special training but want of sympathy and local knowledge . . . a certain aloofness and assumption of superiority [leads them to think] "I belong to a superior race. I condescend to come among you but should never think of living with you or even eating with you." The Arabic teacher will squat round some calabash and dip his hand in the same dish. . . . We must make ourselves neighbourly.[21]

The Muslim theme in Harris' work may also have served another purpose. Muslim clerics viewed the coming of Christianity with alarm, an attitude easily reciprocated on the Christian side. African Muslim clerics and the new charismatic leaders shared a suspicion of missionaries, which suggests that opposition to missionaries should be distinguished from opposition to Christianity itself. The missionary movement was perceived as a rival power, with foreign agents in serious competition with Muslim representatives and local Christian leaders. When the pioneer CMS missionary in Nigeria Rev. David Hinderer returned to Ibadan in 1853 after his furlough, he found that his host Chief Agbakin had died in his absence, and that Muslims had circulated a message not to receive him back. The Muslims said that Hinderer was an evil omen, or perhaps even a sorcerer who would cause peoples' lives to be cut short. "Many were afraid even to shake hands with him, and said they had buried charms in the road to prevent him coming again from Abeokuta."[22] Christianity and Islam were competing in the common idiom of spirit power, not just in the idiom of political influence or of abstruse theological doctrine.

However, in spite of pleas for a change of direction, missionary policy did not budge or yield to field experience. Displaying a singular lack of ecumenical sensitivity, officials wasted little time in rushing to assess and claim Harris' achievement as a credit to the West. While the Harrist movement was in full spate, the Methodist minister Stephen J. Gibson wrote that "in countless ways, small in themselves, but powerful in the aggregate, superstition is being undermined by what we usually sum up as 'civilization.' The gates are being lifted up."[23]

Despite the unimpeachable eyewitness testimony of the great mass movement he witnessed from Harris's preaching, William Platt was undaunted in his confidence in the long-term and permanent salvific benefits of Western civilization. He, too, foresaw a beneficial floodtide swamping all of old Africa before it, and affirmed jubilantly: "Two of the most powerful influences 'undermining' ancient belief and practice in West Africa are Trade and Colonization. It might be said that every new village shop opened is one more blow struck at the slowly dying body of African fetishism, every Ford car performing its marvels on Africa's bush roads is another nail in the coffin of 'Darkest' Africa."[24] Platt returned to this view, saying, "We doubt not that once we, as a Mission, show them [the Harrist converts] that we mean business, they will prefer the enlightenment of that state to the illiteracy which now prevails."[25] It completely escaped Platt that the conversion tide was surging without literacy.

Paul Wood and Antoine Léthel, two French missionaries under the aegis of the Protestant Paris Mission, opted to trump up a justification for essential missionary work in the aftermath of Harris' evangelistic campaign. They did so by concocting a picture of overwhelming need, and thus gave themselves credit for their role in the heroic rescue of heathen Africa. The prospect of foreign paternalism subverted reality, so that what Harris achieved was seen to lack merit. It bolstered claims that the cultural deficit of Africans was justification for European intervention. Wood and Léthel observed that, in spite of their evident enthusiasm, the Africans who came to Christianity through Harris were prominent for "their deep ignorance; their untrained teachers can only repeat distant echoes gathered from the Protestants of the Gold Coast, Liberia, or Sierra Leone; superstition is still great . . . , and morality is weak. But all are aware of their ignorance and have a burning desire for learning, and it is enough to see the warmth with which we have been received to realise the intensity of the universal desire for the true Gospel of Jesus."[26] The statement firmly puts missionaries in the limelight; otherwise it is not a true reflection of the circumstances. Its underlying refrain is: what Harris could not do, missionaries could and would. It stands in striking contrast, for instance, to the testimony of Fr. Hartz who was prepared to give Harris his due and to deal with him with respect in spite of their differences.

Wood and Léthel's statement falls into a pattern. For them, as well as for Platt and others, salvation was a stepping stone to civilization, which they regarded as unquestionably better and more desirable than the escapist idea of life in the hereafter. European secularists, it happened, shared that view. Wood and Léthel restated the sentiment with natural conviction. One begins to wonder what motives drove the missionaries. Should one discount all the missionary rhetoric about the necessity of the gospel and instead look to their metropolitan secular presumptions as the true motivation of their action, or was the cultural outcome they had in mind really the new religion that replaced the witness of the apostolic church? It is a delicate issue of style and substance, with local consequences. In missionary thinking, was religion a trailer for high culture, suggesting skepticism about Harris and about the gospel more profound than historical reports first indicated? Or was that skepticism the missionary hazard of viewing things, not from the point of view of *kairos*, God's time, but from the short end of the colonial telescope?

For their part, converts made a crucial distinction between gospel and civilization; they were willing to embrace Christianity but resisted the drive to bring their lands under colonial control, and the general political primacy of the West. For new converts with little exposure to the West, Christianity was a revealed religion, and it was only incidentally that it became associated with European civilization. It made sense that whites should belong to a religion like Christianity that brought heaven and earth together in singular testimony to the power of God. At any rate, belief in God was a deeply rooted idea and was not something of foreign vintage that would make God into little more than a piece of foreign costume. An original religious spirit enabled Africans not to be bedazzled by the shimmering trophies of civilization into acquiescing in colonial rule as God's mandate. God was for everyone, especially for the powerless. Many in West Africa, for example, took comfort in the victory of Japan in the Russo-Japanese War of 1905, saying Japan's victory echoed that of David over Goliath, in that a world power was humbled by a small country. It echoes Aeschylus' celebration of the defeat of Xerxes as an example of the law of righteousness by which God rules the world. Christianity offered an interpretation of historical events that favored underdogs and, on that ground, there was hope for Africans against colonial domination.

Where Others Sowed

Africans asked whether apostolic witness required civilization as an alibi, and whether it was credible for the West to claim to be exclusive host of the things of God. Could one access Christianity outside the cultural scheme of the West? Peter is the Rock, but was instructional stonewalling a helpful or necessary obstacle? Had Catholics squandered an opportunity of solidarity in faith with the Africans against colonial subjugation? Should John Calvin and John Wesley be the litmus test of Christian conversion? Was Schweitzer justified in his view that high Christology was required to shield Jesus from heathen naïveté?

The colonial and missionary officials gave little merit to the culture of illiterate Africans. As far as the officials were concerned, there was no such thing as illiterate Christianity; the milieu of African oral tradition was deemed unsuitable for the religion. Europe's was a superior civilization, and any compromise of that would be a setback for the Christian order. For officials of such persuasion, "the idea that the interests of an assortment of barbaric, ideal-less and untutored tribesmen, clothed in sheep's fat, castor oil or rancid butter—men who smelt out witches, drank blood warm from the throats of living cattle and believed that rainfall depended on an arrangement of a goat's intestines—should be exalted above those of the educated European would have seemed to them fantastic."[27] Whites who took a pro-African view were guilty of a weakness, and earned the derogatory sobriquet of "flannelfoot" (gullible liberal). Sir Richard Burton, for one, blamed such pro-African views on the missionary movement, saying missions impeded the machinery of colonial hegemony by transfusing its muscular agenda with "homoeopathic doses of scientific political economy."[28] He referred to mission-educated Africans in the "pejorative singular" as the half-reclaimed, semi-clad tribesman stained by the defects of the species.[29]

The Harrist resurgence gave an resounding answer to those aspersions by proclaiming the gospel under local conditions in the present tense, without the intervening adverbial delays, subjunctive distrust, prejudiced modifiers, and subject-object antagonism of the colonial discourse. For Harris and the other new charismatic prophets, the serial origin of Christianity meant that new local beginnings in faith did not need to be tied to overseas sponsorship. Bethlehem was in the heart of the believer—any believer, anywhere.

For these new prophets, the Christian faith was universal in origin, local in character, indigenous in agency, and global only under metropolitan colonial presumptions, presumptions that lurked in the designation of global Christianity. But Westerners were mistaken to think that the science, technology, and communication systems they dominated invested them with the right to make religious generalizations. As Roland Allen pointed out, many people enjoyed the benefits of Western civilization without in the least being predisposed toward Christianity, and many others enjoyed the blessings of Christianity while being adversely impacted by the effects of Western civilization. The West's global projects had, more often than not, trailed adversity.

John Colenso (1814–83), an Anglican missionary to South Africa, echoed these sentiments, saying there was irrefutable evidence to show Progress as the

Destroyer, evidence other than "the heaps of Zulu dead under the guns of the British army." When Colenso lamented conditions and circumstances not only unfavorable but also preclusive of the virtue of godliness—such as grinding poverty, ignorance of good and evil, and vicious, morbid tendencies inherited from vicious parents, all of it surrounded by an atmosphere of vicious feeling and example—he had the great over-grown cities of Europe in mind, not Africa. Colenso continued: "Must modern civilisation, we ask, in its triumphant onward course, pass like the car of Juggernaut over the heads and hearts of these little ones?"[30] The advance of progress had led to the decay of the modern city, Colenso said, and the acids had eaten their way into "the home, the family, the centre and fountain of reverence, of self-respect, of love and moral excellence [causing them to be] obliterated in the over-crowded lodgings."[31] Echoing Adam Smith, Colenso asserted that Western civilization brought its share of misery and wretchedness for non-Western societies in its wake, and was far from being the boon for Africans that missionaries presented it as.

Catholic missionaries might disagree with their Protestant counterparts about who had first claims on the loyalty of the Harrist converts, but both sides assumed that they had civilization in their favor and that alone was enough to settle the argument about whether there was any future for the Africans Harris failed to salvage out of their heathen customs.

In one description, this note of Western superiority is struck insistently although the enthusiastic response of the people to the church is obviously because of its firm anchor in African life and customs. The Vicar General of the *Missions Africaines*, Fr. Lacquerie, testified in 1929 about the warm welcome he received in areas Harris influenced.

> There is singing, there are cries of joy; it is difficult to maintain order.
> These courageous folks want to spread out their garments in the
> path of the Monsignor, but he forbids it; to compensate, they gather
> closely around the hammock which will carry him to the village. A
> chief must never go on foot, and the bishop is a chief. The procession swells as we approach the village. The brass band, which came to
> meet us, performs with such vigour that one fears the horns might
> burst. We cross the village in grand procession to reach the church,
> large, clean, [and] wonderfully adorned. The church fills up as the
> crowd pours in, happy and proud to receive their Pastor for the very
> first time. I am moved when I think that Christianity here is only a few
> years old (i.e. since 1920 when Catholics first arrived!), and that
> these people are but rarely visited by the Fathers. One feels that many
> are instinctively attracted to us, pagans, protestants, and particularly

Harrists, whose chief, a good young man [called André Blagou], has courageously resisted the influences which the heretical pastor [Pierre Benoît] wished to exert over him.[32]

This account minimizes Harris' role and discounts the significance of the definitive primal response to Christianity. Without being oblivious to the divisions of Christianity, Harris was consumed with the work of angels and saw converts of his preaching, not as denominational prizes, but as souls primed for God's favor. That was their primal value, and it explains why he welcomed Catholic and Protestant missions equally to share in that fundamental work of making disciples. It seems like sour grapes to claim the fruits of his labor while disparaging and discounting him as their instrument. Many of the Harrist converts reacted to this inconsistency by subsequently establishing separate communities of their own—and who could blame them?

Right from the beginning, national feelings were stirring in the movement. When Platt arrived in Abidjan in April 1924, expecting to be welcomed as the anointed fulfillment of Harris' prophecy about missionaries coming to teach his people, he was confronted by a leader, Djobe Djako, who demanded of him: "What has this Whiteman come to look for? The village belongs to us and we are not going to observe what he has told us."[33] Platt threatened colonial retribution to silence the criticism; but he knew that if force was required to establish his authority, it was not a convincing sign that the people would welcome him. Platt had wandered into a field not of his own sowing.

One-Sided Story

Missionary jealousy stands to explain a good deal of the ambivalence toward Harris. A leader of the Harrist church reported that "at the bidding of the whites our ancestors buried or burned their fetishes, or threw them into the sea, but then they had nothing with which to replace them. Then they took their fetishes back. They thought that because they had no more fetishes, they had no strength and nothing worked well. They brought back their fetishes and with them they found their strength and freedom again. Each time the whites told them to get rid of their fetishes, they tried to, but they received no replacement. Then Harris came."[34] Africans heard the same message from Harris, but with a vital difference. Harris promised to replace the old emblems of religion with the unrivaled power of the Christian baptism. "Harris said once you are baptized, the fetishes will have no more power over you. Baptism will change your life. You should build a temple and worship God."[35]

Unlike the missionaries, Harris preached a threshold message that God was able to intercede in situations of personal crisis and was needed to effect visible change. Missionaries condemned traditional healing practices and divination as magical superstition, and forbade their converts to practice them. Instead, missionaries prescribed the taking of pills for remedy of ailments, and in so doing severed illness and its remedy from any religious underpinning, Christian or primal.

When Harris dismissed traditional healing as powerless, his converts asked him for an alternative. "His reply was, in effect, take native medicine if you have to; but while you gather the leaves, pray to God; while you prepare the medicine, pray to God; when you take it, pray to God."[36] The pill bottle was the functional equivalent of traditional medicine, but was it, like fetish, disconnected from faith? Missionaries believed so, but Harris' people did not agree. For support, the people could turn to the testimony of Scripture about the tree of life on either side of the river, whose leaves were for the healing of the nations (Rv 22:2).

Alphonse Aké, a Harrist follower, argued that traditional healers looked for short cuts to retain the faith of their patients, thus opening the way for manipulation and abuse. Aké's critique recognized the need for Christianity to contest the ground with traditional healers by making the patient a conscious partner in the healing process. The goal was to shift the patient's trust in merely human means to God as the source of life and health. Here is Aké's exposé of the local herbalist: "Thus, in the case of the fight against this or that sickness, the herbalists first crush the leaves, seeds, or roots of plants which are considered capable of treating the sickness before giving it to the patient for treatment. In this way, the patient is never able to know the origin of this plant, and finds himself obliged to trust his herbalist once more."[37] For Harris, faith in an invisible God was the all-purpose cure for the soul and for the suffering and needy; that message stuck, in contrast to the preaching of the missionaries.

Harrist converts retained a lively sense of religious healing, which allowed Harris to attach the related idea of faith healing: since God was the author of life and of wellbeing, and since evil forces worked to bring about death and misfortune, believers should choose God for their needs against the evil powers. Prayer was a request for healing, whether of body or spirit made no difference. In the battle between good and evil, medicine was not neutral. There was good medicine and bad medicine. Good medicine was God's gift and thus could heal, while bad medicine was the work of evil powers and wrought harm. Both kinds of medicine worked, and both belonged to the world of hidden causes. Thus, good doctors were also good agents and allies in God's work of healing and salvation, while bad doctors harmed their patients. "Thou shall do no harm" of the Hippocratic oath is commensurate with God's mission of healing the broken hearted and binding wounds (Ps 147:3).

The translation enterprise sometimes brought unsuspecting missionaries to the realization that medicine played a complex double role in African societies. In the Luganda version of the Bible, for example, the word "charmer" or "wizard" was rendered as *basawo*, as in Dt 18:10–11: "There shall not be found among you any one that maketh his son or daughter to pass through the fire, or that useth divination, or an observer of times, or an enchanter, or a witch, or a charmer, or a consulter with familiar spirits, or a wizard, or a necromancer." When later medical missionaries arrived in Uganda, they were also called *basawo*. With the Bible in their hand, the local people claimed that Scripture prohibited the practice of medicine. Thanks to this confusion in translation, a movement was launched to shun doctors as enchanters,[38] suggesting that the roots of healing were alive with social sensibility. When missionaries sifted Harris' teaching for magic and superstition, they overlooked the crucial connection between medicine and its spiritual roots. Missionaries used modern medicine to eradicate disease, but also to wipe out superstition; what was left of religion was little more than an irrelevant supplement. Were the missionaries, in fact, bewitched by modern medicine and in need of deliverance, Africans wondered? This cultural conception explains the widespread mistrust of medical missions.

In conditions of colonial subjugation, it was understandable for missionaries to be jealous of Harris' success, with the circumstances of military defeat tempting missionaries to extol the power and efficacy of Western technology against local superstition. The dramatic thrust of French power in the country, exacerbated by the forces unleashed by a market economy, upset the established order and threatened old assurances. An unsettling generation gap opened, pitting a rootless, mobile group of young people against the older generation and scrambling the lines between the sexes. The priests of the Mando cult and other diviners, for example, frequently poisoned young men, and witchcraft accusations became rampant, requiring draconian measures to establish guilt and punish offenders. Some of the ethnic groups, such as the Agnis of Sanwi, used the Harrist movement as justification for defying French colonial intrusion. The Dida people refused to pay taxes and plotted ways to resist French claims over their country. Many more groups believed the popular mobilization resulting from the Harrist resurgence would help them escape the colonial subjugation that they regarded as intolerable.

This is all evidence of widespread collective insecurity and of general strain on the traditional value system. Change ruled the day, and the people felt the need to make a radical choice between the old and new. The work of Prophet

Harris, as of his peers, has to be seen in that light. "Harris had told his converts that they must become Christian or face certain destruction."[39] What Harris accomplished and the methods and means he employed suggest a creative adaptation of inherited ideas and practices to resolve new challenges without incurring the old sanctions. Missionaries were largely ineffectual in responding to those challenges, at least as far as the teachings of the standard Western catechism were concerned, which might explain why missionaries looked to colonization to bring about the outcome they wanted. Colonization demonstrated the fact that Africans were helpless and dependent on the West, whatever the achievements of Harris or others like him. The readiness with which missionaries held up the benefits of Western civilization as the real need of Africans showed in what respect Harris could not compete with Europeans. That missionary attitude was no insignificant factor in complicating the choices Africans faced.

Yet none of these reasons can entirely absolve missionaries from being so unappreciative of the potential of primal religions for responding to the apostolic message. Harris was the gift horse they looked in the mouth. Missionaries believed that only the safety valve of civilization could control the flow of Christian ideas and values and safeguard the religion from syncretism (at least from the syncretism of the subjects, if not of the masters). That attitude provided fodder for scholars who wished to construe mission as cultural imperialism, for it was true that mission represented power. Organized mission was funded and maintained by white people; it represented range and reach beyond the capability of local African bodies; its bureaucracy was self-replenishing; its order and hierarchy more robust and versatile than the oral character of traditional chieftaincy rule; and its network of economic contacts and global outreach far superior to the subsistence economies and sporadic tribal councils of pre-industrial, pre-literate societies. In terms of sheer power, missions were without rival in the field.

Religion and the Irrational

Still, those very considerable advantages imposed a limitation on the ability of missions to operate effectively in the oral milieu of primal societies where religion was not a matter simply of bureaucratic organization, external institutions, once-a-week church attendance, and official nomenclature, but a matter of the spirit, of the unseen, of protection from evil spirits, and of belief in the life hereafter. Power and authority alone could not explain the depth of the spirit or pursue the spirit through its many challenging manifestations.

Africans had, in Christianity, a system of ideas they could connect to the old framework. A chief wrote to a missionary informing him that the chief and his people had already received Christianity but felt in need of instruction. His main motivation in requesting help was because he saw Christianity as a defense against the devil. The chief feared that the return of the devil was imminent. "To avoid the devil visiting us any more, we pray that your Church supplies our need by sending a teacher here before the close of the month."[40]

In the African resurgence, evil, like healing, remained a major preoccupation, and the new charismatic leaders gave it close attention. A leader of the new Pentecostal movement in Ghana named Apostle Opoku Onyinah produced a handbook on the subject, *Ancestral Curses*, in which he scanned the Bible, assembling materials and dividing them into appropriate subject matters in order to diagnose and prescribe remedies for affliction. He offered Christianity as the power to render the curse null and void, saying faith in Christ dissolved the potency of the undeserved curse, citing Proverbs to that effect: "Like a fluttering sparrow or a darting swallow, an undeserved curse does not come to rest."[41]

However, that still left the deserved curse to contend with. Apostle Onyinah dealt with the issue in the present tense. He stressed that the curse was the result of disobedience to God, and the remedy was obedience to God; the very God who made provision in Scripture for His people, Israel, to avert the consequences of the curse. The fruit of the curse was death, while the fruit of obedience was life. On that point, Onyinah cited Paul: "Just as sin entered the world through one man, and death through sin and in the same way death came to all men, because all have sinned."[42] Onyinah elaborated: "Without the fall of Adam, no other curse would have occurred. It is the root cause of all man's problems. The fallen nature is an enemy of God and seeks to do its own [thing]. The attempt to do one's own thing without God is disobedience, which is the basic cause of a curse."[43] To remove the tree of affliction, Onyinah dug under the root.

Believers in God acquired a new status, having not only been cleansed of evil but also assuming the role of moral agents. Onyinah cited the Gospel: "For by your words you will be acquitted, and by your words you will be condemned."[44] The redeemed in Christ held in their hands the key to their own wellbeing as well as to their own affliction. Submission to God stemmed from the same source as disobedience to God—the moral will. However, not all misfortune was the result of a curse. Onyinah pointed out that Jesus attributed the chronic affliction of a man born blind from birth not to the man himself or to his parents but to God so that His works might be displayed in the man's life.[45]

Onyinah stressed that Christians were not exempt from suffering. "I must say positively that the Scripture also speaks about Christians suffering."[46] This view of affliction represented a fundamental alteration in traditional systems of explanation by introducing into the equation, for the first time, a God of salvation. Onyinah described the culmination of the entire kerygmatic process begun by Abraham by citing Scripture: "Christ redeemed us from the curse of the law by becoming a curse for us, for it is written, 'Cursed is everyone who is hung on a tree.' He redeemed us in order that the blessings given to Abraham might come to the Gentiles through Christ Jesus, so that by faith we might receive the promise of the Spirit."[47] Christianity was the solution for overcoming demons, Onyinah claimed in a study of that title.[48]

For much of the time, this theological reflection eclipsed issues of rank and social status (although it contained an implicit critique of social and physical deprivation by addressing social and physical need as part and parcel of the answer Christianity offered to all and sundry). The verdict of E. Bolaji-Idowu, one of Africa's most influential theologians, is pertinent here. Bolaji-Idowu argued that Christianity enlarged the people's vision, freed their minds from the shackles of superstition and the irrational, and liberated their spirits from besetting fears.[49] For him, the idea of divine transcendence did not mean divine remoteness or indifference; it meant transcendent solutions for spiritual and social problems. In the face of life's enigmas, God was dependable, and that fact drained the universe of its bogeys and jinxes.

By the same token, divine omnipotence meant simply that God's power was greater than the aggressive colonial version that was entering the land, for political control lacked the potency and permanence of faith in God. Africans remembered that administrators were dismissive of religion while they were bent on extending their power uncontested. Yet for Africans, material authority could not ultimately prevail over the effects of hidden causes that were more potent; in any case, Apostle Onyinah assured his followers that both were evidence of God's undivided sovereignty. Africans were aggrieved that missions did not share a view of God's work as something greater than the claims of colonial subjugation and scientific superiority, work that made little moral distinction among levels of economic, intellectual, or cultural attainment. For the missionaries, Christianity was religion without the irrational elements.

Missionaries might have recalled the sentiments expressed by Lactantius, the fourth century North African theologian who brokered the Christian faith to its cultured despisers of the age. Lactantius spoke about the one God who gave being and life to all, who wished us all to be equal, and to be alike in our moral dignity as we are in our moral inadequacies. Human beings had the same terms of life, and an equal longing for eternal fellowship. No one was excluded from the benefits of heaven, or from a place in the daylight. It was the one power that nurtured the earth for the benefit of all, and sustained us, not as slave or master, but as free and worthy. Within the divine providence, no one was exempt from the obligations of the moral life or from its privileges. The salvific benefits of Christ made no invidious distinction or grudging concession, as the Gentile experience showed. The apostolic practice in that regard laid down the precept that, where it was necessary, Christians must violate the taboo of cultural exclusion in order to fulfill the promises God first made to the Jewish nation and subsequently to the Gentiles: "If you are Christ's, then you are Abraham's offspring, heirs according to promise."

Awakening in Weakness

The *Missions Africaines* to which Father Lacquerie belonged was founded by Cardinal Lavigerie, who made respect and identification with African life and culture—what he termed "my beloved Africa"—a central plank of his missionary vocation. "I have loved everything about Africa," he wrote effusively, "her past, her future, her mountains, her clear sky, her sunshine, the great sweep of her deserts, the azure waves that bathe her coasts." Lavigerie made it a requirement for missionaries of his order to adhere, without exception, to his rule of love for Africa and for Africans, and "he harshly upbraided any White Father whose letters or reports bore traces of revulsion or disdain that appeared to belie such love."[50] The reality, however, was often different, as Lacquerie and his colleagues showed.

Undeterred by missionary willfulness or shortcomings, Harris and his charismatic cohorts pressed on with their agenda. Harris himself was a tangible, embodied expression of Christianity's primal affinity; a Christianity not drained of its founding appeal. Helmut Thielicke, a German theologian, once observed that angels could not have been effective bearers of the gospel because their celestial attributes would have disqualified them from sharing in the lives of ordinary persons, nor could personalities of marble character have succeeded because their impassive natures would have made them a sarcasm upon human feebleness and a mockery of human needs. Yet by their aloof self-contentment, missionaries took on the attributes of remote agents with little sensitivity to local people and, by doing so, placed the Gospel beyond reach, threatening to make it irrelevant.

Harris and his transnational movement averted such a negative outcome for Christianity. The new prophets were transitory figures, go-between personalities who straddled the waning world of the old spirits and rising world of the new order. Harris modeled the power of a primal medium; his oracular pronouncements echoing the warnings, commandments, and directives of the old oracles, now transformed with the new message of hope. In his hands, Christianity was loosened from its Western frame and given primal range. Missionary antagonism to Harris was, in part, a reflection of the distance separating missionaries from the African reality. Missionaries were just not able to command the indigenous idiom with the authority of Harris. This showed their inadequacy, and they blamed Harris for this shortcoming.

It required no explanation for Harris' converts to appreciate the deeply suggestive connection between their world and the world of the Bible. Against that, the connection missionaries made with material benefits of civilization lacked religious force. The resulting political fallout were the objections that trailed the religion in its post-Western resurgence. True to form, Harris warned of unforeseen challenges, saying people could act to avert disaster. The choice was moral in nature, specifically a choice about Christian reconciliation and forgiveness. Aware that conflict and suffering were widespread, Harris still enjoined patience and a spirit of forgiveness by his converts. There was not the slightest hint or the vaguest suggestion that militancy had any role in his religious revolution, notwithstanding reprisals from officials.

Harris would not flinch and abandon his peaceful mission under pressure, nor did his converts. The point is underlined in the standard Harrist catechism, by posing the question about whether we should help and love our enemies. The catechism responds that we should, for only God reserves the right to judge and avenge wrong, stressing the fact that even though he was manhandled and insulted by the authorities, Harris lifted not a finger.[51] We should recognize the scale of this achievement for local potential. Post-Western Christianity has been remarkable for its forbearance in the face of overwhelming power and suffering, and for instilling hope and trust in people. Christianity banished the demons of fear and vengeance.

Equally striking was the absence of a call to utopian idealism. The suffering and dilemmas of existence did not produce a flight from the world or, equally significantly, a judgmental attitude toward others. Theological nitpicking was foreign to the leaders, allowing them, in the depths of affliction and the mystery of life, to cultivate a spirit of charity and forgiveness among their followers.[52]

The resurgence had, in Harris, a spectacular instance of large-scale cultural recomposition and spontaneous personal transformation. The involvement of missionary societies extended the Harrist resurgence to Europe and beyond. Even though missionaries were ambivalent about Harris—gladly recognizing his value to them, but reluctant to allow that he accomplished much of lasting quality—they could not evade the fact that Harris was a unique spectacle. The effort to annex him as a client of missions acknowledged his importance. Still, Harris' local agency was downgraded in favor of missionary initiative. Yet the Harris awakening provided the cover for missionaries to enter the country, placing missionaries in the awkward position of having to look to Harris as their religious ally while supporting the colonial administration in its opposition to Harris. It called for an urgent critical reassessment of the whole issue of mission, which is the subject of the next chapter.

7

Civilization and the Limits of Mission

Critical Pillar

Cultural Prelude

Two vexing issues nip at the heel of a world Christianity student: the first is the criticism that Christianity was already so firmly anchored in the Enlightenment milieu of its origins in the modern West that in whatever forms it emerged in the rest of the world it was bound to sow the seeds of its formative Western character. What is worldwide about Christianity is what the West did to the religion in the wake of the West's colonial expansion. The second is that, insofar as it was the offspring of the West, a reconstructed Christianity is little compatible with indigenous societies and cultures, and as such the concept of world Christianity is historically inaccurate. Christianity became a world religion only because Europe was a world power. Hillaire Belloc was right: Europe is the faith.

That political view is connected to the idea that the religion's cultural traits are unalterably Western. It is the reason that Westernized Christians hold a decisive advantage over their local counterparts, and can exercise an influence far greater than their numbers indicate. A legitimate Christianity must everywhere be integral with that clear, Western imperative. Accordingly, when we speak of "world Christianity" we evade the West's global ascendancy as the driving force and channel of the religion, and distort an important historic fact about the world the West dominated. If the concept of world Christianity is intended to deny its global Western character, then it is invalid. Christianity is a postcolonial religion and properly belongs with post-colonial studies. Accordingly, deconstruction is the method most appropriate to the subject.

Without, however, gainsaying the fact of European imperial domination, we may still question whether without qualification that extended to the missionary movement in its *local effects*. Under the maritime expansion of Spain and Portugal, for example, the idea that Christendom would promote European civilization overseas hit major obstacles on the ground and was abandoned, or else was significantly modified. Still, the surviving intellectual habits continued to project a Christian commonwealth as the goal of missions. I have in previous remarks assessed that claim with respect to vernacular and frontier demands, arguing that to the extent that they engaged the reality on the ground, missions came into tension, if not into conflict, with their civilizational role. I shall now expand on that by turning to the critical ferment that cross-cultural practice and reflection generated. That is best done with the experience of two former missionaries, one Protestant and the other Catholic, whose criticisms put them at odds with the civilizational view of the subject, and with a post-colonial characterization of the religion. Mission encountered limits to the relative effectiveness of Europe's cultural mandate, while at home new waves of immigration upset confidence in the cultural mandate.

Roland Allen and the Post-Western Reckoning

We begin with Roland Allen (1868–1947), an English missionary who served in China from 1895 under the auspices of the Society for the Propagation of the Gospel (SPG). In a deeply ironic way Allen was the restless soul of a post-Christian West and the inaudible voice of post-Western Christianity. Ill health forced him to return to England in 1903 after a brief missionary spell in China. With his career in China effectively cut short, he retired from missionary service. Yet he felt no longer at ease in his own church, and so, after briefly serving in parish work in England, he resigned under protest and devoted himself for the next twenty years or so to writing and publishing books on mission. Finally, in the 1930s, he immigrated to Kenya, where his son and daughter were living. He died there in June 1947 and is buried there.

Allen wrote perspicaciously on missionary methods and principles as well as on the philosophy of cross-cultural mission, offering critical reflections on the role of civilization and the Enlightenment in Christianity in general, and in missions in particular. Without realizing it, Allen had set out to delineate the nature of post-Western Christianity at a time when the church and his contemporaries thought almost exclusively in Eurocentric, Christendom terms. That he did so with such undeviating consistency and unflagging commitment is testimony to his unique talents and Christian gifts. He was a voice crying in the wilderness, a prophet without honor in his own country. And yet the future that he shaped by his ideas, a future he so keenly discerned and so eloquently expressed, arrived too late to claim and to be claimed by him. For one thing, Allen ceased much too early to be an active missionary, and, for another, his remarks were directed to missionaries whose energies were absorbed in institutional, in-house demands. The church that Allen described was an imagined community in contrast to the flesh-and-blood issues of emerging churches of which Europe was only too dimly aware. The gap between Allen's ideas and the realities of mission made his views feel remote and speculative. Yet that takes nothing away from their force.

When he challenged Europe's selective engagement with the gospel Allen meant no disrespect to his country or to the Western heritage whose greatness he did not minimize or misrepresent. Indeed, as the valiant champion of the rights of those least able to defend themselves, Allen was an honor to his country. He remained restless, nevertheless, about the growing gap between the church's stated objectives and the conflicting means employed to reach them. He was all too aware, and too deeply troubled, by the easy assumption that mission and colonial rule were ordained copartners in a joint enterprise, and he turned that restlessness into a searching critique. For Allen, mission was the work of the spirit, not just in the flaky sense of bustling excitement and disorderly enthusiasm but in the sense of openness to the mind of Christ and to the witness of the apostles, especially to that of Paul. Europe's cultural ascendancy in the expansion of Christianity held little merit for Allen because he felt New Testament eschatology was not beholden to linear rules of historical sequence.

That root theological conviction enabled Allen to transcend his own cultural limitations and, equally momentously, enabled him to see a natural bridge between New Testament Christianity and the missionary enterprise in China. The fundamental basis of human identity for Allen was not cultural but theological: human beings were first and last subjects of God's redemptive work in Christ, and their cultural state carried no prior moral entitlement or disqualification. The superiority of Western culture was not Christianity's remedy for the inferiority of non-Western cultures because in both cases the gospel superceded claims of superiority and inferiority.

Missionaries, for instance, decided that it was impossible for them to dwell among the people and to share their life because it would have seemed like sharing the sinful life of unredeemed heathens even if it were physically feasible to do so. Europeans could not be nomads, wandering teachers, passing from village to village, pausing here a while, and there a while, to instruct any who cared to listen to them. Instead, missionaries settled permanently, acquired land, built houses, and established mission stations somewhat removed from the people. To these quarantined stations missionaries brought their wives and raised their families.

The stations were imagined little bits of Europe rolled up and transplanted to a foreign country. Their walls contained a European civilization, and outside them were heathen, unenlightened elements of culture. Missions represented the boundary delineating one world from another, the age of civilization from the age of heathen customs. The West's immense cultural achievement spawned the sentiment of cultural righteousness, and demanded maturity in converts as a condition of Christian acceptance. The call to repentance and to faith was the call to renounce non-Western customs and to repose faith in the ameliorative projects of mission. The kingdom of heaven fetched pictures in the mind stirringly reminiscent of the prime real estate known as the Home Counties.

Allen noted that when Europeans built the first houses in the mission compounds they were taking a step that seemed the simplest and the most logical. It made eminent sense to have houses fit for Europeans to live in, and so they were built and furnished to the standard of European tastes. As the Wesleyan missionary to South Africa, Henry Dugmore, explained, native huts were so low and smoky "that European clothes can scarcely be borne in them, and the loose kaross and squatting posture seem an almost necessary accompaniment to their habitation." His answer was "the use of walled houses."[1] Nothing else made any sense.

Conversion to Christianity was construed in similar terms. To educate and to civilize local people meant to inculcate in them the taste for European habits and the skill to make European-style houses and other artifacts. Technical ability and the accompanying economic affluence would lead to the proliferation of modern houses, which in turn would lead to the multiplication of Christian families wishing to live in those houses. The existence of the house was far more important than anything else that happened in the native village. Before any converts arrived, the house was there. The success of Christian mission would thereby be assured, and easy to measure and count. One could plan for it on the basis of precise, quantitative goals.

In that view, the material constituents of mission were wholesome fruits of the spirit of God, and were a measure of the cultural gap between missionaries and the people they came to convert. Progress could be gauged by the narrowing gap. Yet, argued Allen, the missionaries' material culture got in the way of their message. European culture immobilized the force of Christianity, and signaled that the missionaries intended to be in permanent occupation of the land. When missionaries proclaimed Christian salvation as God's act, their cultural habits contradicted them while local opposition reinforced the contradiction. On the ground the gospel appeared not to fit so well into the system Europeans all along assumed to be its indispensable corollary.

Converts or Clients?

This concentration on missionary life as the model Christian life required converts to be dislodged from their cultural system and to be cast on the goodwill of missionaries. Converts suffered a double jeopardy. They were uprooted from their culture only to be cast adrift on the fringes of the missionary community as adopted clients. Suddenly and unexpectedly, converts found themselves bogged down in an untenable contradiction, for the very attributes missionaries fashioned for them denied their roots in the societies of their birth. It was as if a stranger entered your home to declare you an alien there.

When someone wanted to become a Christian the missionaries told him or her that his or her customs were contrary to the gospel. The question was whether to give the convert time to abandon the customs gradually or whether to insist on abandoning them at once. Missionaries, who in any case forbade the customs and tolerated no compromise on the matter, insisted on converts immediately and totally severing their ties with the old way of life. It did not occur to the missionaries that their converts were open to hostility and persecution by local people, until after the fact.

The principle of missionary judgment that salvation was the antithesis of damnation was alien to the Chinese mind. "There is no one in heaven judging sin," Chu Hsi, the greatest Confucian sage of the later ages, once said.[2] The goal of Chinese religion was not salvation or life after death; it was the good life based on right conduct here on earth. Prophetic passion was as foreign to Chinese religious thought as snow in Timbuktu. The missionary encounter with China set up an endemic tension in the sense that the converts missionaries made came to Christianity for things Christianity was not allowed to offer, and brought with them things Christianity did not want to accept.

Utterly deaf to local voices, missionaries persisted with the old certitudes by assembling an experimental community chosen by artificial selection. The brightest and fittest students would rise to the top in mission schools, to be creamed off for recruitment into various branches of missionary service.

The cycle would be self-generating and self-sustaining, except that it would not be self-supporting or self-reliant. The English missionary bishop of Madagascar and later general secretary of the Society for the Propagation of the Gospel, Bishop Copland King, wrote in 1909 about the steps necessary to create a native pastorate. The first step was to identify and select the best and most promising pupils of the school and to take personal responsibility in tutoring them. The majority would be incapable of receiving a good education, and, though of good character, they were really stupid. But a few, perhaps three or four, "the best elements of the race," might make the grade. These would be quick-witted, young boys who could be whipped into shape. They would be later siphoned off, trained, and equipped as faithful clones. Such young talent would become the most assured channel for the mediation of Western civilization, and the weapon with which to undermine the authority structure of the village elders long considered impediments to civilization.

The second stage was for the students to become teachers or catechists under missionary supervision. To raise the teachers and catechists to the next stage a college must be founded, organized on a three- to five-year cycle. From the ranks of such trained people missionaries would recruit persons of impeccable character and sound intellect to form a local clergy. Finally, and only after the lapse of considerable time, bishops would be created to assume responsibility for the church, with missionary oversight as safeguard. Bishop King maintained that "the first Christian Churches were bits broken off the local synagogues, and that there were usually to be found among the earliest converts men who had been well trained in the faith, the morals and the devotional life of Judaism."[3] Missions, Bishop King argued, should sublet Christianity as the achievement of Western civilization just as Christianity had once been a subapostolate of Judaism. Third World churches were hind-bits broken off the block of the Western masterpiece. In Bishop King's view, the ascendancy of Europe foreclosed any choice in the matter, and made apprenticeship under missionary superintendency a tenet of discipleship. By virtue of its unrivaled preeminence, Europe was anointed by God to be the exclusive host for the benefits of salvation. That was what Bishop King understood as the historic challenge of Christianity and its global mission.

Allen objected strongly to this viewpoint, saying such views were a contradiction of the deepest and strongest convictions of the people because they dissociated the church at the very foundation from the people's natural conceptions of order and authority. That argument, Allen protested, stood in open defiance of apostolic teaching and example.[4] Besides, the prospects of success for such a conception of Christianity's global mission were bleak in the extreme. It was the case of mission being all hook and little bait, or as the sand-wich without the meat.

It was not the domination of individual missionaries that was the prob-lem but the domination of a system "which we deliberately uphold."[5] Such domination had no warrant in Scripture, in the early history of the church, or even in the history of the conversion of England. In the history of England's first six centuries, it is rare to find an example of a foreign missionary bishop succeeded in his diocese by another foreigner. Augustine was consecrated bishop of Canterbury in 597. Seven years later, two other bishops were ap-pointed in Rochester and London. In 644 a native Englishman was conse-crated at Rochester who in turn consecrated the first native bishop of Can-terbury in 654.

Similar indigenous leadership quickly took root elsewhere. In 627 Felix, a Burgundian, was consecrated to Dunwich. The only foreign bishops were Theodore of Tarsus in 668 at Canterbury, and Parisians Agilbert in 650 at Dorchester and Leutherius in 670 at Winchester. Between 669 and 687 Theodore consecrated twenty bishops, of whom only one was not an English native. A glance at the sees established in England from 656 shows that all the bishops listed there were native: those in Lichfield founded in 656, those in Lindsey created in 678, those in Dunwich after 627, those at Elmham in the years between 673 and 1055, those at Worcester between 680 and 1095, and those at Hereford between 676 and 1079. "If men speak of civilization as they do, China is a far more civilized land than was England in those days," Allen declared.[6]

Evidence of Western obstruction and local resistance could be had from examples of converts who were rejected, driven from their homes or villages, and otherwise stigmatized. Cut adrift in the crosscurrents of an assertive Eu-ropean political order and a rising local reaction, converts became driftwood. Persons could not live without some social order, and converts were torn from their roots in their own society to wilt in an alien missionary environment. They once had a home. Now, thanks to Christianity, they had none. Their communities disgorged them, and missionaries received them with tongue firmly in cheek. Christianity dispossessed them of their natural ties without giving them a real stake in missionary culture. The new civilization centered on the mission compound had no root, and when converts flocked to these compounds they were as tossed leaves. The missionaries taught them stan-dards of cleanliness and hygiene, imbued them with polite manners and mild sentiments, and put them in European clothes, but instead of feeling honored and appreciated they felt violated and mocked. After all, that was not their culture, and they could ill afford to claim it on any other ground. European civilization became the religion's trap, and theirs, too. In China, for example, an idea took root and quickly spread that to become a Christian involved submission to foreign domination. That belief had a powerful effect in deterring people from approaching the missionary or from receiving missionary teaching with open minds and moral conviction.[7]

In time an earthquake rocked Christianity's cultural shibboleths when predictably the nationalist reaction arose and threatened to overwhelm it. The prohibitions and impositions of Christendom only pinned down the religion sufficiently to allow local reaction to assail it with unrelenting accuracy. Local converts turned upon their foreign teachers: "It is you who hold us down: it is your insistence upon your Western creeds which has crippled our thought: it is you who will not put us into positions of authority: it is you who will not trust us with the money which you have taught us is necessary for any religious expansion."[8]

Allen said missionaries believed that they were training their converts for freedom and found they had only exasperated them, and driven them into revolt. The true domination of the foreign missionaries was not so much a lust to keep power in their own hands as an inability to see that to nurse converts in the beginning, and to act as their patrons, was to become lords over them, and that to stifle their first unrecognized, unspoken instinct for self-expression was to make certain first of sterility and then of sterile revolt. As Conor Cruise O'Brien observed of Catholic and Protestant missionaries in the Congo, even the humane act of feeding the hungry was a weapon when its goal was to secure submission. "It is true . . . that it is better that the [local] people were fed than that they should have starved: 'warfare' by feeding people is better than 'warfare' by killing and burning. Yet the two kinds of warfare were systematically interconnected: the stick for those who refused to submit . . . , the carrot for those who submitted because they did not wish to starve."[9] If Christianity survived the legacy of local resentment it would be by reason of a post-Western cultural euthanasia, by reason of a radical act of self-redefinition. To light the candle of faith, missions must first extinguish themselves. Allen had shown why this is necessary.

Cultural Osmosis

Allen asked what might be wrong with the picture missionaries created of their work, and suggested that it was the Western cultural captivity of the gospel. He said missionaries assumed that it was their responsibility to set and maintain the Christian standard of morality when in fact that was not their business or in their power. Insofar as the moral life had its seat in the unfettered conscience of the person, missionaries could not go there to maintain it. All they could do was to enforce external law, such as that which colonial administrators enforced, although that was not the remit of missions. When missionaries assumed the role of enforcer, they defeated the very purpose of their announced vocation. They became like the Judaizers in the early church, the people against whom Paul railed for being obstacles to the church's mission. Mission as European cultural righteousness contradicted the gospel as God's irrevocable gift of salvation to all people. Apostolic faithfulness, not to say anything of the gospel's vernacular merit, demanded repudiation of mission as Western civilization.

Allen then drew briefly on the Islamic comparison to show where and how Western missions went wrong. Islam, he said, had a fixed, established code of morals and ethics. Muslims operated by a deliberate external code. Yet Muslims admitted converts before they had learned the code or before they had even advanced in their understanding of it. Muslims did so in the conviction that in time converts would acquire the habits and knowledge requisite to correct belief and to canonical practice. Once converts had attained to such a standard, they acquired a permanent status within Islam, Allen argued.

Christianity, he urged, could not behave like Islam and expect to retain its moral authority. Only disaster lay on that path. Yet, surprisingly, mission seemed set on that path, which made Christianity appear like Islam but without the advantage Islam enjoyed as *Dár al-Islám*, as worldly domain. Earthly dominion succeeded in projecting Islam's power and ideals, but it ruined the church's reputation everywhere. The kingdom of God could not share a common fence with the kingdom of Mammon without the cross-contamination that made faith the tenet of national glory, and Mammon the standard of cultural righteousness. What tempted missions into invoking the wraith of Islam, Allen warned, could not be the spirit of the Christ of apostolic teaching. To all intents and purposes missions had slipped from that apostolic benchmark, Allen charged. It was safe to assume that those converts who, upon entering the church, received a new moral law by virtue of external imposition would sooner or later recognize no moral necessity for it. Missionaries could not ask converts to place their social relations on the chopping block in exchange for Christianity as a mere token in their kinship idiom and expect lasting results. It was missions strangling the gospel.

The Failure of Success

Allen noted that the civilization mandate saddled missions with a distracting message and a crushing burden. The distraction came about by way of split priorities as missionaries spoke variously of the gospel of enlightenment, the gospel of healing, the social gospel, and the gospel of sex equality. Missions stretched their resources to cover medical, educational, and social work as forms of preaching the gospel. Social uplift became the goal and rationale of the gospel. The work of Christ was construed as lifting people out of poverty and backwardness. Accordingly, "missionary work was preparing for the day when races and tribes and peoples instructed in Christian ethics, strengthened by Christian science, enriched by Christian sociology, would recognize the source of all this blessing, and would be able to worship and serve Christ duly as Christians ought to do."[10] Yet, insisted Allen, Paul deliberately rejected any means of propagating the faith that might distract people from the truth that the Christian faith was founded not in a human philosophy but in the power of God.[11] Missions had a thousand plans, but God had only one. Salvation was not by the thousand capillaries of cultural assimilation.

The crushing burden on missions came about because of the shifting social contours missionaries devised for their work. Large institutions, guilds, clubs, halls, and structures were created and staffed with an army of expensive recruits. Heavy machinery was purchased, transported, and, at great cost, maintained by skilled expatriate specialists who were brought into remote areas that had scarcely the means to inherit or to perpetuate such top-heavy elaborate infrastructure. Missions were consumed in the creation of offices and departments, with directors, clerks, and accountants, divided and subdivided. Organization was an end in itself by overshadowing the end for which it existed. Samuel Butler painted a disturbing picture of the power of machines over people when he showed people destroying their machines because they were afraid that they might become the machines' slaves, tending and feeding them for their lives. "May not man himself become a sort of parasite upon the machines; an affectionate, machine-tickling aphid? The servant glides by imperceptible approaches into a master; and we have come to such a pass that, even now, man must suffer terribly on ceasing to benefit the machines."[12]

Missionaries' love of organization misled them into misguided priorities, such as expecting spiritual results from institutions. The effectiveness and continuity of missionary work depended on the strength and continuity of organization. Organization was the vehicle for globalizing the Christian faith, and missionaries looked to it to produce ends it was ill designed for. The organization network created its own momentum and rationale. The large output of tracts and leaflets designed for missionary intercession, with its emphasis on appeals for gifts of money, might lead an unsuspecting observer to conclude that the authors of these leaflets and tracts had discovered not the power of intercession, but a silver mine. Technical gear for fund-raising was mounted to facilitate appeals for money, and that became a cause in its own right. It fostered an environment of unhealthy competition. English missionary bishops, for example, urged the Church of England not to allow itself to be outmatched in funds and numbers by American Presbyterians and Wesleyans.

The day would come when the West would continue to hold the purse strings of the church, but at the same time Christianity would cease to be the monopoly of the West. Allen foresaw that time to be one of no small strife. That is part of the culture clash that has now erupted between a post-Christian West and a post-Western Christianity. Can the wealth of the Western church purchase the agreement or acquiescence of Third World Christian leaders in the West's radical social agenda? How might a post-Christian West respond to post-Western developments and tip the balance on the side, say, of the liberalism of Desmond Tutu against the traditionalism of Nigeria's Peter Akinola? What weight does organized religion carry in societies with few institutional assets but with strong charismatic appeal?

For his part, Allen felt that bequeathing the heavy baggage of a professional institutional missionary organization in societies with few institutional assets was a stubborn disregard of realities. In the meantime, the machinery of mission appeared as a formidable obstacle to conversion on the ground. It was the first and last barrier local people must cross to make it into the church. Yet the fact that many crossed it without seeing the need at the same time of joining the church stripped civilization of its religious mystique and challenged converts to drop the Christian requirement, in other words to rebel. Civilization just kept compounding the problem of missions, which explains Roland Allen's impassioned and urgent plea for separating the two.

Allen attacked the deleterious consequences of Western materialism and its drag on missionary impetus. With words he placed in the mouth of an imaginary Muslim interlocutor, he articulated those sentiments, of which a paraphrase might be as follows. The Muslim muses to himself about Christian missionaries who pour out their money and who establish all this extravagant machinery. In spite of it all they make only a few converts. Their work will do Muslims more good than harm. The converts know not the power of a true religion. While the missionaries labor at these material things, Muslims advance by their own spiritual power. Missionaries organize and build, and toil and sweat to convert by material methods; Islam grows with much less toil and sweat. With all their money and their talents missionaries purchase a few converts only, and then they must begin all over again in the same costly way to make a few more. One convert to Islam is the sure firstfruits of a great harvest. Islam advances automatically. God works without material aid by outsiders.[13] Allen's picture, it has to be observed, was a rhetorical device, and although it might succeed in rallying the troops, it scarcely reflected the complex character of the mission of Islam.

The material question was not whether separating civilization and Christianity should be undertaken, but whether an alternative boundary was at all conceivable for Christianity in its post-Western phase. Was Christianity conceivable without Western civilization or without globalization? The cumulative weight of practice and the distractions of the call to social action were against the idea. In numerous subtle and obvious ways post-Western Christianity carried the purebred genes of its European origins. Yet the cost of persisting with mission on that basis was too high to be sustainable in the *long durée*. The impasse shows the inevitable fate of missions as Western civilization, and it suggests that, however well endowed, missions could not be salvaged in their foreign character but only in their vernacular character as locally led churches. Allen hinted at that shift as a question of methods, and thus failed to lift it up as a matter fundamentally of vernacular structural reconceptualization. But it seemed the only way to slip the civilizational trap he identified and to establish local priority for Christianity.

Technically, Allen was correct in his diagnosis of the problem. Missions subordinated Christ to their social preconditions, conditions that favored stationary centers built under European direction. Those conditions became the preoccupation of missions; they crowded out the gospel. The logic of requiring intellectual, moral, and social advance before faith in Christ, Allen confessed, assumed that intellectual enlightenment and moral and social advance were based on a foundation other than trust in Christ. When missionaries assumed that enlightenment and improvement would issue in acceptance of faith in Christ, they made it reasonable to conclude that faith in Christ was not the foundation but the copingstone of social and moral progress. They put the cart before the horse. Other well-intentioned people had also made that strategic mistake.

For Allen, the procedure was flawed from the start. Enlightened and socially advanced local groups could and did cling to their newly acquired cultural status without feeling the least need or inclination to pay any regard to Christianity, except to demand that cultural achievement should be disentangled from the need to profess the Christian faith. Of a piece with that was the fact that enlightened and socially advanced ideas could be and were used to deleterious ends, which left Christians having to fight, or at the least to disown, the very thing their own agency created. Nothing demonstrated the futility of Christian teaching better than the indifference or hostility of the class of cultured despisers it raised. The fact that missionaries were blind to that showed how complete was their own cultural captivity. Complacency was a more deadly foe of the gospel than persecution.

Allen recalled that Roman slaves who lived in social conditions deeply repugnant to what the West called the Christian life still converted to Christianity before any ameliorative social remedies were available to them. The Christian life embraced slaves and concubines without bashfulness or reservation while they were slaves and concubines because the Christian life did not make social disadvantage a disqualification of membership. We saw that fact clearly demonstrated among New World slaves and other social victims during the Great Awakening. While the gospel acted to dissolve social stigma and to empower the cause of equality and justice, the offer of salvation was not made conditional on that. The tail did not wag the dog.

Redrawing the Boundary

Roland Allen asked for critical honesty from his missionary colleagues. When they spoke of "Christian civilization," they had in mind, frankly, the civilization of Christian England: Western civilization. Allen objected that that was not Christian civilization. To a life devoid of Christian faith missionaries more willingly gave the name of "Christian" than to a life devoted to Christ and inspired by Christ under conditions the missionaries regarded as uncivilized. Allen protested the notion of the church as cultural establishment, declaring: "Ignorant men speak as if Christ and His Church had nothing to offer which is not the natural inheritance of every Englishman, nor any right to lay down rules and conditions on which those gifts may be obtained; because they see every man, whatever his belief or his character, admitted without question to the highest privileges which the Church can bestow."[14]

It was a mistake to believe that it was possible to introduce Christian social conditions apart from the Christian faith, Allen pointed out. Educational work, medical work, agricultural work, and social work have been called Christian work only because Christians happened to do them. But they were work that non-Christians had done, too, and often with distinction. Not to see that was to be blinded by force of the ideological gospel. Allen quoted a writer from Japan who noted that Japan had, to all intents and purposes, adopted the accoutrements of modern civilization without any sign that it paid, or wished to pay, any heed to Christianity. Japan did not confound civilization with Christianity, it was clear, and so why did missionaries?

To teach people that Christianity was civilization, and vice versa, was to mislead them by sowing seeds of disenchantment. Yet that was the outcome missionaries courted when they assumed the role of civilizing Christian agents. The iniquity intrinsic in the system of civilization was all too obvious to local populations who saw Christian civilization as merely a cloak for justifying European ideas and customs, and social doctrines in order to impose them as divine law. Geoffrey Allen, himself a missionary to China but no relation to Roland Allen, said there were grave dangers in the Western control of Christianity because of the risk that "the name of Christ may become identified [in the eyes of the Chinese] with all that is slovenly, and antiquated, and ill-equipped" in Western institutions.[15]

What missionaries failed to notice, or what they preferred to conceal from themselves, was that material progress had acquired the force of first principles. The material outcome they desired became a substitute for Christianity. As such, the outcome became the message, and the means of its propagation. Missionaries tinkered with the original idea that the Christian message should have a useful outcome and then went on to promulgate the rule and requirement that Christianity itself should be useful, or it would cease to be Christianity. For that reason Roland Allen thought that missionaries were on the verge of forsaking their true calling, of losing their identity, and abandoning the people entrusted to their care. His focus remained on the missionaries, and that limited audience inevitably narrowed his range, though it considerably sharpened his focus.

When he turned from missionaries to the local scene, Allen expressed serious doubts about the value of the work of civilization missionaries put their hands to. Organization, for example, looked very different from the ground. The erection of buildings, the management of property, and the maintenance of a vast corps of professional preachers were all made necessary by missions' civilizational mandate, but were absurd in frontier cultures. You did not want an elaborate system of structures and institutions to propagate faith and values. You needed faith and values from the outset. Monetary rewards subverted the religious motive. Naturally, missionaries seemed like cultural mercenaries. The stationary mission station as the model structure for establishing Christianity in foreign lands was misconceived. It was the diocesan structure transferred root and branch to conditions unlike anything in Europe. In a nominally Christian society, such as Europe, synods, church councils, committees, schools, halls, and bureaucratic organization were what you needed to shepherd a flock largely anonymous and largely irregular in its religious habits. In the mission field that was historically non-Christian, totally different needs had to be addressed by totally different ideas and practices. Missionaries seemed unequipped for that task.

Such a verdict pointed firmly to the need for a fresh, radical overhaul of Christianity's characteristic missionary enterprise, and in a 1913 work, *Missionary Methods*, Allen devoted some general thoughts to that issue. The missionary he had in mind did not go out to persuade others that the religion in which they were brought up was a bad one and that the missionary's religion was to be preferred. The question, he said, was not one of cultural innocence, namely, that Eastern nations had religions appropriate to their cultural needs just as the West had a religion equally appropriate for it. Some people objected to mission because they felt non-Western societies were too far behind on the scale of civilization to be able to comprehend Christianity's sophisticated system of ethics and theology. It was wrong to force Christianity on such people before they were ready for it. In any case, the simple religions of non-Western populations were far more effective for their equally simple needs, and missionaries should not interfere with what God had seen fit to leave in place. Allen rejected that form of cultural relativism for Christian mission, calling on Paul for support.

Unusual for his time and among his missionary colleagues, Roland Allen was unflinching in his criticism of what he saw as wrong with mission and with the Western cultural captivity of the gospel. Repeatedly, he made the point that undertaking mission in colonized societies should be carefully distinguished from colonial ideas of power and the superiority of Western civilization. Allen was writing in an era of high nationalist agitation when notions of Europe's unquestioned mastery over all spheres of life, including missionary societies, were under attack. Allen was, accordingly, unrelenting in his attack on the folly and hazard of Christian missions proclaiming civilization. He remained a man of his time in speaking almost by reflex of indigenous people as heathen and primitive, but he roiled the complacency of those who felt entitled to rule the heathen and primitive world unchecked and unquestioned. Even though he was a child of his culture, the missionary vocation compelled Allen to undertake a searching critique of the European order and its shortcomings in a world of rising and shifting expectations. His thought moved very much in the currents of Christianity's local promise, though it was a later generation that grasped fully the challenge of context for Christian life and thought.

The structural basis of nineteenth- and twentieth-century missions was the voluntary association that was, for the most part, supported by the sacrificial gifts, donations, and offerings of lay members. Much of the responsibility for the organization, support, networking, and administration of these voluntary missionary societies fell on the broad shoulders of women, who also led in the field as nurses, teachers, and educational leaders. That structural feature accounted for the fact that the modern missionary movement received less support from governments than in any period of the history of the religion since the enthronement of Charlemagne. The relative freedom of missionary societies from government financial control made room for discerning missionaries like Allen to plant ideas of voluntarism in societies where religion was an official franchise—as it had been in Allen's own home country. That spirit of voluntarism stimulated the emergence of unofficial agents and figures in the spread of Christianity: catechists, evangelists, nurses, preachers, teachers, exhorters, colporteurs, readers, tradesmen, and so on. They were the invisible line of advance that steadily pushed Christianity forward and outward across hinterland districts and country trails. They were the real missionaries to their people, though leaden-footed Europeans claimed the credit for their success.

It happened that Roland Allen never had the opportunity to create a plan to carry out his well-thought-out ideas and deep convictions in any mission field. He developed his ideas and opinions specifically with China in mind, though the model of mission he put up for emulation was that of the apostle Paul. And Paul's model of mission, Allen argued, "was not peculiarly St. Paul's. The method in its broad outlines was followed by his disciples, and they were not all men of exceptional genius. [The method] is indeed universal, and outside the Christian Church has been followed by reformers, religious, political, social, in every age and under most diverse conditions."[16]

Yet we may point to something else as being possibly more crucial in Paul's missionary approach than the fact that reformers of every stripe copied it, and that was Paul's uncompromising insistence that embracing the Gentiles as full and ungrudging members of the fellowship was the sine qua non of the church's mission. The church could not be the church without equal access for those previously considered to be ritually impure. On that issue, Paul staked his reputation, and even his life. An important implication for missionary practice of the kind Allen criticized was whether the requirements of civilization could be reconciled with that Pauline standard, at the heart of which was the matter of the completeness of salvation for Gentiles without permanent Mosaic vetting or temple oversight.

Allen said the Gentile boundary had been a formidable one for the early Christians to breach, but breach it they did. The Mosaic code seemed an insuperable obstacle. Jesus appeared in the world within the Mosaic system and upheld its impeccable authority. He appointed his apostles within the terms of the covenant. Though in one rare case he commended a Gentile for his faith, saying he had "not found so great a faith, no, not in Israel" (Lk 7:9), he appointed no Gentile to preach the gospel to Gentiles. The thought of preaching Christ without the law was inconceivable. How, then, could the disciples of Jesus have gone outside the covenant, outside the Mosaic system, and admitted or recognized as servants of Christ those who were not within the covenant? The answer was that the witness of the Holy Spirit to the redemptive work of Jesus made that move necessary and inescapable. To deny that or to undo it would have been a blatant contradiction of practice and principle.

The covenant was accordingly expanded to make room for Gentiles who "desired communion with the apostles. The apostles acknowledged that they had the Spirit. Being led themselves by the Spirit, they put aside all the countless and crushing objections which could be raised, they put aside all the serious disabilities under which these new converts laboured, they recognized the fact and accepted the consequence. God gave the Holy Spirit; they admitted at once that nothing more was needed for salvation, nothing else was needful for communion."[17] That was the fact that the enforcers of civilization evaded or defied, but which Allen demanded they heed. "For thirty years he pleaded that the Church (overseas) be placed on its own feet, that is, for an indigenous Christianity. This, he held, could not be imposed from outside[,] for an indigenous Church is not simply a Church that is master in its own house, but a Church that had the gift of the Holy Spirit and knew what this gift meant for its own life."[18]

In his assessment of *The Indigenous Church* (1928), an essay by Sidney J. W. Clark (1862–1930), Allen commended the "Three Self" movement, which was self-governing, self-supporting, and self-propagating local churches freed of missionary control.[19] For Clark, the idea of an indigenous church, Allen agreed, "was not the idea of something which might emerge after a century or two of training, something ideal and remote; it was something real and present. [It was something] embodied in little local Churches widely scattered over the world, not indeed necessarily scattered widely apart, far distant from one another, but widely scattered over wide areas." That was the vision Allen had of China, so that "in every market town in China, in every centre of population all over the world [there would be] the Church which could grow and expand without any direction from foreigners."[20]

As a contemporary of the pivotal changes China underwent in the Communist revolution, Allen was surprisingly tight-lipped on Christianity's encounter with Marxism. Yet few things have affected Christian prospects in China more, as will be made clear in chapter 8. For Allen, however, Christianity was a world religion because Christianity had real and present worldwide appeal, not because it had a Western mandate. Indeed, Allen contended that the Western mandate all too often hindered or inhibited its indigenous potential. His confidence in the future of the church was bound up with his theological conviction about faith as local embodiment, and that carried an implicit rejection, for example, of the merits of a foreign Marxist ideology.

Vincent Donovan and the Catholic Response

In the 1960s, nearly half a century after Allen, a Catholic missionary bound for East Africa stumbled on Roland Allen's writing, and it had a dramatic effect on how the missionary subsequently understood his calling personally, and the role of mission generally. The missionary in question was Fr. Vincent Donovan, a Spiritan Catholic missionary who served among the Maasai between 1955 and 1973.[21] After many years of struggling with cross-cultural obstacles to Western mission, Donovan discovered the works of Roland Allen, whose argument that missionaries should look to the apostolic missionary example as a corrective felt like an open door for him; through that door was a world of limitless possibilities for him.

Although Catholic missionary policy and practice differed greatly from Allen's background, there was still a great deal of relevant merit in what he had to say. In spite of the stunning changes spawned by the nationalist movement, and the different sets of issues with which missions were confronted since Allen left China, "the main and general insights and questions of this remarkable man are as valid today as they were when they first stunned and disturbed the church of his day.... Roland Allen's insights and questions challenged most of the missionary theories I had ever heard, and would make it all the more necessary for me to proceed cautiously from real practice and experience towards a new and different theory of mission."[22]

Square Pegs in Round Holes: Old Catholic Mission and Local Indifference

In spite of Donovan's resolve to follow Allen's insights regarding missions, the legacy of Western missions in East Africa was not entirely reassuring on that front. When Donovan began work among the Maasai, there were 33,000 Catholic missionary priests in the world, and yet together with Protestant missionaries they could not claim to have evangelized more than 18 percent of the world. Donovan said that record of results was not so much an achievement as a dismal failure, and the reason for it was clear. When in 1928 the apostolic visitor to East Africa met with a gathering of bishops in Dar es Salaam, he told them point-blank: "Where it is impossible for you to carry on both the immediate task of evangelization and your educational work, neglect your churches in order to perfect your schools."[23] Following the apostolic visitor's advice, missionaries toiled for souls in their stony meadows and returned empty.

The new doctrine of missionary work placed the emphasis on moving developing countries forward on the path to economic abundance. Conversion was out of the question. A new breed of missionaries as ecclesiastical Peace Corps arrived on the scene, and one might find them behind the plow, laying pipes, digging wells, introducing miracle grains, and ushering in progress and development throughout the Third World. Yet nothing could mask the fact that missionary work was in shambles. Born in an age of slavery, distracted by the mounting demands of the school system, caught unprepared by the onset of political independence, and whipped by the twists and turns of nation building, missions in East Africa lost their way badly. After more than a hundred years in East Africa some 1,951 priests could show little for their labor.[24] Reflecting on that grim truth, Donovan admitted, "I became discouraged in a way it would be hard to describe. More than that, before I began to see the way out of the mire, I was ready to give up. I was ready to announce to the church that had sent me, and to anyone else who wanted to listen, that Christianity was not valid—not valid for these Masai, perhaps not valid even for me."[25] When Donovan convinced himself of the false assumption about the moral necessity of civilization, he suffered a crisis of faith. The situation was as Allen described it, that converts who were offered the precondition of civilization would necessarily not be detained by Christianity when it was its turn, because the religion could be postponed indefinitely. As Donovan admitted, he felt weary from being required to deal with mounting material demands amid diminishing religious prospects. It felt like the ordeal of the mythical Sisyphus, who was doomed to push a boulder uphill for eternity.

The Missionary Mandate Restated

Finally, in May 1966, out of long frustration and with a fistful of filial daring, Donovan fired off a letter to his bishop. Priests had gone to the Maasai, built and equipped four schools and a hospital, detailed the mission car to run community errands, attended social occasions in the kraals where they drank milk and honey beer, and done things like that for years, he recounted.

But never, or almost never, is religion mentioned on any of these visits. The best way to describe realistically the state of this Christian mission is the number zero. As of this month, in the seventh year of this mission's existence, there are no adult Masai practicing Christians from Loliondo mission. The only practicing Christians are the catechist and the hospital medical dresser, who have come here from other sections of Masailand.

That zero is a real number, because up until this date no Catholic child, on leaving school, has continued to practice his religion, and there is no indication that any of the present students will do so.

Having frankly described this situation as totally devoid of result, Donovan said he could not go on from there to offer a credible justification for persisting with mission in the old style. "I suddenly feel the urgent need to cast aside all theories and discussions, all efforts at strategy—and simply [to] go to these people and do the work among them for which I came to Africa."[26] Casting aside all theories and all efforts at a strategy meant breaking free also of the schools, hospitals, and other bits of missionary machinery and their burdensome maintenance and cost. It meant transgressing hallowed boundaries, including ideas of church.[27]

Such a move involved upending and redefining a century or more of missionary practice and teaching. The move might begin by assailing the whole basis of the claim that heathen society was sinful. On that point Donovan asked rhetorically: "Are Masai pagans further away from salvation than European and American Christians? Is endemic and incurable cattle thieving further removed from salvation than assassinating and killing and selling deadly weapons and cheating in business and lying in advertising?"[28]

Donovan said he was in no doubt about the answer. Western missionaries must renounce the view that civilization was required to disinfect indigenous people and render them tidy enough to receive the gospel. It was more consistent and truer to the New Testament spirit to assume that the message of Christianity in terms of God's revelation "was for everyone, for the entire human race, for every people in every segment of that human race—as they are, where they are, now. Or else we would have to retranslate the mission mandate to: 'Preach the gospel to all the nations—except to those who are not ready.'"[29]

Retranslating the message in that form was out of the question for Donovan, for that was what he thought had hampered and corrupted mission in the first place, and what, in his turn, Roland Allen had dissected so persuasively. As Allen pointed out with repetitive emphasis, the issue at stake was whether the gospel could be a cultural blueprint and still have anything left worth calling the gospel. Again, the answer was obvious to Donovan. The gospel was not progress or development; it was not nation building or adult education; it was not a school system, a health campaign, a five-year plan, or an economic program; it was not a ranching scheme or water development; it was not an independence movement, a creed for freedom fighters, or a slogan for flag bearers. The gospel was adaptable and applicable to all human situations, and although it took its bearings from life and experience in the real world, it was not exclusively synonymous with any or all of these things. The gospel had its religious roots in the deeds and actions of a redemptive God whose claim on faith and obedience was absolute and nonnegotiable. True human development, according to Donovan, began with affirmation of human dignity as God's unique, sovereign gift, whence development became participation in God's work in creation, and that carried no cultural or political strings.[30] Civilization was not an alibi, and that view freed civilization to be a servant of the truth, not its master.

Donovan testified that as he began again to ponder how he might evangelize the Maasai he felt he had to start with the fundamental assumption that God enabled a people, any people, to reach salvation through their culture and tribal, racial customs and traditions. "In this realization would have to rest my whole approach to the evangelization of the Masai."[31] At the heart of that shift of understanding was what missionaries were typically afraid of, namely, "that no Christianity has any meaning or value if there is not the freedom to accept or [to] reject it. . . . The acceptance of it would be meaningless if rejection were not possible." The Christianity of a cradle Catholic merely as birthright, says Donovan, is a dead and useless thing.[32] Cultural entitlement was a barrier to the gospel's intercultural potential.

Donovan's perspective on gospel and culture is crucial for the whole rationale and justification of mission, for it foregrounds the indigenous framework and sidelines missionary assumptions. Transmission of the message yielded pride of place to the translation of the message, with Donovan insisting that that was where the real heartbeat of the gospel could be found. It was ironic that so much of conventional mission was in open disagreement with that.

It was not only Paul's method but also Paul's spirit that seemed resonant in Donovan's statements. Just as Jesus the Messiah of the Jews plausibly became Christ the Greek philosopher, just so as the Lion of Judah (Hos 5:14) could he become the Maasai Warrior. In a revealing testimony, a Maasai elder assured Donovan that the Maasai people did not search for him as a priest to come to them. Donovan came to them and followed them into the bush, into the plains, into the steppes where their cattle were, into the hills where they took their cattle for water, into their villages, and into their homes. Donovan told them about the High God, and about how the Maasai must search for Him and try to find Him even if that meant leaving their land and their people.

Indigenous Discovery of the Gospel

At this point the elder came to the punch line: it was not the Maasai who had searched for God, but God who had searched for the Maasai. He continued: God "has searched *us* out and found us. All the time we think we are the lion. In the end, the lion is God."[33] It was a stunning statement about the purpose of mission as being nothing more than a prompter of what was at heart an indigenous process, and it came from the lips of a village elder. The statement represented a reordering of priorities. Face to face with the gospel, the Maasai saw the issue not so much as missionaries discovering the Maasai and preparing them, as about God being there for the Maasai even while they thought they were somewhere else. The insight belied the image of the Maasai as beginners in the faith; it was, in fact, a huge stride in mature discipleship, and it blew away all the meandering stratagems and hesitant steps of organized mission.

Donovan took the message to heart, and at the next opportunity applied it with effect. He described the story of Ole Sikii, a young Maasai warrior who exhibited a particular gift for taking on challenges, including the challenge of religion. He decided once to pursue his religious interest by setting out to find God, whose abode was at the top of a volcanic mountain where the lava still simmered. It was a seventy-mile trip. Welcoming the challenge, Ole Sikii set out for his destination. He spent three lonely and weary days perched on the rim of the crater looking for God. Not seeing God there, Ole Sikii descended from the mountain, a disappointed and exhausted man, his faith in tatters.

Yet, undaunted warrior that he was, Ole Sikii was in the midst of feverish preparations for a return trek to the mountain to find God when Donovan came upon him and decided to address him with the words he learned from the Maasai elder. Ole Sikii told Donovan that he had tried as hard as a human being could to look for God. Ole Sikii had left his father, his family, and his home to go in search of God up the terrible mountain. He had tracked God to His lair, like a lion tracks a wildebeest. In the meantime, Donovan assured, God had been on the prowl for him. It was Donovan's turn to show he had learned an invaluable lesson at the hands of the Maasai. His ears still ringing with the memorable words of the Maasai elder, Donovan relished his newfound role as an elder to Ole Sikii: "You did not send for me or look me up. I was sent to you. You thought you were searching for Engai. All this time he has been searching for you. God is more beautiful and loving than even you imagined. He hungered for you, Ole Sikii. Try as we might, we cannot reach up by brute force and drag God down from the heavens. He is already here. He has found you. In truth, Ole Sikii, we are not the lion looking for God. God is the lion looking for us. Believe me, the lion is God."[34]

Ole Sikii might have been reminded of the words of Isaiah (49:15–16): "Can a woman forget her sucking child, that she should have no compassion on the son of her womb? Even these may forget, yet I will not forget you. Behold, I have graven you on the palms of my hand; your walls are continually before me."[35] The Maasai had tutored Donovan well. "They taught me something that no other people in Africa had ever taught me. But it took a long time for that lesson to sink in."[36] The gifts of a Maasai elder saved a missionary, and now a missionary vocation. The receivers of the message turned effective givers, too, as Donovan's story made clear. Donovan suggested that missionaries should only accept the part assigned to them in Christianity's serial expansion rather than try to run the whole show themselves. Why that should be controversial or why, so late in the missionary enterprise, it should still require Donovan to stake his vocation on it, should be food for thought. Donovan was constrained to observe: "The final missionary step as regards the people of any nation or culture, and the most important lesson we will ever teach them—is to leave them."[37] The *missio Dei* could not be held hostage to Europe's rule of cultural assimilation.

Sartor Resartus: Rediscovery of Christianity

In his frank and honest appraisal of his work, Donovan offered himself as a live specimen of the ironic logic of mission in which the reception of the message took precedence over its transmission. Mission did not spare him: he became his own first convert. What happened to him, he wrote, was long overdue, but also inevitable in the nature of the case. Those missionaries who left the field unscathed had done so because they had not taken the vocation at face value. For Donovan to become a missionary required having his expatriate cultural organs removed, and that procedure was best carried out in the field, preferably in some tribal homestead screened from civilization rather than in the mission clinic. In that primal environment the natives could observe with unfiltered eyes everything happening to him. The procedure was rough and ready, interspersed with moments of great clarity and relief along with revealing clumsiness and stupidity. He needed to be a willing participant in his own stripping to spare himself needless pain, especially if he wanted to claim some credit for the result.

The procedure had four unsettling stages. Flouting an elementary rule of etiquette, the first stage was Donovan's decision to pitch tent among people who were no relatives of his. The people, accordingly, interrogated him in so many different and subtle ways about who asked him to come to them, and in as many different and subtle ways he tried to dance around that question. It only postponed the showdown. The second stage was his need for the people to befriend, protect, assist, and guide him. That was not the role he imagined of the missionary. After all, he came to preach, not to learn—yet it was too late for anything other than learning now. The third stage was his discovery that God could speak, and, indeed, has spoken to the people in their own language and through their own culture. When he recovered sufficiently from the shock of that realization, Donovan felt guilty for making Christianity the tribal religion of the West, and Jesus a cultural client. The fourth and final stage was his ripe conviction that his work was scarcely done while the people had failed to repossess the gospel without his vetting or approval.

The procedure culminated in another ironic twist, namely, the production of a permanent, written record of his experience, and for that Donovan used his academic training, not to justify but to unmask himself. He staged an attack against himself. He was at the receiving end of Christianity's frontier meta- morphosis that had no parallel in his own Western heartland experience. A new feature was the organic connectivity in the field between life and faith, between community and identity. So Donovan wrote down his experience in a minor key, one part confession and one part indictment, vibrant with the spirit of real-life adventure. As his own first convert he was now qualified for the role of reverse missionary, acquiring with it a sense of new discovery, in fact, a sense of Christianity rediscovered, the apt title of his book.

What role did that leave the missionary? Donovan answered that it would help to redefine the work of missionaries. Donovan said that missionaries stood at the cutting edge of the church in the world, and for that reason missionaries were positioned at the leading edge of development and libera- tion. There would be work to do, not only for missionaries, and certainly not just for establishing and maintaining a mission station, Donovan affirmed. In response to a critic of his book, Donovan gave an example of the role of missionaries. With fear and trembling he described one situation where he felt constrained to question hallowed Maasai custom. He was asked by Maasai men to grant an exception to them by allowing them to forego eating the Com- munion hosts in front of the women. The men asked whether they could be allowed simply to rub their foreheads with the sacred elements and return them. That way they would avoid the contamination that came from "eating them in front of the women, because women pollute every food they are near." Donovan refused, for "it struck me as such a lamentable distortion of the meaning of the Eucharist—the sign of unity and the bond of love—and of the meaning and position of women, that I judged such a ceremony would stand as a countersign to the gospel which was my primary responsibility."[38] Cultures were not entirely innocent and impervious. It is relevant to point out that when the Spiritans shifted their mission from schools to homesteads to individuals, "Maasai women joined the church in increasing numbers, while Maasai men generally avoided the church."[39]

At several points in his observations, Donovan drew a contrast between the highpoints in the Maasai reception of Christianity and the official teaching of the church, his intention being to demonstrate how Maasai understandings threw fresh light on the truth of the gospel. It seemed as if the Maasai had recommissioned and reoutfitted Donovan to undertake a new mission to deliver the West from its false gods. Given the benefit of the new Maasai milieu, Donovan thought the church's opposition was wrongheaded. It was not that the Maasai were proposing to depart from Christian teaching; it was that they were proposing to enter more deeply into it. It was imperative for the West to welcome that fact.

As an example of faithfulness, Donovan pointed to the Masaai's African Creed. In the creed the Maasai spoke of believing as a community rather than as isolated persons, and, instead of casting their creed in cognitive abstract terms of the seen and unseen, of Christ as eternally begotten of the Father, God from God, light from light, begotten not made, and so on, the Maasai spoke of a journey of faith in a God who out of love created the world and everyone, how they once knew the High God in darkness but now knew this God in the light. The creed continued with God's promises in Scripture, history, and momentously in Jesus, "a man in the flesh, a Jew by tribe, born poor in a little village, who left his home and was always on safari doing good, curing people by the power of God," until finally he was rejected by his people, tortured and nailed hands and feet to a cross, and died. Then the irony of the historical Jesus is clinched with a stunning understatement with the words, "He lay buried in the grave, but the hyenas did not touch him, and on the third day he rose from the grave." A note of eschatological joy and hope swells to conclude the creed, "We are waiting for Him [Jesus]. He is alive. He lives. This we believe. Amen."

The Jesus of the African Creed is a solid historical figure, steeped in his Jewish culture, swept up in the controversies of the day, put to death without being shamed, witnessed to by Scripture, anointed and abiding through the

Holy Spirit, a channel of God's grace, and present in the world through sacrament, mission, and service to one another. This Jesus is not smothered in cultural conceits but instead is allowed to rise in his own power, and to be met on his own terms. There is intervention, but it is God's intervention, not the intervention of theological experts.

There is little sign in the African Creed, as there is, for example, in the Nicene Creed, of the words "smelling of the [litigious] lamp,"[40] of the scars of bitter theological strife, of rubbing in the noses of the vanquished, of haunting heresy, or of the West's twilight mood. Maasai ideas of God were not as prickly, in large part because the Maasai did not think of faith as a strategy against their enemies, as reward for their achievement, or as jousting with the heretics. Accordingly, their creed resounds with gratitude and with their sense of God's honor. Their attention was focused strictly on God rather than on them or on anyone else. The whole point of their creed was not that it should be a study document for scholars but a testament of faith and devotion for believers. Tribal valor or ancient grudges had no part in the creed. On the contrary, its whole spirit was animated by hope and trust in God in the sense in which Christians had grounds to hope and trust, namely, by acknowledging God in their midst. It is not too far from what Roland Allen meant when he spoke about the gift of the Holy Spirit in communities of local discernment.

So little noticed at the time, Donovan's field findings soon assumed new significance in the face of the coming post-Western awakening. The first signs that something momentous was afoot were evident in the 1980s when the *World Christian Encyclopedia*, published from Nairobi, not far from Tanzania where Donovan was based, drew attention to the shift. The *Encyclopedia* provided mounting evidence of the gathering momentum, confirming an unsettling gap with the situation in the post-Christian West, which Donovan and Allen had predicted. China would dramatize the change.

8

Christian Awakening and the New China

Bamboo Pillar

Two Foreigners, One Country

Rudyard Kipling had his finger on a vital pulse when he quipped that Asia was not going to be civilized after the methods of the West because there was too much of Asia and because Asia was too old. Indeed, Kipling's jest sums up the checkered history of relations between the two civilizations fairly well, as Europe's global range failed to advance intercultural exchange. For much of that history the wisdom that Asia was too big and too old was flouted, and the failure of communication between Europe and Asia resulted in a wall of estrangement blocking interactions with China, leaving national officials determined to seek ways of protecting themselves from the unpleasant facts of Western expansion.

Two central issues have defined China's encounter with the Western Christian movement: one was the demand for indigenous control against missionary domination, and the other was China's role in recent global Marxist movements. Christianity was a target on both fronts: one time as an obstacle to local empowerment, and another as an antagonistic ideology. On both issues Christianity yielded ground; first with respect to China's national interests, and next with respect to China's place in global revolutionary movements.

Despite this conflict, China's preoccupation with Christianity seldom faltered, though leaders on both sides misconstrued the nature of Christianity's local awakening. Antagonism to Christianity as a foreign religion coexisted incongruously with the exclusive espousal of the foreign ideology of Marxism. The demand of absolute conformity to state dogma under penalty of summary justice did not change the fact that Marxism was without indigenous roots, nor render Christianity illegitimate for being foreign. Perhaps Mao was too mindful of his nemesis in the Christian-inspired Kuomintang nationalist movement led by Sun Yat-sen (d. 1925), and later by Chiang Kai-shek (d. 1975), to ignore Christianity as an ideological foe.

At any rate, at a critical juncture of its history China welcomed the message of revolution it wanted to hear and sequestered the message of salvation it was determined to contest, having decided in both cases that the available indigenous options were inadequate or unacceptable. It remains a puzzle, however, why prominent Western observers—including religious scholars—thought that China's adoption of Marxist revolution was authentically Chinese while Christianity should be repudiated for not being genuinely Chinese, an attitude accompanied by a virtuous appeal to respect for local culture. Yet Marx condemned Asia for its brutalizing worship of nature and for having degraded human beings to the position of falling down on their knees in adoration of Hanuman, the monkey, and Sabbal, the cow.

Undeterred by such aspersion, Western apologists insisted that "it has never been more than a misunderstanding of mission for the missionary to try to short-circuit the process by which individual human beings decide their ultimate loyalties and manifest their decisions externally."[1] Yet Mao's prescription for China's problems instituted precisely such an external blueprint by way of Marx, though Western observers were too deafened by the echoes of their own eager applause for Mao to hear the signals that would fuel the coming indigenous Christian response. Seeing in China's revolution what they expected to see, Western observers overlooked the obvious strides Christianity was poised to take.

After the dust settled and missionaries were no longer on the scene, the Christian movement remained a viable contender in the field in spite of its heavy baggage. China—embattled or liberated—was seldom far from the Christian mind, whether abroad or at home. Indeed, the Christian mind was formed by being Christ-indwelled, not by being a transplant attitude with built-in local antipathy. Christianity fostered that local advantage by enabling converts to transcend a Christendom complex, including the Western guilt complex that abandoned any hope of local Christian re-engagement. Progressive voices in the West led a well-rehearsed movement to revamp the Christian enterprise altogether and to denounce the capitalist West that supported it. Their goal was that the new mission of what they continued to speak of as Christendom, should be concerned with *"leavening the world* [rather] *than of churching the people."*[2] They claimed this was an advance; and it became, in effect, the flight of the lemmings.

Nemesis of History

The historical trail leading to this orchestrated cultural retreat is well laid, and its traces have persisted through the centuries. When he ascended the Dragon Throne in 1724, the emperor Yung-cheng reversed his father's policy of openness to the Jesuits. At a meeting with the Jesuits in Beijing, he predicted that naval force would eventually accompany European missionary intrusion into China. He did not mince words with the Jesuits, his sentiments being an accurate reflection of the doctrine that missions were to be pursued with the dual swords of both civil and ecclesiastical power. That was precisely how the Franciscan Fr. Paulo da Trinidade had expressed it regarding Goa in 1638. Emperor Yung-cheng weighed in:

> You say that your law is not a false law. I believe you. If I thought
> it was false, what would prevent me from destroying your churches
> and driving you away from them? What would you say if I sent a
> troop of Bonzes and Lamas into your country to preach their doc-
> trines? You want all Chinese to become Christians. Your law demands
> it, I know. But in that case what will become of us? Shall we be-
> come the subjects of your King? The converts you make will recog-
> nize only you in time of trouble. They will listen to no other voice but
> yours. I know that at present there is nothing to fear, but when
> your ships come by the thousands then there will probably be great
> disorder.... The (K'ang-hsi) emperor, my father, lost a great deal
> of his reputation among scholars by the condescension with which he
> let you establish yourselves here. The laws of our ancient sages will
> permit no change, and I will not allow my reign to be laid open to
> such a charge.[3]

The emperor issued the Edict of Expulsion and Confiscation, resulting in the widespread wrecking of churches or their conversion to granaries, schools, or public halls. Some 300,000 Christians were affected by the persecution. Survivors were subject to public restrictions and penalties. For hundreds of years, Christianity was regarded as a foreign intrusion, and converts as cultural turncoats.

Resistance

That historical background colored China's view of the foreigners and their creed, and it supplied irrefutable evidence of foreign bad faith. Henceforth, the shadow of an acquisitive West loomed large in the Chinese mind with respect to Christianity, provoking long-standing opposition and distrust of the West. When, in October of 1949, Mao Tse-tung made the dramatic announcement, "The Chinese people have stood up," he ended more than a century of ignominy at the hands of Europeans and reminded the world of China's importance. Nothing better illustrates China's humiliation by foreigners than the Opium Wars of the nineteenth century.

The British East India Trading Company, for example, saw a particularly lucrative source of riches in selling opium to China. China's subsequent resistance was crushed by British military invasion, and the treaty ending the First Opium War in 1842 legalized the opium trade, gave control of Hong Kong to the British rather than China, and established five "treaty ports" on the Chinese coast where special privileges were reserved for Europeans. China's first Protestant Church was built in Amoy in 1848. These high-handed terms were extended after the Second Opium War of 1856. Between 1840 and 1940 China languished under the debilitating terms of these "unequal treaties," generating intense anti-Western sentiment among the Chinese. According to a report, by 1909 there were eight Protestant mission stations with 75 congregations, 8,000 baptized members, 30 pastors, a Union boys' Middle School, Union Theological College, 80 schools, and 10 hospitals; all with fewer than 100 missionaries.[4] It did not help matters that Christian missionaries declared universal support for the Taiping Rebellion of 1854. The London Missionary Society missionary Griffith John said, in 1860, that he was convinced the Rebellion was a sign that God had intervened in China to uproot idolatry and prepare to establish Christianity in the country. With Western military help, the insurrection was finally put down in 1864. Possibly twenty million Chinese died in the conflict. The Rebellion burned the specter of Christianity as national menace into China's official memory.

All of this feeling led to periodic bursts of violence, such as the Boxer Uprising in 1900, in which 230 Western missionaries (called "Primary Devils") were among those killed,[5] and the establishment of the Chinese Communist Party in 1921 where Marxism, Leninism, and Stalinism were mixed inconclusively with Confucianism and Taoism. The Chinese proverb that says that three ways lead to one goal does not, unfortunately, reckon with ambushes. When Japan invaded China in 1937, the Nationalists under Chiang Kai-shek and the Communists under Mao buried the hatchet temporarily and joined forces finally to drive out the Japanese enemy in 1945. The three ways then became two as the civil war resumed, culminating in the Communist victory in 1949.

It may be useful to comment briefly on the intellectual background to the Communist uprising in China. China had watched the course of the Russian Revolution—the dates of which coincided with the First World War—with close interest, and saw it as a war fomented by the Christian nations of Europe. Russia was popular in China for having renounced her extra-territorial rights and special privileges. By denouncing Christianity and adopting atheism as a philosophy, the Russians acted in ways consistent with the criticisms Confucian scholars had made against Buddhism; namely, that the superstitions of religion contained falsehoods and malice detrimental to the good of society. Russia tore down the mask hiding the true face of Christianity and demonstrated that the Chinese suspicion of missions as a foreign conspiracy was all too true. The Chinese felt that Christianity was without intrinsic merit, that it had failed demonstrably in Europe, and that Russia's actions exposed the religion's nefarious designs for the world to see. China felt vindicated in its view that missionaries wanted to spread Christianity in China for no other reason than to promote foreign interests.

In China itself, the leaders abandoned any hope of embracing Christianity, emboldened by the fact that what was left of Christianity—even in its cultural stronghold of Europe—now seemed to be in rapid decline, with no future. The leaders regarded missions as a throwback to a discredited past, with little positive influence to contribute to China. Christianity was no longer the vanguard of Western civilization, as many students abroad came to acknowledge. These educated Chinese youth had felt estranged from their elders, but returned home with a pronounced disenchantment with Christianity as the solution to China's problems. The Chinese felt that they must lay the ghost of Christianity to rest in order to give birth to a new society in China.

Understandably, Mao regarded Western perfidy as the single greatest injustice that had to be avenged. He recalled that missionaries applauded the era of the "unequal treaties" as God's will, ensuring by their attitude that Christianity would carry a foreign stigma. The Chinese felt that missions opened a third front of the West's war on China by making cultural imperialism a part of the West's political and economic aggression. The goals of Westernizing China and Christianizing China were one and the same for the missionaries. As C. P. Fitzgerald stated, "The missionaries of both the Reformed and the Catholic churches found that the greatest obstacle to their progress was not the fanatical devotion of the Chinese to some pagan creed, but their tolerance."[6] It explains why Roland Allen protested missionary endorsement of Western political interests as a betrayal of their vocation. In any case, Mao gave Christianity no quarter even though, in theory, the Communists guaranteed freedom of religion. He launched a permanent peasant-led two-tier revolution against what he called "antagonistic contradictions" from without and "non-antagonistic contradictions" from within. There were, at that time, about three million Catholics and one million Protestants in China.

Mao noted that the Chinese Communist authorities would not and could not abolish religion by state fiat, or force people not to believe in religion. Even though, for him, politics was his religion and his religion politics, Mao declared that coercion or repression would not settle the issue. That did not, however, mean Christianity should be tolerated. On the contrary, religion qua religion was for the wealthy. The poor had the Eighth Route Army. The matter would ultimately be settled by the political instrument. In an interview with the Western journalist Anna Louise Strong, Mao asked her what the heart of the Christian religion was. "To free the captives," Strong responded, to which Mao retorted, "And what exactly have you done to achieve that?"[7] Protestant Christian leaders responded with the three-self movement led by Y. T. Wu, the secretary of the Chinese YMCA and a graduate of Union Seminary in New York. The "Christian Manifesto" was issued in 1950 to promote the cause of an indigenous Chinese Christianity, that is to say, a politically acquiescent Christianity. The three-self movement changed its name in 1954 to the Protestant Three Self Patriotic Movement. It resolved permanently and completely to sever all relations with Western missions and, as it were, to march to the chant of "What a comrade we have in Jesus." The era of religious tutorial in political correctness had arrived.

For its part, the Catholic Church was called upon to repudiate Archbishop Antonio Riberi (1897–1967) who denounced the Communists and forbade Catholics to join the Communist Party. Riberi was placed under house arrest in May 1951, and subsequently expelled from China. In June, Fr. John Tung was invited by the officials to condemn Riberi. In his speech, however, Tung declined to attack Riberi, saying such attacks would eventually be extended to the pope and to Christ himself. He was arrested and sent to work in a labor camp in a remote part of China. By the end of 1952, sixteen Catholic priests, missionaries, brothers, and sisters had been thrown out of China. By the end of 1953, more than three hundred Chinese Catholic priests were languishing in jail.

Caving in to official pressure, a number of Catholic priests and lay people organized the "Preparatory Committee of the Chinese Catholics' Patriotic Association" in July 1956, which led to the convening of the Chinese Catholics' Patriotic Association the following year. The Association adopted a resolution to the effect that: "The Catholic Church in China must implement a policy of autonomy and independence whereby Chinese Catholics, cleric and lay, take charge of their own affairs. With our country's independence and dignity foremost in mind, we shall maintain purely religious relationships with the Vatican, obeying the Pope only in matters pertaining to faith and church law while completely severing all political and economic ties with the Vatican and resolutely opposing its [the Vatican's] use of religion as a pretext to undermine the sovereignty of our country and to sabotage our just cause of anti-imperialist patriotism."[8] Thus, by state fiat, the Catholic community was being required to embrace the role of quasi-official sponsor of national mandates. But a papal statement rejected the official policy whose aim, it said, was:

> to join the clergy and the faithful in love of their religion and their country, with these objectives in view: that they might foster patriotic sentiments; that they might advance the cause of international peace; that they might accept that species of socialism which has been introduced among you and, having accepted it, support and spread it; that, finally, they might actively cooperate with civil authorities in defending what they describe as political and religious freedom. And yet—despite these sweeping generalizations about defense of peace and the fatherland, which can certainly deceive the unsuspecting—it is perfectly clear that this association is simply an attempt to execute certain well-defined and ruinous policies. For under an appearance of patriotism, which in reality is just a fraud, this association aims primarily at making Catholics gradually embrace the tenets of atheistic materialism, by which God Himself is denied and religious principles are rejected.

Fishing in Troubled Waters

A time of new leniency opened in May 1956 when Mao launched what he called the Hundred Flowers Period, during which time open criticism of government policies was allowed by Protestant voices. But a year later, in June 1957, the experiment in openness was abruptly halted and a chill descended on the churches. In the Great Leap Forward campaign, which began in 1958, Christian groups started targeting each other in a bid to curry favor and to establish their legitimacy with the government.

For Christians in China, trying to find their bearings in the shifting currents of change was like playing cat's cradle with the thicket of official pronouncements and directives. Christians groped their way through the maze of revolutionary propaganda, not knowing if the command to fight "the four pests" of flies, rats, mosquitoes, and sparrows included rooting out unpatriotic elements in the churches, or if the government's decree on the Fight-the-Locusts campaign should be augmented by mobilizing Sunday worship services and Sunday schools as propaganda mills. In the Hand-the-Heart-to-the-Party campaign in the late 1950s, for example, Chinese Protestant leaders felt the campaign should include a public denunciation of the U.S. National Council of Churches for their meddlesome claim that Chinese Christians were persecuted by their government. The irony was that Mao himself had written in July 1937 that what he called the "phrase-mongering of the 'Leftists' "—letting flowery slogans take precedence over concrete action—was antagonistic evidence of the "breach between the subjective and the objective, by the separation of knowledge from practice."[9] Christians soon learned that in the milieu of revolution, even religion could not atone for the sin of phrase-mongering.

It became a cruel Kafkaesque game of victims beating themselves with a rod fashioned from the dark suspicion, innuendo, and rumors directed at them. In a famous assertion in the 1960s, Bishop K. H. Ting denied categorically that the Chinese Church had suffered any discrimination or persecution. On the contrary, he insisted, Christians held high public office in China. The Communist-inspired Christianity of China, Ting declared, was a sign to the nations and the beginning of a new outpouring of Christ's presence in the world. Right-minded Christians should see that the ground was thick with fellow comrades, and class solidarity the greatest commandment. Progressive audiences in the West welcomed the suggestion that party vanguards might find Jesus a hearty trooper of the cause, even though a far different reality was unfolding on the ground. It pointed to the uncomfortable truth that religious denial of persecution was, in fact, proof of political repression.

The party diehards brandished their trophies by rehearsing the claim that religion was false consciousness, no more legitimate as a self-deception than as a deception of others, and that Christian leaders who insinuated themselves into Communist ranks did so by fake solidarity. By accepting the Marxist philosophy, Christians admitted that their own teaching was bogus, and condemned themselves before anyone else did. In the Great Proletarian Cultural Revolution (starting in 1966), a New China was conceived in which religion was put in its place. The party carried out purges; closing schools, freeing students from their classes to conscript them in ideological training camps, and hounding scholars, now considered "stinking" social debris. A four-headed monster was wheeled out and targeted at the "four olds"—old ideas, old culture, old customs, and old habits—all of that erupting into the formidable guise of the Red

Guards, the youthful party vanguards. Revolutionary virtue turned hysteri-cal, as some seventeen million urban youth were thus deployed to stalk the countryside.

The Red Guards wreaked havoc in every sector of Chinese society, and the churches were overwhelmed by the turmoil. By September 1966, all the churches were closed, their leaders rounded up, and their properties confis-cated. The Red Guards attacked the site of the ancient Nestorian stele of 781, unearthed in 1623, and destroyed the main building of the Da Qin monastery in their campaign to stamp out any visible trace of religion across China. The destructiveness of the Red Guards reached a climax in August 1966, when images of the Buddha were torn down, and statues, icons, crucifixes, and other religious symbols were destroyed in a fit of uncontrolled revolutionary rage. The (Catholic) Southern Cathedral in Beijing was closed, its crossremoved, and the building turned into a storage facility. Amidst the repression, not a word was said about the constitutional guarantee of freedom of religion. The *Little Red Book* of Chairman Mao became the authorized scripture of the rulership cult that was on the rampage, as the party updated the Heavenly Mandate of the Confucian tradition with a hefty dose of Marxism-Leninism. It created such heady extremism that even Mao's attempt in 1968 to rein in the overzealous Red Guards was ineffectual. According to some observers, it took until 1976, the year of Mao's death, to disarm the behemoth and to bring matters under control.

Appeasement

One could interpret the upheavals of the Cultural Revolution as an example of the collision between an implacable foreign ideology and the indefatigable spirit of China—the results certainly left little doubt of a rupture with the old China. Yet the events found powerful sympathetic voices in the West, such as Joseph Needham (1900–95) of Cambridge University, recognized as among the most respected historians of China's cultural achievement (and who was a major influence in the shaping of UNESCO). His monumental series, *Science and Civilization in China* had appeared in seventeen volumes by the time of his death. His achievements were celebrated by the establishment of the Need-ham Institute at Cambridge.

Needham wrote in 1972 that the Chinese revolution had created the ideal society, which was much closer to the kingdom of God than Western soci-ety. He went on: "It would seem that the China which broke the heart of mis-sionaries has accepted the spirit of Christ from another source, namely, [from]

Marxism. . . . The Chinese society of the present day is, I think, further on the way to the true society of mankind, the Kingdom of God if you like, than our own. I think China is the only truly Christian country in the world in the present day, in spite of its absolute rejection of all religion." Needham said that Christ was to be found in China because China was "where the good are, and where good things are done. That means appreciating what is happening in China at the present day."[10]

Needham's sentiments were echoed in numerous other statements to the effect that modern China had fulfilled all the high moral expectations of the *Magnificat* and the *Sermon on the Mount*, and that Maoism was God's saving power in China and had replaced the church as God's redemptive presence in Chinese society. The report of the Louvain conference testified that the work of Christ and the work of Mao converged in China. " 'Love your neighbour to the point of denying yourself' is the ethical core of the Gospel. 'Fight selfishness; serve the people' is the ethical core of Mao Tse-tung Thought. 'By their fruits you shall know them' is the decisive criterion of the Gospel. Marxism has sworn by the same test of 'fruits' or 'practice,' and in the case of China at least has both preached and practiced 'continuing revolution' in its name."[11]

In this fashion, the fiery chariot of Mao's nationalist revolution overtook the juggernaut of nineteenth-century missionary domination of China and crushed it. "Here was a phenomenon of incalculable historical significance. Through Marxism, humanism, and pacifism, through the liberation struggles of nations, races, and other repressed groups, and now through an officially sanctioned ferment in the Churches, both Protestant and Catholic, a new perception was growing in the West that there was a larger and worthier war to wage than the Cold War, and its lines of battle did not have to leave all Christians on one side and all Communists on the other. . . . What made the New China a 'yellow peril' to the establishments was precisely what made it a 'Red hope' to the alienated and [to] their counter-cultures."[12] If in a previous era, Christians could claim to know on the basis that "the Bible told me so," now they could say because Mao told them so.[13] Yet the claim raised a basic question: could China be Marxist and assert that it was anti-foreign at the same time? As a Marxist champion of Third World rights and aspirations, China was applauded for repudiating the old China.[14] The Jesuit theologian William van Etten Casey compared Chinese society to one "huge Jesuit novitiate," where the pursuit of virtue predominated. C. S. Song, the Presbyterian minister, said Mao's Long March was the inauguration of a new stage in the history of salvation. China was the New Israel, he contended; on the tacit grounds, perhaps, that "Old Israel" in terms of old China was now defunct. Salvation history, he declared, had to do with God's acts in history, and—thanks to the changes wrought by the Chinese Communist Party—that was being acted out in the transition from the old China to the new China.

The theologians were in no doubt whatsoever on whether Marxist China could also be Christian.[15] The meaning of the cross as the central Christian symbol, they affirmed, supported the attempt in China to relate love and power by rejecting servility, indifference, and cringing in the face of tyrannical power. In China's context, nonviolent struggle against injustice, however desirable, was not an option. Armed struggle was.[16]

With all this revisionist fervor, the theologians found, in China, a providential platform for global ecumenical solidarity on the new gospel according to Mao. In growing numbers, Catholic theologians joined the ranks to swell the chorus of praise for Communist China's achievements. Jean Charbonnier and Léon Trivière echoed the refrain that China's revolution was part of salvation history, and that those who suffered in order to build the New China had shared in the redemptive passion of the Savior. Dries van Coillie, who had served as a Catholic missionary in China, claimed that China had achieved a state of total grace with the establishment of unselfishness, helpfulness, honesty, endurance of hardship, modesty, self-criticism, dignity, courage, generosity, concern for the exploited and oppressed, and equality.[17] Joachim Pillai, another Catholic theologian, said he discovered Christ's redemptive presence in Maoist China, alongside the all too regrettable absence of Christ in the West.[18] Pillai thought that was confirmation of the insight of faith that Christ appeared where we least expected Him. Donald McInnis felt that the new spirit alive in the Chinese people brought out the best in each individual.

The Lutheran World Federation and the Catholic organization, *Pro Mundi Vita*, held a consultation that embellished this optimistic picture of China. The organizers issued a call to end missions to China, to reject the need for the survival of the church in China, and to affirm God's redemptive action in the Chinese revolution. The communiqué went on:

> The liberation movement in China led by Mao Tse-tung is not excluded therefore from our understanding of God's saving work in history. The Christian can affirm the gains of the Chinese revolution, insofar as these have contributed to the humanization process, while at the same time recognizing that liberation in China is not complete or final. In China to an impressive degree, basic human needs have been met, dignity has been restored, people have been freed to participate in the decision-making process that affects their

daily lives, and in this the Christian may rejoice. The Chinese revolution is seen as part of God's saving action. . . . From a Christian
viewpoint, what we see happening in contemporary China seems to be
God's intensive wrestling with the Chinese people . . . for an eventual
fulfillment of [God's] saving purpose. The social and political trans-
formations brought about in China through the application of the
Thought of Mao Tse-tung have unified and consolidated a quarter
of the world population into a form of society and life-style at once
pointing to some of the basic characteristics of the kingdom of
God. . . . We believe that here power greater than China, the power
which transcends history and yet works within history, is at work
making China a sign to the nations[19]

The communiqué insisted that the time had passed when Christianity
could raise questions for China, pointing out that these questions were already
settled for Chinese Christians who had long ago reached the conclusion that
Christianity was, at best, irrelevant and, at worst, inimical to China's interests.
Christianity was regarded as alien and subversive for plausible reasons, with no
future in China except as a secret conspiracy. The "chief problem for Christians about the China-and-Christianity question is the fact that it has to all
appearances ceased to be a question in China itself."[20] Nothing was more apt
for China than for Christianity's God to be the one "who knew the way of the
grave."[21] The Christian West must learn to forego its claim to be the arbiter of
Christianity. "The new China challenges us to give up our attitudes of superiority and to acknowledge the quality of the new leadership which has emerged
in China. Christians . . . have to free themselves from the parochial Western
context in which many of their Churches have developed and realize that the
Gospel might be more powerfully expressed and fulfilled in the new type of
society which is promoted in China."[22]

For the now-marginal post-Christian West, the implications were clear,
according to the Louvain communiqué. Western Christianity had been far
too closely involved with the bourgeois capitalist system and its imperialist
schemes for it to play any meaningful role in post-Western developments. For
far too long, the church had acquiesced in a society in which the strongest
minority made profit at the expense of the weakest majority, and reflected that
bias in its schizoid message of theoretical love and practical apathy. Depending
on the financial support of an unjust system, the church became inured to the
needs and concerns of the poor. "The result in the West is a Church with a
sterile lack of words and deeds of liberating power."[23] This exploitative view of
the church was perpetuated in the post-Western world, lending support to the

charge that Christianity was a moral injustice willfully perpetrated upon the world. It needed and deserved Mao to set it straight.

Backing Down

Historical events, however, caused a shift in attitudes, and Chinese leaders became less starry-eyed about Mao and less fearful about the gospel. In 1978, at the beginning of the government's liberalization program, Deng Xiaoping declared that the revolution's leaders had had second thoughts and would embark on a program of easing restrictions on religion. In 1979, Deng challenged the Chinese Communist Party to "seek truth from facts," code for deserting Mao's legacy. It was an acknowledgment that something had gone badly wrong and that the solution could be found in new openness. China could not afford the doctrinaire inflexibility that was uncluttered by evidence[24]—and neither, in a way, could the coming theologians.

As the flood receded, the rock reappeared. Churches bounced back as the government made good on promises of restitution for properties seized and wrongs committed. In the revised Constitution of 1982, religious rights were reaffirmed under article 36, followed by the publication of Document 19 concerning religious policy in China. The document essentially repudiated the excesses of the Cultural Revolution against religion as a "leftist mistake." Churches must be rebuilt, clergy educated, and believers protected, the declaration said. Some 4,000 Protestant and 2,000 Catholic churches were thus reopened or rebuilt.[25] It did not take long for high-ranking officials to declare open sympathy for religion, and by 1986 the thaw had created a vigorous spate of official endorsements, including subsidies for church reconstruction projects. According to a report in 2003, in addition to the 45,000 registered churches in existence, between 30,000 and 40,000 groups affiliated with the Protestant Three-Self Patriotic Movement were still waiting for their turn to register. The windfall of the new awakening created a bottleneck and caused a pent-up demand for pastoral training and leadership.[26]

The official about-face amounted to a dramatic repudiation of the bitter fruits of the revolutionary labor camps that theologians had breezily attributed to God's redemptive action in China. Under threat of abandonment, Mao's messianic mystique had been refurbished in 1971 by the Gang of Four, led by Mao's wife, Jiang Qing, who rounded up suspect dissident supporters of the disgraced premier, Zhou Enlai. In 1974 a mass movement was launched to eradicate the influence of Lin Piao, who had died in 1971 after an abortive attempt on Mao's life. Lin Piao was denounced for propagating Confucianism, a tradition the Communists attacked for perpetuating the retrograde values of the old China. An officially sanctioned haul was staged of some 4,000 Chinese Christian leaders who, in 1974, were attending an underground Christian training session in Fangcheng County, Henan Province.

In the cruel irony of violent historical reversal, in 1976 the Gang of Four was overthrown for bringing Mao's Messianic legacy into disrepute, and its members were arrested as China awoke wearily from the nightmare of the Cultural Revolution. With the insecure reflexes of recovering stalwarts, senior apparatchiks began to poke holes in the ideological lantern they once tended by converting to Christianity. One disgraced member of the Gang of Four movement, Fang Tiancai, inquired incredulously of the person he met in prison (whom he had been instrumental in sending to death row), "Are you Li Tianen?" When told that he was, Fang declared, in tones one part remorse and one part indictment, "God in Heaven, you are an awesome power! I was ready to execute you three times, but the Jesus you believe in protected you. Marx was not able to save me. Now I believe the Gospel you believe in is real."[27]

Li was released from prison in 1979 after all the charges against him were quietly dropped, though he was assigned menial jobs cleaning toilets, mopping floors, and emptying out trash at the Shanghai Municipal Hospital Number Four. Before he left prison, Li agreed to Fang's request to pray for him. It is a strange irony that Chinese leaders should be willing to repent while Western theological leaders persisted in extolling China's controversial record. What these theologians called signs of Christ's redemptive passion were to be found not, as they claimed, in China's violent swings of fortune, but instead in forces set to ignite the coming Christian awakening.

Christianity's spontaneous grassroots appeal may be gauged from the following report. In a detailed study of Protestantism in one province, it was found that on a given Sunday some 800 worshipers—mostly illiterate peasants—gathered in church of whom the vast majority were peasants and illiterates. "A few in attendance were Party cadres, and one out of the 800 had a Bible."[28] More than 54 percent of the people there said they embraced Christianity for reasons that had to do with their personal physical health, not with sympathy with foreign interests.

Theological assessments of China's Christian prospects were dominated by a debilitating Western guilt complex that substituted Mao's earthly kingdom for God's heavenly one. In a deeply sympathetic study of the issues, one report said the experience of Christianity in the West showed what it called a multiple law of diminishing returns. It identified four such laws: first, conversion was meaningless where everyone was already converted; second, conversion as a personal act had little merit in a society where Church membership was a social norm; third, where church membership was the social norm the bid to make it the norm for everyone made it more ambiguous—cultural Christians made Christianity a mere padding; fourth, a world that had touched the limits of physical and psychic living space was not a world that would allow itself to be polarized by religious claims.[29] That assessment was blind to the new spirit of the post-Western Christian resurgence and to a role for the West that was being pushed to the unaccustomed position of new Christian margins. Perhaps Chinese Christian thought would do better and demonstrate creative critical engagement with the new reality. As it was, detached from the facts on the ground, the West's cultural axiom made it difficult to acknowledge the Southern/Eastern shift in Christianity's center of gravity, or even to conceive of a plan of action based on the premise that the worldwide Christian resurgence was more local than Western.[30]

Second Wind

What all this pointed to was that Christian life in China had shared in the unsettled political climate, especially because the government inserted itself into how the churches must relate to the West.[31] Official policy had been against outside involvement on the grounds that such involvement would not be consistent with China's sovereignty. This nettled the Catholic Church by forcing it to decide between adhering to Catholic teaching on the universal authority of the pope and China's demand of exclusive loyalty to the government. The Chinese Catholic leaders' assurance of their patriotic commitment failed to sway the government if they combined that assurance with filial obedience to the pope. It merely confirmed the official suspicion that, manipulated by Rome, Christianity had covert political designs on China.

By the same token, when the officially authorized Patriotic Association of Christians made a gesture of accommodation to Rome, it was viewed with incredulity and as a ruse to create an independent Chinese Catholic church in contravention of Church teaching. It seemed to place Chinese Catholics in an awkward position, while making the "official" and "underground" or "registered" and "unregistered" distinction a tenuous one at best. Bishop Aloysius Jin Luxian of Shanghai, for example, acknowledged government approval as indispensable to a functioning Catholic church, including the operation of seminaries, preaching openly, and writing and publishing books. In return, Bishop Aloysius kept Rome at arm's length and defended himself with a theory of the church as follows: "Every local Church is fully Church. Every local Church has full rights. They must be united in one Church, but equally as [in] the Holy Trinity."[32]

Sitting in the eye of the storm, the Catholic bishop of Beijing, Fu Tieshan, was more critical of the Vatican, claiming the Vatican had collaborated with powers of aggression against China and had exploited its connection with Chinese Catholics to act against the will of Christ and the interests of China. The refusal of the Vatican to recognize the authority of democratically elected bishops, Bishop Fu charged, showed bad faith and made it hard to trust Vatican proposals for a rapprochement with China. Bishop Zong Huaide, the president of the Chinese Patriotic Catholic Association, also backed this hardline position. He said the decision by Catholic Chinese to participate fully in the work of socialist construction was unwisely opposed by the Vatican, showing hostility to China and lack of respect for the autonomy of the Chinese Catholic Church.

For many church leaders, however, the issue was unimportant in the overall scheme of things. The leaders simply ignored the "official" and "unofficial" distinction and participated in the Mass of both camps. As Fr. John-Baptist Zhang of the Catholics' Patriotic Association testified, "People don't care very much any more about the divorce between the official and unofficial church. The Vatican is very clear that it will not get into conflict with the government."[33]

Nevertheless, the Vatican's relations meanwhile with the Chinese government suffered a major setback in May, 2006, when, against papal protest, the government went ahead with the consecration of Ma Yinglin as bishop of Kunming. A papal spokesman called the consecration of Ma a "grave wound to the unity of the church."[34] In response the Vatican authorized going ahead with the consecration of Pei Junmin, whose appointment had been jointly approved with the government although the government had not agreed to the timing of the consecration—the reports are confusing as to what is cause and what is consequence here. In any case, the incident brought to a head the simmering tension between Liu Bainian, the leader of the Patriotic Association and often referred to as "China's Pope," and Hong Kong's Cardinal Joseph Zen Ze-kiun. The general expectation of a thaw in relations between the Vatican and Beijing has been set back, though neither side is willing to force a confrontation. Father Jeroom Heyndrickx, a Belgian priest and the Vatican's point man in relations with Beijing, for example, is slow to pin all the blame on Liu Bainian for the adversarial nature of the relationship with Beijing, saying Liu should not be held more accountable than his role as a minor official warrants—a conciliatory gesture that would not go unnoticed.

All these and other changes have shown that a profound change has overtaken the Catholic Church in China. "The result today is a church that is to all appearances self-assured and confident, independent of Vatican control, democratic in structure, giving real power to the laity, on the way to overcoming sexism, and contributing in every way it can to the material and spiritual well-

being of the Chinese masses."[35] The catalyst and moving force for this transformation was an ideological atheist state, and, as a consequence, "Christianity
has given birth to something genuinely new."[36] Christianity absorbed repression into its internal combustion to drive the surge.

The central question remained: whither the church in China? Much uncertainty still abounded about how relevant the Chinese experience was in the
general context of post-Western Christianity. In spite of its avowed sympathy
for Maoist China, even the Louvain communiqué was convinced that the gospel
would fuel a critical phase in China's future. "We believe that the revolution
will prove to need the Gospel . . . to keep it radical, honest and human. A Church
witnessing to such a gospel needs to be one that is soaked in the Chinese tradition and in the thought and life of the new China, and has learned to understand and love the whole [society] in the light of Christ."[37] But that hope
could not sidestep the issue of a state-imposed patriotic litmus test that inhibited open Christian profession in China, shrank the church's margin of free
association, and blocked its wish to contribute to the worldwide church. The
government's demand that Chinese Christianity become more Chinese by becoming less Western seemed to imply that Chinese Christianity should also
become less Christian. As J.S. Mill (1806–1873) once observed, a state which
dwarfs its people as men and women, in order that they may be more docile
instruments in its hands even for beneficial purposes, will find that with small
people no great thing can really be accomplished. By agreeing to be thus treated,
Christians would concede that they were part of both a Western and local conspiracy with no intrinsic credibility of their own.

The Louvain memorandum contended that Christians had a role in
fashioning the new China "through the way their breaking of the ground [for
the seeds of the Gospel] helped to break the spell of the Chinese past." In this
assessment, Christians needed to face up to the fact that "there are values in
China which a Christian ought simply to recognize as Christian values, that
many of them are there as much in spite of as because of the Christians of
history, and that all of them can contribute to making Christianity more truly
Christian as surely as they can contribute to making China more truly Chinese."[38] Thus, what might be new about "patriotic" Christianity in China
might also be the bracing foreign ideology that promulgated it.

The Role of Women in the Church: New Wind of Change

Meanwhile, the Anglican Church was involved in a project of genuine indigenization quite independent of political events, though it coincided with them.

Showing frontier Christianity at one of its critical and creative turning points, the project assumed the form of an initiative for a fundamental reform of the clerical office. Accordingly, a movement was launched, unprecedented in the Anglican Communion, to advance the cause of women's ordination. It came to a head with the ordination of the first woman, Florence Lei, in 1944, which sparked a revolt in the Church of England. It was the kind of smoking gun the standard bearers of the West needed to confirm their worst fears about the hazards of an unsupervised, immature post-Western Christianity. In spite of pleas from China and at home, Rev. Lei was pressured to repudiate her ordination and to resign. She did so, she said, for the sake of the greater good of the church. Her supporters, on the other hand, had every reason to wonder if that cause was not already hers.

In response to the fiasco, an international committee was convened to draft a document in 1948, entitled *A Memorandum to the Lambeth Conference*, which called for the adoption of the principle of the ordination of women and for their recognition in every respect as the equals of men. The *Memorandum* was submitted as a resolution of the Chung Hua Sheng King Hui, and it set out the case for women's ordination in clear, uncompromising language. The denial of Holy Orders to women, the *Memorandum* affirmed, could not be defended by reason or practice. "In principle any and every freedom which is open to men is open to women also and equally. Such freedom may properly be regulated but it cannot be taken away," the *Memorandum* stated. Christian freedom was something intrinsic by virtue of the action of the Holy Spirit in creation. Our response to God was made possible by the freedom God had seen fit to bestow on us.

The cause for the ordination of women rested on that unimpeachable foundation. Furthermore, the idea had behind it the advantages of practical expediency and spiritual need, not only of the church in China but also in every other part of what the *Memorandum* called "world Christianity itself." The pressure to embrace the full equality of women in the life of the church, the *Memorandum* observed, was coming from the mission frontier from where "come reports of converts to Christianity—often made by women evangelists— left for long periods without the sacraments of the Church for lack of Clergy to Administer them." A sense of new possibilities for Christian life and practice was developing in post-Western Christianity, whose leaders believed that Christianity stood to recapture its New Testament spirit outside the Western frame. In England, for example, the shortage of priests was typically solved by consolidating parishes, thus shelving the question of ordaining women. In China, however, that option was out of the question. Instead, the *Memorandum* continued, "A more courageous note has been struck which has resulted in the enquiry which is now before the Lambeth Conference."

The resolution tabled at Lambeth was submitted by the Diocesan Synod of Kong Yuet and circulated by it to all the other Diocesan Synods. The document urged the ordination of women on the grounds "that God is using China's age-long respect for women, and her traditional confidence in women's gifts for administration and counsel, to open a new chapter in the history of the Church." The *Memorandum* noted that the request of the church in China for the ordination of women had local reasons and support but that "the principles and considerations involved are of importance for the whole Anglican Communion." The implicit challenge of the *Memorandum* was for the West to accept the consequences that Christianity was a world religion. "A conservative adherence to traditions which are not of the essence of the Gospel may be proclaimed as loyalty to the Faith and yet, in reality, involve a misunderstanding and a denial of its essential meaning," which in this regard meant extending full equality to women. Only then could the church be recognized as true to the gospel.

The church in China mobilized a campaign at home and abroad in England to press the Lambeth Conference to adopt its *Memorandum*. It led to the drafting of "A Memorial by the Anglican Group for the Ordination of Women," delivered to Lambeth in support of the Chinese *Memorandum*. The "Memorial" went into detail on the historical, missionary, theological, psychological, pragmatic, and administrative arguments in support of the ordination of women. The church must be open to the world beyond the West and its settled consensus. Temporizing in the circumstances would be fatal to all that the church stood for. An important historical document, the "Memorial" requires serious attention even today, as the following summary makes clear.

The "Memorial" called on the Lambeth Conference to rid itself of all residual prejudice and baseless fears against women and to reverse centuries of sex discrimination. The challenge of the Chinese church to open its doors to women was one that implicated church practice everywhere else. The church owed it to itself to recognize its unique and irreplaceable debt to faithful women of great distinction, such women as St. Teresa of Avila, St. Catherine of Siena, St. Hilda, Abbess of Whitby, and St. Joan of Arc; they had shown that women might encourage kings, and even whole nations, might rebuke popes, and might instruct saints. Names, too, like those of Elizabeth Fry, Florence Nightingale, Josephine Butler, Evelyn Underhill, and countless others— including missionaries, nurses, educationists, and even martyrs (Primitive, Catholic, Protestant, and Modern)—had proved beyond question that women had a distinctive spiritual quality, and that they manifested it in public and on the widest stages (p. 5). The small step the Chinese church took in ordaining its first woman seemed like a leap in the dark only because the Western church was blind on the matter.

The "Memorial" cautioned that post-Western Christianity was a salutary reminder that the reality of the world was firmly set against the forces of inertia, inequality, and resistance, and—challengingly—against a world dominated by men. After all, many societies beyond the West had been matrilineal as well. The "peculiarly interesting and relevant feature of our present-day civilization is that it is becoming less and less one-sided every day, and is evolving [into] something new—an approximation to a balance, rather than [to] a conflict, of the claims of the two sexes. The position is now regarded as complementary, and even the exercise of jurisdiction is falling increasingly to merit rather than to sex. Modern civilization is becoming more and more concerned with what is HUMAN, human as such, rather than [with] men; and [it is] as human beings that we stand before God" (p. 4). Mission was Christianity's forward impulse, and the call for change from China evidence of its post-Western potential.

The "Memorial" contended that the Chinese church, far from being unfaithful, was on the cutting edge of history; the call of the Chinese church for the ordination of women showed it to be a boundary marker, in contrast to the church in the West which was still set in its old ways. The decision to ordain women was ultimately inevitable, it said, and, failing that, all the church could do was simply to temporize and delay at enormous cost to its vocation. The immense losses that would ensue would take generations to recover. In being conservative and averse to change, the "Memorial" charged, the church in the West was out of step with the wind of change as the harbinger of the real work of God in the world.

The "Memorial" reminded its readers that the restoration of the Order of Deaconesses, which had been hailed with fanfare by the 1897 Lambeth Conference, was inexcusably abandoned by the action taken in 1920 to reverse the church's course. Since 1920, and especially after the setback suffered in 1930, there had been a steady decline in the position of women in the church. New measures being considered for adoption at the 1948 Lambeth Conference were harsh and retrogressive, and wholly undesirable. The sexist argument that an "unordained" male lay reader might perform functions not permitted to ordained deaconesses damaged the sacrament by making the grace that was intrinsic in ordination a mere accessory to the "grace of sex," leading to the notion that ordination was one thing for men, and another for women. "Ordained or semi-ordained (whichever theory we adopt), a woman is still on a lower level than a man. This is a view highly derogatory to women—all women, as such, and not merely deaconesses. It is an attack upon the spiritual status of all women as a sex, and an attempt to commit the Church of England, for the first time (at least since the Reformation), to an official endorsement of their inferiority" (p. 8).

There was a paramount, unavoidable, and compelling moral obligation for the church to repudiate what was patently unjust and to take the action that alone could restore it to the place God appointed for it. The "Memorial" concluded: "If men and women were considered first and foremost in respect of their COMMON REDEEMED HUMANITY; that is, the things they have, as Christians, in common and not in difference, if they were considered, in short, as human beings, not as sexes, they could come forward freely, and fall naturally into their place in one common diaconate, one common priesthood, even as they do already in one common laity. There is no other way. 'All are one in Christ Jesus' means what it says" (p. 9). For all their prophetic passion and compelling logic, the *Memorandum* and the "Memorial" failed to sway the 1948 Lambeth Conference.

Yet these eloquent views show a remarkable ripening of the thought emerging between progressive voices in the West and church leaders on the missionary frontier, and may be a helpful correction to the standard depiction of post-Western Christianity as a reactionary phenomenon. It is a reminder of the rich mutual benefit to be had from an interdependence that is duly acknowledged and rightly embraced. As the Louvain communiqué put it, China proved that there was a very healthy trend for all peoples, cultures, and religions to draw closer to each other because of their common humanity under one God. Religion offered a new and radical way to build confidence in the importance of affirming the unity—rather than uniformity—of the world.[39]

New Hope

By 1992, the Catholic Church and the state had reached a degree of *modus vivendi*, with the state withdrawing from direct intervention in church life, though it continued to view the church as part of its "People's Propaganda System." For example, the government commended the Catholic Church in Shandong for not taking part in the Tiananmen Square demonstration in 1989 by presenting the church with a silk banner in appreciation (which, ultimately, says more about state perception than about the church).

In June 2004, police arrested one hundred house church leaders in Wuhan city. Among those detained was Xing Jinfu, thirty-nine, who was arrested on three previous occasions for church-related activities. The leadership of the Protestant China Gospel Fellowship has also come under heavy pressure, crushing hopes for a relaxation of religious restrictions under the new Communist leadership of President Hu Jintao.

External pressure on the church has combined with internal struggles between the "open," officially sanctioned registered church and the unregistered "underground" church under papal jurisdiction to complicate the whole question of growth of the church in China. The challenges and opportunities of the church require that we pay attention to the existing political context, for expansion has carried the double burden of secret believers assembling in unauthorized places and of officially co-opted members gathering in licensed churches. In the handbook, *Global Catholicism: Portrait of a World Church*,[40] the number of Catholics in mainland China is put at 7.5 million. China itself is divided into mainland China, Hong Kong, Macau, and Taiwan. The Catholic population outside mainland China is just below 750,000.

At the other extreme of the statistical picture are figures that seek to reflect the dynamism believed to be at work in the underground church movement. Those figures vary widely, some sources estimating between 30 and 50 million believers, while the *World Christian Encyclopedia* lists 89 million.[41] The official Public Security Bureau gives the figure of 25 million Christians in China, but that figure does not include unofficial "house churches." Beside those official and unofficial Christians, there are Chinese intellectuals, who have been described as "cultural Christians," whose names do not appear on lists. In this field, as in many others, it would be extremely hazardous to be dogmatic about a statistical silver bullet. We should, instead, look for the underlying trends.

The expansion points to the strategic role Christianity is poised to play in China. In certain crucial areas, the government has put on the clamps, especially since the Falun Gong outbreak of 1999 and the subsequent publication of "Office 610," designed to combat what are called "evil cults." In other instances, the government gives tacit encouragement to religion. For example, in a front-page memorial notice on the faith of John Paul II, *Faith Fortnightly*[42] (a national Catholic newspaper), noted that the late pope addressed over 4 billion people in his extensive travels. It published pictures of rejoicing among Chinese Catholics on the occasion of the reception of new members at the year's Easter Vigil. Fresh hope seemed to stir with the election of Pope Benedict XVI,[43] whose namesake, Pope Benedict XV (1914–22), paid close attention to the church in China and is credited with establishing the first Chinese hierarchy. In his apostolic letter, *Maximum Illud*, issued on November 1, 1919, he summoned the church to develop local clergy. His letter led to the convening of the first Synod of Bishops in China: the *Primum Concilium Sinense*, or the Shanghai Synod. Six Chinese bishops were ordained in Rome in October 1926, and later consecrated by Pius XI. Both registered and unregistered Catholics in China warmly greeted Pope Benedict XVI's election.

Nevertheless, challenges persist. The new path of material advancement that China has adopted with zeal has led to a strategic opening of China to new relations with the West. Yet, paradoxically, that has not necessarily improved the situation of Christians in China. Indeed, the wheels of rapid economic change have brought a collision with Catholic social teaching that much closer, if still no less undesirable. Commenting on his visit to China undertaken at the invitation of officials there, Cardinal Roger Mahony, archbishop of Los Angeles, said that Catholics "realize that a new type of cultural collision is beginning to take place in China as [they recognize that] the values of the Gospel and [of] Jesus Christ are in sharp contrast to the new Chinese values of making money and having more and more possessions."[44]

The sudden removal of traditional safeguards of family and community support has created a deep crisis of youth disenchantment and urban dislocation. According to reports, China's high school and university students have shown symptoms of stress and depression because of the scarcity of jobs and an uncertain future. A study by the *Society Survey Institute of China* of 1,000 University students in major cities—including Beijing, Shanghai, Guangshou, Nanjing, and Wuhan—reported severe mental health problems, including suicidal tendencies, mood disorders, and psychosis. Similar problems are reported in other studies, such as the one conducted by the Hubei Provincial Education Department in central China. Counseling hotlines and medical institutions have tried to respond.[45] The pace of rapid social change has thus had severe adverse repercussions, without enough social service infrastructures able to deal with the situation.

In the midst of the ferment, sympathy for religion seems to run deep, as does official unease. Officially authorized religious practice is easier to document, if also less reliable, while uninhibited forms of religion seem a more reliable metronome of local developments, though far less accessible. The revival flame fuels the state repression on which it feeds, making religious practice disorganized, state control uneven, and record keeping uncertain. It makes historical inquiry an inexact science.

The underlying trend, however, is toward a reconfiguring of the Chinese intellectual landscape. A generation of educated senior Chinese growing up under the "open door" policy of Deng has been influenced by works such as R. H. Tawney's *Religion and the Rise of Capitalism*, resulting in revisionist changes to the ideology of a command economy. Similarly, the one-child policy that the government has enforced has altered the basic family structure and is fueling a culture of individualism, which can be fertile ground for Christianity's message of individual salvation. Jiang Zeming, the Communist Party leader, is reported to have responded to a question in early 2002 about the kind of legacy he would like to leave in China by saying he would propose to make Christianity the official religion of China, replacing ideology with a faith-based order.[46]

Many observers credit the growth of Christianity to the impact of the Charismatic/Pentecostal movement that has been able to spread without the handicap of top-heavy organizational machinery and the need for hierarchical coordination and direction. The movement is set to exploit the restrictions placed on open Christianity by dispensing with the need for card-carrying Christians and instead focusing on heartfelt religion (which is less suscepti-ble to organized manipulation). However, evidence that Charismatics are mak-ing strides against official sanction has been used to justify a policy of tight state control to check the prospects, feared or real, of social disruption. Studies of the Charismatic/pentecostal renewal movement in China estimate that by 2025 some ninety million may be involved. The total Christian population by 2010 is estimated to be at 119.5 million.[47] The growth is hard to explain under existing restrictions; perhaps the fact that, as an example of religious compli-ance as well as of unpredictable growth, the charismatic/pentecostal move-ment is both cause and consequence of official surveillance has had an impact.

The available statistics leave no impression other than that significant changes are still underway.[48] The whole environment is necessarily compli-cated by the mixed signals being sent by the government, with measured Western-style economic liberalization accompanied by careful internal regu-lation of religion and of Western contacts. Reports in 2005 spoke of some 90,000 people being baptized in 2003. But the reports also noted how cau-tious the bishops were about what the numbers signified.[49] The real question for the church in China is not about succeeding in winning converts, for that seems assured on present trends, but about what role the church might and should play in a reawakened China.

The Christian Corridor and Its Chinese Axis

In his report on recent developments in Christianity in China, David Aikman, a former *Time* magazine Beijing bureau chief, offered the opinion that China is in the process of becoming Christianized "in some ways like rolling thun-der."[50] The Christian proportion of China's population is likely to be between 20 and 30 percent in a few decades, according to Aikman. Carol Hamrin concurs with that assessment, noting that "there is an unprecedented opening for Christianity to become the mainstream of belief in China."[51] The statistical Christian impact, Aikman believes, will mean that a Christian worldview will become the dominant worldview of China's senior elites. That Christian worldview will be Augustinian in nature; that is to say, it will be marked by a sense of international responsibility supported by the values of restraint, justice, and stability—including a culture of choice, if we take full account of Augustine's teaching. China's bid for a superpower stake in the counsels of the world has been seriously hampered by the lack of a moral center in national life. Christianity is set to fill that vacuum, which gives the religion a defining public role. In that scenario, the ideals of human rights and national generosity would guide and inspire the exercise of power and economic influence.

Aikman speculates that a Christianized China might also tip the balance in favor of Christianity in the Middle East, which would fulfill at long last Ramon Lull's Crusade-era dream for a Europe strategically united with populations beyond Europe through the Christian heritage. Lull realized the strategic advantage a Mongol conversion to Christianity would hand Europe in its relations with Islam. Instead, the Mongols converted to Islam. In the post 9/11 world, China's Christian worldview would predispose it to join the West in combating terrorism, Aikman conjectures. A resurgent Christianity in China, according to him, will be evangelical in ethos, but he did not say whether or not that means it will also be ecumenical.

Thinking only of Protestant prospects in a reawakened China, Thomas Alan Harvey maintained that the growth of Christianity in China at the annual rate of 7 percent means that China will soon contain the largest group of Protestants of any country in the world. "Like Christians throughout the developing world, Chinese Christians represent the vanguard of the church in the twenty-first century."[52] For his part, Aikman is confident that the future greatness of China lies on the path of not only pro-Western liberalization, but in a fundamental cultural change in which "the Chinese dragon is tamed by the power of the Christian Lamb."[53]

Although Aikman states that the process may have already started in the works of China's house church leaders, it is not clear why Catholicism should be omitted from that list, certainly not on the basis of its history or of present trends in conversion, change, and renewal. Cardinal Roger Mahony reported on this renewal after his visit to China, stressing that he found no signs of despair among the Catholic community. On the contrary, Catholics "are filled with deep zeal and new energy to bring fuller evangelization to their people." He continued, saying youthful leadership now in place will ensure that "the Gospel permeates the rich and enduring values of the Chinese culture."[54]

Mahony's point about the historic moment of the church in China correlates with the spirit of John Paul II, who was a self-conscious witness to history in a way few popes before him were. He sought truth in history by promoting the church's full involvement in global geopolitical and national struggles.[55] The Chinese Catholic leadership seemed aware of the new spirit, with Bishop Aloysius of Shanghai declaring on the occasion of the five hundredth anniversary of St. Francis Xavier that now the "relay baton of evangelization is in our hands."[56]

The Christian reckoning in China would likely reengage China's immense cultural heritage as it moves to fashion a role for itself on the world stage. China has been opening to the world on two fronts, at home and abroad. Economic liberalization has opened China to the world market, but it has also created a vibrant diaspora culture of Chinese immigrants in the United States, Europe, Panama, Australia, Canada, Korea, Myanmar, Thailand, Indonesia, the Philippines, Singapore, Malaysia and South Africa—estimated at a total of 35 million people. It is likely that Chinese Christians in these and other diaspora communities will reconnect with the new religious developments in China and extend China's outreach.[57]

Pius XI stressed China's importance in a message to the apostolic delegate to China in August 1928.[58] The pope insisted that "full recognition [should] be given to the legitimate aspirations and rights of the nation, which is more populous than any other, whose civilization and culture go back to the earliest times, which has, in past ages, with the development of its resources, had periods of great prosperity, and which—it may be reasonably conjectured—will become even greater in the future ages, provided it pursues justice and honor." This papal view of Christianity in China was not about darning and patching, but about a fundamental reconditioning of the gospel that also affected other places.[59]

With their ambivalent policy toward Christianity, the leaders of China's Communist revolution helped summon a banished church from the shadows. I referred earlier to Chu Hsi's remark about there being no one in heaven judging a person's sin, and noted that prophetic passion is completely foreign to the Chinese religious outlook. In his rejection of China's spiritual heritage as something superstitious and inert, however, Mao became the summary judge of cultural sins and, in the course of his rule, introduced extreme messianic passion into China's reckoning.[60] According to one assessment, from the combination of influences stemming from the church which God saw and the church human beings spoke of, " 'a messianic fire [was] cast on the earth' which [Chinese] Marxism scattered so far from the hearths of Christendom."[61] In any case, as Daniel Bays noted, the state in China has had religious dimensions for a long time. "The contemporary state structure and Communist Party domination of public life have inherited this tradition and have built upon it a pattern of ritual, vocabulary and public discourse which is similar to that of theocratic organizations."[62] Mao might be far from Christendom, but not far enough to avoid rousing the Christian ghost from the mountain recluses and political backwaters to which rhetoric banished it. The political mission of China seemed too evocative of the Christian mission it combated for it to succeed without the Christian alibi. And that alibi came to haunt the gatekeepers of the revolution.

If present trends continue, China's political leaders will have to go farther than just tinkering with the ideology of total power and abandon "the administrative maze of parallel hierarchies" vis-à-vis Christianity. By construing Christianity as a hostile parallel Marxist organization, the Chinese Communist Party seemed to entangle itself with its own ideology and to prevent Christianity from becoming a beneficial peaceful influence in the stream of social progress. The wary steps recently taken in economic reform should find positive reinforcement in Christianity, freed of the bugbear of Christendom.

Having emerged from the *Sturm und Drang* of political and cultural upheaval, the Catholic Church in China did not, to amend Ronald Knox, "haul down [its] colors, and pipe to this new generation in the airs [the vanguard] had grown accustomed to, in the hope that it would dance."[63] On the contrary, the church was unapologetic as it sounded the note of faithfulness to the gospel as its *raison d'être*. Pius XII anticipated that response in 1944 when he said that the church was the herald of the gospel, not the franchise of a transplanted European order.

Numerous official Catholic statements reiterate the point that China's Christian fulfillment will only vindicate what properly belongs with China's place in the world Christian movement. The good government that is characteristic of such a society is not, as John Henry Newman expressed it, what makes the state strong but what makes the nation great in terms of the unfettered enterprise of citizens and of constitutional safeguards of state power. Private enterprise is the source of civil philanthropy and personal responsibility, Newman affirmed. Marked by Christian openness, China's global role would be to contribute with unprecedented resources "for the welfare of the world and for the prevalence of peace," in the words of Tertullian (ca. 160–ca. 240).[64]

China's place in the Christian movement has not been the propagation of Christendom and Western hegemony, as nearly everyone now agrees—in reality, Christendom has long been a historical anachronism. As Huo Shui, a former government political analyst, observes, the Christian idea of love has introduced a new value system in China, including the idea of repentance "which is lacking in Chinese culture." He writes of a moral revolution in the New China where the "Christian faith became more indigenous . . . you can no longer say that Christianity is a foreign religion. The Churches are led by Chinese. You see Chinese Bibles. You hear Chinese worship songs. You experience a Chinese style of worship. The church looks and feels Chinese . . . Christianity has finally taken root in *Shenzhou*—in China, the land of God."[65] All this suggests that a China strengthened by its own resources and renewed in its own identity would be a China well endowed to assume a leadership role in the scheme of post-Western Christian developments.

When he came to reflect on a lifetime of scholarship on China, John Fairbank urged an opening of minds on both sides of what had been the bamboo curtain and an extension of friendship to advance prospects of intercivilizational understanding and respect. Although he was writing in the decade or so before Hong Kong was handed over to the jurisdiction of mainland China in 1997—the "return to the heart of the dragon" —Fairbank's words are no less pertinent. Writing in 1983, he said "American-Chinese relations today still lie precariously on a fault line where different values and interests grind against each other. Our hope," he pleaded, "must be that a mutual understanding of our discordant motivations can help us accept our differences. Today we Americans have an opportunity for friendship with China, both in Taiwan and on the mainland, based on genuine cooperation in facing common problems. This cooperation—in respect of education, industrialization, arms control, energy, food, population, pollution, and so on—can draw us all together. It is an opportunity we should seize."[66] World Christianity has helped to shape that defining moment, as China's close attentiveness to the subject has acknowledged, and as should the rest of the world.

9

Conclusion

*Third Wave Awakening and Concurrent
Cultural Shifts: Renewal and Convergence
in Comparative World Order Perspective*

Post-Western Fault Line

The convergence of the modern missionary movement with the rise of
European empires complicated Christianity's position in colonized
societies. Despite their role as allies of the empire, missions also developed the vernacular that inspired sentiments of national identity
and thus undercut Christianity's identification with colonial rule.
Instead of monastic withdrawal from the world, the new Christians
embraced social action and engagement. In time there emerged a
vigorous new wave of Christian renewal trailing anticolonial sentiments. Yet on the ideological side of the equation missions maintained their colonial links. It was in that context that church leaders hit
on the revolutionary idea of convening in 1910 the epoch-making
World Missionary Conference at Edinburgh. Unforeseen at the time,
the conference changed the face of modern Protestantism at home
and abroad, and marked the checkered beginning of the modern ecumenical movement, which attempted to unite the various Protestant
churches and denominations. This struck a chord with the leaders
of the younger churches of Africa and Asia who felt increasingly that
the word *mission* carried the unsavory odor of European domination
and financial control, while the focus on church unity rightly drew
attention to indigenous leadership and responsibility.

The conference tackled Christianity's role in a new global
environment: rising nationalism in China, India, and Japan, the

challenge of non-Christian religions, particularly Islam, and secularism. The conference organizers were right about a new awakening in the air, but, except for Islam, misconstrued it as a political awakening. In his book *The Decisive Hour of Christian Missions* (1910), John R. Mott, for example, took up the challenge of Islam, warning that Africa would become a Muslim continent if existing trends continued. To respond to that challenge, leaders at Edinburgh spoke grandiloquently of the need for a "comprehensive plan for world occupation," an echo of the late nineteenth-century American Student Volunteer Movement's slogan, "the evangelization of the world in this generation."[1]

In 1910 Europe was still the powerhouse of Christianity, not yet even dimly aware of the religion's worldwide appeal. Accordingly, only 17 of the more than 1,200 delegates came from the Third World: 8 from India, 4 from Japan, 3 from China, 1 from Burma, and 1 from Korea. There was not a single delegate from Africa.

What no one at the time knew was that Edinburgh 1910 would be the last time that the Western missionary movement would hold center stage, not because the religion would decline, but because expansion of the church would exceed anything the leaders could have dreamed of. "The extraordinary growth of Christianity in Africa, for example, was not foreseen by any of the Edinburgh delegates."[2] The most visionary of missionary statesmen had not the vaguest intimation that they were at a historical fault line and that Christianity would soon embark on its course to become a more widespread and diverse religion than at any other time in its history. It would be the era of unprecedented missionary surge.

It happened that the two currents of church unity and missionary expansion in time diverged. When in 1948 the ecumenical movement was eventually institutionalized as the World Council of Churches, the missionary impulse was annexed as the Commission on World Mission and Evangelism, and was eventually abandoned, suggesting the irony of the success of the ecumenical movement requiring the repudiation of mission. At Edinburgh the signs of tension between church and mission, between Europe as the faith and Christianity as a post-Western phenomenon, were already apparent, and several delegates commented on it. Even a figure as sympathetic as the Indian churchman V. S. Azariah urged the mission agencies to commend not just self-sacrifice but Christian friendship; in other words to support a shift from missionary paternalism to indigenous leadership and mutual solidarity.[3] Little did Azariah imagine that without paternalism mission would cease.

Edinburgh 1910 was a watershed, and was followed by a series of missionary consultations and ecumenical conferences, all of which produced further radical moves concerning the mission of the church in the twentieth century. However, the spirit of optimism and high resolve that sounded at Edinburgh was much more muted in subsequent meetings. The reason was obvious. In the aftermath of World War I, a measured hesitation, a self-conscious realism, perhaps even a loss of Christian self-confidence, beset the churches. Among serving missionaries, there was a crisis of confidence about the value of the gospel in light of the destruction and upheaval of the Great War. This forced a sharp question on missionaries: if evangelized Christian countries of Europe could make war on one another, what was the use of evangelizing non-Western societies? Why should people give up their own imperfection for the imperfection that Christianity had proved to be? One missionary at the time concluded that either Christ had failed, or the church had failed. This debilitating introspection was the first sign of the transition of the modern West to a post-Christian phase, and it left leaders to ponder what the new worldwide role of the church might be. They could no longer assume that Europe was the heartland of the gospel.

Accordingly, at the second World Missionary Conference held in Jerusalem in 1928, a revisionist understanding of the mission of the church was put forward. In its essential outlines, this revisionist view was that the Christian claim about the uniqueness and finality of Christ was no longer tenable in view of the reality of other faiths. Whereas in an earlier age Christians ventured into the world in seasonal waves, sowing seeds of a fully formed Baptist, Lutheran, Catholic, Presbyterian, or Methodist grain, now Christians should position themselves in the world with an attitude of humility, equality, and interdependence. In this thinking there could be no exclusive salvation through Christ alone, for other religions provided equally valid salvific vehicles for their followers. The most reasonable outcome for all religions, it was argued, was for them to forge an enlightened synthesis in which all their exclusive claims were set aside as offensive and the truth of all subsumed in a progressive, global unity. That view became the mantra of ecumenism.

In the meantime, the mission of the church was to lead the way into that future by specifically abjuring any claim to mission and conversion, and by committing itself to economic and social structures of national life and the new international order. As one missionary leader commented, the Jerusalem conference sounded the note of "End Missions Imperialism Now!" For this leader, a most crucial issue was Christianity's relation to other religions, and on that the churches should simply surrender their claim to authoritative truth.[4] Only relative truth could safeguard humanity's precious unity.

This line of thinking had radical theological implications for Christianity and for the church, as was eventually demonstrated by the 1960 conference of the World's Student Christian Federation at Strasbourg, whose theme was

"The Life and Mission of the Church." The shift now afoot assumed that the church was not the repository of unchanging truths but the axis of a new realism, that religious virtues like faith and hope were not charters for resignation and fatalism but the warrants for self-improvement; that the Last Judgment was not the end of the world but the summons to social justice; and everlasting life was not a blissful, deathless existence beyond time and space but a free, prosperous, and happy life here and now. This mood ripened into a radical call for flexible, mobile Christian social groups to set out to "deontologize" the church, which means, in effect, to shun primacy of doctrine and to commit instead to contextual social engagement.[5] As a report from the World Council of Churches put it, it is the world, not the church, that now wrote God's agenda.[6] The world in this context was the world of advanced industrial Europe. It was in that mood that R. Elliott Kendall in 1978 wrote his candid assessment of Christian prospects in Africa and elsewhere in a work called *The End of an Era*.[7] There he urged his fellow Western missionaries essentially to concede defeat.

Yet it was clear by the end of the twentieth century that neither the rapid collapse of the colonial empires nor the surge of nationalist movements had been the decisive setback for religion that everyone believed. One sign of the consternation was in the form of a letter I received from the Russian Academy of Sciences in the early 1990s inviting me to a conference on the topic "The Problem of Religion." With its hints alternately of alarm and incredulity, the title was proof that the organizers were in what in classical Islam was called "a state between two states" (*manzila bayna manzilatayn*), neither persuaded of the truth of religion nor dismissive of the fact of its return. Standing amid the debris of the collapsed Soviet Empire, the organizers were disconcerted by the improbable reality of religion having made a comeback against considerable odds.

The Weathercock's Reward

The facts, though, seem impressive enough for what might be called the Third Awakening. The total world population in 1900 was 1.6 billion; Muslims numbered just below 200 million, Christians 558 million. In 1970, total world population was 3.7 billion with a Muslim population of 549 million and Christians at 1.2 billion. In 2005, Muslims numbered 1.3 billion and Christians 2.1 billion, including 1.3 billion Catholics.[8] The numbers of Buddhists and Hindus remained stable, with natural increase rather than conversion accounting for growth. The statistics for one twelve-month period at an early phase of the return of religion show that twenty-five million people changed their religious affiliation, of whom eighteen million were converts to Christianity, and seven million defectors from Christianity to other religions, making Christianity the most active religious frontier in the world.[9]

The pace of religious expansion in Africa entered its most vigorous phase following the end of colonial and missionary hegemony, with the dramatic collapse of postcolonial states fueling the expansion. In 1900 the Muslim population of Africa was 34.5 million, compared to roughly 10 million Christians, a ratio of better than 3:1. By 1985 Christians outnumbered Muslims for the first time. Of the continent's total population of 520 million, Christians (including self-styled evangelicals) numbered 271 million, compared to about 216 million Muslims. In 2000 the number of Christians in Africa grew to 346 million, with 330 million Muslims concentrated mostly in the Arabic-speaking regions of Egypt and North and in West Africa. The projected figure for 2005 was 390 million Christians, with 600 million estimated for 2025. It is a continental shift of historic proportions.

In 1900 Europe (including Russia) and North America had a combined Christian population of under 428 million—82 percent of the world's Christians, compared to 94 million for the entire rest of the world. The figures do not include Pentecostals and other non-denominational groups. By 2005, Europe and North America's 758 million Christians were far fewer than the 1.4 billion for the rest of the world—a decline to 35 percent of the total. Thus, 65 percent of the world's Christians now live in the Southern Hemisphere and in East Asia, areas that have become Christianity's new stronghold. Increasingly, Europe is a new Christian margin.

Charismatic Christianity has been the driving engine of the Third Awakening, and is largely responsible for the dramatic shift in the religion's center of gravity. Pentecostal Christians are a distinct denomination, though the charismatic spirit that typically defines them is more widespread. Pentecostals are charismatics, but not all charismatics are Pentecostals. The reason is obvious. Many of those swept up in charismatic movements joined the mainline churches, both Catholic and Protestant, while others formed a distinct Pentecostal ecclesiastical bloc. The statistics, accordingly, reflect the complex character of the phenomenon. Even there the figures are impressive: in 1970, there were over 72 million Pentecostals/Charismatics; in 2005, nearly 590 million. Projections estimate that by 2025, Pentecostals/Charismatics will number nearly 800 million. Now exploding in Brazil, Mexico, Russia, and China, Pentecostal Christianity may become the most widespread form of the religion, with as yet unquantifiable effects on mainline churches and on global politics.[10] As David Martin has shown, in Latin America the prominence of

TABLE 9.1. The Worldwide Religious Profile

Year	1900	1970	2000	2006	2025 estimate
World	1.6 billion	3.7 billion	5.7 billion	6 billion	7.8 billion
Buddhists	127 million	233.4 million	364 million	382.4 million	418 million
Christians	558 million	1.2 billion	2 billion	2.15 billion	2.6 billion
Hindus	203 million	462.5 million	811 million	877.5 million	1 billion
Muslims	200 million	553.5 million	1.1 billion	1.3 billion	1.7 billion
Pentecostals/ Charismatics	981,000	72.223 million	523 million	588.502 million	800 million

female Pentecostals has affected the *machismo* culture of the traditional military establishment.[11] Female politicians are accordingly drawing on the energy of the Pentecostal movement to effect social change.

Pentecostalism is also riding the wave of Latin American demographic movements, including currents of immigration into the United States. Of about thirty-seven million Latino immigrants in the United States, the vast majority is Pentecostal, with a strong Catholic overlay.[12] The convergence of U.S. evangelical groups, such as the Christian Coalition, adherents of the health-and-wealth gospel, and the burgeoning megachurch phenomenon, along with Latin American immigration have raised the political stakes in mainstream America and driven the evangelical missionary agenda.[13]

A growing number of U.S.-born members is being swept up in the Pentecostal/Charismatic movement. In fact, one study estimates that 54 percent of the Pentecostals are U.S.-born, of which 24 percent are white, 29 percent Hispanic, and 35 percent black. There are said to be 59 million Pentecostals in North America. In New York City alone over 4,000 churches with a membership of some 800,000 are counted in this number. Mainline churches

TABLE 9.2. The World Christian Resurgence: New Center of Gravity

Year	1900	2000	2005 (projected)	2025 (projected)
Africa	8.75 million	346.4 million	389.304 million	600 million
North America	59.57 million	212 million	222 million	250 million
North America and Europe (combined) *includes Russia in 1900	427.779 million (82% of the world's Christians)	748 million	757.765 million (35% of the world's Christians)	767.9 million
Rest of the World (i.e., without North America and Europe)	93.7 million	1.2 billion	1.378 billion (65% of the world's Christians)	1.85 billion

TABLE 9.3. Comparative Resurgence in Africa

Year	1900	1985	2000	2025
Africa's Population	107.8 million	520 million	784 million	1.3 billion
Muslims	34.5 million	216 million	315 million	519 million
Christians	8.7 million	270.5 million	346.5 million	600 million

Tables adapted from various sources, including the *World Christian Encyclopedia*, 2nd edition, 2001; The *IBMR*, January issues for 2004 to 2007; and Burgess and Van Der Maas, editors, *The New International Dictionary of Pentecostal and Charismatic Movements*, 2003.

have responded to the awakening by embracing Pentecostalism's intimate and earnest worship style.[14]

When they assessed Christian fortunes in China in 1974, the authors of a joint study predicted that Christianity, which was already a non-Western religion, would, from the vantage point of the year 2000, "appear from the standpoint of most of Asia more as a declining religion of the First and Second Worlds than as a rising religion of the Third."[15] With respect to the post-Christian West, that prediction was on the mark; the prediction went astray, however, when describing Christianity as a declining post-Western religion, which unquestionably it is not. Instead, the religion commenced a vigorous expansion. It is as if the river, instead of eddying out into a dry bed, had grown more vigorous as it proceeded downstream. As G.K. Chesterton quipped, a dead thing can go with the stream, but only a living thing can go against it. Christianity confronted obstacles major and minor of reversal, rejection, and resistance, only to burst forth in its post-Western awakening with something of the precocious ferment of its original mission.

The Roman Catholic Dimension: The African Synod

Convened first at Rome in May 1994, and finally at Yaoundé, Cameroon, in September 1995, the African Synod was a milestone in the evolution of mission and Christianity in Africa. The synod was a major step in applying the statements of Vatican II to Africa. The synod was convened under the apostolic leadership of Pope John Paul II, who traveled to Cameroon in September 1995 to preside over its substantive deliberations.

The synod's detailed and extensive pronouncements, contained in the Propositions and introduced with a list of protocols describing the nature, scope, tasks, hopes, goals, and future direction of the work,[16] marked a decisive step in the church's understanding of engagement in Africa, a far cry from the jingoist effusions of the imperial era known as the Scramble for Africa, and from the sanguine assumptions of Catholic Europe. In its statement on "The Missions," Vatican II laid down lines of development for what were called the young churches. These churches were seen as diminutive versions of their mature Western counterparts. It was as if the authors of the Vatican II document "were wishing on the new churches of the world all the difficulties that have rent and torn and wounded the European-American church." They could "imagine no church different in form from their own."[17] The African Synod took that lesson to heart and affirmed that the church was in Africa, this time not to dominate and confiscate, but to share and replenish. It was a time of restitution and restoration.

The synod in effect conceived the church as a local faith community that was indigenously led and as such committed to engagement with Africa's critical development needs. The synod placed special emphasis on the continent's immense human potential and what that could contribute to global solidarity for peace, justice, and opportunity. If, as one of its documents states, Vatican II was, in part, an attempt by the church to come to terms with the modern world, then another equally important part was coming to terms with the implications of Third Wave Christian resurgence. This required that the younger churches of Asia and Africa not be absorbed into preexisting European structures and institutions; instead, the church must reinvent itself to respond to changes in the former mission fields. The church should accept the local implications of Christianity's new cultural manifestations. It helped that the vernacular Mass opened the way for the fundamental rethinking that was required, yet it took the African Synod to draw out in a timely, concrete way the new paths to be followed in Africa. The papacy worked in a collegial spirit with African bishops to manage the practical implications of the fact that Christianity was a world religion.

The obstacles, however, are formidable, and perhaps insurmountable, though the costs of inaction and delay are high. With little by way of infrastructure, churches are confronted with elementary problems of nation building following the dramatic collapse of postindependent states. Routine issues of governance and civil society are compounded by endemic structural corruption. The AIDS epidemic—which claimed over 2.4 million lives in Africa in 2002, a daily rate of over 6,575—is more than a health emergency. It is not much short of a social calamity. The relative youth of those infected with HIV means that much of Africa's future is being foreclosed unless the churches can step into the breach. Trade reforms, including access to world markets, are important, yet responsible indigenous engagement is necessary to make economic benefits meaningful to the young and deserving poor. With some 175 million members in Africa, the Catholic Church responded with the African Synod by forging partnerships that go beyond programs of external relief and charity to social renewal and commitment to peace and justice. With its cultural variety and human dynamism Africa is at the same time fast becoming a Christian continent for the first time. The new directions for the religion reflect the realignment underway.

The Artichoke and the Political Weapon

African Christian life has been in search of relevance and fresh voices. The African Synod is one such response. Another is Christian Independency, which splintered off into varieties of "Ethiopianism," that is, into forms of protest and resistance defined by racial and political issues. In its essentially religious temper, however, Independency assumed the charismatic and revivalist tones of Zionism. This showed considerable continuity with African religions, and radically transformed Christianity into an African religion. Here, too, we see Christianity profiting from positive as well as negative circumstances. Colonial repression fomented Ethiopian sentiments, and national independence removed the brakes on indigenous potential. That double process of provocation and attraction created the conditions for the indigenous discovery of Christianity, and laid the groundwork for Christianity as a world religion reshaped by the values and idioms of non-Western cultures. The original language of religion was the mother tongue, and it happened that Africa abounded in the gift of tongues.

Africa's role on the national as well as world stage has been bitterly contested by nationalist leaders, with churches and ordinary Christians paying a deadly price. The suspicion, misunderstanding, and outright hostility of colonial and missionary authorities to Christian localism converged with nationalist hostility to the new awakening to place old and new Christians under crushing restrictions. In the colonial environment, officials for the most part relied on the force of law to restrict unauthorized forms of the religion. Postcolonial national leaders inherited that legal weapon and transformed it into an implacable anti-Christian dogma. In a postcolonial Algeria, for example, the Catholic Cathedral in Algiers was commandeered and converted into a public library. In India Christians were reduced to the status virtually of an outside caste,[18] while in Angola and Mozambique the nationalist leaders declared open war on Christianity.[19]

In Ethiopia the regime of Mengistu Haile Mariam was perhaps the most extreme example of the fate that haunted Christianity in the new postcolonial world. Mengistu Haile Maryam inaugurated a Red Reign of Terror in the mid-1970s in which the Ethiopian Orthodox Church became a target for harsh repression. In February 1976, the patriarch Thewophilos was dismissed for heading a church termed a "cave of exploiters."

The government adopted what it called the "artichoke method" of eviscerating the church in steps. First, it abrogated the special status of Ethiopian Christianity by adopting a policy of religious toleration, thus placing the church on an equal status with Islam. Then it bore down on the new religious groups, which had a tenuous hold on people's loyalty and which could be dealt with in a bid for popular support. Next, it stripped the agencies, programs, and initiatives that extended the church's reach in society. It followed that up by cherry-picking gullible members of the clergy to spread the illusion that Christianity and Communism are compatible. It next looted valuable and precious holy objects from the church and sent them to friendly countries abroad to be put on public display, in order to violate their sacred value. Then it infiltrated the abbeys and monasteries with agents provocateurs trained in satellite Communist states that committed flagrant obscene acts calculated to scandalize the church.[20] Finally it mounted the coup de grâce against the exposed core itself—the Orthodox Church—and smashed it.

The strategy worked to perfection, with the Ethiopian Orthodox Church cooperating with the state in attacking missions and related new Christian groups as foreign agents and as enemies of Ethiopia. Orthodox authorities thus took the poisoned chalice, recognizing the government's power to decide which forms of religion were treasonous, a logic then extended to the Orthodox Church itself. The government swiftly declared religion to be the opiate of the people, and Orthodoxy thereby became an enemy. A remorseless state-directed propaganda war followed, setting members of the clergy against one another, arousing long-suppressed Muslim grievances against the church, and rounding up church officials, members of the clergy, their associates and allies, and subjecting them to revolutionary vengeance. The ideological purge became a rite of passage for political initiation. Amnesty International reported that some half a million people were killed in 1974 and 1975.[21]

E Pluribus Unum

The post-Western awakening has occurred in the midst of religious diversity and cultural tension, making these important pillars of World Christianity. In his prescription for a post-Christian Europe, Lesslie Newbigin suggests that variety and diversity need not be in conflict with "truth and commitment" (to adopt Pope Benedict XVI's formulation), and that the call for a Christian society is not an exclusive demand for a Christian state. In its encounter with Islam, Christianity cannot avoid the issue of the role of faith and the public order, Newbigin maintains. For his part, Philip Jenkins sees a double jeopardy in the onset of talk about new Crusades as well as a cultural clash with liberal Christianity.[22] Splits in the Anglican Communion over the Episcopal Church USA appointing gay clergy are thus intraconfessional shrapnel with global range. There are few denominations without ecumenical segments, and, therefore, few policy issues without international import. Going beyond national loyalty, Christian experience has become increasingly "catholic."

The unraveling taking place in the Western heartland of Christianity is in striking contrast to the thrust of the religion in the rest of the world. The conversion of northern Europeans culminated in the great public institutions and systems of literature, philosophy, art, architecture, music, crafts, and science and technology that have defined the heritage of the West. Christianity today is faced with a dramatic challenge to this impressive and complex heritage. Even though many would applaud a post-Western triumph similar to that of the West, they would still be reluctant to accept its religious nature. That intellectual resistance is the sticking point, and it abandons the field to sectarian radicalism.

The debates about a Christian society and religious pluralism are relevant to post-Western Christianity. In China, for example, the West's secular modern priorities, including its language of liberation, seem remote, implausible, and strikingly outdated.

The misadventure of the Cultural Revolution caused the architects of China's Communist revolution to budge, and that made a rapprochement with Christianity no longer improbable. The changes of the 1980s helped to reset the religious calendar. China became a logical trailway of Christianity's long march, so to speak, with the religion surviving China's turbulent relations with the West. China's story belongs with the eastward thrust of Christianity in the earliest centuries as well as with the transition from "Christendom" to world Christianity. An Anglican Chinese clergyman based in Beijing in 1957 pointed out the irony of the humiliation but also the hope of a Christianity born on the fringes of one world and abandoned on the fringes of another. Given China's central place in the whole scheme of world history, Chinese Christianity can on no reasonable grounds be considered a fringe phenomenon. The long breaks in China's Christian history make it easy, though by no means excusable, to forget the country's role in the religion's history.[23]

That the "Church of the East" should spread to China from Persia was due in no small part to the fact that the 'Abbásid caliphate dominated the West and made missionary work there impossible. Instead, thanks to the Old Silk Route, missions headed out by way of the Black Sea and the Russian rivers toward northern and central Europe and eastward into Asia as far as China. There were more Christians in China at the peak of missions there than in the ancient Christian heartland at the peak of the 'Abbásids, a dramatic indication of the religion's shifting center of gravity. In China we had the remarkable convergence of the historic Gentile impulse of mission and its sustained local appeal. It is clear that in the religion's eastward shift what happens to the church in China will have incalculable consequences for the rest of the world generally, and for the post-Christian West in particular. China could correct the one-sidedness of Western Christianity.[24]

Given Christianity's winding, historical course and spontaneous appeal, that possibility seems warranted, though only a few years ago the picture was very different as voices in the West called for an end of the missionary era in China, and, indeed, of the church itself. A linear trajectory for Christian history saw China fading at the far end of the road. Under Mao, it was widely believed, China had achieved what the church could not, and the Communist Revolution should be embraced as the foreordained answer to devout Christian prayers. Marxist ascendancy in China, it was said, was the long-delayed secular upheaval needed to expose Christianity as an extinct volcano. These voices in the West were taken seriously, in part because of the weight they carried, and in part because a postcolonial guilt complex had spooked the post-Christian West. Gripped by a *fin de siècle* tough-mindedness, the West was in no mood to contemplate with equanimity the prospects of a Christian resurgence anywhere, least of all in China. Christianity was appropriately a casualty of historical inevitability.

Yet, in the end and characteristically, Christianity emerged to master the adverse circumstances of state repression. As occurred under the Roman Empire, the Christian movement under China's totalitarian government adapted to state-imposed disabilities, and continued to grow in many different ways. The so-called "house churches" were reminiscent of what Tertullian described of the branded "underground" church in the Roman Empire.

> We assemble to read our sacred writings, if any peculiarity of the times makes either forewarning or reminiscence needful. With the sacred words we nourish our faith, we animate our hope, and we make our confidence more stedfast [sic]. But we are your brethren as well, by the law of our common mother nature. Give the congregation of Christians its due, and hold it unlawful, if it is like assemblies of the illicit sort; by all means let it be condemned, if any complaint can be

validly laid against it, such as lies against secret factions. But who has
ever suffered harm from our assemblies? We are in our congregations
just what we are when separated from each other; we are as a community what we are [as] individuals; we injure nobody, we trouble
nobody. When the upright, when the virtuous meet together, when
the pious, when the pure assemble in congregation, you ought not to
call that a faction, but a *curia*—[i.e., the court of God].

That might stand equally for an effervescent, if also hard-pressed Christianity
in today's politically dynamic China. China's fluctuating religious policy makes
it impossible to ignore the subject, if also difficult to predict the precise outcome. The checkered course of Christian developments there has parallels
elsewhere in the world.

It is important to reiterate what is distinctive about the pluralism that
Christianity engendered. The roots go back to Christian origins in the Jewish
environment. From the beginning, Jewish monotheist ideas and ethical examples shaped the religion in its Gentile rehabilitation without cramping its
intercultural impulse. The Gentile frontier placed the church on the path of
open plural encounter, and that allowed Christianity to achieve its peculiar
effect by dumping the old colonial cargo and surging in its post-Western phase.

Some examples capture the spirit of the Catholic response to the intercultural process of conversion. One is best exemplified by the spirit of Gregory
the Great: preserve the old temples, but rededicate them to the worship of the
one true God. That avoids imposing external restrictions and cramping local
imagination, while setting a new direction for frontier experience. It allowed
for new styles of church and mission to thrive. A study of the "pastoral anthropology" of the Catholic Church in Tanzania picks up this theme of direction and local adaptability by conceiving a special role for university students, seafarers, fishermen, and market women as religious agents. The White
Fathers organized the people into "small Christian communities."[25] Sometimes frontier experience led to radical choice, as in the case of a Tanzanian
Catholic bishop who exchanged his comfortable episcopal residence for life
with his flock in an *ujamaa* cooperative village.

Vincent Donovan, the apostle to the Maasai, offers reflections on how the
post-Western awakening offers a corrective perspective on the church in the
West. He argues that, notwithstanding the pervasive skepticism, mission is
the way for the Western church to recover its apostolic heritage. It is clear,
Donovan notes, that the norms and styles of the priesthood and church life
embraced by the West were appropriately shaped by the structures of society.
One culture, such as the West and its built-in authoritarian, individualistic,

hierarchic structure, responded to Christianity with its own valid form of clerical order. Another culture, such as an African one, with its communitarian,
nonhierarchic structure, should have an equal right to respond with its own
valid form of the priesthood. That can be done only by a cultural interpretation of Christianity, Donovan contends.[26] That view parallels the idea that an
"original" Christianity involves historical construction necessarily. Undertaking such interpretation raises the bar of self-reflection, and spares no shibboleths. It generates the intercultural aspect of the Christian movement.

Donovan says the parish council characteristic of Western church life is
an anachronism. A parish council filled with elections and politicking and vying for position with functions and rivalries can hardly be considered a healthy
community and should not be relied on as far as its judgments and actions are
concerned. Paul said as much to a group among the early Corinthians with
similar traits and penchants, even as far as their Eucharist was concerned: "Do
you really think what you are doing and eating is the Lord's Supper?"[27] The
idea of church on the frontier requires a radical change, says Donovan. He
described a scenario in which ordinary Maasai constituted the church in
the only sense in which it mattered: an illiterate elder, a young literate elder, a
woman gifted in singing and evangelism, and others with charismatic gifts.
"They were all members of a Christian community newly baptized.... I was
preparing them to take over their Christian communities. I was training them
for the priesthood."[28]

Protestant examples of frontier awakening followed a similar pattern. An
Anglo-Catholic layman, Edmund John Sepeku, gave up a lucrative government
job at Radio Tanzania after he heard a voice calling him to follow Jesus Christ.
"I had been paid highly ... I left all that. [I had] a nice car ... I left all that. [I had]
a telephone in my house and office. I left all that [in order to] accept Jesus'
call."[29] Experiments in new forms of church and styles of prayer and worship
were adopted. Mobile and itinerant groups were created, such as Bible study
groups, women's evangelization groups, women's drama performances, groups
specializing in collecting the life histories of individual church members, revival fellowship groups, choral groups, and home visitation groups.

A novel concept was an ecumenical fellowship group in Tanzania called *Liro*,
an acronym for *L*utherans, *I*slam, and *Ro*man Catholicism. Formed in 1979, it
engaged in joint educational and social projects. In 1985 the group changed
its name to *Umaka*. Women emerged into leadership positions, sometimes as
widows, divorcees, independent entrepreneurs, and particularly as primary
school teachers in which role they had been the critical agents of formation for
families and communities throughout Africa. Women founded and led credit
associations, intratribal dance societies, and mutual aid societies. "It is often

overlooked that the politically involved women are at the same time prominent in the women's groups of their Church."[30] A Pan-African women's politica convention convened in 1962 in Dar es Salaam was hosted by women who were also active in the church.

As these and numerous other examples suggest, once the religion broke loose of its colonial moorings, it underwent spontaneous awakening at the hands of local agents, an awakening surprising for its scope, depth, and resilience. The new awakening echoes the theme Constantine-Cyril once enunciated, namely, that God's rain falls upon all equally, that just as we all breathe air in the same way so is God freely available to us, and that Christianity should not be banished to the outskirts of the three tongues of Hebrew, Greek, and Latin, for that would condemn all other nations and tribes to the triple affliction of being blind, deaf, and mute.[31] Converts did not have to forego their culture to become loyal Christians, but neither did they have to be blind to their own shortcomings and inadequacies to be responsible citizens. For these converts, the reality of personal agency, cultural diversity, social options, and the multiplicity of languages and of religions has been constitutive of their view of faith and discipleship. Nothing is more conducive to that sense of vocation than an indigenous Christianity. In periods or in societies where people have been denied a choice and where religion is exclusively a matter of enforceable national custom, the Christian identity centered on God as boundary-free truth has come under tremendous pressure, with the larger society reflecting that fact in a shrinking capacity for tolerance.

Whatever the attendant tensions and suspicions, conversion to Christianity has expanded Christianity's plural idiom and multicultural range while also helping to promote choice, however negligible that may appear on the grand scale of things. The new awakening has fostered a culture of civic virtue, with moral appeal to conscience and individual liberty. Attesting to the indomitable faith and forbearance of Catholic Chinese, for example, Betty Ann Maheu described what she called a typical Catholic scene: villages in rural areas consisting mostly of poor farmers, where arrests of bishops and the faithful are common but not decisive for faith and hope. She continued, saying attending an early-morning Mass in one of these villages can be a moving experience. On one occasion when she traveled with two women from the German Office of Aid to the Church in Need, one of them found herself unprepared for the spectacle of faith and devotion she encountered and felt "she could not stay to greet the people after Mass. She went off alone and wept."[32] It was tantamount to a cultural shift in expectations in which the church in need was discovered to be the church awake. It showed the convergence of poverty and faith that the post-Christian West had long left behind. Yet that scenario of faith and poverty abounds everywhere in the post-Western awakening, and expatriates typically come upon it with something of a shock. It is not how the world looks from the vantage point of an agnostic, secular West.

A dynamic World Christianity has worked against cultural deadlock and has affected, sometimes for the good, the climate of interethnic and interracial encounter. Ethnic intolerance has been exchanged for ethnic trust. The bitter conflict of Matthew Ajuoga with the Anglican Mission in Kenya illustrates this fact. Ajuoga subsequently broke away to form the Church of Christ in Africa (CCA). The vernacular Bible was a major impetus. In 1953 the Luo Old Testament was published, and Ajuoga, a Luo himself, noticed that the word missionaries translated as *hera*, from the Greek *philadelphia*, was the same as the English *love*. Ajuoga protested that *hera*, "brotherly love," was absent in missionary treatment of Africans.

After years of fruitless protest and debate aimed at changing missionary policy and culture, in 1957 Ajuoga and his followers joined the new awakening and founded the CCA. It was at that stage essentially a Luo ethnic church, but not for long. "By 1965 the CCA claimed members among fifty-six of the tribes and sub-tribes of Kenya, Uganda and northern Tanzania; by 1967 eight dioceses had been formed in the three nations. Among its seventy clergy then there were two Teita, two Kikuyu, six Luyia (including one archdeacon) and one Gusii—all from Bantu tribes traditionally somewhat hostile to the Luo."[33] African ancestors might be reclaimed as Christians, but in that case they forfeited their role as ethnic idols. Even the Anglican Mission was not shut out entirely, as is evident from the survivals in the CCA of Anglican forms and liturgical practice. The awakening conserved ethnic interest without excluding interethnic and interracial acknowledgment.

In its own right this Third Wave of the Christian awakening reflects the tempo of world history, suggesting new possibilities for historically suppressed and marginalized people and appealing for a change of heart of the post-Christian West. While the process of Westernization is not necessarily the cause of the Christian resurgence, it has sometimes coincided with it, and in other ways has not impeded it. World Christianity has not been hampered by the politics of Western economic ascendancy. Yet even in that fortuitous sense, the disciples of Westernization could ill afford to ignore their neighbors and likely allies in the new awakening.

Instructively, while the world has become better integrated by the communications revolution, it has not become more reconciled. Newly acquired economic advantage, for example, has not engendered to the same degree a shared commitment to global problems nor made for a more open intercultural process. In spite of, and sometime because of, the challenges they face, new believers are in a special position to offer plausible models of personal initiative, ethical reconciliation, and intercultural solidarity. The fact that disadvantaged peoples and their cultures are buoyed by new waves of conversion has created alignments of global scope at the margins of power and privilege. The paradigm nature of the realignment compels a fundamental stocktaking of Christianity's frontier awakening, and an imperative of partnership with it. When opportunity knocks the wise will build bridges while the timorous will build dams. It is a new day.

Notes

INTRODUCTION

1. Acts 11:26.

2. II Cor. 5:19.

3. Acts 10:28–29.

4. Acts 10:34.

5. The issue of the historicity of Acts is beyond the scope of this book, but see, for example, Colin J. Hemer, *The Book of Acts in the Setting of Hellenistic History* (Tübingen: Mohr [Paul Siebeck]), 1989; repr. Winona Lake, Ind.: Eisenbrauns, 1990), 244–76, 308–64.

6. In the institutional life of the church the idea of Christianity being bounded by no religious or cultural system has not always been observed, though in the 2006 reflections on the Catholic lectionary on Acts 10:25–29, for example, the Archdiocese of Chicago lifted the idea by affirming that baptism followed by confirmation is not an exclusive order for membership in the church. "The Holy Spirit descended upon the unbaptized," it said. "Surely," the commentary continued, "we are to learn from this that nothing can inhibit God's will to bestow grace and redemption upon every race and nation. Our theologians may speak in dogmatic tones about a 'sacramental system,' but the Spirit of God cannot be enclosed or limited by it. Sometimes in our efforts to codify our faith, we can forget that God's love and mercy are beyond any code or system."

7. R. G. Collingwood, "Reason Is Faith Cultivating Itself," *Hibbert Journal* 26, no. 1 (1927–28): 4.

8. Adolf von Harnack, *The Mission and Expansion of Christianity in the First Three Centuries.* 2 vols. (New York: Putnam, 1908), i, 64.

9. 1 Cor 1:24; 2:7; Eph 3:10.

10. C. H. Dodd, *The Meaning of Paul for Today* (London: Fontana, 1964), 73–74, 80.

11. Acts 22:1–5.

12. Acts 22:1–5, 12–16.

13. Acts 26:10–11.

14. Rom 12:1; 1 Cor 3:16; 6:19.

15. F. F. Bruce, *Paul: Apostle of the Heart* (London: Paternoster: Grand Rapids, Mich.: Eerdmans, 1977), 173–87.

16. Andrew F. Walls, "Converts or Proselytes? The Crisis over Conversion in the Early Church," *International Bulletin of Missionary Research 28*, no. 1 (January 2004): 2004.

17. Mt 1:21; Lk 24:21; Acts 3:24–26.

18. Acts 21:20.

19. Acts 2.

20. Acts 15.

21. Walls, "Converts or Proselytes?" 5.

22. Acts 9:2; 18:26; 24:14.

23. 1 Cor 1:9; Eph 3:9; Phil 2:1; 1 Jn 1:3.

24. Rom 6:3–4; Col 2:12–13.

25. Harnack, *The Mission and Expansion of Christianity*, i, 56.

26. 2 Cor 11:24.

27. Gal 2:11–21.

28. Galatians 2:16; Arthur Cushman McGiffert, *A History of Christianity in the Apostolic Age* (Edinburgh: T. & T. Clark, 1897, repr. 1951), 192–324.

29. Jaroslav Pelikan, *Jesus through the Centuries: His Place in the History of Culture* (New Haven, Conn.: Yale University Press), 1985, 19.

30. Rom 15:26–27.

31. Rom 3; 11:24, 28–32.

32. Karl Marx, *Selected Writings*, edited by Lawrence H. Simon, Indianapolis: Hackett Publishing Company, 1994, p. 25.

33. Walls, "Converts or Proselytes?", 6.

34. Though accepted in theological writing, inculturation is still an unwieldy term. I use it here of necessity but only in the limited sense of critical indigenous appropriation as distinct from the unheeding imposition of foreign institutions or ideas. The term now has a history, and so merits acknowledgment.

35. Gal 3:24–29.

36. J. S. Trimingham, *Christianity among the Arabs in Pre-Islamic Times* (London: Longman; Beirut: Librairie du Liban, 1979), 205.

CHAPTER 1

1. Mt 18:20.

2. *Christi mors potentior erat quam vita* ("the death of Christ was more effective than his life")

3. Malachi 1:11.

4. Psalms 32:7; 90:1; 119:114.

5. *Plutarch's Lives*, vol. 2, (New York: Random House Publishing, 2001), 416.

6. Lactantius, *Divine Institutes Book V, chap. xv, The Ante-Nicene Fathers*, vol. 7 (Edinburgh: T. & T. Clark; Grand Rapids, Mich.: Eerdmans, 1994). This translation by Oliver O'Donovan and Joan Lockwood O'Donovan, *From Irenaeus to Grotius; A Sourcebook in Christian Political Thought* (Grand Rapids, Mich.: Eerdmans, 1999), 46–55.

7. Peter Brown, *The Rise of Western Christendom: Triumph and Diversity*, AD 200–1000, 2nd ed. (Oxford: Blackwell, 2003), 418.

8. Christian ideas of chastity, for example, contrasted sharply with prevailing classical ideas.

9. Mary Beard, John North, and Simon Price, *Religions of Rome*, vol. 1: *A History* (Cambridge: Cambridge University Press, 1998), 1:212.

10. Ibid., 1:214.

11. For a detailed study, see Peter Richardson, *Herod: King of the Jews and Friend of the Romans*, introd. by I. Howard Marshall (Edinburgh: T. & T. Clark, 1996; repr., Fortress, 1999).

12. Beard, North, and Price, *Religions of Rome, A History*, 2:277.

13. Ibid., 2:280.

14. *First Apology*, chap. xiv.

15. The legend is echoed in the Qur'an, *súrah* 18.

16. Diogenes (ca. 400–ca. 325 BC) lived an eccentric life in Athens where he was a founder of the Cynics. Among his surviving legends is one that has him carrying a lantern in daylight, saying he was looking for one honest person.

17. Tertullian, *Apologia*, chap. xxxix.

18. Ibid., chap. xxxii.

19. Jaroslav Pelikan notes that Tertullian saw natural law, not the Christian *logos*, as the bridge with pagan society. See Jaroslav Pelikan, *The Emergence of the Catholic Church (100–600)* (Chicago: University of Chicago Press, 1971), 32.

20. *Meminisse Iuvat*, "On the Persecuted Church," July 14, 1958. Renewed controversy now surrounds Pius XII's role in the Nazi occupation. The Vatican has brushed aside the criticisms by canonizing Pius XII.

21. John Boswell, *The Kindness of Strangers* (New York: Pantheon, 1988), 445–46. In his encyclical, *Quemadmodum*, of January 6, 1946, Pius XII made a plea on behalf of the world's destitute children.

22. Lewis Mumford, *The City in History* (New York: Harcourt, Brace, and World, 1961), 147.

23. Edward Gibbon, *The Decline and Fall of the Roman Empire* (New York: Modern Library, n.d.), 2:714–15.

24. Cited in John Ferguson, 1973, 50.

25. Cited in Adolf von Harnack, *The Mission and Expansion of Christianity in the First Three Centuries* (New York: Putnam, 1908), 2:176.

26. *Against Heresies*, chap. ii.

27. Cited in Harnack, *The Mission and Expansion of Christianity*, 2:152.

28. Maxwell Staniforth, ed. and trans., *Early Christian Writings* (Harmondsworth, England: Penguin Classics, 1968), 176–77. Pius XII cited this passage to stress the worldwide character of the church's mission. See *Evangelii Praecones* 33, June 2, 1951.

29. R. G. Collingwood, *The Idea of History* (Oxford: Clarendon, 1961), 49–50.

30. In his attempt to uncover an original Christianity, Isaac Newton devised an ingenious system based on the idea that the Bible had existed in a language of perfect and exact signification that could be discovered by a mystical rule of analogy. The language of Scripture, Newton maintained in his *The Philosophical Origins of Gentile Theology* (1678), was unlike any of the languages of the world in its capacity to defy difference and historical contingency, for only such a language was worthy of the one universal God who spoke it. Such views mirror the claims Muslims make about the Arabic of the Qur'an, though it is unclear if Newton really intended to emulate Islam on this question. Newton's work is in H McLachlan, editor. *Theological Manuscripts* (Liverpool: Liverpool University Press), 1950, 119.

31. Lamin Sanneh, *Translating the Message: The Missionary Impact on Culture* (Maryknoll, N.Y.: Orbis, 1989), 211–38.

32. J. S. Trimingham, *Christianity among the Arabs in Pre-Islamic Times* (London: Longman; Beirut: Librairie du Liban, 1979), 94.

33. Harnack, *The Mission and Expansion of Christianity*, 2:145, 467–68.

34. Ibid., 2:145.

35. Ibid., 1:20–21.

36. Cited in ibid., 1:22n.

37. Ibid., 1:105.

38. For an astute assessment of Gibbon, see Louis Dupré, *The Enlightenment and the Intellectual Foundations of Modern Culture* (New Haven, Conn.: Yale University Press, 2004), 210–19.

39. On the provinces of the empire, see Theodor Mommsen, *The Provinces of the Roman Empire*, 2 vols., rev. ed. (London: Macmillan, 1909, reprinted New York: Barnes & Noble, 1996).

40. Moses Hadas, *A History of Rome: From Its Origins to 529 AD as Told by the Roman Historians* (New York: Doubleday Anchor, 1956), 131.

41. 1 Thess. 1:9; 1 Cor 10:21–22.

42. Harnack, *The Mission and Expansion of Christianity*, 2:296–97.

43. Trimingham, *Christianity among the Arabs*, (London: Longman; Beirut: Librairie du Liban, 1979), 56, 66, 75, 118, 150–51.

44. Traditional exegesis connects *súrah* 85:4–9 to this battle.

45. Axel Moberg, ed. and trans., *The Book of the Himyarites* (London: Oxford University Press, 1924).

46. Irfan Shahid, *The Martyrs of Najran: New Documents* (Bruxelles: Soc. des Bollandistes, Bd. Saint-Michel, 1971), 24; Trimingham, *Christianity among the Arabs* (London: Longman; Beirut: Librairie du Liban, 1979), 289, 299.

47. Alphonse Mingana, "Early Spread of Christianity in India," *Bulletin of the John Rylands Library of Manchester*, no. 10 (1926): 32ff.

48. Kenneth Scott Latourette, *The History of the Expansion of Christianity*, vol. 2: *The Thousand Years of Uncertainty, 500 AD to 1500 AD* (New York and London: Harper & Brothers), 1937–45; repr. Grand Rapids, Mich.: Zondervan, 1970), 2:282 1966: Harper & Row Publishers.

49. Benedict Vadakkekara, *The Origin of India's St. Thomas Christians: A Historiographical Critique* (Delhi: Media House, 1995), 184f.

50. For more details, see Erica C. D. Hunter, "The Church of the East in Central Asia," *Bulletin of the John Rylands Library of Manchester* 78, no. 3 (1996).

51. Bede, *Ecclesiastical History of the English People*, trans. Leo Sherley-Price (Harmondsworth, Penguin, 1984), 126. The opening words echo Luke 1:68–71. The scene is interestingly reminiscent of an encounter recorded in the eleventh century between the king of ancient Mali in West Africa and a visiting Muslim cleric. The king wished an end to drought for which the cleric prescribed conversion to Islam.

> O King, if you only believed in God the most high and acknowledged his oneness, and in Muhammad—on him be salat and peace—and acknowledged his prophethood, and accepted all the laws of Islam, I could assure you of relief from what you are suffering, and that God's mercy would be over the people of your land and that your enemies would envy you because of that.

Joseph Kenny, *The Spread of Islam through North to West Africa, 7th to the 19th Centuries: A Historical Survey with Relevant Arabic Documents* (Lagos: Dominican Publications, 2000), 85.

52. Keith Feiling, *A History of England: From the Coming of the English to 1918* (London: Macmillan, 1963), 47.

53. Brown, *The Rise of Western Christendom*, 351–52.

54. Alister E. McGrath, *In the Beginning: The Story of the King James Bible and How It Changed a Nation, a Language, and a Culture* (New York: Doubleday, 2001).

55. Thomas Babington Macaulay, *The History of England* (London, Longman, Brown, Green, 1849–1861). 1:6.

56. D. Greene, "Some Linguistic Evidence Relating to the British Church," in *Christianity in Britain 300–700: Papers Presented to the Conference on Christianity in Roman and Sub-Roman Britain*, Held at the University of Nottingham, 17–20 April, 1967, eds. M. W. Barley and R. P. C. Hanson (Leicester: Leicester University Press, 1968), 86.

57. Dag Strömbäck, *The Conversion of Iceland*, trans. and ed. Peter Foote (London: Viking Society for Northern Research, University College, 1975), 16.

58. Ibid., 54.

59. Ibid., 58–59.

60. Edward Kylie, trans. and ed., *The English Correspondence of Saint Boniface* (London: Chatto & Windus, 1924), 61–67.

61. H. P. R. Finberg, *The Formation of England: 550–1042,* (London: Paladin Books, 1974), 46–47.

62. Feiling, *A History of England*, 47–48. A similar theme is taken up in *Beowulf*, an Old English epic poem of uncertain date that combines vernacular and Christian religious elements.

63. Bede, *Ecclesiastical History*, 247.

64. Feiling, *A History of England*, 47.

65. Brown, *The Rise of Western Christendom*, 2003), 215, 377.

66. Bede, *Ecclesiastical History*, 86–87.

67. Hugh Williams, *Christianity in Early Britain* (Oxford: Clarendon, 1912).

68. Raphael Loewe, "The Medieval History of the Latin Vulgate," in *The Cambridge History of the Bible*, vol. 2, G. W. H. Lampe, ed. (Cambridge: Cambridge University Press, 1988).

69. C. White, *The Correspondence between Jerome and Augustine of Hippo* (Lewiston, N.Y. Edwin Mellen, 1990).

70. *Ut nullus credit quod nonnisi in tribus linguis Deus adorandus sit. Quia in omni lingua Deus adoratur et homo exauditur si justa patierit.* See Francis Dvornik, *Byzantine Missions among the Slavs: SS Constantine-Cyril and Methodius* (New Brunswick, N.J.: Rutgers University Press, 1970), 367.

71. Adriaan H. Bredero, *Christendom and Christianity in the Middle Ages* (Grand Rapids, Mich.: Eerdmans, 1994), 16f.

72. The phrase is: *zillu-l-llâhi fi-l-ard.*

73. Significantly, unlike the Muslim caliphs, Charlemagne lacked an original jihad warrant from his religion's founder, but he made up for that in the ad hoc methods he employed that would, under the rules of jihad, be considered a flagrant breach of orthodox rules. Under jihad rules, for instance, conversion is not required, and sometimes is not even encouraged; only subjection to Muslim authority is necessary. It shows Europe trying to catch up with Islam and lagging behind in this regard.

74. John Michael Wallace-Hadrill, *The Frankish Church* (Oxford: Clarendon, 1983), 378, 380–81.

75. John Coakley Andrea Sterk, eds., *Readings in World Christian History*, vol. 1: *Earliest Christianity to 1453* (Maryknoll, N.Y.: Orbis, 2004), 308.

76. Lk 23:38,

77. Psalm 116:1; Acts 2:11; Phil 2:11; 1 Cor 14:4.

78. Harnack, *The Mission and Expansion of Christianity*, 1:22; 2:456.

79. John Philip, *Researches in South Africa: Illustrating the Civil, Moral, and Religious Condition of the Native Tribes.* 2 vols. (London: James Duncan, 1828), 1:204; 2:359.

80. 2 Cor 3:2–3.

81. James Adam, *Religious Teachers of Greece* (Edinburgh T.&T. Clark, 1908), 306–7.

82. Charles Norris Cochrane, *Christianity and Classical Culture: A Study of Thought and Action from Augustus to Augustine* (New York: Oxford University Press, 1957), 474.

83. Brown, *The Rise of Western Christendom*, 14.

84. *Evangelii Praecones*, 60, 63, June 2, 195.

CHAPTER 2

1. Phil 2:15; 3:14.

2. Mt 5:14.

3. *Early Christian Writings: The Apostolic Fathers* (tr. Maxwell Staniforth, Penguin Books, Harmondsworth: England, 1968, reprinted by Penguin Books, 1982) 235.

4. While living and teaching in Milan, Augustine met a friend by the name of Ponticianus, an African, who introduced him to Antony's life:

> The Egyptian monk, whose name was in high repute among [God's] servants, though up to that time not familiar to us. When Ponticianus came to know this, he lingered on that topic, imparting to us a knowledge of this man so eminent, and marveling at our ignorance. . . . What is wrong with us. . . . The unlearned start up and 'take' heaven, and we, with our learning, but wanting heart, see where we wallow in flesh and blood.

See Augustine, *Confessions*, book viii, chaps. 6, 8. Perhaps that is what Augustine means when he says that he is a question to himself.

5. Peter Brown, *The World of Late Antiquity: AD 150–750* (New York: Norton, 1971), 98.

6. Robin Lane Fox, *Pagans and Christians* (San Francisco: HarperSanFrancisco, 1988), 375ff.

7. Adolf von Harnack, *The Mission and Expansion of Christianity in the First Three Centuries. 2 vols. (New York: Putnam, 1908), i, 200–208.

8. Bengt G. M. Sundkler, *The Christianity Ministry in Africa* (Uppsala: University of Uppsala, 1960); also Bengt G. M. Sundkler, *Bantu Prophets in South Africa*, 2nd edition, (London: Oxford University Press for the International African Institute, 1961), 238–94.

9. R. P. C. Hanson, *Saint Patrick: His Origins and Career* (Oxford: Clarendon, 1968), 207. Patrick's claim, "I woke up," suggests he was asleep and that what he had was a dream of the lucid kind. Visions in *stricto senso* belong with being awake.

10. Cited in Jaroslav Pelikan, *Jesus through the Centuries: His Place in the History of Culture* (New Haven, Conn.: Yale University Press 1985), 115.

11. Irfan Shahid, "Arab Christianity in Byzantine Palestine," *Aram Periodical* 15 (2003): 228–29; Haim Goldfus, "Urban Monasticism and Monasteries of Early Byzantine Palestine: Preliminary Observations," *Aram Periodical* 15 (2003): 71–79. Pius XII offered an extensive assessment of the missionary significance of Boniface in his encyclical, *Ecclesiae Fastos*, from June 1954.

12. The dating of the *Odes* to the late first century would have implications for the much later dating of the *Gospel of John*, which the *Odes* quote liberally.

13. J. H. Charlesworth, ed. and trans., *The Odes of Solomon: The Syriac Texts* (Oxford: Clarendon), 1973.

14. Sozomen, *The Ecclesiastical History* in *The Nicene and Post-Nicene Fathers of the Christian Church*, second series, vol. II (Edinburgh: T&T Clark, Grand Rapids, Mich.: Wm. B. Eerdmans Publishing Company, 1989), 293.

15. Cited in J. S. Trimingham, *Christianity among the Arabs in Pre-Islamic Times* (London: Longman; Beirut: Librairie du Liban, 1979), 106. See also Robin Lane Fox, *Pagans and Christians* (New York: HarperSanFrancisco of HarperCollins Publishers, 1988), 18–20.

16. The Arabic is *aqímú al-dín wa lá tatafarraqú fíhi.*

17. Qur'an 42:13

18. Qur'an 3:47–49; 9:30-32; 19:35–37; 43:64–67.

19. Kenneth Cragg, *The Arab Christian: A History in the Middle East* (Louisville: Westminster John Knox, 1991), 39.

20. Qur'an 12:2; 20:113; 41:3; 42:7; 43:3.

21. Trimingham, *Christianity among the Arabs*, 107, 141.

22. Ibid., 308–11.

23. W. Montgomery Watt, *Muslim-Christian Encounters: Perceptions and Misperceptions* (London: Routledge, 1991), 2.

24. Richard Bell, *The Origin of Islam in Its Christian Environment: The Gunning Lectures* (Edinburgh University, 1926; repr. 1968), 4–5. The Coptic Church fared no better in its encounter with Western missions. See Alastair Hamilton, *The Copts and the West, 1439–1822* (New York and Oxford: Oxford University Press, 2006).

25. Watt, *Muslim-Christian Encounters*, 7.

26. Peter Brown, *The Rise of Western Christendom: Triumph and Diversity, AD200–1000*, 2nd ed. (Oxford: Blackwell 2003), 377.

27. Jaime Lara, *City, Temple, Stage: Eschatological Architecture and Liturgical Theatrics in New Spain* (Notre Dame: University of Notre Dame Press, 2004), 122.

28. Qur'an 9:34; 57:28.

29. "Ibn Mubárak," *Encyclopaedia of Islam*, 2nd ed., 3:879.

30. Edward Gibbon, *The Decline and Fall of the Roman Empire* (New York: Modern Library, n.d.), 1:418.

31. S. M. Burstein, ed., *Ancient African Civilizations: Kush and Axum* (Princeton, N.J.: Marcus Wiener, 1998), 96.

32. G. H. R. Horsley, *New Documents Illustrating Early Christianity*. 2 vols. (North Ryde, New South Wales: Macquarie University Press, 1981–82), 1:143–44.

33. Constance B. Hilliard, ed., *Intellectual Traditions of Pre-Colonial Africa* (Boston: McGraw Hill, 1998).

34. Roberto Sanchez Valencia, "The Monophysite Conviction in the East versus Byzantium's Political Convenience: A Historical Look to Monothelism in Palestine," *Aram Periodica* 15 (2003); also D. A. Hubbard, "The Literary Sources of the Kebra Nagast" (Ph.D. diss., St. Andrews University, 1957).

35. Getatchew Haile, "A Christ for the Gentiles: The Case of zä-KRESTOS of Ethiopia," *Journal of Religion in Africa* 15, no. 2 (1985).

36. E. R. Dodds, *Págan and Christian in an Age of Anxiety* (New York: Norton, 1970), 134ff.

37. 2 Tm 1:5.

38. Rom 8:19; 2 Cor 5:17; Col 2:12.

39. Eusebius, *The History of the Church* (Harmondsworth: Penguin, 1984), 65–69, 73.

40. W. O. E. Oesterley and Theodore H. Robinson, *A History of Israel.* Vol. 2, *From the Fall of Jerusalem, 586 BC to the Bar-Kokhaba Revolt, AD135* (Oxford: Clarendon, 1932; repr. 1957), 2:422–23.

41. J. N. D. Kelly, *Golden Mouth: The Story of John Chrysostom: Ascetic, Preacher, Bishop* (Ithaca, N.Y.: Cornell University Press), 1995.

42. Erica C. D. Hunter, "The Transmission of Greek Philosophy via the 'School of Edessa,'" in *Literacy, Education and Manuscript Transmission in Byzantium and Beyond,* ed. Catherine Holmes and Judith Waring (Leiden: Brill, 2002).

43. Sydney H. Griffith, "The Monks of Palestine and the Growth of Christian Literature in Arabic," *The Muslim World* 78, no. 1 (January 1988): 22.

44. Trimingham, *Christianity among the Arabs,* 145.

45. S. Gero, "Byzantine Iconoclasm during the Reign of Leo III," *Adversus Constantinum Caballinum* (1973); Steven Derfler, "The Byzantine Church at Tel Kerioth and Religious Iconoclasm in the Eighth Century: The 1991–1994 Seasons of Excavation," *Aram Periodical* 15 (2003): 39–47.

46. Henri Pirenne, *Mohammed and Charlemagne* (London: Unwin University Books, 1968), 160.

47. Franz Rosenthal has documented this in painstaking detail. See Rosenthal, *The Classical Heritage in Islam* (London: Routledge & Kegan Paul, 1975; German edition, Zürich: Artemis Verlags-AG, 1975).

48. Translation and original Arabic text in Ameer Ali, *The Spirit of Islam: A History of the Evolution and Ideals of Islam, with a Life of the Prophet* (London: Chatto & Windus, 1964), 368–69.

49. Averroës, *Middle Commentary on Aristotle's 'De anima,'* ed. and trans. Alfred L. Ivry (Provo, Utah: Brigham Young University Press, 2002).

50. A. J. Arberry, ed., *Aspects of Islamic Civilization: As Depicted in the Original Texts* (London: Allen & Unwin, 1964; repr., Ann Arbor: University of Michigan Press, 1967), 122, 123.

51. The "Nestorian Church" is a misapplied term, the partisan result of the Christological controversies of Chalcedon. Historians have now corrected the designation to "The Assyrian Church of the East." See S.P. Brock, "The 'Nestorian' Church: A Lamentable Misnomer," *Bulletin of the John Rylands Library of Manchester,* vol. 78, no. 3, Autumn, 1996, 23–35.

52. Qur'an 19:17; 21:91.

53. Psalms 2:2–12; 33:6; 89:19; 90:1, 4; 104:4, 30; 107:20; 110:3; 148:5.

54. Genesis 1:26; 11:7; Dt 6:4; Jb 1:21; Mt 5:45; 28:19; 1 Cor 2:10; Heb 1:1.

55. John W. Coakley and Andrea Sterk, eds., *Readings in World Christian History,* vol. 1: *Earliest Christianity to 1453* (Maryknoll, N.Y.: Orbis, 2004), 242.

56. Qur'an 16:107.

57. Qur'an 6:119.

58. Qur'an 3:27.

59. Ibid.

60. R. Strothmann, "Takíya," *Shorter Encyclopaedia of Islam*, ed. H. A. R. Gibb and J. H. Kramers (Leiden: Brill, 1961), 36.

61. Genesis 16.

62. Qur'an 19:17

63. Coakley and Sterk, eds., 304. Constantine-Cyril is doing some telescoping here. The verse in question says only: "Then We sent unto her Our Spirit (*fa-arsalná ilayha rúhaná*) that presented himself to her a man without fault." It is in a different passage that Mary's virgin status is affirmed: "And she who guarded her virginity (*w'alláti ahsanat farjahá*), so We breathed into her Our spirit and appointed her and her son to be a sign unto all beings" (21:91–92). Ibn Taymiyya (d. 1328) asserts that Qur'án 19:17 is a refutation of the specious claims of Christians.

64. Richard Walzer, "Arabic Transmission of Greek Thought to Europe," *Bulletin of the John Rylands Library of Manchester* 29 (1945–46); W. Montgomery Watt, *The Influence of Islam on Medieval Europe* (Edinburgh: Edinburgh University Press, 1972), 58–71, 79–80; Watt, *Muslim-Christian Encounters*, 52–58.

65. Syrian Monophysites, so named after James Baradai (d. 553).

66. Cited in R. Dozy, *Spanish Islam: A History of the Muslims in Spain* (London: Chatto and Windus, 1913), 576. On Islam and other religions, see Jacques Waardenburg, "World Religions as Seen in the Light of Islam," in *Islam: Past Influence and Present Challenge*, eds. Alford T. Welch and Pierre Cachia (Edinburgh: Edinburgh University Press, 1979), 245–75.

67. Al-Ghazálí wrote under the misapprehension that John's Gospel was originally written in Coptic.

68. Arberry, ed., *Aspects of Islamic Civilization*, 303.

69. Miguel Asín Palacios, *Islam and the Divine Comedy* (New York: Dutton, 1926).

70. Rom Landau describes Ibn 'Arabí as an important influence on Jung, in *The Philosophy of Ibn 'Arabí* (London: Allen & Unwin), 1959.

71. Aziz Ahmad, *A History of Islamic Sicily* (Edinburgh: Edinburgh University Press, 1975), 95.

72. Jane Ellen Harrison, *Themis: A Study of the Social Origins of Greek Religion* (Cambridge: Cambridge University Press, 1912), 487.

73. Denis R. Janz, *World Christianity and Marxism* (New York: Oxford University Press, 1998).

74. Ernest Wolf-Gazo, "Weber and Islam," *ISIM Review* 16 (Autumn 2005): 44.

75. Max Weber, *Economy and Society: An Outline of Interpretive Sociology*, ed. Guenther Roth and Claus Wittich (Berkeley and Los Angeles: University of California Press, 1978), 1:625; 2:1076, 1096–97, 1183; Brian S. Turner, *Weber and Islam: A Critical Study* (London and Boston: Routledge & Kegan Paul, 1974).

76. *Chronicle of Zuqnín*, ed. and trans. Amir Harrak (Toronto: Pontifical Institute of Medieval Studies, 1999), 329–30.

77. Muhammad b. Jarír al-Tabarí, *Ta'ríkh al-rusul wa'l-mulúk*, 2 vols., (Leiden: 1964; 2 Cairo: Dár al-Ma'ríf, 1969), 2:1372.

78. Moshe Gil, *A History of Palestine, 634–1099*, trans. from the Hebrew by Ethel Broido (Cambridge: Cambridge University Press, 1992), 151.

79. *Chronicle of Zuqnín*, 322–23.

80. Constantin- François Volney, *Travels through Egypt and Syria in the Years 1783, 1784 and 1785* (New York: J. Tiebout for E. Duyckinck, 1798); Youssef Courbage and Philippe Fargues, *Christians and Jews under Islam* (London and New York: I. B. Tauris, 1997), 52–90; 'Abdul-Rahim Abu Husayn, "Duwayhi as a Historian of Ottoman Syria," *Bulletin of the Royal Institute for Inter-Faith Studies* 1, no. 1 (Spring 1999).

81. Richard Hakluyt, *Voyages and Discoveries* (Harmondsworth: Penguin, 1972), 250–51.

82. Aylward Shorter, *The Cross and the Flag in Africa: The "White Fathers" during the Colonial Scramble, 1892–1914* (Maryknoll, N.Y.: Orbis, 2006), 1.

83. Virgil Elizondo comments on the appeal of Mary and Jesus for long-suffering Mexican American women—grandmothers, mothers, wives, girlfriends. Like Mary, these women stand by silently as injustice and violence are done to their kin. For example, critics dismiss the Good Friday burial service as evidence only of morbid tendencies whereas, in fact, the clandestine burial of Jesus takes on a special significance for people whose loved ones were taken away by officials, condemned, and disappeared into obscurity and whose memory is hallowed and honored in a ritual that is a standing indictment of official guilt. Called *nuestro Diosito en la cruz* ("our little God on the cross"), Jesus is at the center of an existential reality. See Elizondo, "Living Faith: Resistance and Survival," in *Mestizo Worship: A Personal Approach to Liturgical Ministry*, ed. Virgil Elizondo and Timothy Matovina (Collegeville, Minn.: Liturgical, 1998), 17.

84. Franz Babinger, *Mehmed the Conqueror and His Time*, ed. William C. Hickman; trans. from the German by Ralph Manheim. (Princeton, N.J.: Bolingen Series 96 of Princeton University Press, 1978), 411.

85. Myron P. Gilmore, *The World of Humanism: 1453–1517* (New York: Harper, 1952; repr. 1962), 18.

86. Gibbon, *The Decline and Fall of the Roman Empire*, 2:626.

87. H. McKennie Goodpasture, ed., *Cross and Sword: An Eyewitness History of Christianity in Latin America* (Maryknoll, N.Y.: Orbis, 1989), 6–7.

88. Francesco Gabrieli, *Arab Historians of the Crusades*, trans. from the Italian by E. J. Costello (London: Routledge & Kegan Paul, 1969; repr. Berkeley and Los Angeles: University of California Press, 1984). First published as *Storici Arabi delle Crociate* (Turin: Giulio Editore S.p.A.), 101

89. Cited in Bernard Lewis, *The Emergence of Modern Turkey*, 2nd ed. (London: Oxford University Press, 1968), 28.

90. See, for example, Trevor Royle, *Crimea; The Great Crimean War 1854–1856* (London and New York: Palgrave Macmillan, 2004.)

CHAPTER 3

1. H. McKennie Goodpasture, ed., *Cross and Sword: An Eyewitness History of Christianity in Latin America* (Maryknoll, N.Y.: Orbis, 1989), 32–33.

2. Ibid., 34.

3. Ibid., 44–45.

4. Eric Williams, *From Columbus to Castro: The History of the Caribbean* (New York: Vintage, 1984), 406.

5. Ibid., 34. On the status and role of blacks, see Herman L. Bennett, *Africans in Colonial Mexico: Absolutism, Christianity, and Afro-Creole Consciousness, 1570–1640* (Bloomington: Indiana University Press, 2003).

6. Goodpasture, *Cross and Sword*, 12.

7. Eric Williams, *From Columbus to Castro*, 33.

8. Ibid., 33–34.

9. Adam Smith, *The Wealth of Nations*, edited by Edwin Cannan (New York: Modern Library Edition of Random House, 1994), 605. It is relevant here to note that a similar fate overtook the Australian Aborigines. Originally numbering perhaps up to half a million at the time of Captain Cook's arrival in 1770, they numbered only around 10,000 by 1850, killed off, for the most part, by white settlers.

10. Goodpasture, *Cross and Sword*, 64.

11. Maxwell E. Johnson, *The Virgin of Guadulupe: Theological Reflections of an Anglo-Lutheran Liturgist*, Lanham, MD: Rowan & Littlefield Publishers, Inc., 2002, 23.

12. Stafford Poole, *Our Lady of Guadalupe: The Origin and Sources of a Mexican National Symbol, 1531–1797* (Tucson: University of Arizona Press, 1997), 106–07, 219, 224–25.

13. In 1940, Graham Greene (1904–91) devoted one of his novels, *The Power and the Glory*, to the bitter consequences of that anticlerical theme.

14. To their alarm, Portuguese officials learnt in the Autumn of 1608 that Pope Paul V had decided to take over control of the missions, thereby stripping the Portuguese Crown of its patronal privileges. When in 1610 the pope commissioned the Discalced Carmelites to embark on a mission to Kongo from Portugal, Philip III blocked the mission by preventing its departure from Lisbon. A Portuguese official objected to the new papal policy, arguing that "a monarchy that has lost its reputation, even if it has lost no territory, is a sky without light, a sun without rays, a body without a soul." He had unwittingly spoken also for the papal monarchy stripped of its missionary mandate. Richard Gray, "The Papacy and Africa in the Seventeenth Century," *Il Cristianesimo nel Mondo Atlantico nel Secolo XVII*, Rome: Libreria Editrice Vaticana, Citta del Vaticano, 1997, 287.

15. Cited in Bailey W. Diffie and George D. Winius, *Foundations of the Portuguese Empire, 1415–1580*, vol. 1 (Minneapolis: University of Minnesota Press, 1977), 254.

16. Cited in Vincent Cronin, *A Pearl to India: The Life of Robert de Nobili* (London: Rupert Hart Davis 1959), 29.

17. Cited in C. R. Boxer, *The Portuguese Seaborne Empire, 1415–1825* (London: Hutchinson & Co., 1977), 145.

18. See Edward H. Spicer, *Cycles of Conquest: The Impact of Spain, Mexico, and the United States on the Indians of the Southwest, 1533–1960* (Tucson: University of Arizona Press, 1962).

19. Eric Williams, *From Columbus to Castro*, 1984, 36.

20. Bartholomew de Las Casas, *History of the Indies* (New York: Harper & Row), 1971, 149.

21. Ian Linden has discussed a related issue in his book. See Ian Linden, *A New Map of the World* (London: Darton, Longman & Todd, 2003).

22. "To found a great empire for the sole purpose of raising up a people of customers may at first sight appear as a project fit only for a nation of shopkeepers. It is, however, a project altogether unfit for a nation of shopkeepers; but extremely fit for a nation whose government is influenced by shopkeepers." Adam Smith, *The Wealth of Nations*, 663.

23. Ibid., book IV, chap. 2, 484–85.

24. John Maynard Keynes, "The Resilience of Capitalism," *Atlantic Monthly* 149, no. 5 (May 1932): 521–26.

25. Richard Gray, "The African Origins of the Missio Antiqua," in *Clavis Scientiae* (Rome: Instituto Storico Dei Cappucini, 1999), 406.

26. L. Jadin and M. Dicorato, trans. and ed., *Correspondence de Dom Afonso, roi du Congo 1506–1543* (Brussels: Koninklijke Academie Voor Overzeese Wetenschappern, 1974), letter 24.

27. Cited in John Baur, *2000 Years of Christianity in Africa: An African History, 62–1992* (Nairobi: Paulines Publications of Africa, 1994), 75.

28. Anne Hilton, *The Kingdom of Kongo* (Oxford: Clarendon, 1985), 179ff.

29. Basil Davidson, editor, *The African Past: Chronicles from Antiquity to Modern Times* (Harmondsworth, Middlesex, England: Penguin Books, 1966), 194–95.

30. Harold G. Marcus, *A History of Ethiopia* (Berkeley and Los Angeles: University of California Press, 1994), 30–47.

31. Job Ludolphus, *A New History of Ethiopia: Being a Full and Accurate Description of Abessinia* (London: Samuel Smith, 1682), 357; Balthazar Tellez, *Travels of the Jesuits in Ethiopia* (London: J. Knapton, 1710), 242.

32. Ludolphus, *A New History*, 364.

33. Edward Gibbon, *The Decline and Fall of the Roman Empire*, 3 vols. (New York: Modern Library: n.d.) ii, 863.

34. For a summary of Kongo and slavery see Roland Oliver, *The African Experience: Major Themes in African History from the Earliest Times to the Present* (New York: IconEditions of HarperCollins, 1991), 127–28.

35. J. H. Parry, *The Age of Reconnaissance* (New York: Mentor, 1964), 33.

36. Cited in Jean Comby, *How to Understand the History of Christian Mission* (London: SCM, 1996), 60.

37. Eric Williams, *From Columbus to Castro*, 44.

38. Richard Gray, "The African Origins of the Missio Antiqua." In *Clavis Scientiae* (Rome: Instituto Storico Dei Cappucini, 1999).

39. Richard Gray, *Black Christians and White Missionaries* (New Haven, Conn.: Yale University Press, 1990), 23.

40. The Capuchins had a long history of antislavery experience. Between 1585 and 1589, for example, they set out as papal emissaries for North Africa to ransom slaves, many of whom were Italians. In that period they indemnified some one thousand

slaves from Algiers and Tunis. Robert C. Davis, *Christian Slaves, Muslim Masters: White Slavery in the Mediterranean, The Barbary Coast, and Italy, 1500–1800* (New York, Palgrave Macmillan, 2003), 167.

41. Henry J. Koren, "The Legacy of Francoise Libermann," *International Bulletin of Missionary Research* 28, no. 4 (October 2004).

42. For an account of these developments, see Richard Gray, "The Catholic Church and National States in Western Europe during the Nineteenth and Twentieth Centuries from [the] Perspective of Africa," *Kirchliche Zeitgeschichte, Internationale Halbjahreszeitschrift für Theologie und Gescchichtswissenschaft* 14, no. 1 (2001): 148–55.

43. John C. Van Horne, ed., *Religious Philanthropy and Colonial Slavery: The American Correspondence of the Associates of Dr. Bray, 1717–1777* (Urbana and Chicago: University of Illinois Press, 1985), 2.

44. Hugh Barnes, *Gannibal: The Moor of Petersburg* (London: Profile, 2005).

45. Herman L. Bennett, *Africans in Colonial Mexico: Absolutism, Christianity, and Afro-Creole Consciousness, 1570–1640* (Bloomington: Indiana University Press, 2003), 16.

46. W. E. B. DuBois, *The Suppression of the African Slave Trade to the United States of America: 1638–1870*, 1898; repr., New York: Russell & Russell, 1965, 30–31. Cambridge, MA: Harvard Historical Studies, 1898.

47. Samuel Hopkins, *Dialogue Concerning the Slavery of the Africans* (Norwich: Judah Spooner, 1776; and New York: Robert Hodge, 1785), 56, 63.

48. Aylward Shorter, *The Cross and the Flag in Africa: The "White Fathers" during the Colonial Scramble, 1892–1914* (Maryknoll, N.Y.: Orbis, 2006), 77ff.

49. Ibid., 78.

50. J. W. Loguen, *The Rev. J. W. Loguen, as a Slave and as a Freeman: A Narrative of Real Life*, Syracuse, NY: J.G.K. Truair, Office of the Daily Journal, 1859, ix.

51. Anthony Kirk-Greene, David George: The Nova Scotian Experience," *Sierra Leone Studies*, new series, 14 (December 1960), 110-111.

52. Robin Winks, *The Blacks in Canada* (New Haven, Conn.: Yale University Press, 1972), 60.

53. Bruce Hindmarsh, *John Newton and the English Evangelical Tradition: Between the Conversions of Wesley and Wilberforce* (Oxford: Clarendon, 1996).

54. Elie Halévy, *A History of the English People in the Nineteenth Century: England in 1815* (London: Ernest Benn; New York: Barnes & Noble, 1961).

55. Paul Cuffee, *Paul Cuffe's Logs and Letters: 1808–1817: A Black Quaker's 'Voice from Within the Veil,'* edited by Rosalind Cobb Wiggins (Washington, D.C.: Howard University Press, 1996), 341–43.

56. Rosalind Cobb Wiggins, *Logs and Letters*, 1996, 342.

57. Ibid., 342.

58. Henry Noble Sherwood, "Paul Cuffe," *Journal of Negro History* 8 (April 1923): 204.

59. Thomas Clarkson, "Society for the Purpose of Encouraging the Black Settlers at Sierra Leone, and the Natives of Africa Generally, in the Cultivation of Their Soil,

and by the Sale of Their Produce," January 28, 1814, Public Record Office, London, CO 267/41.

60. Paul Sherwood, "Paul Cuffe," *Journal of Negro History*, 8 (April 1923), 195–96.

61. In Freetown Cuffee reminded Locke that Locke had complained in America about being denied his liberties and was again murmuring because he was called upon to serve as a juror. "Go and fill thy seat and do as well as thou canst," Cuffee told him. *Logs and Letters*, 434.

62. Mary Kingsley, *West African Studies* (London: Macmillan, 1899; repr. London: Frank Cass, 1964), 128.

63. Sherwood, "Paul Cuffe," 213.

64. *First Annual Report of the American Colonization Society*, 5; ibid., 220.

65. The Moravian Church was founded in 1457 following the martyrdom of John Hus in 1415, with a worldwide following presently of fewer than a million. Today, the Moravians have entered into unity agreements with other Protestant churches.

66. Cited in Shorter, *The Cross and the Flag*, 176.

67. The British and Foreign Bible Society was also founded in 1804, with the inspiration coming from Thomas Charles's desire to supply Bibles in Welsh to his parishioners. William Wilberforce and John Thornton were among its first vice presidents.

68. *The Works of the Reverend Sydney Smith* (London: Longman, Brown, Green, Longmans and Roberts, 1859), 136–37.

69. Sierra Leone became a crown possession after 1807.

70. Psalm 95:11.

CHAPTER 4

1. Geoffrey Moorhouse, *The Missionaries* (Philadelphia: Lippincott, 1973), 93.

2. Ibid., 94.

3. Ibid., 94.

4. I shall return to the subject of the role of missions in cultural imperialism in a later chapter.

5. Cited in Edwin W. Smith, *The Shrine of a People's Soul* (London: Livingstone 1929), 79.

6. Other historians give that credit to the Indian "mutiny" of 1857.

7. Philip Woodruff, *The Men Who Ruled India* (New York: Schocken, 1954, 2 volumes), vol. 2, 193–203.

8. A. Trevor Clark, "Eye-Witnesses of the Coercion of the Old Guard Emir Yakubu III of Bauchi," *African Affairs* 94, no. 376 (July 1995).

9. Edwin Smith, *The Golden Stool: Some Aspects of the Conflict of Cultures in Modern Africa* (London: Holborn, 1926), 311.

10. Jean Comaroff and John Comaroff, *Of Revelation and Revolution: Christianity, Colonialism, and Consciousness in South Africa* (Chicago: University of Chicago Press, 1991), 309–10.

11. A historical study of Catholic missionary translation notes that it took great skill and sensitivity for missionaries to achieve the results they wanted. The dialogue entailed "was far from being an unequal contest between the missionary and the African, between a linguistic manipulator and a 'passive object of literacy.' It often took considerable time for missionaries to acquire an accurate idea of African traditional religion," and without that knowledge missionary effort was in vain. Only African agency availed in the end. See Aylward Shorter, *The Cross and the Flag in Africa: The "White Fathers" during the Colonial Scramble, 1892–1914* (Maryknoll, N.Y.: Orbis, 2006), 163–66.

12. Edwin W. Smith, *The Shrine of a People's Soul*, 190.

13. Lewis argues "that those who read the Bible as literature do not read the Bible. . . . I think it very unlikely that the Bible will return as a Book unless it returns as a sacred book." C.S. Lewis, *Selected Literary Essays* (Cambridge; Cambridge University Press, 1969), 144.

14. Comaroff and Comaroff, *Of Revelation and Revolution*, 213–15, 311.

15. R. Delavignette, *Freedom and Authority in French West Africa* (London: Oxford University Press, 1950), 17.

16. Anthony Benezet, *Some historical account of Guinea: its situation, produce, and the general disposition of its inhabitants: with an inquiry into the rise and progress of the slave trade, its nature, and lamentable effects* (London: J. Phillips, 1788).

17. Basil Davidson, editor, *The African Past: Chronicles from Antiquity to Modern Times* (Harmondsworth, Middlesex, England: Penguin Books), 1964, 178.

18. Adam Smith, *The Wealth of Nations*, ed. Edwin Cannan (New York: Modern Library Edition of Random House, 1994), book IV, chap. 7, 675. A disciple of Smith berated abolitionists for not turning their attention to West Indian free trade rather than to the humanitarian campaign for slaves. See David Brion Davis, *The Problem of Slavery in the Age of Revolution, 1770–1823* (Ithaca, N.Y.: Cornell University Press, 1975), 355n.

19. Lesslie Newbigin, *Foolishness to the Greeks: The Gospel and Western Culture* (Geneva: World Council of Churches 1986), 107–8.

20. A former student of mine at Harvard Divinity School, Jean Fairfax, reported that when she visited Schweitzer at Lambaréné, she could not help noticing how Schweitzer, standing on his verandah, disbursed money to African workers by simply throwing coins on the ground. A scramble would ensue, which appeared to satisfy the great man. Ms. Fairfax confirmed the report when I recalled it at a conference at the University of Michigan, Ann Arbor, May 18, 2005. For a critique of Schweitzer's philosophy see A. G. Hogg, "The Ethical Teaching of Dr Schweitzer," *International Review of Missions* 14 (1925): 237–51.

21. Cited in Andrew Ross, *David Livingstone: Mission and Empire* (London and New York: Hambledon & London, 2002), 70.

22. Ross, ibid., 242–43.

23. George Shepperson and Thomas Price, *Independent African: John Chilembwe and the Origins, Setting, and Significance of the Nyasaland Native Rising of 1915* (Edinburgh: Edinburgh University Press 1958; reprinted 1987), 162.

24. Cited in ibid., 163–64.

25. "Mark Twain on American Imperialism," *The Atlantic* 269, no. 4 (1992): 46–65, 49.

26. Rev. Mojola Agbebi, *Inaugural Sermon*, New York, 1903, extract in J. Ayo Langley, ed., *Ideologies of Liberation in Black Africa, 1856–1970* (London: Rex Collings, 1979), 77.

27. His intellectual biographer, Shlomo Avineri, while reflecting on the plight of the Jewish people in communist Russia, examines this theme in Marx's thought. Avineri, *The Social and Political Thought of Karl Marx* (London: Cambridge University Press 1968).

28. Patrick Keatley, *The Politics of Partnership* (Harmondsworth: Penguin, 1963), 124, 467.

29. Ibid., 124–25.

30. Ibid., 121.

31. Livingstone, cited in Roland Oliver, *The Missionary Factor in East Africa* (London: Longman, 1970), 10.

32. Ross, *David Livingstone*, 239.

33. Arthur Keppel-Jones, *Rhodes and Rhodesia: The White Conquest of Zimbabwe, 1884–1902* (Kingston and Montreal: McGill-Queen's University Press 1983), 419.

34. Ibid., 533.

35. Arnold J. Toynbee, *Civilization on Trial* (New York: Oxford University Press, 1948), 80.

36. David Ayalon, "The Historian al-Jabarti," in *Historians of the Middle East*, edited by Bernard Lewis and P. M. Holt (London: Cambridge University Press, 1962), 395.

37. The ancient epic of Sunjata in the Penguin Classics illustrates this theme. See Bamba Suso and Banna Kanute, *Sunjata: The Mande Epic* (London: Penguin, 1999).

38. Cheikh Hamidou Kane, *Ambiguous Adventure* (London: Heinemann Education Book, 1972; Paris: René Julliard, 1962), 46–7. For a discussion of the theme in historical narratives, see William B. Cohen, *The French Encounter with Africans: White Responses to Blacks, 1530–1880* (Bloomington: Indiana University Press, 1980; repr. 2003).

39. Alan Cowell, "Christians are Torn in the Land of Dr. Livingstone," *New York Times*, December 28, 1982, A2.

40. Marion M. Preminger, *The Sands of Tamanrasset: The Story of Charles de Foucauld* (New York: Hawthorn, 1961), 55. Also Foucauld, *Meditations of a Hermit: The Spiritual Writings of Charles de Foucauld*, translated by C. Balfour (London: Burns & Oates, 1981).

41. Rushdie writes: "Mélange, hotch-potch, a bit of this and a bit of that is *how newness enters the world*. It is the great possibility that mass migration gives the world, and I have tried to embrace it. The *Satanic Verses* is change-by-fusion, change by conjoining. It is a love-song to our mongrel selves. [People] are leaking into one another, as a character of mine once said, *like flavours when you cook*." Salman Rushdie, *In Good Faith* (New York: Viking, 1990), 4.

42. *Facing Mount Kenya*, 259.

43. Ibid., 259–60.

44. *"Mngu"* in Kenyatta.

45. See F. B. Welbourn, *East African Rebels: A Study of Some Independent Churches* (London: SCM, 1961), 135ff.

46. 42. *Facing Mount Kenya*, 264.

47. Ibid., 267–8.

48. E. W. Blyden, *The Return of the Exiles and the West African Church* (London: W. B. Whittingham, 1891).

49. Fiona Macleod [William Sharp], *Winged Dynasty: Studies in the Spiritual History of the Gael* (London: Chapman and Hall, 1904), 223.

50. A theological review in 1978 seemed still tone deaf to the significance of translation in Christianity, for it stated that while French is suitable for Cartesian analysis, and English for pragmatic thought, "Arabic can strike the heart and mind by its affirmative and incantatory power. Participants in dialogue would do well to remember that not all languages have the same kerygmatic force, nor the same inclination to serenity." *Pro Mundi Vita Bulletin* 74 (Sept.–Oct., 1978), 45.

51. F. B. Welbourn, *East African Rebels*, 169ff.

52. Ibid., 172–73.

53. Ernest Llewlellyn Woodward, *Christianity and Nationalism in the Later Roman Empire* (New York: Longmans, Green, 1916).

54. David Maxwell, "Historical Christian Independency: The Southern African Pentecostal Movement," *Journal of African History* 40, no. 3 (1999).

55. Douglas Bush, *English Literature in the Earlier Seventeenth Century, 1600–1660* (New York and London: Oxford University Press, 1945), 9.

56. H. A. Junod, *Life of a South African Tribe* (London: Macmillan, 1927), 449. Catholic Missionaries in East Africa experienced a similar culture shock regarding African responses, though in their case they came eventually to a positive view. One such missionary was inspired to say that, ignorant of the vices of corrupt civilization, African Pagans were not as far from the Kingdom of God as one might otherwise think. See Shorter, *The Cross and the Flag in Africa*, 158.

57. Welbourn, *East African Rebels*, 127–28.

58. Bengt G. M. Sundkler, *Bantu Prophets in South Africa*, 2nd ed. (London: Oxford University Press for the International African Institute, 1961), 30.

59. The sentiment is echoed across the Jewish diaspora. Marc Chagall, for example, explained his choice of being nonresident in Israel, saying in a poem, "only that land is mine that lies within my soul." See "The Soul in the City," cited in Kenneth Cragg, *Semitism, The Whence and Whither ('How Dear Are Your Counsels')* (Brighton, England: Sussex Academic Press, 2005), 163.

60. In 1892 the Imperial British East Africa Company (IBEA) intervened during a civil war on the side of the Protestants against the existing Catholic minority. Frederick (later Lord) Lugard lent armed support to the Protestants. Léon Livinhac, Lavigerie's successor, traveled to London in 1893–94 to intercede with the British government on behalf of the hard-pressed Catholic mission in Uganda. In 1898 the British

government finally agreed to a payment of £10, 000 as an indemnity to the Uganda Catholic Mission for the damage it suffered, though without admitting liability for the IBEA. See Shorter, *The Cross and the Flag in Africa*, 14. In the postcolonial era that bitter legacy remained a thing of the past, thankfully.

61. Terry Barringer, "The Drum, the Church, and the Camera: Ham Mukasa and C. W. Hattersley in Uganda," *International Bulletin of Missionary Research* 20, no. 2 (April 1996): 67.

62. Sometimes the bell was a second choice. Charles Domingo wrote to Charles Booth in March 1912 asking for a bell for his church because "the drum which we use in calling people for services, Sabbath School as well as Day School is partly torn and hardly can [produce any] sound at all." Shepperson and Price, *Independent African*, plate 11.

63. Psalms 149:5; 150:1ff.

64. II Samuel 6:14, 16.

65. After initial reservation, Catholic missionaries in East Africa acquired new-found respect and appreciation for African music and dance, and welcomed them in the church. See Shorter, *The Cross and the Flag in Africa*, 158–59.

66. French colonial authorities, for example, debated about whether to promote primal religions to prevent a potent Islam from taking root across the imperial path (even if primal religions conflicted with the French agenda of a progressive social order), or whether to exploit Islam's cosmopolitan potential as a universal faith even though that might foment Pan-Islamic anticolonial sentiment. That characteristic logical clarity only dramatized the problem of the French. It was this secular essentialism that Pius XII criticized as the nemesis that plunged the world into total war in the twentieth century.

CHAPTER 5

1. The resemblance with the discontinuity of the Muslim *Jáhiliyáh* is illusory, for in the Islamic instance it is not the case that the secular, nonreligious state is a necessary or lesser evil; it is a necessary good. See chapter 2 above.

2. Kenneth Scott Latourette, *The History of the Expansion of Christianity* vol. 5, *The Great Century in the Americas, Australasia, and Africa, 1800–1914* (New York and London: Harper & Brothers, 1943, 234.

3. Reported in *The Times* of London, 18 July, 1984.

4. Article 34 of the Articles of Religion of the Anglican Church supports Agbebi on this point. The article states: "It is not necessary that Traditions and Ceremonies be in all places one, or utterly like; for at all times they have been diverse, and may be changed according to the diversities of countries, times, and men's manners, so that nothing be ordained against God's Word." On the BCP in Chinese, for example, see S. I. J. Schereschewsky, *The Bible, Prayer Book, and Terms in Our China Missions* (New York: [1888?]), 6ff. Stephen Neil estimated that the BCP has been translated into more than 200 languages. See Neil, *The Christian Society* (London: Collins, The Fontana Library of Theology and Philosophy), 1952, 135.

5. Rev. Mojola Agbebi, *Inaugural Sermon*, New York, 1903, extract in J. Ayo Langley, ed., *Ideologies of Liberation in Black Africa, 1856–1970* (London: Rex Collings, 1979), 72–77.

6. F. B. Welbourn, *East African Rebels: A Study of Some Independent Churches* (London: SCM, 1961), 201ff.

7. John V. Taylor, *Process of Growth in an African Church*, IMC ("International Missionary Council") Research Pamphlets 6 (London: SCM, 1958), 15f. A striking contrast was the case of the Ugandan John Sentamu who was appointed Archbishop of York in June 2005, a historic first such appointment. Instead of the love and loyalty Taylor speaks of, Sentamu received racist abuse and insults from people who objected to his appointment, with some of the letters containing human excrement. Sentamu ignored the insults.

8. The first evidence of the existence of a Mau Mau underground movement came to light in 1948, with the movement's pledge to rid the country of Europeans. The Mau Mau administered oaths of blood loyalty in secret rituals, drawing on Christian symbolism. The colonial government proscribed it, and Jomo Kenyatta was tried as a Mau Mau leader. See Caroline Elkins, *Imperial Reckoning: The Untold Story of the End of the Empire in Kenya* (New York: Henry Holt, 2005), 31ff. A prominent Mau Mau leader was Gakaara wa Wanjau. Educated at a Presbyterian mission school, he returned embittered as a soldier from World War II, turning henceforth to the nationalist cause. In 1952 he published his *Creed of Gikuyu and Mumbi* in which he joined belief in "God the Almighty, Creator of Heaven and Earth" with faith "in Gikuyu and Mumbi our dear ancestral parents to whom God bequeathed this our land. Their children were persecuted in the era of Cege and Waiyaki by the clan of white people, and they were robbed of their government and their land and relegated to the status of humiliated menials. Their children's children had their eyes opened, they achieved the light of a great awareness, and they fought to restore their parents to their seats of glory." Wanjau concludes his *Creed* with reaffirmation of faith in what he called "the holy religious ceremonies of Gikuyu and Mumbi," in the leadership of Kenyatta, "and the everlastingness of the Gikuyu nation." See Wanjau, *Mau Mau Author in Detention*, 1988, 250.

9. W. M. Eiselen, "Christianity and the Religious Life of the Bantu," in *Western Civilization and the Natives of South Africa*, ed. I. Schapera (London: Routledge, 1934), 76.

10. Sundkler, 1976, 291.

11. Welbourn, *East African Rebels*, 11–12.

12. *For All God's People: Ecumenical Prayer Cycle* (Geneva: World Council of Churches, 1978), 161.

13. Cited in Bengt G. M. Sundkler, *Bantu Prophets in South Africa*. 2nd ed. (London: Oxford University Press for the International African Institute, 1961), 31.

14. James Melvin Washington, *The Origins and Emergence of Black Baptist Separatism, 1863–1897* (Ph.D. diss., Yale University, 1979), 172.

15. Robin Lane Fox, *Pagans and Christians* (San Francisco: HarperSanFrancisco, 1988), 402ff. For a study of dreams in African Christianity, see Nelson Osamu

Hayashida, *Dreams in the African Church: The Significance of Dreams and Visions among Zambian Baptists* (Amsterdam and Atlanta: Editions Rodopi), 1999.

16. See also Richard Carwardine *Trans-atlantic Revivalism, 1790–1865* (Westport, Conn.: Greenwood, 1978), 199.

17. David B. Barrett, *Schism and Renewal in Africa* (Nairobi: Oxford University Press, 1968), chapter 18.

18. Ibid., 169.

19. Kelefa Sanneh, "Pray and Grow Rich," *The New Yorker* (October 11, 2004).

20. Paul Seaver, *The Puritan Lectureships: The Politics of Religious Dissent, 1560–1662* (Stanford, Calif.: Stanford University Press, 1970), 144.

21. Austa Malinda French, *Slavery in South Carolina and the Ex-Slaves; Or, The Port Royal Mission* (New York: Winchell M. French, 1862), 131.

22. Cited in Andrew F. Walls, "A Christian Experiment: The Early Sierra Leone Colony," in *The History of the Church and the Propagation of the Faith, Studies in Church History*, vol. 6, edited by G. J. Cuming (Cambridge: Cambridge University Press, 1970), 119.

23. Cited in Andrew F. Walls, "A Colonial Concordat: Two Views of Christianity and Civilization," in *Church, Society, and Politics*. Vol. 12 of *Studies in Church History*, ed. Derek Baker (Oxford: Blackwell, 1975), 301.

24. John Blassingame, *The Slave Community: Plantation Life in the Antebellum South*, rev. ed. (New York: Oxford University Press, 1979), 145.

25. Anna Maria Falconbridge, *Narrative of Two Voyages to Sierra Leone, during the Years 1791–2–3, in a Series of Letters, &c.* (London, 1794, repr. London: Frank Cass, 1967), 201. A newer edition of the work is available by Christopher Fyfe (Liverpool: Liverpool University Press, 2000).

26. French, *Slavery in South Carolina*, 127.

27. Paul Cuffee, *Cuffe's Logs and Letters: 1808–1817: A Black Quaker's 'Voice from Within the Veil,'* ed. Rosalind Cobb Wiggins (Washington, D.C.: Howard University Press, 1996), 116–17.

28. Grant Gordon, ed., *From Slavery to Freedom: The Life of David George* (Hantsport, N.S.: Lacelot Press for Acadia Divinity College, 1992), 139–41.

29. On the political uses of the Bible in Africa and elsewhere, see Philip Jenkins, *The New Faces of Christianity: Believing the Bible in the Global South* (New York: Oxford University Press, 2006).

30. Edwin W. Smith, *The Shrine of a People's Soul* (London: Livingstone, 1929), 195.

31. Ibid., 195–96.

32. Ibid., 196.

33. Floyd J. Miller, *The Search for a Black Nationality: Black Emigration and Colonization, 1787–1863* (Urbana: University of Illinois Press, 1975), 203.

34. Martin R. Delany and Robert Campbell, *Search for a Place: Black Separatism and Africa* (Ann Arbor: University of Michigan Press, 1969), 112–13.

35. Diedrich Westermann, "The Place and Function of the Vernacular in African Education," *International Review of Mission* (January 1925): 26–27, 28. Defending the

Bible as an instrument of education in the building of moral character, Thomas Huxley protested against its exclusion in schools in England. "By the study of what other book," he asked, "could children be so humanized?" Cited in Edwin W. Smith, *The Shrine of a People's Soul* (London: Livingstone, 1929), 198–99.

36. Smith, ibid., 44.

37. Edwin Smith, *The Golden Stool: Some Aspects of the Conflict of Cultures in Modern Africa* (London: Holborn, 1926), 295, 303.

38. J. H. Oldham, "Educational Policy of the British Government in Africa," *The International Review of Missions* 14 (1925).

39. P. N. C. Molokwu, "Vernacular in Ishan Schools," *The Nigerian Teacher* 1, no. 5 (1935): 53.

40. Abubakar Tafawa-Balewa, "The City of Language," *The Nigerian Teacher* 1, no. 4 (1935): 52.

41. Molokwu, "Vernacular in Ishan Schools," 53–55, 54.

42. Ibid.

43. John Philip, *Researches in South Africa: Illustrating the Civil, Moral, and Religious Condition of the Native Tribes*. 2 vols. (London: James Duncan, 1828), 1:357.

44. Walter R. Miller, *Yesterday and Tomorrow in Northern Nigeria* (London: Student Christian Movement, 1938), 177–78.

45. Philip Woodruff, *The Men Who Ruled India*. 2 vols. (New York: Schocken, 1953), 1:334.

46. Paul E. H. Hair, "Archdeacon Crowther and the Delta Pastorate: 1892–99," *Sierra Leone Bulletin of Religion* 5, no. 1 (June 1963), 23. Emphasis in original.

47. Lamin Sanneh, *Abolitionists Abroad: American Blacks and the Making of Modern Africa* (Cambridge, Mass.: Harvard University Press, 1999), 126–29, 139–81.

CHAPTER 6

1. J. D. Y. Peel, *Aladura: A Religious Movement among the Yoruba* (London: Oxford University Press for the International African Institute, 1968), 95.

2. Cited in J. D. Y. Peel, " 'For Who Hath Despised the Day of Small Things?' Missionary Narratives and Historical Anthropology," *Comparative Study of Society and History* 37, no. 3 (July 1995): 603.

3. See E. Adeolu Adegbola, "The Church of the Middle Class Elite," in *Christianity and Socio-political Order in Nigeria*, ed. S. A. Adewale (Ibadan: Nigerian Association for Christian Studies, 1987).

4. "The weakening of the old order is symbolized in the story of how there was a gentle oracular spirit who lived in the forest by Efon, where she looked after the wild creatures and answered people's queries; in 1927 she told Alajedare, the Alaye [chief], that 'her pot of indigo dye had been broken by the new road, and that she was leaving Efon to return no more'—so the old gods were leaving as the new order advanced." See Peel, *Aladura*, 94.

5. 1 Kings 18:20ff.

6. Godwin Tasie, *Christian Missionary Enterprise in the Niger Delta: 1864–1918* (Leiden: Brill 1978), 193ff.

7. Peel, *Aladura*, 91.

8. Ibid., 91–2.

9. The Southern Baptist Theological Seminary issued a statement in 2007 barring professors and administrators from endorsing charismatic practices, proof of the continuing Protestant opposition to charismatic religion.

10. Bradley P. Holt, "Healing in the Charismatic Movement: The Catholics in Nigeria," *Religions* 2, no. 2 (December 1977): 38–58.

11. Cited in J. D. Hargreaves, *France and West Africa: An Anthology of Historical Documents* (London: Macmillan, 1969), 249–50.

12. Ibid., 251.

13. Cited in Sheila S. Walker, *The Religious Revolution in the Ivory Coast: The Prophet Harris and the Harrist Church* (Chapel Hill: University of North Carolina Press, 1983), 57.

14. David Shank, *Prophet Harris, "The Black Elijah" of West Africa* (Leiden: Brill, 1994), 255.

15. Gordon MacKay Haliburton, *The Prophet Harris: A Study of an African Prophet and His Mass-Movement in the Ivory Coast and the Gold Coast 1913–1915* (London: Longman, 1971), 177.

16. Louvain was not the last or only example of such cultural blindness. When I returned to Yale Divinity School in 2005 after a sabbatical leave, I discovered that my course on World Christianity had been reassigned to a different place in the curriculum called "Non-Christian Religions."

17. David A. Shank, "The Taming of the Prophet Harris," *Journal of Religion in Africa* 27, no. 1 (February 1997), 72ff.

18. William J. Platt, *From Fetish to Faith: The Growth of the Church in West Africa* (London: Cargate 1935), 87.

19. Platt, *From Fetish to Faith*, 87–88; Haliburton, *The Prophet Harris*, 177.

20. Charles W. Armstrong, *The Winning of West Africa* (London: Wesleyan Methodist Missionary Society, 1920), 39–40. Armstrong was stationed on the Gold Coast, now Ghana. For the effects of the Harris movement on Ghana, see Christian G. Baëta, *Prophetism in Ghana: A Study of Some "Spiritual" Churches* (London: SCM, 1962).

21. William Maude cited in Barbara Prickett, *Island Base: A History of the Methodist Church in the Gambia, 1821–1969* (Bo, Sierra Leone: Bunumbu 1971), 164–65.

22. J. D. Y. Peel, *Religious Encounter and the Making of the Yoruba* (Bloomington: Indiana University Press, 2000), 128.

23. *The Foreign Field*, 1920. Cited in James R. Krabill, *The Hymnody of the Harrist Church among the Dida of South-Central Ivory Coast (1913–1949)* (Frankfurt: Peter Lang, 1995), 273.

24. *The Foreign Field* (September 1922). Cited in Krabill, *The Hymnody of the Harrist Church*, 274.

25. Cited in Haliburton, *The Prophet Harris*, 177.

26. Ibid., 180.

27. Cited in Jeremy Murray-Brown, *Kenyatta* (London: Allen & Unwin, 1972), 61.

28. Richard Burton, *Wanderings in West Africa*, 2 vols. (New York: Dover, 1952), 2:48.

29. Burton, *Wanderings in West Africa*, 1:217; 2:72–3. The phrase "pejorative singular" occurs in O'Brien, *To Katanga and Back* (New York: Grosset and Dunlap, 1966), 161.

30. Jeff Guy, *The Heretic: A Study of the Life of John William Colenso, 1814–1883* (Pietermaritzburg: University of Natal Press, 1983), 299.

31. Ibid.

32. Cited in Krabill, *The Hymnody of the Harris Church*, 275–76.

33. Haliburton, *The Prophet Harris*, 176.

34. Walker, *The Religious Revolution in the Ivory Coast*, 40.

35. Ibid.

36. Andrew F. Walls, "The Significance of Christianity in Africa," Church of Scotland (Edinburgh: St. Colin's Education Centre and College, 1989), 18.

37. "*Ainsi, en cas de lutte contre telle ou telle maladie, ils écrasaient d'abord les feuilles, les écorces ou les racines des plantes susceptibles de guérir le malade avant de les lui confier pour le traitement. De cette manière, le malade ne pouvait jamais connaitre l'origine de cette plante, et se trouvait dans l'obligation de se confier à son féticheur une autre fois.*" Alphone Boyé Aké, *Le Harriste Face a sa Religion* (Abidjan,1980), 7.

38. Edwin W. Smith, *The Shrine of a People's Soul* (London: Livingstone 1929), 193.

39. Walker, *The Religious Revolution in the Ivory Coast*, 168.

40. Armstrong, *The Winning of West Africa*, 41.

41. Proverbs 26:13.

42. Rom 5:12.

43. Opoku Onyinah, *Ancestral Curses* (Accra, Ghana: International Missions Office, 1994), 27.

44. Matthew 12:37. This verse echoes another one: "The righteous one shall live by his fidelity" (Hb 2:4).

45. John 9

46. Onyinah, *Ancestral Curses*, 37.

47. Gal 3:13–14.

48. Opoku Onyinah, *Overcoming Demons* (Accra, Ghana: Pentecostal Press International Missions Office, 1995).

49. E. Bolaji-Idowu, *Olodumare: God in Yoruba Belief* (London: Longmans, 1962), 209.

50. Aylward Shorter, *The Cross and the Flag in Africa: The "White Fathers" during the Colonial Scramble, 1892–1914* (Maryknoll, N.Y.: Orbis, 2006), 157.

51. *Premier Livret de l'Education Religieuse a l'usage des Missions Harristes* (Petit-Bassam August 1956), 10.

52. In this respect, the tragedy of the 1994 Rwanda genocide still defies explanation. Perhaps the failure to develop a post-Western idiom in the form of a distinc-

tively African Christian movement allowed the introduction of Christianity to proceed along official lines of political and economic stratification. In that way, civilization got in the way of the gospel, and also in the way of African-directed transformation of ethnic identity. It happens that the warring Tutsi and Hutu share the same culture and language, their differentiation being the result of Belgian policy in the 1920s to favor the taller, cattle-owning Tutsi over the stockier, peasant Hutu cultivators. The height criterion gave Tutsi access to education while excluding the Hutu. Social stratification reinforced invidious distinctions, as did official Christianity's dogma that it was entitled to reproduce itself in its European forms among non-European races. Africans could not engage or confront themselves as Africans in someone else's idiom. This left few safeguards in Rwanda against the politics of suspicion, retribution, and getting even. For a field report on the genocide see Nancy Gibbs, "The Killing Fields of Rwanda," *Time*, May 16, 1994.

CHAPTER 7

1. Noël Mostert, *Frontiers: The Epic of South Africa's Creation and the Tragedy of the Xhosa People* (London: Jonathan Cape, 1992; repr. London: Pimlico, 1993), 955.

2. Many prayers in the pre-Ch'in Dynasty China (221–207 BC) take up the subject of sin, but only in terms of making restitution. Of this, Mo Tzu (fl. fifth–fourth centuries BC) said:

> I do not know if I have sinned against the deities of the upper and lower worlds. The good man I dare not keep in obscurity, the sinner I dare not pardon. The examination of them is by Thy mind, O God. If the people of the myriad regions committed offences, let these offences rest on my person. If I, in my person, have committed offences, let them not be attributed to the people of the myriad regions.

See Bartholomew P. M. Tsui, "Ancient Chinese Prayers: A Collection," *Ching Feng: Quarterly Notes on Christianity and Chinese Religion and Culture* 19, nos. 3 and 4 (1976): 59. Mo Tzu's defense of the cause of the common people evokes the spirit of Amos.

3. Cited in Roland Allen, *The Spontaneous Expansion of the Church and the Causes Which Hinder It* (London: World Dominion, 1927), 179.

4. Ibid., 171–95.

5. David M. Paton, ed., *The Ministry of the Spirit: Selected Writings of Roland Allen* (London: World Dominion, 1960), 178.

6. Ibid, 179.

7. Roland Allen, *Missionary Methods: St Paul's or Ours?* (London: World Dominion, 1912; repr. 1927), 78.

8. Paton, ed., *Ministry of the Spirit*, 180.

9. Conor Cruise O'Brien, *To Katanga and Back*, 1966, 165.

10. Roland Allen, *Spontaneous Expansion*, 1927, 110.

11. Ibid., 119.

12. Cited in ibid., 134–35.

13. Ibid., 142.

14. Paton, ed., *Ministry of the Spirit*, 194.

15. Geoffrey Allen, *The Theology of Missions* (London: Student Christian Movement, 1943), 70.

16. Roland Allen, *Missionary Methods*, 5.

17. Paton, ed., *Ministry of the Spirit*, 57.

18. Ibid., xvi.

19. For a study of the Three-Self Movement see Philip L. Wickeri, *Seeking Common Ground: Protestant Christianity, the Three-Self Movement, and China's United Front* (Maryknoll, N.Y.: Orbis, 1988).

20. Roland Allen, introduction to *The Indigenous Church*, by Sidney J. W. Clark (London: World Dominion, 1928), 8.

21. I use throughout the standard form "Maasai" rather than the archaic "Masai" of Donovan's book.

22. Vincent Donovan, *Christianity Rediscovered* (Maryknoll, N.Y.: Orbis, 1978; rev. ed., 2003), 25

23. Cited in ibid., 7.

24. Ibid., 28.

25. Ibid., 10–11, 47–48.

26. Ibid., 13. Paul V. Kollman regards Donovan's view as too harsh. See Kollman, *The Evangelization of Slaves and Catholic Origins in Eastern Africa* (Maryknoll, N.Y.: Orbis, 2005).

27. Donovan, *Christianity Rediscovered*, 92ff.

28. Ibid., 43.

29. Ibid.

30. Ibid., 126–29.

31. Ibid., 23.

32. Ibid., 82. In this regard, Pope Benedict XVI affirms that view of the subject. "Nobody is born a Christian, not even in a Christian world and of Christian parents. Being Christian can only ever happen as a new birth." See Joseph Ratzinger (Pope Benedict XVI), *Truth and Tolerance: Christian Belief and World Religions* (San Francisco: Ignatius, 2004), 87.

33. Donovan, *Christianity Rediscovered*, 48.

34. Ibid., 87.

35. Ibid., 33.

36. Ibid., 82.

37. Ibid., 121.

38. Vincent Donovan, "Response to Reflections on *Christianity Rediscovered*," *Missiology: An International Review* 18, no. 3 (July 1990): 276–78, 277.

39. Dorothy L. Hodgson, *The Church of Women: Gendered Encounters between Maasai and Missionaries* (Bloomington: Indiana University Press, 2005), 180.

40. In his assessment of Demosthenes' oratory, Plutarch described it as being contrived for real effect and seriousness, "not smelling of the lamp," meaning not designed, like Cicero's, for the partisan disadvantage of his antagonists. See *Plutarch's Lives*, vol. II 2001, 2:442

CHAPTER 8

1. "The Churches and China," 20.

2. "The Churches and China," 20. Italics in the original source.

3. Cited in C. R. Boxer, *The Portuguese Seaborn Empire, 1415–1825* (London: Hutchinson & Co., 1969; repr. 1977), 242.

4. Philip Wilson Pitcher, *In and About Amoy* (Shanghai and Foochow: Methodist Publishing House, 1909).

5. Roland Allen, described in a previous chapter, was an eyewitness of the Boxer Uprising, which he described in his *The Siege of the Peking Legations, Being the Diary of the Rev. Roland Allen, with Maps and Plans* (London: Smith, Elder, 1901).

6. C. P. Fitzgerald, *The Birth of Communist China* (Baltimore: Penguin, 1964), 126.

7. Dennis R. Janz, *World Christianity and Marxism* (New York: Oxford University Press, 1998), 128. This part of the interview was omitted in Fremantle's anthology of Mao's writings.

8. Anthony S. K. Lam, *The Catholic Church in Present-Day China through Darkness and Light* (Hong Kong: The Holy Spirit Study Center, 1997), 34–5.

9. Mao, "On Practice," Anne Fremantle, *Mao Tse-tung: An Anthology of His Writings* (New York: Mentor, 1962), 212.

10. "A Christian Perspective on the Chinese Experience," *Anticipation* (Geneva) (August 1973), 24, 28, 29. Also in "China and the Churches in the Making of One World," *Pro Mundi Vita* 55 (1975): 16–7.

11. "China and the Churches," 21.

12. Ibid., 15.

13. "The Louvain Consultation" adopted Mao's teaching that "human nature is class-determined, and it is only after exploitation and class oppression have been overcome that a common nature and universal love will be possible." Mao was correct in saying that "policies and actions cannot be based on the assumption of a common human nature as a present reality." Mao's teaching of hating the enemy was not a contradiction of Christian teaching about loving those who hate you. "Animosity is that which gives a dynamic or animating element to love. To love means to be animated and enlivened for struggle against all that which is opposed to love and genuine human community," p. 24.

14. "China and the Churches," 9.

15. This view was echoed in the opinions of such Protestant theologians as K. H. Ting; Y. T. Wu, the American; Randolph Sailer, the British theologian and colleague of Roland Allen; David Paton; and the Canadians Edward Johnson and James

G. Endicott. Philip L. Wickeri, *Seeking Common Ground: Protestant Christianity, the Three-Self Movement, and China's United Front* (Maryknoll, N.Y.: Orbis, 1988), 7ff. While recognizing the Chinese Communist revolution as the watershed that it was, Newbigin felt there was much in the theological rethinking that was not sufficiently profound.

16. "The Louvain Consultation," 24–5.

17. Janz, *World Christianity and Marxism*, 140.

18. In his book, *The Victory of Reason: How Christianity Led to Freedom, Capitalism, and Western Success* (New York: Random House, 2005), Rodney Stark sounds a note of confidence that stands in striking contrast to this pessimism. For a critical review of the book, see Mark C. Henrie, *Commentary* (July–August 2006).

19. "The Louvain Consultation, 23–4.

20. "China and the Churches," 3.

21. Ibid., 11. The phrase is adapted from G. K. Chesterton who meant something entirely different by it. Christianity had had five deaths by his time, he said, and "risen again" because "it had a god who knew the way out of the grave." See Chesterton, *The Everlasting Man*, chapter 6, "The Five Deaths of the Faith" (London: Hodder & Stoughton, 1953).

22. "The Louvain Consultation," 27.

23. Ibid., 29.

24. The tide seems to have taken a decisive turn when new history textbooks in China skimped on any mention of the communist revolution, including socialism. Only a single sentence is devoted to the Communist Revolution in China before the 1979 reforms. As for Mao, he is mentioned only once in a chapter on etiquette. "Nearly overnight the country's most prosperous schools have shelved the Marxist template that had dominated standard history texts since the 1950s." The changes are part of a broader effort to present a more stable and less violent view of Chinese history, a view that serves the country's economic and political goals. "Where's Mao? Chinese Revise History Books," *New York Times*, September 1, 2006.

25. "The Catholic Church in the People's Republic of China," *Pro Mundi Vita Studies* 15 (June 1990): 13–4.

26. Erik Burklin, "The Greatest Need in the Chinese Church: The China Christian Council Confronts the Task of Theological education," *ChinaSource* 5, no. 1, (Spring 2003): 8–9.

27. David Aikman, *Jesus in Beijing: How Christianity Is Transforming China and Changing the Global Balance of Power* (Washington, D.C.: Regnery, 2003), 70.

28. Janz, *World Christianity and Marxism*, 145–46.

29. "China and the Churches," 19–20.

30. Religious scholars were not the only ones to have been seduced by events in China of the 1970s. Secular pundits were equally ebullient about the new utopia set to unfold in China. The magazine, *Mother Jones*—advertising itself as the standard bearer of "smart, fearless journalism"—carried a report in its issue of February/March 1979 to the effect that the People's Republic of China was "on the verge of breaking into industrial statehood in a big way" and to become "the world's first post-petroleum

culture." The report said that the likelihood of Shanghai becoming the Detroit of the Far East was remote. Richard Parker, "The First Post-Oil Society?" *Mother Jones* (February/March 1979).

31. Confronted with the Falun Gongg incident of 1999, the government tightened its surveillance of religious groups under an edict called "Office 610," promulgated to combat what the government called "evil cults."

32. Janz, *World Christianity and Marxism*, 144.

33. Aikman, *Jesus in Beijing*, 219.

34. Jim Yardley and Keith Bradsher, "A Bitter Game: Beijing Battles with Vatican," *New York Times*, May 13, 2006.

35. Janz, *World Christianity and Marxism*, 145.

36. Ibid.

37. "The Louvain Consultation," 30.

38. "China and the Churches," 24.

39. "The Louvain Consultation," Appendix: Contemporary Church, Contemporary China by Herbert Dargan, *Pro Mundi Vita*, 54, 1975, 37.

40. *Global Catholicism: Portrait of a World Church*, 178–80.

41. For the sake of comparison, the same source gives 19 million Christians in South Korea, 62.3 million in India, and 27.8 million in Indonesia. See *World Christian Encyclopedia*, 2nd ed. (New York: Oxford University Press, 2001).

42. *Faith Fortnightly*, April 15, 2005.

43. In a congratulatory letter to the new pope, Anthony Li Du'an, bishop of Xi'an diocese, spoke of his confidence in the work of the church in China. Reported in the Italian Catholic journal, *30 Days* [www.30giorni.it].

44. *Hong Kong Sunday Examiner*, November 2005.

45. *China Church Quarterly* (Summer 2006): 6.

46. Jiang formally relinquished power at the Party Congress convened from November 7–15, 2002, when he was succeeded by Hu Jintao.

47. Todd M. Johnson and Sandra S. Kim, "The Changing Demographics of World Christianity," *World Christian Database* (www.worldchristiandatabase.org), 2006.

48. Daniel H. Bays, "Chinese Protestant Christianity Today," *The China Quarterly* 174 (June 2003): 491.

49. "[Chinese] Bishops Visit Europe," *China Church Quarterly*, no. 61 (Winter 2005).

50. David Aikman, "Chinese Christianity: Turning the Nation Around," *China-Source* 5, no. 1 (Spring 2003): 1–4, and *Jesus in Beijing*, 285ff.

51. Carol Lee Hamrin, "History, Myth and Missions," *ChinaSource* 5, no. 4 (Winter 2003): 4.

52. Thomas Allen Harvey, *Acquainted With Grief* (Grand Rapids, Mich.:, 2002), 159.

53. The Christian outcome in China may be more complex, according to Choan-Seng Song (1990), who speaks of "the cross in the lotus world," indicating thereby the importance of the perennial Buddhist tradition. See C.S. Song.

54. *Hong Kong Sunday Examiner*, November 2005. See also Betty Ann Maheu, "The Catholic Church in China," *America* 193, no. 14 (November 7, 2005).

55. Paul Elie, "The Year of Two Popes: How 'Mr. Inside' Stepped into the Shoes of 'Mr. Outside,' and What it Means for the Catholic Church," *The Atlantic* (January/ February 2006).

56. Cited in *China Church Quarterly*, no. 65 (Winter 2006).

57. Kim-kwang Chan, "Missiological Implications of Chinese Christianity in a Globalized Context," *Quest: An Interdisciplinary Journal for Asian Christian Scholars* 4, no. 2 (November 2005): 55–74; also the same author's "Chinese Christianity and Global Mission," *ChinaSource* 8, no.1 (Spring 2006): 4–6.

58. *Acta Apostolicae Sedis* 20 (1928), 245.

59. In his encyclical *Rerum Ecclesiae* of February 28, 1926, Pius XI issued instruments for the creation of an African clergy. For example, in 1928 St. Augustine's Training College was established in Ghana to train candidates for the priesthood. After the completion of the construction project in 1930, enrollment was expanded.

60. Jung Chang and Jon Halliday, *Mao: The Unknown Story* (New York: Knopf, 2005).

61. "China and the Churches," 24.

62. Bays, "Chinese Protestant Christianity Today," 492.

63. Ronald A. Knox, *On Englishing the Bible* (London: Burns Oates, 1949), 15. The allusion is to Mt 11:16–7.

64. Tertullian, *Apologia*, chap. xxxi, page 46.

65. Huo Shui, "View from the Wall: China, the Greatest Christian Nation in the World?" *ChinaSource* 5, no. 4 (Winter 2003): 10.

66. John King Fairbank, *The United States and China* (Cambridge, Mass.: Harvard University Press, 1983), xvii.

CONCLUSION

1. On the SVM, see Nathan Showalter, *End of a Crusade: The Student Volunteer Movement for Foreign Missions and the Great War* (Lanham, Md.: Scarecrow, 1998).

2. Kenneth Ross, "The Centenary of Edinburgh 1910: Its Possibilities," *International Bulletin of Missionary Research* 30, no. 4 (October 2006): 177.

3. On Azariah, see Susan Billington Harper, *In the Shadow of the Mahatma: Bishop V. S. Azariah and the Travails of Christianity in British India* (Grand Rapids, Mich.: Eerdmans, 2000).

4. Hugh Vernon White, "End Missions Imperialism Now!" *The Christian Century*, February 14, 1934. White was an official of the American Board of Commissioners for Foreign Missions.

5. See, in this regard, Arend van Leeuwen's influential work, *Christianity in World History* (London: Edinburgh House Press, 1964).

6. *The Church for Others*, 20–23.

7. R. Elliott Kendall, *End of an Era: Africa and the Missionary* (London: SPCK, 1978).

8. David B. Barrett, George T. Kurian, and Todd M. Johnson, eds. *World Christian Encyclopedia: A Comparative Survey of Churches and Religions in the Modern World*, 2nd ed. (Oxford and New York: Oxford University Press, 2001), 1:12ff.

9. *Encyclopaedia Britannica World Data*, 1992.

10. Daniel H. Bays, "Indigenous Protestant Churches in China, 1900–1937: A Pentecostal Case Study," in *Indigenous Responses to Western Christianity*, ed. Steven Kaplan (New York: New York University Press, 1995).

11. David Martin, *Tongues of Fire: The Explosion of Protestantism in Latin America* (Oxford: Blackwell, 1990). See also Paul Freston, Evangelicals and Politics in Asia, Africa and Latin America (Cambridge: Cambridge University Press, 2001).

12. Barrett, Kurian, and Johnson, eds., *World Christian Encyclopedia*, 1:191–98; Stanley M. Burgess and Eduard M. Van Der Maas, eds., *The New International Dictionary of Pentecostal and Charismatic Movements*, rev. and exp. (Grand Rapids, Mich.: Zondervan, 2003), 286ff.

13. See leader article in *The Economist*, "In the World of Good and Evil," September 16–22, 2006; on U.S. evangelical missions abroad, see Steve Brouwer, Paul Gifford, and Susan D. Rose, eds., *Exporting the American Gospel: Global Christian Fundamentalism* (New York: Routledge, 1996); Paul Gifford, ed., *Christian Churches and the Democratization of Africa* (Leiden: Brill, 1995); Paul Gifford, *African Christianity: Its Public Role* (London: Hurst, 1998); and Paul Gifford, *Ghana's New Christianity: Pentecostalism in a Globalizing African Economy* (London: Hurst, 2004). A *New York Times* ([January 14, 2007], 33) report observed that the Pentecostal groups are "natural allies for the Republican Party, which has courted Latino Pentecostals . . . with government grants for churches that run 'faith-based' social services."

14. David Gonzalez, "A Sliver of a New York Storefront, and a Faith on the Rise," *New York Times*, January 14, 2007, 33.

15. "China and the Churches in the Making of One World," *Pro Mundi Vita* 55 (1975), 20.

16. Maura Brown, ed., *The African Synod: Documents, Reflections, Perspectives* (Maryknoll, N.Y.: Orbis, 1996).

17. Vincent Donovan, *Christianity Rediscovered* (Maryknoll, N.Y.: Orbis, 1978; rev. ed., 2003), 97.

18. Chandra Mallampalli, *Christians and Public Life in Colonial South India, 1863–1937: Contending with Marginality* (London and New York: Routledge Curzon, 2004).

19. On the church in Angola see W. Henderson, *The Church in Angola: A River of Many Currents* (Cleveland, Ohio: The Pilgrim Press, 1992). For Mozambique see Jan van Butselaar, "The Role of Churches in the Peace Process in Africa; The Case of Mozambique Compared," chapter in Lamin Sanneh and Joel A. Carpenter, editors, *The Changing Face of Christianity: Africa, the West, and the World* (New York: Oxford University Press, 2005).

20. Haile Mariam Larebo, "The Orthodox Church and the State in the Ethiopian Revolution, 1974–84," *Religion in Communist Countries* 14, no. 2 (1986): 155ff.

21. Ricardo Orizio, "The Lion Sleeps Tonight," an interview with Mengistu Haile Mariam. Translated from the Italian by Avril Bardoni. *Transition* 11, issue 89. For a Muslim point of view, see Hussein Ahmed, "Coexistence and/or Confrontation? Towards a Reappraisal of Christian-Muslim Encounter in Contemporary Ethiopia," *Journal of Religion in Africa* 36, no. 1 (2006).

22. Philip Jenkins, *The Next Christendom: The Coming of Global Christianity* (New York: Oxford University Press, 2002).

23. The clergyman in question, Chao Fu-san, said that Christian Chinese were twice victims of history: "We did not weep with them that wept in [the] old China, neither do we now rejoice with them that rejoice in the new. We seem to have become pitiful strangers in our own country and among our own people." See "China and the Churches in the Making of One World," *Pro Mundi Vita* 55 (1975): 14.

24. Foreseeing a time when missions no longer dominated the field, Edwin Smith wrote: "The foreign mission is not a permanent institution; it will pass away, even as it ceased to be in our own land; the Church remains. . . . The Church in China, for example, will one day be as independent of the Church in England as the English Church is of the Chinese." See Edwin Smith, *The Shrine of a People's Soul* (London: Livingstone, 1929), 201.

25. Bengt Sundkler and Christopher Steed, *A History of the Church in Africa* (Cambridge: Cambridge University Press, 2000), 1013.

26. Donovan, *Christianity Rediscovered*, 110.

27. Ibid., 109.

28. Ibid., 114.

29. Sundkler and Steed, *A History of the Church in Africa*, 1014.

30. Ibid., 1016.

31. John W. Coakley and Andrea Sterk, eds., *Readings in World Christian History*, vol. 1: *Earliest Christianity to 1453* (Maryknoll, N.Y.: Orbis 2004), 1:308.

32. Betty Ann Maheu, "The Catholic Church in China," *America* 193, no. 14 (November 7, 2005): 11.

33. David B. Barrett, *Schism and Renewal in Africa* (Nairobi: Oxford University Press, 1968), 260–61.

Select Bibliography

Abulafia, David. *Frederick II: A Medieval Emperor*. London: Penguin, 1988; repr. London: Pimlico, 1992.

Aburish, S. *The Forgotten Faithful: The Christians of the Holy Land*. London, 1993.

Acta Apostolicae Sedis 20, 1928.

Adam, James. *Religious Teachers of Greece, Being the Gifford Lectures on Natural Religion Delivered at Aberdeen*. Edinburgh: T. & T. Clark, 1908.

Adegbola, E. Adeolu. "The Church of the Middle Class Elite." In *Christianity and Socio-political Order in Nigeria*, ed. S. A. Adewale. Ibadan: Nigerian Association for Christian Studies, 1987.

Ahmad, Aziz. *A History of Islamic Sicily*. Edinburgh: Edinburgh University Press, 1975.

Ahmed, Hussein. "Coexistence and/or Confrontation? Towards a Reappraisal of Christian-Muslim Encounter in Contemporary Ethiopia," *Journal of Religion in Africa* 36, no. 1 (2006).

Aikman, David. "Chinese Christianity: Turning the Nation Around," *ChinaSource* 5, no. 1 (Spring 2003).

———. *Jesus in Beijing: How Christianity Is Transforming China and Changing the Global Balance of Power*. Washington, D.C.: Regnery, 2003.

Ajami, Fouad. *The Foreigner's Gift: The Americans, the Arabs, and the Iraqis in Iraq*. New York: Free, 2006.

Aké, Alphone Boyé. *Le Harriste Face a sa Religion*. Abidjan, 1980.

Ali, Ameer. *The Spirit of Islam: A History of the Evolution and Ideals of Islam, with a Life of the Prophet*. London: Chatto & Windus, 1964.

Allen, Geoffrey. *The Theology of Missions*. London: Student Christian Movement, 1943.

Allen, Roland. *Missionary Methods: St Paul's or Ours?* London: World Dominion, 1912; repr. 1927.

———. *Essential Missionary Principles.* New York: Fleming H. Revell, 1913.

———. "Introduction." In *The Indigenous Church,* by Sidney J. W. Clark. London: World Dominion, 1928.

———. *The Spontaneous Expansion of the Church and the Causes Which Hinder It.* London: World Dominion, 1927.

Alton, Lord David. "Roman Catholic Responses to Religious Persecution," *Review of Faith and International Affairs* 3, no. 3 (Winter 2005–2006).

Anstey, Roger. *The Atlantic Slave Trade and British Abolition: 1760–1810.* Atlantic Highlands, N.J.: Humanities, 1975; and London: Macmillan, 1975.

Arberry, A. J. ed., *Aspects of Islamic Civilization: As Depicted in the Original Texts.* London: Allen & Unwin, 1964; repr. Ann Arbor: University of Michigan Press, 1967.

Armstrong, Charles W. *The Winning of West Africa.* London: Wesleyan Methodist Missionary Society, 1920.

Asamoah-Gyadu, J. Kwabena. "African Initiated Christianity in Eastern Europe: Church of the 'Embassy of God' in Ukraine. *International Bulletin of Missionary Research* 30, no. 2 (April 2006).

Athanasius of Alexandria. *The Life of Antony (The Coptic Life and the Greek Life),* trans. Tin Vivian and Apostolos N. Athanassakis. Kalamazoo, Mich.: Cistercian, 2003.

Averroës (Ibn Rushd). *Middle Commentary on Aristotle's 'De anima,'* ed. and trans. Alfred L. Ivry. Provo, Utah: Brigham Young University Press, 2002.

Avineri, Shlomo. *The Social and Political Thought of Karl Marx.* London: Cambridge University Press, 1968.

Ayalon, David. "The Historian al-Jabartí." In *Historians of the Middle East,* edited by Bernard Lewis and P. M. Holt. London: Oxford University Press, 1962.

Baba, Ahmad. *Mi'ráj al-Su'úd: Ahmad Baba's Replies on Slavery,* ed. and trans. John Hunwick and Fatima Harrak. Rabat: Institute of African Studies, University Mohammed V, 2000.

Babinger, Franz. *Mehmed the Conqueror and His Time,* ed. William C. Hickman. Translated from the German by Ralph Manheim. Princeton, N.J.: Bolingen Series 96 of Princeton University Press, 1978.

Babur, Emperor. *The Baburnama: Memoirs of Babur, Prince and Emperor,* ed. and trans. Wheeler M. Thackston. New York: Modern Library, 2002.

Badger, G. P. *The Nestorians and their Rituals.* 2 vols.: London: J. Masters, 1852.

Baëta, Christian G. *Prophetism in Ghana: A Study of Some "Spiritual" Churches.* London: SCM, 1962.

Barbour, Hugh. *Ts'ai Yung-ch'un's Life and Work: Fully Chinese and Fully Christian.* New Haven, Conn.: Yale Divinity School Library, 2000.

Barker, Ernest, ed. and trans. *Social and Political Thought in Byzantium: From Justinian I to the Last Palaeologus: Passages from Byzantine Writers and Documents.* Oxford: Clarendon, 1961.

Barley, M. W., and R. P. C. Hanson, eds. *Christianity in Britain, 300–700: Papers Presented to the Conference on Christianity in Roman and Sub-Roman Britain, Held at the University of Nottingham, 17–20 April, 1967*. Leicester: Leicester University Press, 1968.

Barnes, Hugh. *Gannibal: The Moor of Petersburg*. London: Profile, 2005.

Barrett, David B. *Schism and Renewal in Africa*. Nairobi: Oxford University Press, 1968.

Barrett, David B., George T. Kurian, and Todd M. Johnson, eds. *World Christian Encyclopedia: A Comparative Survey of Churches and Religions in the Modern World*, 2nd ed. 2 vols. Oxford and New York: Oxford University Press, 2001.

Barringer, Terry. "The Drum, the Church, and the Camera: Ham Mukasa and C. W. Hattersley in Uganda," *International Bulletin of Missionary Research* 20, no. 2 (April 1996).

Baur, John. *2000 Years of Christianity in Africa: An African History, 62–1992*, Nairobi: Paulines Publications of Africa, 1994.

Bays, Daniel H. "Indigenous Protestant Churches in China, 1900–1937: A Pentecostal Case Study," In *Indigenous Responses to Western Christianity*, edited by Steven Kaplan. New York: New York University Press, 1995.

———, ed. *Christianity in China: From the Eighteenth Century to the Present*, Stanford: Stanford University Press, 1996.

———. "Chinese Protestant Christianity Today," *The China Quarterly* 174 (June 2003).

Beard, Mary, and Michael Crawford. *Rome in the Late Republic: Problems and Interpretations*. Ithaca, N.Y.: Cornell University Press, 1985.

Beard, Mary, John North, and Simon Price. *Religions of Rome*. Vol. 1, *A History*; Vol. 2, *A Sourcebook*. Cambridge: Cambridge University Press, 1998.

Becken, Hans-Jürgen, Irving Hexam, and G. C. Oosthuizen, trand. and ed. *The Story of Isaiah Shembe: History and Traditions Centered on Ekuphahameni and Mount Nhlangakazi*. Lewiston, N.Y.: Mellen 1996.

Bede. *Ecclesiastical History of the English People*, trans. Leo Sherley-Price. Harmondsworth: Penguin, 1955; repr. 1984.

Bedoyere, Guy de la, *Roman Britain: A New History*, London: Thames and Hudson, 2006.

Bell, Richard. *The Origin of Islam in Its Christian Environment: The Gunning Lectures, Edinburgh University*, 1925. London: Frank Cass, 1968.

Bennett, Herman L. *Africans in Colonial Mexico: Absolutism, Christianity, and Afro-Creole Consciousness, 1570–1640*. Bloomington: Indiana University Press, 2003.

Benezet, Anthony. *Some historical account of Guinea: its situation, produce, and the general disposition of its inhabitants: with an inquiry into the rise and progress of the slave trade, its nature, and lamentable effects*, London: J. Phillips, 1788.

Berliner, A. "Zur Ehrenrettung des Maimonides." In *Moses ben Maimon: sein Leben, seine Werke und sein Einfluss Zur Erinnerung an den siebenhundertsten Todestag des Maimonides*. 2 vols. Leipzig: 1914.

Birúní, Muhammad al-. *Alberuni's India*, ed. and trans. Edward C. Sachau. 2 vols. London: Kegan Paul, Trench, Truner, 1910.

Blassingame, John. *The Slave Community: Plantation Life in the Antebellum South*, rev. ed. New York: Oxford University Press, 1979.

Blyden, E. W. *The Return of the Exiles and the West African Church*, London: W. B. Whittingham, 1891.

Bodde, Derk. *Peking Diary: 1948–1949: A Year of Revolution*. New York: Fawcett World Library, 1967.

Bolaji-Idowu, E. *Olodumare: God in Yoruba Belief*. London: Longmans, 1962.

Boswell, John. *The Kindness of Strangers*. New York: Pantheon, 1988.

Bovill, E. W. *The Golden Trade of the Moors*, 2nd ed. London: Oxford University Press, 1968.

Boxer, C. R., ed. *South China in the Sixteenth Century*. London: Hakluyt Society, 1953.

––––––. *The Portuguese Seaborne Empire, 1415–1825*. London: Hutchinson & Co., 1977.

Bredero, Adriaan H. *Christendom and Christianity in the Middle Ages*. Grand Rapids, Mich.: Eerdmans, 1994.

Encyclopaedia Britannica World Data, 1992.

Brock, S. P. "The 'Nestorian' Church: A Lamentable Misnomer," *Bulletin of the John Rylands Library of Manchester*, no. 3 (Autumn 1996).

Brockelmann, Carl. *History of the Islamic Peoples*. New York: Capricorn, 1960; German edition: Munich, 1939.

Brouwer, Steve, Paul Gifford, and Susan D. Rose, eds. *Exporting the American Gospel: Global Christian Fundamentalism* New York: Routledge, 1996.

Brown, Maura, ed., *The African Synod: Documents, Reflections, Perspectives*. Maryknoll, N.Y.: Orbis, 1996.

Brown, Peter. *The World of Late Antiquity: AD 150–750*. New York: Norton, 1971.

––––––. *The Rise of Western Christendom: Triumph and Diversity, A.D. 200–1000*, 2nd ed. Oxford: Blackwell, 2003.

Browne, E. G. *Literary History of Persia*. 3 vols. Cambridge: Cambridge University Press, 1929.

Bruce, F. F. *Paul: Apostle of the Heart*. London: Paternoster; and Grand Rapids, Mich.: Eerdmans, 1977.

Budge, E. A. W. *A History of Ethiopia, Nubia and Abyssinia*. London: Methuen, 1928.

Buell, Denise Kimber. *Why This New Race? Ethnic Reasoning in Early Christianity*. New York: Columbia University Press, 2005.

Burgess, Stanley M., and Eduard M. Van Der Maas, eds. *The New International Dictionary of Pentecostal and Charismatic Movements*, rev. and exp. Grand Rapids, Mich.: Zondervan, 2003.

Burklin, Erik, "The Greatest Need in the Chinese Church: The China Christian Council Confronts the Task of Theological education," *ChinaSource* 5, no. 1 (Spring 2003).

Burleigh, Michael. *Earthly Powers: The Clash of Religion and Politics in Europe from the French Revolution to the Great War*. New York: HarperCollins, 2006.

Burstein, S. M., ed. *Ancient African Civilizations: Kush and Axum*. Princeton, N.J.: Marcus Wiener, 1998.

Burton, Richard. *Wanderings in West Africa*. 2 vols. London: Tinsley Brothers, 1863; repr. New York: Dover, 1991.

Bush, Douglas. *English Literature in the Earlier Seventeenth Century, 1600–1660*. New York and London: Oxford University Press, 1945; repr. 1952.

Butler, A. J. *The Ancient Coptic Churches of Egypt*. London: Oxford University Press, 1884.

Butselaar, Jan van, "The Role of Churches in the Peace Process in Africa; The Case of Mozambique Compared," chapter in Lamin Sanneh and Joel A. Carpenter, editors, *The Changing Face of Christianity: Africa, the West, and the World* (New York: Oxford University Press, 2005).

Cahill, E., *The Framework of a Christian State*. Harrison, N.Y.: Roman Catholic Books, Division of Catholic Media Apostolate, 1932.

Cambridge History of Africa. Vol. 5: *c.1790–c.1870*, ed. John E. Flint. Cambridge: Cambridge University Press, 1976.

Carretta, Vincent. *Equiano, the African: Biography of a Self-Made Man*. Athens: University of Georgia Press, 2005.

Carretta, Vincent, Paul E. Lovejoy, Trevor Burnard, Jon Senbach. "Olaudah Equiano, the South Carolinian? A Forum," *Historically Speaking, The Bulletin of the Historical Society* 7, no. 3 (January/February 2006).

Carwardine, Richard, *Trans-atlantic Revivalism, 1790–1865*. Westport, Conn.: Greenwood, 1978.

Chan, Kim-kwang. "Missiological Implications of Chinese Christianity in a Globalized Context," *Quest: An Interdisciplinary Journal for Asian Christian Scholars* 4, no. 2 (November 2005): 55–74.

———. "Chinese Christianity and Global Mission," *ChinaSource* 8, no. 1 (Spring 2006).

Chang, Jung, and Jon Halliday. *Mao: The Unknown Story*. New York: Knopf, 2005.

Charlesworth, J. H., ed. and trans. *The Odes of Solomon: The Syriac Texts*. Oxford: Clarendon, 1973.

Chesterton, G. K., *The Everlasting Man*, London: Hodder & Stoughton, 1953.

"The Louvain Consultation on China," *Pro Mundi Vita* 54 (1975).

"China and the Churches in the Making of One World," *Pro Mundi Vita* 55 (1975).

"[Chinese] Bishops Visit Europe," *China Church Quarterly*, no. 61 (Winter 2005).

China Church Quarterly, no. 65 (Winter 2006).

Chronicle of Zuqnin, Parts 3 and 4: A.D. 488–775, translated from Syriac with notes and introduction. by Amir Harrak. Toronto: Pontifical Institute of Medieval Studies, 1999.

Ciholas, Paul. *The Omphalos and the Cross: Pagans and Christians in Search of a Divine Center*. Macon, Ga.: Mercer University Press, 2003.

Clark, A. Trevor. "Eye-Witnesses of the Coercion of the Old Guard Emir Yakubu III of Bauchi," *African Affairs* 94, no. 376 (July 1995).

Clarkson, Thomas, "Society for the Purpose of Encouraging the Black Settlers at Sierra Leone, and the Natives of Africa Generally, in the Cultivation of Their Soil, and by the Sale of Their Produce," January 28, 1814, Public Record Office, London, CO 267/41.

Cleary, Edward L. *Resurgent Voices in Latin America: Indigenous Peoples, Political Mobilization and Religious Change.* New Brunswick, N.J.: Rutgers University Press, 2004.

Coakley, John W., and Andrea Sterk, eds. *Readings in World Christian History.* Vol. 1: *Earliest Christianity to 1453.* Maryknoll, N.Y.: Orbis, 2004.

Cochrane, Charles Norris. *Christianity and Classical Culture: A Study of Thought and Action from Augustus to Augustine.* New York: Oxford University Press, 1957.

Cohen, William B. *The French Encounter with Africans: White Responses to Blacks, 1530–1880.* Bloomington: Indiana University Press, 1980; repr. 2003.

Collingwood, R. G. "Reason Is Faith Cultivating Itself," *Hibbert Journal* 26, no. 1 (1927–28).

———. *The Idea of History.* Oxford: Clarendon, 1961.

Collins, John J. *Jewish Wisdom in the Hellenistic Age.* Louisville: Westminster John Knox, 1997.

Comaroff, Jean, and John Comaroff. *Of Revelation and Revolution: Christianity, Colonialism, and Consciousness in South Africa.* Chicago: University of Chicago Press, 1991.

Comby, Jean. *How to Understand the History of Christian Mission.* London: SCM, 1996.

Comfort, Philip Wesley, ed. *The Origin of the Bible.* Wheaton, Ill.: Tyndale House, 1992.

Courbage, Youssef, and Philippe Fargues, *Christians and Jews under Islam.* London and New York: I. B. Tauris, 1997.

Cowell, Alan, "Christians are Torn in the Land of Dr. Livingstone," *New York Times,* December 28, 1982.

Cragg, Kenneth. *The Arab Christian: A History in the Middle East.* Louisville: Westminster John Knox, 1991.

———. *Semitism, The Whence and Whither ('How Dear Are Your Counsels').* Brighton, England: Sussex Academic Press, 2005.

———. *The Qur'án and the West.* Washington, D.C.: Georgetown University Press, 2006.

Cronin, Vincent. *A Pearl to India: The Life of Robert de Nobili.* London: Rupert Hart Davis, 1959.

Crummey, Donald Edward. "The Ethiopian Revolution," *Canadian Journal of African Studies* 9, no. 2 (1975).

Cuffee, Paul. *Paul Cuffe's Logs and Letters: 1808–1817: A Black Quaker's 'Voice from Within the Veil.'* Edited by Rosalind Cobb Wiggins. Washington, D.C.: Howard University Press, 1996.

Cuoq, Joseph. *Jabarti, journal d'un notable du Caire Durant l'expédition francaise d'Égypte (1788–1800).* Paris: Albin Michel, 1979.

———. *Islamisation de la Nubie Chrétienne.* Paris: Librairie Orientaliste Paul Geuthner S.A., 1986.

Daniel, Norman. *The Arabs and Mediaeval Europe.* London: Longman; Beirut: Librairie du Liban, 1979.

———. "The Impact of Islam on the Laity in Europe from Charlemagne to Charles the Bold." In *Islam: Past Influence and Present Challenge,* edited by Alford T. Welch and Pierre Cachia. Edinburgh: Edinburgh University Press, 1979.

———. *Islam and the West: The Making of an Image.* Oxford: Oneworld, 1993.

Dargan, Herbert. "The Louvain Consultation," Appendix: Contemporary Church, Contemporary China, *Pro Mundi Vita*, 54, 1975.

Daube, David. *The New Testament and Rabbinic Judaism*. London: Athlone, 1956.

Davidson, Basil, ed. *The African Past: Chronicles from Antiquity to Modern Times*. Harmondsworth, England: Penguin Books, 1966.

Davis, A. J. "Coptic Christianity," *Tarikh* 2, no. 1 (1967).

Davis, David Brion. *The Problem of Slavery in the Age of Revolution, 1770–1823*. Ithaca, N.Y.: Cornell University Press, 1975.

———. *The Problem of Slavery in Western Culture*. New York: Oxford University Press, 1988.

Davis, Robert C. *Christian Slaves, Muslim Masters: White Slavery in the Mediterranean, The Barbary Coast, and Italy, 1500–1800*, New York: Palgrave Macmillan, 2003.

Dawson, Christopher. *Religion and the Rise of Western Culture*. London: Sheed and Ward, 1950.

Delany, Martin R., and Robert Campbell. *Search for a Place: Black Separatism and Africa*. Ann Arbor: University of Michigan Press, 1969.

Delavignette, R. *Freedom and Authority in French West Africa*. London: Oxford University Press, 1950.

Derfler, Steven. "The Byzantine Church at Tel Kerioth and Religious Iconoclasm in the Eighth Century: The 1991–1994 Seasons of Excavation," *Aram Periodical* 15 (2003): 39–47.

Diffie, Bailey W., and George D. Winius. *Foundations of the Portuguese Empire, 1415–1580*, vol. 1. Minneapolis: University of Minnesota Press, 1977.

Dodd, C. H. *The Meaning of Paul for Today*. London: Fontana, 1964.

Dodds, E. R. *Pagan and Christian in an Age of Anxiety*. New York: Norton, 1970.

Donovan, Vincent. "The Naked Gospel: Stamping out Ready-to-Wear Christianity," *U.S. Catholic* 46, no. 6 (1981).

———. "Response to Reflections on *Christianity Rediscovered*," *Missiology: An International Review* 18, no. 3 (July 1990).

———. *Christianity Rediscovered*. Maryknoll, N.Y.: Orbis, 1978; rev. ed., 2003.

Dozy, R. *Spanish Islam: A History of the Muslims in Spain*. London: Chatto and Windus, 1913; repr. London: Frank Cass, 1972.

DuBois, W. E. B. *The Suppression of the African Slave Trade to the United States of America: 1638–1870*, Cambridge, MA: Harvard Historical Studies, 1898; repr. New York: Russell & Russell, 1965.

Du Plessis, J. *A History of Christian Missions in South Africa*. London: Longmans, Green and Co., 1911; repr. Cape Town: C. Struik, 1965.

Dupré, Louis. *The Enlightenment and the Intellectual Foundations of Modern Culture*. New Haven, Conn.: Yale University Press, 2004.

Dupré, Willem. "Religious Plurality and Dialogue in the Sermons of Nicholas of Cusa," *Studies in Interreligious Dialogue* 15, no. 1 (2005): 76–85.

Du Toit, Bryan M. "Religion, Ritual, and Healing among Urban Black South Africans." In *African Healing Strategies*, edited by Brian M. du Toit and Ismail H. Abdalla. Buffalo, N.Y.: Trado-Medic Books of Conch Magazine, 1985.

Dvornik, Francis. *Byzantine Missions among the Slavs: SS Constantine-Cyril and Methodius.* New Brunswick, N.J.: Rutgers University Press, 1970.

Earhart, Victoria L. "The Church of the East during the Period of the Four Rightly-Guided Caliphs," *Bulletin of the John Rylands Library of Manchester* 78, no. 3 (Autumn 1996).

"Ebionism." In *Encyclopaedia of Religion and Ethics*, vol. 5, edited by James Hastings. New York: Charles Scribner's Sons, 1981.

Eiselen, W. M. "Christianity and the Religious Life of the Bantu," In *Western Civilization and the Natives of South Africa*, edited by I. Schapera. London: Routledge, 1934.

Elie, Paul, "The Year of Two Popes: How 'Mr. Inside' Stepped into the Shoes of 'Mr. Outside,' and What it Means for the Catholic Church," *The Atlantic* (January/February 2006).

Eliot, T. S. *Christianity and Culture: The Idea of a Christian Society and Notes Towards the Definition of Culture.* New York: Harcourt Brace Jovanovich, 1968. First published 1940.

Elizondo, Virgil. "Living Faith; Resistance and Survival." In *Mestizo Worship: A Personal Approach to Liturgical Ministry*, edited by Virgil Elizondo and Timothy Matovina. Collegeville, Minn.: Liturgical, 1998.

Elkins, Caroline. *Imperial Reckoning: The Untold Story of the End of the Empire in Kenya.* New York: Henry Holt, 2005.

Ellsberg, Robert, ed. *Charles de Foucauld: Selected Writings.* Maryknoll, N.Y.: Orbis, 1999.

Equiano, Olaudah. *Interesting narrative of the life of Olaudah Equiano, or Gustavus Vassa, the African, written by himself: authoritative text, contexts, criticism; edited by Werner Sollors.* New York: Norton, 2001.

Eusebius. *The History of the Church.* Harmondsworth: Penguin, 1984.

Fairbank, John King. *The United States and China*, 4th enl. ed. Cambridge, Mass.: Harvard University Press, 1983.

Falconbridge, Anna Maria. *Narrative of Two Voyages to Sierra Leone, during the Years 1791–2–3, in a Series of Letters, &c.* London, 1794; repr. London: Frank Cass, 1967.

Faith Fortnightly, a publication of the Catholic Church in China.

Feiling, Keith. *A History of England: From the Coming of the English to 1918* (London: Macmillan, 1963.

Feldman, Noah. "Out of One, Many." *The New York Times Book Review* (July 30, 2006).

Ferguson, John. "Aspects of Early Christianity in North Africa," *Tarikh* 2, no. 1 (1967).

———. *The Heritage of Hellenism.* London: Thames and Hudson, 1973.

———. *The Religions of the Roman Empire.* London: Thames and Hudson, 1982.

Fiddles, Edward. "Lord Mansfield and the Sommersett Case," *The Law Quarterly Review*, CC (October 1934).

Finberg, H. P. R. *The Formation of England: 550–1042*, London: Hart-Davis MacGibbon, 1974; repr. London: Paladin Grafton, 1986.

First Annual Report of the American Colonization Society.

Fitzgerald, C. P. *The Birth of Communist China.* Baltimore: Penguin, 1964.

Flint, John E., ed. *Cambridge History of Africa*, vol. 5: *c.1790–c.1870*. Cambridge: Cambridge University Press, 1976.

For All God's People: Ecumenical Prayer Cycle (Geneva: World Council of Churches, 1978).

Foucauld, Charles de. *Meditations of a Hermit: The Spiritual Writings of Charles de Foucauld*. Translated by Charlotte Balfour. London: Burns & Oates, 1981.

Fox, Robin Lane. *Pagans and Christians*. New York: HarperSanFrancisco of HarperCollins Publishers, 1988.

Fremantle, Anne. *Mao Tse-tung: An Anthology of His Writings*. New York: Mentor, 1962.

French, Austa Malinda. *Slavery in South Carolina and the Ex-Slaves; or, The Port Royal Mission*. New York: Winchell M. French, 1862; repr. New York: Negro Universities Press, 1969.

Frend, W. H. C. *The Rise of Christianity*. Philadelphia: Fortress, 1984.

Freston, Paul. *Evangelicals and Politics in Asia, Africa and Latin America*. Cambridge: Cambridge University Press, 2001.

Friedmann, Yohanan. *Tolerance and Coercion in Islam: Interfaith Relations in the Muslim Tradition*. Cambridge: Cambridge University Press, 2003.

Froehle, Bryan T., and Mary L. Gautier. *Global Catholicism: Portrait of a World Church*. Maryknoll, N.Y.: Orbis, 2003.

Fück, J. W. "Islam As an Historical Problem in European Historiography Since 1800." In *Historians of the Middle East*, edited by Bernard Lewis and P. M. Holt. London: Oxford University Press, 1962.

Fyfe, Christopher. *A History of Sierra Leone*. London: Oxford University Press, 1962.

Gabrieli, Francesco. *Arab Historians of the Crusades*. Translated from the Italian by E. J. Costello. London: Routledge & Kegan Paul, 1969; repr. Berkeley and Los Angeles: University of California Press, 1984. First published as *Storici Arabi delle Crociate*. Turin: Giulio Editore S.p.A., 1957.

George, David. "An Account of the Life of Mr. David George, from Sierra Leone in Africa, Given by Himself in a Conversation with Brother Rippon of London, and Brother Pearce of Birmingham." In *The Annual Baptist Register for 1790, 1791, 1792, and Part of 1793*, edited by John Rippon.

Gero, S. "Byzantine Iconoclasm during the Reign of Leo III," *Adversus Constantinum Caballinum* (1973).

Gibbon, Edward. *The Decline and Fall of the Roman Empire*, 3 vols. New York: Modern Library: n.d.

Gibbs, Nancy, "The Killing Fields of Rwanda," cover story, *Time*, May 16, 1994.

Gifford, Paul, ed. *Christian Churches and the Democritization of Africa*. Leiden: Brill, 1995.

———. *African Christianity: Its Public Role*. London: Hurst & Company, 1998.

———. *Ghana's New Christianity: Pentecostalism in a Globalizing African Economy*. Bloomington: Indiana University Press, 2004.

Gil, Moshe. *A History of Palestine, 634–1099*. Translated from the Hebrew by Ethel Broido. Cambridge: Cambridge University Press, 1992; repr. 1997.

Gillman, Ian, and Hans-Joachim Klimkeit. *Christians in Asia Before 1500.* Ann Arbor: University of Michigan Press, 1999.

Gilmore, Myron P. *The World of Humanism: 1453–1517.* New York: Harper, 1952; repr. 1962.

Gladstone, William E. *The State and Its Relations with the Church.* 2nd ed. London, 1839.

Goldfus, Haim. "Urban Monasticism and Monasteries of Early Byzantine Palestine: Preliminary Observations," *Aram Periodical* 15 (2003): 71–79.

Gonzalez, David. "A Sliver of a Storefront, A Faith on the Rise," *New York Times*, January 14, 2007.

Goodell, William. *Slavery and Anti-Slavery: A History of the Great Struggle in Both Hemispheres, with a View of the Slavery Question in the United States.* New York: William Harned, 1852.

Goodpasture, H. McKennie, ed. *Cross and Sword: An Eyewitness History of Christianity in Latin America.* Maryknoll, N.Y.: Orbis, 1989.

Gordon, Grant, ed. *From Slavery to Freedom: The Life of David George.* Hantsport, N.S.: Lacelot Press for Acadia Divinity College, 1992.

Gottfried, R. S. *The Black Death: Natural and Human Disaster in Medieval Europe.* New York: Free, 1983.

Grant, Frederick G., ed. *Ancient Roman Religion.* New York: Liberal Arts, 1957.

Gray, John M. *Early Portuguese Missionaries in East Africa.* London: Macmillan, 1958.

Gray, Richard. *Black Christians and White Missionaries.* New Haven, Conn.: Yale University Press, 1990.

———. "The Kongo Kingdom and the Papacy," *History Today* (January 1997).

———. "The Papacy and Africa in the Seventeenth Century." In *Il Christianesimo Nel Mondo Atlantico nel Secolo 17.* Vatican City: Libreria Editrice Vaticana, 1997.

———. "The African Origins of the Missio Antiqua." In *Clavis Scientiae.* Rome: Instituto Storico Dei Cappucini, 1999.

———. "The Catholic Church and National States in Western Europe during the Nineteenth and Twentieth Centuries from [the] Perspective of Africa," *Kirchliche Zeitgeschichte, Internationale Halbjahreszeitschrift für Theologie und Gescchichtswissenschaft* 14, no. 1 (2001).

Greene, D. "Some Linguistic Evidence Relating to the British Church." In *Christianity in Britain 300–700: Papers Presented to the Conference on Christianity in Roman and Sub-Roman Britain, Held at the University of Nottingham, 17–20 April, 1967.* Edited by M. W. Barley and R. P. C. Hanson. Leicester: Leicester University Press, 1968.

Griffith, Sydney H. "The Prophet Muhammad, His Scripture and His Message, According to the Christian Apologies in Arabic and Syriac from the First Abbasid Century." In *La vie du prophète Mahomet*, edited by Toufic Fahd. Paris: Presses Universitaires de France, 1983.

———. "The Monks of Palestine and the Growth of Christian Literature in Arabic," *The Muslim World* 78, no. 1 (January 1988).

Griggs, W. Wilfred. *Early Egyptian Christianity from Its Origins to 451 CE.* Leiden: Brill, 1990.

Grislis, Egil. "Luther and the Turks, Parts 1 and 2," *The Muslim World* 64 (1974): 180–93, 275–91.

Grunebaum, Gustave E. von. *Medieval Islam: A Study in Cultural Orientation*, 2nd ed., Chicago: University of Chicago Press, 1953; repr. 1966.

Gunner, Liz, ed. and trans. *The Man of Heaven and the Beautiful Ones of God (Umuntu Wasezulwini Nabantu Abahle Bakankulunkulu): Isaiah Shembe and the Nazareth Church*. Scottsville, Natal: University of KwaZulu-Natal Press, 2004.

Gutiérrez, Gustavo. *Las Casas: In Search of the Poor of Jesus Christ*. Maryknoll, N.Y.: Orbis, 1993.

Guy, Jeff. *The Heretic: A Study of the Life of John William Colenso, 1814–1883*. Pietermaritzburg: University of Natal Press, 1983.

Hadas, Moses, trans. and ed. *A History of Rome: From Its Origins to 529 A.D. as Told by the Roman Historians*. New York: Doubleday Anchor, 1956.

Haile, Getatchew. "A Christ for the Gentiles: The Case of zä-KRESTOS of Ethiopia," *Journal of Religion in Africa* 15, no. 2 (1985): 86–95.

Hair, Paul E. H. "Archdeacon Crowther and the Delta Pastorate: 1892–99," *Sierra Leone Bulletin of Religion* 5, no. 1 (June 1963).

Hakluyt, Richard. *Voyages and Discoveries*. Harmondsworth: Penguin, 1972.

Halévy, Elie. *A History of the English People in the Nineteenth Century: England in 1815*. London: Ernest Benn; New York: Barnes & Noble, 1961.

Haliburton, Gordon MacKay. *The Prophet Harris: A Study of an African Prophet and His Mass-Movement in the Ivory Coast and the Gold Coast 1913–1915*. London: Longman, 1971.

Hamilton, Alastair. *The Copts and the West, 1439–1822*. New York and Oxford: Oxford University Press, 2006.

Hamrin, Carol Lee, "History, Myth and Missions," *ChinaSource* 5, no. 4 Winter 2003.

Hancock, David Leslie. *Citizens of the World: London Merchants and the Integration of the British Atlantic Community: 1735–1785*. Cambridge: Cambridge University Press, 1995.

Hanson, R. P. C. *Saint Patrick: His Origins and Career*. Oxford: Clarendon, 1968; repr. 1997.

Hargreaves, J. D., ed. *France and West Africa: An Anthology of Historical Documents*. London; Macmillan, 1969.

Harnack, Adolf von. *The Mission and Expansion of Christianity in the First Three Centuries*. 2 vols. New York: Putnam, 1908.

Harper, Susan Billington. *In the Shadow of the Mahatma: Bishop V. S. Azariah and the Travails of Christianity in British India*. Grand Rapids, Mich.: Eerdmans, 2000.

Harrison, Jane Ellen. *Themis. A Study of the Social Origins of Greek Religion*. Cambridge: Cambridge University Press, 1912.

Hartch, Todd. *Missionaries of the State: The Summer Institute of Linguistics, State Formation, and Indigenous Mexico, 1935–1985*. Tuscaloosa: University of Alabama Press, 2006.

Harvey, Thomas Allen. *Acquainted with Grief*. Grand Rapids, Mich.: Brazos, 2002.

Hastings, Adrian. *The Church in Africa, 1450–1950*. Oxford: Oxford University Press, 1994.

————, ed. *A World History of Christianity*. Grand Rapids, Mich.: Eerdmans, 1999.

Hayashida, Nelson Osamu. *Dreams in the African Church: The Significance of Dreams and Visions among Zambian Baptists*. Amsterdam and Atlanta: Editions Rodopi, 1999.

Henrich, Sarah, and James L. Boyce. "Martin Luther—Translations of Two Prefaces on Islam: Preface to the *Libellus de ritu et moribus Turcorum* (1530), and Preface to Bibliander's Edition of the Qur'an (1543)." *Word and World: Theology for Christian Ministry: Islam* 16, no. 2 (Spring 1996): 250–66.

Henrie, Mark C., review of Rodney Stark, *The Victory of Reason: How Christianity Led to Freedom, Capitalism, and Western Success* (New York: Random House, 2005), *Commentary* (July–August 2006).

Herlihy, D., ed. *The Black Death and the Transformation of the West*. Cambridge, Mass.: Harvard University Press, 1997.

Hemer, Colin J. *The Book of Acts in the Setting of Hellenistic History*. Tübingen: Mohr (Paul Siebeck), 1989; repr. Winona Lake, Ind.: Eisenbrauns, 1990.

Henderson, W. *The Church in Angola: A River of Many Currents*, Cleveland: The Pilgrim Press, 1992.

Herodotus. *The Histories*. Translated by George Rawlinson, 1910; repr. New York: Everyman's Library, Knopf, 1997.

Hilliard, Constance B., ed. *Intellectual Traditions of Pre-Colonial Africa*. Boston: McGraw Hill, 1998.

Hilton, Anne. *The Kingdom of Kongo*. Oxford: Clarendon, 1985.

Hindmarsh, Bruce. *John Newton and the English Evangelical Tradition: Between the Conversions of Wesley and Wilberforce*. Oxford: Clarendon, 1996.

Hiney, Tom. *On the Missionary Trail, A Journey through Polynesia, Asia, and Africa with the London Missionary Society*. New York: Atlantic Monthly Press, 2000.

Hirst, Michael. "Pushed to the Periphery," *America* (June 19–26, 2006): 10–13.

Hochschild, Adam. *Bury the Hatchet: Prophets and Rebels in the Fight to Free an Empire's Slaves*. Boston: Houghton Mifflin, 2005.

Hodgson, Dorothy L. *The Church of Women: Gendered Encounters between Maasai and Missionaries*. Bloomington: Indiana University Press, 2005.

Hogg, A. G. "The Ethical Teaching of Dr Schweitzer," *International Review of Missions* 14 (1925): 237–51.

Holt, Bradley P. "Healing in the Charismatic Movement: The Catholics in Nigeria," *Religions* 2, no. 2 (December 1977).

Hong Kong Sunday Examiner.

Hopkins, J. F. P., and N. Levtzion, eds. *Corpus of Early Arabic Sources for West African History*. Cambridge: Cambridge University Press, 1981.

Hopkins, Jasper, ed. and trans. *Nicholas of Cusa's De Pace Fidei and Cribratio Alkorani*. Minneapolis: Arthur J. Banning, 1994.

Hopkins, Samuel. *Dialogue Concerning the Slavery of the Africans*. Norwich: Judah Spooner, 1776; and New York: Robert Hodge, 1785.

Hornblower, Simon, and Antony Spawforth, eds. *The Oxford Classical Dictionary*, 3rd ed. New York: Oxford University Press, 1996.

Horsley, G. H. R. *New Documents Illustrating Early Christianity*. 2 vols. North Ryde, New South Wales: Macquarie University Press, 1981–82.

Hourani, Albert. *Arabic Thought in the Liberal Age, 1798–1939*. London: Oxford University Press for the Royal Institute of International Affairs, 1962; repr. 1970.

Hubbard, D. A. "The Literary Sources of the Kebra Nagast." PhD diss., St. Andrews University, 1957.

Hunter, Erica C. D. "The Church of the East in Central Asia," *Bulletin of the John Rylands Library of Manchester* 78, no. 3 (1996).

———. "The Transmission of Greek Philosophy via the 'School of Edessa.' " In *Literacy, Education and Manuscript Transmission in Byzantium and Beyond*, edited by Catherine Holmes and Judith Waring. Leiden: Brill, 2002.

Hunwick, John, and Eve Troutt Powell, eds. *The African Diaspora in the Mediterranean Lands of Islam*. Princeton, N.J.: Markus Wiener, 2002.

Husayn, 'Abdul-Rahim Abu. "Duwayhi as a Historian of Ottoman Syria," *Bulletin of the Royal Institute for Inter-Faith Studies* 1, no. 1 (Spring 1999).

Ibn Battuta. *Travels in Asia and Africa: 1325–1354*. Edited and translated by H. A. R. Gibb. London: Routledge, 1929; repr. New York: A. M. Kelley, 1969.

"Ibn Mubárak," *Encyclopaedia of Islam*, 2nd ed, vol. 3, Leiden: E.J. Brill, 1960–2002.

Irwin, Dale T., and Scott W. Sunquist. *History of the World Christian Movement*. Maryknoll, N.Y.: Orbis, 2001.

Jabarti, 'Abd al-Rahman al-. *Chronicle of the First Seven Months of the French Occupation of Egypt*. Edited and translated by S. Moreh. Leiden: Brill, 1975.

Jadin, L., and M. Dicorato, trans. and ed. *Correspondence de Dom Afonso, roi du Congo 1506–1543*. Brussels: Koninklijke Academie Voor Overzeese Wetenschappern, 1974.

James, William. *The Varieties of Religious Experience: A Study in Human Nature*. New York: Modern Library, 1936.

Janz, Denis R. *World Christianity and Marxism*. New York: Oxford University Press, 1998.

Jaulin, Robert. *L'ethnocide à travers les Amériques*. Textes et documents réunis par Robert Jaulin. Paris: Fayard, 1972.

Jenkins, Philip. *The Next Christendom: The Coming of Global Christianity*. New York: Oxford University Press, 2002.

———. *The New Faces of Christianity: Believing the Bible in the Global South*. New York: Oxford University Press, 2006.

———. *God's Continent: Christianity, Islam and Europe's Religious Crisis*, New York: Oxford University Press, 2007.

Jenkins, Romilly. *Byzantium: The Imperial Centuries AD 610–1071*. Toronto: University of Toronto Press for the Medieval Academy of America, 1987.

John Paul II. *The Church in Africa: Ecclesia in Africa, and Its Evangelizing Mission Towards the Year 2000*. Washington, D.C.: United States Catholic Conference, 1995.

Johnson, Maxwell E., *The Virgin of Guadulupe: Theological Reflections of an Anglo-Lutheran Liturgist*, Lanham, MD: Rowan & Littlefield Publishers, Inc., 2002.

Johnson, Todd M. and Sandra S. Kim, "The Changing Demographics of World Christianity," *World Christian Database* (www.worldchristiandatabase.org), 2006.

Junod, H. A. *The Life of a South African Tribe*. London: Macmillan, 1927.

Kane, Cheikh Hamidou. *Ambiguous Adventure*. London: Heinemann Education Books, 1972. Paris: René Julliard, 1962. First published in French as *L'aventure ambiguë*.

Karsh, Efraim. *Islamic Imperialism: A History*. New Haven, Conn.: Yale University Press, 2006.

Keatley, Patrick. *The Politics of Partnership*. Harmondsworth: Penguin, 1963.

Kelly, J. N. D. *Golden Mouth: The Story of John Chrysostom: Ascetic, Preacher, Bishop*. Ithaca, N.Y.: Cornell University Press, 1995.

Kendall, R. Elliott. *End of an Era: Africa and the Missionary*. London: SPCK, 1978.

Kenny, Joseph. *The Spread of Islam through North to West Africa, 7th to the 19th Centuries: A Historical Survey with Relevant Arabic Documents*. Lagos: Dominican Publications, 2000.

Kenyatta, Jomo, *Facing Mount Kenya*, New York: Viking Books, 1938.

Keppel-Jones, Arthur. *Rhodes and Rhodesia: The White Conquest of Zimbabwe, 1884–1902*. Kingston and Montreal: McGill-Queen's University Press, 1983.

Kerenyi, C. *The Religion of the Greeks and the Romans*. London: Thames and Hudson; New York: Dutton, 1962.

Keynes, John Maynard. "The Resilience of Capitalism," *Atlantic Monthly* 149, no. 5 (May 1932).

Kindopp, Jason, and Carol Lee Hamrin, eds. *God and Caesar in China: Policy Implications of Church-State Tensions*. Washington, D.C.: Brookings Institution, 2004.

Kingsley, Mary. *West African Studies*. London: Macmillan, 1899; repr. London: Frank Cass, 1964.

Kirk-Greene, Anthony, "David George: The Nova Scotian Experience," *Sierra Leone Studies*, new series, 14 (December 1960).

Klausen, Jytte. *The Islamic Challenge: Politics and Religion in Western Europe*. New York: Oxford University Press, 2005.

Knox, Ronald A. *On Englishing the Bible*. London: Burns Oates, 1949.

Kollman, Paul V. *The Evangelization of Slaves and Catholic Origins in Eastern Africa*. Maryknoll, N.Y.: Orbis, 2005.

Koren, Henry J. "The Legacy of Francoise Libermann," *International Bulletin of Missionary Research* 28, no. 4 (October 2004): 174–77.

Krabill, James R. *The Hymnody of the Harrist Church among the Dida of South-Central Ivory Coast (1913–1949)*. Frankfurt: Peter Lang, 1995.

Kuczynski, R. R. *Demographic Survey of the British Colonial Empire*. Vol.1: *West Africa*; Vol. 2: *East Africa, etc.*; Vol. 3: *West Indian and American Territories*. London: Oxford University Press, 1948–53; repr. Fairfield, N.J.: Augustus M. Kelley; Sussex: Harvester, 1977.

Kylie, Edward, trans. and ed. *The English Correspondence of Saint Boniface*. London: Chatto & Windus, 1924.

Lactantius, *Divine Institutes Book V, chap. xv, The Ante-Nicene Fathers*, vol. 7, Edinburgh: T. & T. Clark; Grand Rapids, Mich.: Eerdmans, 1994.

Lam, Anthony S. K. *The Catholic Church in Present-Day China through Darkness and Light*. Hong Kong: The Holy Spirit Study Centre, 1997.

Landau, Rom. *The Philosophy of Ibn 'Arabí*. London: Allen & Unwin, 1959.

Langley, J. Ayo, ed. *Ideologies of Liberation in Black Africa, 1856–1970*. London: Rex Collings, 1979.

Lara, Jaime. *City, Temple, Stage: Eschatological Architecture and Liturgical Theatrics in New Spain*. Notre Dame: University of Notre Dame Press, 2004.

Lara, Jesús. *La Poesía Quechua*. Mexico City: Fondo de Cultura Economica, 1947.

Larebo, Haile Mariam. "The Orthodox Church and the State in the Ethiopian Revolution, 1974–84," *Religion in Communist Countries* 14, no. 2 (1986): 148–59.

Las Casas, Bartholomew de, *History of the Indies*, translated and edited by Andrée Collard (New York: Harper & Row), 1971.

Latourette, Kenneth Scott. *The History of the Expansion of Christianity*. Vol. 1, *The First Five Centuries*; Vol. 2, *The Thousand Years of Uncertainty, 500 A.D. to 1500 A.D.*; Vol. 5, *The Great Century in the Americas, Australasia, and Africa, 1800–1914*; Vol. 6, *The Great Century in Northern Africa and Asia, 1800–1914*. New York and London: Harper & Brothers, 1937–45; repr. Grand Rapids, Mich.: Zondervan, 1970.

Lawrence, T. E. *Seven Pillars of Wisdom: A Triumph*. Garden City, N.Y.: Doubleday, 1935; repr. London; Penguin, 1962.

Lee, Joseph Tse-Hei. *The Bible and the Gun: Christianity in South China, 1860–1900*. New York, Routledge, 2003.

Leeuwen, Arend van. *Christianity in World History*. London: Edinburgh House Press, 1964.

Lewis, Bernard. *The Emergence of Modern Turkey*. 2nd ed. London: Oxford University Press, 1968.

———. *The Muslim Discovery of Europe*. New York: Norton, 1982.

———, trans. and ed. *Islam*, 2 vols. New York: Oxford University Press, 1987.

Lewis, C. S. *Selected Literary Essays*. Cambridge: Cambridge University Press, 1969.

Lewis, Bernard, and P. M. Holt, eds. *Historians of the Middle East*. London: Oxford University Press, 1962.

Lewis, Donald M., ed. *Christianity Reborn: The Global Expansion of Evangelicalism in the Twentieth Century*. Grand Rapids, Mich.: Eerdmans, 2004.

Lewis, Naphtali, and Meyer Reinhold, eds. *Roman Civilization: Selected Readings*, Vol. 1, *The Republic and the Augustan Age*; Vol. 2, *The Empire*. 3rd ed. New York: Columbia University Press, 1990.

Lilla, Mark. "Godless Europe," *New York Times Book Review* (April 2, 2006).

Lindblom, John A. "John C. H. Wu and the Evangelization of China," *Logos* 8, no. 2 (Spring 2005).

Linden, Ian. *A New Map of the World*. London: Darton, Longman & Todd, 2003.

Loewe, Raphael. "The Medieval History of the Latin Vulgate."In *The Cambridge History of the Bible*, vol. 2, G. W. H. Lampe, ed. Cambridge: Cambridge University Press, 1988.

Loguen, J. W. *The Rev. J. W. Loguen, as a Slave and as a Freeman: A Narrative of Real Life*, Syracuse, N.Y.: J. G. K. Truair, Office of the Daily Journal, 1859.

Lovejoy, Paul E. "Autobiography and Memory: Gustavus Vassa, Alias Olaudah Equiano, the African," *Slavery and Abolition* 27, no. 3 (December 2006).

Ludolphus, Job. *A New History of Ethiopia: Being a Full and Accurate Description of Abessinia*. London: Samuel Smith, 1682.

Lull, Ramon. *The Book of the Lover and the Beloved*. Translated from the Catalan by E. Allison Peers. New York: Macmillan, 1923.

Ma, Huan. *Ying-yai sheng-lan: "The overall survey of the ocean's shores"* [1433], trans. from the Chinese text, ed. Feng Ch'eng-Chün, with intro., notes, and appendices by J. V. G. Mills. Cambridge: Cambridge University Press for the Hakluyt Society, 1970.

Maalouf, Amin, ed. *The Crusades through Arab Eyes*. London: Al Saqi; New York: Schocken, 1984.

Macaulay, Thomas Babington. "Gladstone on Church and State." In *Essays*. London: George Routledge and Sons, 1887.

———. *The History of England*, 4 vols. London, Longman, Brown, Green, and Longmans, 1849–1861; repr. London: J. M. Dent & Sons, 1906.

Macleod, Fiona [William Sharp]. *Winged Destiny: Studies in the Spiritual History of the Gael*. London: Chapman and Hall, 1904.

MacMullen, Ramsay. *Christianizing the Roman Empire: A.D. 100–400*. New Haven, Conn.: Yale University Press, 1984.

———. *Christianity and Paganism in the Fourth to Eighth Centuries*. New Haven, Conn.: Yale University Press, 1997.

Madsen, Richard. *China's Catholics; Tragedy and Hope in an Emerging Civil Society*. Berkeley and Los Angeles: University of California Press, 1998.

Maheu, Betty Ann. "The Catholic Church in China," *America* 193, no. 14 (November 7, 2005).

Mallampalli, Chandra. *Christians and Public Life in Colonial South India, 1863–1937: Contending with Marginality*. London and New York: Routledge Curzon, 2004.

———. "World Christianity and 'Protestant America': Historical Narratives and the Limits of Christian Pluralism," *International Bulletin of Missionary Research* 30, no. 1 (January 2006).

Marcus, Harold G. *A History of Ethiopia*. Berkeley and Los Angeles: University of California Press, 1994.

Martin, David. *Tongues of Fire: The Explosion of Protestantism in Latin America*. Oxford: Blackwell, 1990.

Massignon, Louis. *The Passion of al-Hallāj: Mystic and Martyr of Islam*. Translated from the French by Herbert Mason. Princeton, N.J.: Princeton University Press, 1982.

Mauny, Raymond. *Tableau géographique de l'ouest africain au Moyen Age*. Dakar: IFAN, 1961.

Maxwell, David. "Historical Christian Independency: The Southern African Pentecostal Movement," *Journal of African History* 40, no. 3 (1999).

McGiffert, Arthur Cushman. *A History of Christianity in the Apostolic Age.* Edinburgh: T. & T. Clark, 1897; repr. 1951.

McGrath, Alister E. *In the Beginning: The Story of the King James Bible and How It Changed a Nation, a Language, and a Culture.* New York: Doubleday, 2001.

McLachlan, H., editor, *Theological Manuscripts,* Liverpool: Liverpool University Press, 1950.

Memorandum to the Lambeth Conference from the Ordination of Women Ad Hoc Committee, 1948.

Memorial submitted to the Lambeth Conference (1948) on Deaconesses by the Anglican Group for the Ordination of Women.

Merriman, N. J. *The Cape Journals of Archdeacon N.J. Merriman, 1848–1855.* Cape Town: Van Riebeeck Society, 1957.

Merton, Thomas *Love and Living.* Edited by Naomi Burton Stone and Patrick Hart. New York: Farrar, Straus, and Giroux, 1979.

Miller, Floyd J. *The Search for a Black Nationality: Black Emigration and Colonization, 1787–1863.* Urbana: University of Illinois Press, 1975.

Miller, Walter R. *Yesterday and Tomorrow in Northern Nigeria.* London: Student Christian Movement, 1938.

———. *Have We Failed in Nigeria?* London: Lutterworth, 1947.

Milton, Giles. *White Gold: The Extraordinary Story of Thomas Pellow and Islam's One Million White Slaves.* New York: Farrar, Straus, and Giroux, 2005.

Mingana, Alphonse. "Early Spread of Christianity in India," *Bulletin of the John Rylands Library of Manchester,* no. 10 (1926).

Moberg, Axel, ed. and trans. *The Book of the Himyarites.* London: Oxford University Press, 1924.

Molokwu, P. N. C. "Vernacular in Ishan Schools," *The Nigerian Teacher* 1, no. 5 (1935).

Mommsen, Theodor. *The Provinces of the Roman Empire,* 2 vols., rev. ed. New York: Charles Scribner's Sons, 1906; London: Macmillan, 1909; repr. New York: Barnes & Noble, 1996.

Moorhouse, Geoffrey. *The Missionaries.* Philadelphia: Lippincott, 1973.

Mosala, I. "Race, Class and Gender as Hermeneutical Factors in the African Independent Churches' Appropriation of the Bible," *Semeia* 73, 43–57.

Mostert, Noël. *Frontiers: The Epic of South Africa's Creation and the Tragedy of the Xhosa People.* London: Jonathan Cape, 1992; repr. London: Pimlico, 1993.

Mo Tzu. *Basic Writings.* Translated by Burton Watson. New York: Columbia University Press, 1963.

Mott, John R., *The Decisive Hour of Christian Missions,* London: Student Volunteer Missionary Union, 1910.

Mumford, Lewis. *The City in History.* New York: Harcourt, Brace, and World, 1961.

Murray-Brown, Jeremy. *Kenyatta.* London: Allen & Unwin, 1972.

Needham, Joseph. *Chinese Astronomy and the Jesuit Mission: An Encounter of Cultures.* London: China Society, 1958.

Neil, Stepehn, *The Christian Society* (London: Collins, The Fontana Library of Theology and Philosophy), 1952.

Newbigin, Lesslie. *The Relevance of Trinitarian Doctrine for Today's Mission.* C. W. M. E. Study Pamphlets No. 2. London: Edinburgh House, 1963.

———. *Honest Religion for Secular Man.* London: SCM, 1966.

———. *The Open Secret: Sketches for a Mission Theology.* Grand Rapids, Mich.: Eerdmans, 1978.

———. *Foolishness to the Greeks: The Gospel and Western Culture.* Geneva: World Council of Churches, 1986.

———. *The Gospel in a Pluralist Society.* Grand Rapids, Mich.: Eerdmans, 1989.

———. *Truth to Tell: The Gospel as Public Truth.* Grand Rapids, Mich: Eerdmans; Geneva: World Council of Churches, 1991.

———. *Unfinished Agenda: An Updated Autobiography.* London: SPCK, 1993.

———. *Proper Confidence: Faith, Doubt and Certainty in Christian Discipleship.* Grand Rapids, Mich.: Eerdmans, 1995.

———. *Truth and Authority in Modernity.* Valley Forge, Pa: Trinity Press International, 1996.

———. *Signs Amid the Rubble: The Purposes of God in Human History*, edited by Geoffrey Wainright. Grand Rapids, Mich.: Eerdmans, 2003.

Newbigin, Lesslie, Lamin Sanneh, and Jenny Taylor. *Faith and Power: Christianity in "Secular" Britain.* London: SPCK, 1998.

Newman, John Henry. *Discussions and Arguments on Various Subjects.* London: Pickering, 1872; repr. Notre Dame: University of Notre Dame Press, 2004.

Ng, Peter Tze Ming. "The Necessity of the Particular in the Globalisation of Christianity: The Case of China," *Studies in World Christianity* 12, no. 2, 2006.

Ngubane, Harriet. *Body and Mind in Zulu Medicine: An Ethnography of Health and Disease in Nyuswa-Zulu Thought and Practice.* New York: Academic, 1977.

Nida, Eugene A. *Customs and Cultures: Anthropology for Christian Missions.* New York: Harper & Brothers, 1954.

Nielsen, Jørgen. *Muslims in Western Europe.* Edinburgh: Edinburgh University Press, 1992.

Norris, Frederick W. *Christianity: A Short Global History.* Oxford: Oneworld, 2002.

———. "Timothy I of Baghdad, Catholicus of the East Syrian Church, 780–823: Still A Valuable Model," *International Bulletin of Missionary Research* 30, no. 3 (July 2006).

O'Brien, Conor Cruise, *To Katanga and Back: A UN Case History.* New York: The Universal Library of Grosset and Dunlap, 1966.

O'Donovan, Oliver, and Joan Lockwood O'Donovan, eds. *From Irenaeus to Grotius; A Sourcebook in Christian Political Thought.* Grand Rapids, Mich.: Eerdmans, 1999.

Oesterley, W. O. E., and Theodore H. Robinson. *A History of Israel,* 2 vols. Vol. 2, *From the Fall of Jerusalem, 586 B.C. to the Bar-Kokhaba Revolt, A.D. 135.* Oxford: Clarendon, 1932; repr. 1957.

Oldham, J. H. "Educational Policy of the British Government in Africa," *The International Review of Missions* 14 (1925): 421–27.

Oliver, Roland. *The Missionary Factor in East Africa.* London: Longman, 1970.

————. *The African Experience: Major Themes in African History from the Earliest Times to the Present*, New York: IconEditions of HarperCollins, 1991.

O'Mahony, Anthony., ed. *Christian Communities of Jerusalem and the Holy Land: Studies in History, Religion and Politics*. Cardiff: University of Wales Press, 2003.

————, ed. *Eastern Christianity: Studies in Modern History, Religion and Politics*. London: Melisende, 2004.

O'Mahony, Anthony, Göran Gunner, and Kevork Hintlian, eds. *Christian Heritage in the Holy Land*. London: Scorpion Cavendish, 1995.

Onyinah, Opoku. *Are Two Persons the Same? How to Overcome Your Weakness in Temperament*. Accra, Ghana: Pentecost Press, 1991.

————. *Ancestral Curses*. Accra, Ghana: International Missions Office, 1994.

————. *Overcoming Demons*. Accra, Ghana: Pentecostal Press, International Missions Office, 1995.

Oosthuizen, G. C. *Religion Alive: Studies in the New Movements and Indigenous Churches in Southern Africa*. Johannesburg: Hodder & Stoughton, Southern Africa, 1986.

Orizio, Ricardo. "The Lion Sleeps Tonight," an interview with Mengistu Haile Mariam. Translated from the Italian by Avril Bardoni. *Transition* 11, issue 89, no. 1.

Ostrogorsky, George. *History of the Byzantine State*. Rev. ed. Translated by Joan Hussey. New Brunswick, N.J.: Rutgers University Press, 1969.

Pacini, Andrea, ed. *Christian Communities in the Arab Middle East: The Challenge of the Future*. Oxford: Clarendon, 1998.

Palacios. Miguel Asín. *Islam and the Divine Comedy*. New York: Dutton, 1926; repr. London: Frank Cass, 1968.

Papal Documents Related to China 1937–2005. Compiled by Elmer Wurth; edited by Betty Ann Maheu. Hong Kong: Holy Spirit Centre, 2006.

Parker, Richard, "The First Post-Oil Society?" *Mother Jones* (February/March 1979).

Parry, J. H. *The Age of Reconnaissance*. New York: Mentor, 1964.

————. *The Spanish Seaborne Empire*. New York: Knopf, 1981.

Paton, David M., ed. *The Ministry of the Spirit: Selected Writings of Roland Allen*. London: World Dominion, 1960.

Peel, J. D. Y. *Aladura: A Religious Movement among the Yoruba*. London: Oxford University Press for the International African Institute, 1968.

————. *Religious Encounter and the Making of the Yoruba*. Bloomington: Indiana University Press, 2000.

Pelikan, Jaroslav. *The Emergence of the Catholic Church (100–600)*. Chicago: University of Chicago Press, 1971.

————. *Jesus through the Centuries: His Place in the History of Culture*. New Haven, Conn.: Yale University Press, 1985.

Pellow, Thomas. *Adventures of Thomas Pellow, of Penryn, Mariner, Three and Twenty Years in Captivity among the Moors*. New York: Macmillan, 1890.

Philip, John. *Researches in South Africa: Illustrating the Civil, Moral, and Religious Condition of the Native Tribes*. 2 vols. London: James Duncan, 1828; repr. New York: Negro Universities Press, 1969.

Phillips, Melanie. *Londonistan*. New York: Encounter, 2006.

Pinault, David. "Losers' Vengeance: Muslim-Christian Relations and Pakistan's Blasphemy Law," *America* 194, no. 13 (April 10, 2006).

Pirenne, Henri. *Mohammed and Charlemagne*. London: Unwin University Books, 1968.

Pitcher, Philip Wilson. *In and about Amoy*. Shanghai and Foochow: Methodist Publishing House, 1909.

Platt, William J. *An African Prophet: The Ivory Coast Movement and What Came of It*. London: SCM, 1934.

———. *From Fetish to Faith: The Growth of the Church in West Africa*. London: Cargate, 1935.

Plutarch's Lives, vol. 2, New York: Random House Publishing, 2001.

Poole, Stafford. *Our Lady of Guadalupe: The Origin and Sources of a Mexican National Symbol, 1531–1797*. Tucson: University of Arizona Press, 1997.

Porter, Andrew. " 'Cultural Imperialism' and Protestant Missionary Enterprise, 1780–1914," *Journal of Imperial and Commonwealth History* 25, no. 3 (September 1997): 367–91.

Premier Livret de l'Education Religieuse à l'usage des Missions Harristes. Petit-Bassam, (August 1956).

Preminger, Marion M. *The Sands of Tamanrasset: The Story of Charles de Foucauld*. New York: Hawthorn, 1961.

Pressler, Titus. *"Christianity Rediscovered: A Reflection on Vincent Donovan's Contribution to Missiology,"* Missiology, 18, no. 3 (July 1990).

Prickett, Barbara. *Island Base: A History of the Methodist Church in the Gambia, 1821–1969*. Bo, Sierra Leone: Bunumbu, 1971.

Prodromou, Elizabeth H. "Turkey between Secularism and Fundamentalism? The 'Muslimhood Model' and the Greek Orthodox Minority," *The Brandywine Review of Faith and International Affairs* 3, no. 1 (Spring 2005).

Pro Mundi Vita Studies, no. 15, (June 1990).

Putnam, H. *L'Eglise et l'Islam sous Timothée I (780–823)*. Beirut: Dar el-Machreq, 1975.

Rabadan, Muhammad. *Mahometism Fully Explained (Written in Spanish and Arabic in the Year 1603 for the Instruction of the Moriscoes in Spain)*. Translated and edited by J. Morgan. 2 vols. London: E. Curll, W. Mears, and T. Payne, 1723–25.

Ranger, Terence O. *Revolt in Southern Rhodesia, 1896–7: A Study in African Resistance*. London: Heinemann, 1967.

———. *The African Voice in Southern Rhodesia, 1898–1930*. London: Heinemann Educational, 1970.

———. *Dance and Society in Eastern Africa, 1890–1970*. Berkeley and Los Angeles: University of California Press, 1975.

Ratzinger, Joseph (Pope Benedict XVI). *Truth and Tolerance: Christian Belief and World Religions*. San Francisco: Ignatius, 2004.

Rea, William Francis. *The Economics of the Zambezi Missions: 1580–1759*. Rome: Institutum Historicum S.I., 1976.

Reeves, Majorie. *The Influence of Prophecy in the Later Middle Ages*. London: Oxford University Press, 1969.

Reichwein, Adolph. *China and Europe: Intellectual and Artistic Contacts in the Eighteenth Century.* London: Kegan Paul, 1925.

Rhodius, Apollonius. *The Argonautica.* Edited and translated by R. C. Seaton. Cambridge, Mass.: Harvard University Press, 1912; repr. 1988.

Ricci, Matteo. *China in the Sixteenth Century: The Journals of Matteo Ricci: 1583–1610.* Translated by Louis J. Gallagher. New York: Random House, 1953.

Richardson, Peter. *Herod: King of the Jews and Friend of the Romans,* introduction by I. Howard Marshall. Edinburgh: T. & T. Clark, 1996; repr., Fortress, 1999.

Roscoe, John. *The Baganda: An Account of Their Native Customs and Beliefs.* London: Macmillan, 1911.

Rosenthal, Franz. *The Classical Heritage in Islam.* London: Routledge & Kegan Paul, 1975. German edition, Zürich: Artemis Verlags-AG, 1965.

Ross, Andrew. *David Livingstone: Mission and Empire.* London and New York: Hambledon & London, 2002.

Ross, Kenneth. "The Centenary of Edinburgh 1910: Its Possibilities," *International Bulletin of Missionary Research* 30, no. 4 (October 2006).

Royle, Trevor. *Crimea; The Great Crimean War 1854–1856.* London and New York: Palgrave Macmillan, 2004.

Rushdie, Salman. *In Good Faith.* New York: Viking, 1990.

Russell, Bertrand. *Religion and Science.* New York: Oxford University Press, 1961.

Sanneh, Kelefa. "Pray and Grow Rich," *The New Yorker* (October 11, 2004).

Sanneh, Lamin. *Translating the Message: The Missionary Impact on Culture.* Maryknoll, N.Y.: Orbis, 1989.

———. *Abolitionists Abroad: American Blacks and the Making of Modern West Africa.* Cambridge, Mass.: Harvard University Press, 2000.

———. *Whose Religion Is Christianity? The Gospel beyond the West.* Grand Rapids, Mich.: Eerdmans, 2003.

Sanneh, Lamin, and Joel Carpenter, eds. *The Changing Face of Christianity.* New York: Oxford University Press, 2005.

Schama, Simon. *Rough Crossings: Britain, the Slaves and the American Revolution.* London: BBC, 2005.

Schereschewsky, S. I. J. *The Bible, Prayer Book, and Terms in Our China Missions.* New York: [1888?], Peking: American Mission Press.

Schnabel, Eckhard J. *Early Christian Mission.* Vol. 1, *Jesus and the Twelve;* Vol 2, *Paul and the Early Church.* Downers Grove, Ill., Intervarsity, 2004.

Schroeder, Roger. "Catholic Church Growing Everywhere—Except in Europe," *International Bulletin of Missionary Research* 30, no. 3 (July 2006).

Schwarcz, Vera. *The Chinese Enlightenment—Intellectuals and the Legacy of the May Fourth Movement of 1919.* Berkeley and Los Angeles: University of California Press, 1986.

Schweitzer, Albert. *Philosophy of Civilization.* Translated by C. T. Campion. New York: Macmillan, 1950.

Seaver, Paul. *The Puritan Lectureships: The Politics of Religious Dissent, 1560–1662.* Stanford, Calif.: Stanford University Press, 1970.

Sen, Keshub Chunder. "India Asks, Who Is Christ?" Lecture delivered at the town hall, Calcutta, on April 9, 1879. Printed and published by M. M. Rukhit. Calcutta: Indian Mirror Press, 1879.

Shahid, Irfan. *The Martyrs of Najran: New Documents*. Bruxelles: Soc. des Bollandistes, Bd. Saint-Michel, 24, 1971.

———. "The Kebra Nagast in the Light of Recent Research," *Le Mouséon* 89 (1976): 133–78.

———. *Byzantium and the Arabs in the Fourth Century*. Washington, D.C.: Dumbarton Oaks, 1984.

———. *Byzantium and the Arabs in the Fifth Century*. Washington, D.C.: Dumbarton Oaks, 1989.

———. "Arab Christianity in Byzantine Palestine," *Aram Periodical* 15 (2003): 227–37.

Shank, David. *Prophet Harris, "The Black Elijah" of West Africa*. Leiden: Brill, 1994.

———. "The Legacy of William Wadé Harris," *International Bulletin of Missionary Research* 10, no. 4 (October 1996).

Shank, David A. "The Taming of the Prophet Harris," *Journal of Religion in Africa* 27, no. 1 (February 1997).

Sharkey, Heather J. "Arabic Antimissionary Treatises: Muslims Responses to Christian Evangelism in the Modern Middle East," and the companion "Arabic Antimissionary Treatises: A Select Annotated Bibliography," *International Bulletin of Missionary Research* (July 2004).

Shepperson, George, and Thomas Price. *Independent African: John Chilembwe and the Origins, Setting, and Significance of the Nyasaland Native Rising of 1915*. Edinburgh: Edinburgh University Press, 1958; repr. 1987.

Sherwin, Byron L., and Harold Kasimov, eds. *John Paul II and Interreligious Dialogue*. Maryknoll, N.Y.: Orbis, 1999.

Sherwood, Henry Noble. "Paul Cuffe," *Journal of Negro History* 8 (April 1923).

Shorter, Aylward. "Christian Presence in a Muslim Milieu: The Missionaries of Africa in the Maghreb and the Sahara," *International Bulletin of Missionary Research* 28, no. 4 (October 2004): 159–64.

Showalter, Nathan. *End of a Crusade: The Student Volunteer Movement for Foreign Missions and the Great War*. Lanham, Md.: Scarecrow, 1998.

———. *The Cross and the Flag in Africa: The "White Fathers" during the Colonial Scramble, 1892–1914*. Maryknoll, N.Y.: Orbis, 2006.

Shui, Huo, "View from the Wall: China, the Greatest Christian Nation in the World?" *ChinaSource* 5, no. 4, Winter 2003.

Smith, Adam. *The Wealth of Nations*. Edited by Edwin Cannan. New York: Modern Library Edition of Random House, 1994.

Smith, Edwin. *The Golden Stool: Some Aspects of the Conflict of Cultures in Modern Africa*. London: Holborn, 1926.

Smith, Edwin W. *The Shrine of a People's Soul*. London: Livingstone, 1929.

———. *In the Mother Tongue*. London: British and Foreign Bible Society, 1930.

Song, Choan-Seng. *Jesus, the Crucified People*. New York: Crossroad, 1990.

Smith, Sydney, *The Works of the Reverend Sydney Smith,* London: Longman, Brown, Green, Longmans and Roberts, 1859.

Southern, R. W. *Western Views of Islam in the Middle Ages.* Cambridge, Mass.: Harvard University Press, 1978.

Sozomen, *The Ecclesiastical History* in *The Nicene and Post-Nicene Fathers of the Christian Church,* second series, vol. II, Edinburgh: T&T Clark, Grand Rapids, Mich.: Wm. B. Eerdmans Publishing Company, 1989,

Spence, Jonathan. *The Memory Palace of Matteo Ricci.* New York: Penguin, 1985.

Spicer, Edward H. *Cycles of Conquest: The Impact of Spain, Mexico, and the United States on the Indians of the Southwest, 1533–1960.* Tucson: University of Arizona Press, 1962.

Ssu-yü, Teng, and John K. Fairbank, eds. *China's Response to the West: A Documentary Survey, 1839–1923.* Cambridge, Mass.: Harvard University Press, 1954; repr. 1979.

Standaert, Nicolas, ed. *Handbook of Christianity in China.* Vol. 1: *635–1800.* Leiden: Brill, 2001.

Staniforth, Maxwell, ed. and trans. *Early Christian Writings.* Penguin Classics, Harmondsworth, Middlesex, England, 1968; repr. Harmondsworth, England: Penguin Books, 1982.

Stark, Rodney. *The Victory of Reason: How Christianity Led to Freedom, Capitalism, and Western Success.* New York: Random House, 2005.

Stern, S. M. "Quotations from the Apocryphal Gospels in 'Abd al-Jabbár," *Journal of Theological Studies* 18, pt. 1 (April 1967).

Stine, Philip C. *Let the Words Be Written: The Lasting Influence of Eugene A. Nida.* Atlanta: Society of Biblical Literature, no. 21, 2004.

Strömbäck, Dag. *The Conversion of Iceland.* Translated and edited by Peter Foote. London: Viking Society for Northern Research, University College, 1975.

Strothmann, R. "Takíya," *Shorter Encyclopaedia of Islam.* Edited by H. A. R. Gibb and J. H. Kramers. Leiden: Brill, 1961.

Sundkler, Bengt G. M. *The Christianity Ministry in Africa.* Uppsala: University of Uppsala, 1960.

———. *Bantu Prophets in South Africa.* 2nd ed. London: Oxford University Press for the International African Institute, 1961.

Sundkler, Bengt, *Zulu Zion and Some Swazi Zionists,* Oxford: Clarendon Press, 1976.

Sundkler, Bengt, and Christopher Steed. *A History of the Church in Africa.* Cambridge: Cambridge University Press, 2000.

Suso, Bamba, and Banna Kanute. *Sunjata: The Mande Epic.* London: Penguin, 1999.

Tabarí, Muhammad b. Jarír al-, *Ta'ríkh al-rusul wa'l-mulúk,* 2 vols., 1 (Leiden: Dar al-Ma'rif, 1964; 2 (Cairo: Dár al-Ma'ríf, 1969).

Tafawa-Balewa, Abubakar. "The City of Language," *The Nigerian Teacher* 1, no. 4 (1935).

Tafla, Bairu. "The Establishment of the Ethiopian Church," *Tarikh* 2, no. 1 (1967).

Tamrat, Taddese. "The Abbots of Däbrä-Hayq, 1248–1535," *Journal of Ethiopian Studies* 8, no. 1 (May 1970).

———. *Church and State in Ethiopia: 1270–1527.* Oxford: Clarendon, 1972.

Tasie, Godwin. *Christian Missionary Enterprise in the Niger Delta: 1864–1918*. Leiden: Brill, 1978.

Taylor, John V., *Process of Growth in an African Church*, IMC ("International Missionary Council") Research Pamphlets 6 (London: SCM, 1958).

Tellez, Balthazar. *Travels of the Jesuits in Ethiopia*. London: J. Knapton, 1710.

Tertullian, *Apology, The Ante-Nicene Fathers*, vol. III, parts I–III, Grand Rapids, Mich.: Eerdmans, 1986.

Thomas, Charles. *Christianity in Roman Britain to AD 500*. Berkeley and Los Angeles: University of California Press, 1981.

Thomas, Norman E., ed. *International Mission Bibliography, 1960–2000*. Lanham, Md.: Scarecrow, 2003.

Thornton, John K. *The Kingdom of Kongo: Civil War and Transition 1641–1718*. Madison: University of Wisconsin Press, 1983.

———. *The Kongolese Saint Anthony: Dona Beatriz Kimpa Vita and the Antonian Movement, 1684–1706*. Cambridge: Cambridge University Press, 1998.

Tibbetts, Gerald Randall, trans. *Arab Navigation in the Indian Ocean before the Coming of the Portuguese (Kitáb al-fawá'id fi usúl al-bahr wa'l qawá'id)*. London: Royal Asiatic Society of Great Britain and Ireland, 1971.

———. *The Navigational Theory of the Arabs in the Fifteenth and Sixteenth Centuries*. Coimbra: Junta de Investigacões do Ultramar-Lisboa, 1969.

Timothy I. *The Apology of Timothy the Patriarch before the Caliph Mahdi*. Edited and translated by A. Minagana. "Woodbrooke Studies," no. 3, in *Bulletin of the John Rylands Library of Manchester* 12, no. 1 (January 1928): 137–298.

Ting, K. H. "The Chinese Church Today," *The Christian Century* (April 10, 1991).

Toynbee, Arnold J. *Civilization on Trial*. New York: Oxford University Press, 1948.

Treadgold, Warren. *A History of the Byzantine State and Society*. Stanford: Stanford University Press, 1997.

Trimingham, J. S. *A History of Islam in West Africa*. London: Oxford University Press, 1962.

———. *Islam in Ethiopia*. Oxford: Oxford University Press, 1952; repr. London: Frank Cass, 1976.

———. *Christianity among the Arabs in Pre-Islamic Times*. London: Longman; Beirut: Librairie du Liban, 1979.

Tsui, Bartholomew P. M. "Ancient Chinese Prayers: A Collection," *Ching Feng: Quarterly Notes on Christianity and Chinese Religion and Culture* 19, nos. 3 and 4 (1976).

Turner, Brian S. *Weber and Islam: A Critical Study*. London and Boston: Routledge & Kegan Paul, 1974.

Túsí, Nasír al-Dín al-. *Contemplation and Action: The Spiritual Biography of a Muslim Scholar*. London and New York: I. B. Taurus for the Institute of Ismaili Studies, 1999. Originally published as *Sayr wa Sulúk*. Edited and translated by S. J. Badakhchani.

Twain, Mark. "Mark Twain on American Imperialism," *The Atlantic* 269, no. 4 (1992): 46–65.

Ullendorf, Edward. *Ethiopia and the Bible.* London: Oxford University Press, 1988.

Vadakkekara, Benedict. *The Origin of India's St Thomas Christians: A Historiographical Critique.* Delhi: Media House, 1995.

Valencia, Roberto Sanchez. "The Monophysite Conviction in the East versus Byzantium's Political Convenience: A Historical Look to Monothelism in Palestine," *Aram Periodica* 15 (2003): 151–57.

Van Horne, John C., ed. *Religious Philanthropy and Colonial Slavery: The American Correspondence of the Associates of Dr. Bray, 1717–1777.* Urbana and Chicago: University of Illinois Press, 1985.

Venuti, Lawrence. *The Scandals of Translation: Towards an Ethics of Difference.* London: Routledge, 1998.

Vitkus, Daniel J. *Piracy, Slavery and Redemption: Barbary Captivity Narratives from Early Modern England.* New York: Columbia University Press, 2001.

Viviano, Frank, and Michael Yamashita. "China's Great Armada," *National Georgraphic* (July 2005): 28–53.

Volney, Constantin-François. *Travels through Egypt and Syria in the Years 1783, 1784 and 1785.* New York: J. Tiebout for E. Duyckinck, 1798.

Waardenburg, Jacques. "World Religions as Seen in the Light of Islam." In *Islam: Past Influence and Present Challenge,* edited by Alford T. Welch and Pierre Cachia. Edinburgh: Edinburgh University Press, 1979.

Wadström, Carl B. *Essay on Colonization, Particularly Applied to the Western Coast of Africa, with Some Free Thoughts on Cultivation and Commerce; also Brief Descriptions of the Colonies Already Formed, or Attempted, in Africa, Including Those of Sierra Leone and Bulama.* 2 vols. London: Darton & Harvey, 1794.

Walker, F. Deaville. *The Story of the Ivory Coast.* London: Cargate, 1926.

Walker, Sheila S. *The Religious Revolution in the Ivory Coast: The Prophet Harris and the Harrist Church.* Chapel Hill: University of North Carolina Press, 1983.

Wallace-Hadrill, John Michael. *The Frankish Church.* Oxford: Clarendon, 1983.

Walls, Andrew F. "A Christian Experiment: The Early Sierra Leone Colony." In *The History of the Church and the Propagation of the Faith, Studies in Church History,* vol. 6, edited by G. J. Cuming. Cambridge: Cambridge University Press, 1970.

———. "A Colonial Concordat: Two Views of Christianity and Civilization." In *Church, Society, and Politics.* Vol. 12 of *Studies in Church History,* edited by Derek Baker. Oxford: Blackwell, 1975.

———. "The Significance of Christianity in Africa." Church of Scotland. Edinburgh: St. Colm's Education Centre and College, 1989.

———. *The Missionary Movement in Christian History: Studies in the Transmission of Faith.* Maryknoll, N.Y.: Orbis, 1996.

———. "Converts or Proselytes? The Crisis over Conversion in the Early Church," *International Bulletin of Missionary Research* 28, no. 1 (January 2004).

Walzer, Richard. "Arabic Transmission of Greek Thought to Europe," *Bulletin of the John Rylands Library of Manchester* 29 (1945–46): 160–83.

Wanjau, Gakaara wa, *Mau Mau Author in Detention,* Nairobi: Heinemann, 1988.

Washington, James Melvin. *The Origins and Emergence of Black Baptist Separatism, 1863–1897.* PhD diss., Yale University, 1979.

Watt, W. Montgomery. *The Influence of Islam on Medieval Europe.* Edinburgh: Edinburgh University Press, 1972; repr. Edinburgh University Press, 1987.

———. *Muslim-Christian Encounters: Perceptions and Misperceptions.* London: Routledge, 1991.

Weber, Max. *Economy and Society: An Outline of Interpretive Sociology,* 2 vols. Edited by Guenther Roth and Claus Wittich. Berkeley and Los Angeles: University of California Press, 1978.

Weigel, George. "The Cathedral and the Cube: Reflections on European Morale," *Commentary* 117, no. 6 (June 2004): 33–38.

———. *The Cube and the Cathedral: Europe, America, and Politics without God.* New York: Basic, 2005.

Welbourn, F. B. *East African Rebels: A Study of Some Independent Churches.* London: SCM, 1961.

Westermann, Diedrich. "The Place and Function of the Vernacular in African Education," *International Review of Mission* (January 1925).

Westermann, Diedrich, *The African To-day and To-morrow,* London: Oxford University Press for the International African Institute, 3rd edition, 1949. White, C. *The Correspondence between Jerome and Augustine of Hippo.* Lewiston, N.Y.: Edwin Mellen, 1990.

"Where's Mao? Chinese Revise History Books," *New York Times,* September 1, 2006.

White, Hugh Vernon. "End Missions Imperialism Now!" *The Christian Century* (February 14, 1934).

Wickeri, Philip L. *Seeking Common Ground: Protestant Christianity, the Three-Self Movement, and China's United Front.* Maryknoll, N.Y.: Orbis, 1988.

Wilford, John Noble. *The Mapmakers.* Rev. ed. New York: Vintage Books of Random House, 2000.

Wilken, Robert L. *The Christians as the Romans Saw Them.* New Haven, Conn.: Yale University Press, 1984.

Williams, A. V. "Zoroastrians and Christians in Sasanian Iran," *Bulletin of the John Rylands University Library of Manchester* 78, no. 3 (Autumn 1996).

Williams, Eric. *From Columbus to Castro: The History of the Caribbean.* New York: Vintage, 1984.

Williams, Hugh. *Christianity in Early Britain.* Oxford: Clarendon, 1912.

———. *Two Lives of Gildas, by a Monk of Ruys, and Caradoc of Llancarfan.* Felinfach, Wales: Llanerch, 1990.

Wilson, Monica, and Leonard Thompson, eds. *The Oxford History of South Africa.* Vol. 1, *South Africa to 1870.* Oxford: Clarendon, 1969.

Wink, André. *Al-Hind, the Making of the Indo-Islamic World.* Leiden: Brill, 1991.

Winks, Robin, *The Blacks in Canada,* New Haven, Conn.: Yale University Press, 1972.

Witte, John Jr., and Frank Alexander, eds. *The Teachings of Modern Christianity on Law, Politics, and Human Nature.* 2 vols. New York: Columbia University Press, 2005.

Wolf, C. Umhau. "Luther and Mohammedanism," *The Moslem World* 31 (1941): 161–77.

Wolf-Gazo, Ernest. "Weber and Islam," *ISIM Review* 16 (Autumn 2005): 44–45.

Woodruff, Philip. *The Men Who Ruled India* 2 vols. New York: Schocken, 1953–54.

Woodward, Ernest Llewellyn. *Christianity and Nationalism in the Later Roman Empire* New York: Longmans, Green, 1916.

Yamauchi, Edwin M. *Africa and the Bible*. Grand Rapids, Mich.: Baker, 2004.

Yu, Ying-shih. "Confucianism and China's Encounter with the West in Historical Perspective," *Dao: A Journal of Confucian Philosophy* a4, no. 2(June 2005): 203–16.

Yule, Henry, and Henri Cordier, eds. *Cathay and the Way Thither*, 4 vols. Rev. ed. London: Hakluyt Society, 1913–16.

Index